NEW GCSE SCIENCE

Separate Sciences

For Specification Units B3, C3 and P3

Edexcel

Series Editor: Gurinder Chadha

**Authors: John Adkins,
David Applin, Gurinder Chadha**

Student Book

Contents

Biology

B3 Using biology

Chemistry

C3 Chemistry in action

Physics

P3 Applications of physics

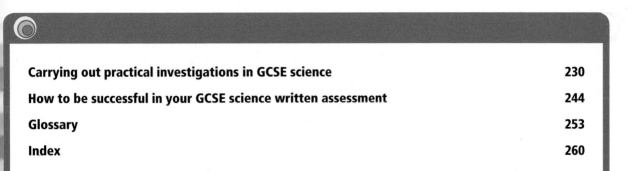

How to use this book

Welcome to Collins New GCSE Separate Sciences for Edexcel!

The main content

Each two-page lesson has three sections:

> The first section outlines a basic scientific idea

> The second section builds on the basics and develops the concept

> The third section extends the concept or challenges you to apply it in a new way. It can also provide information that is only relevant to the Higher tier (indicated with 'Higher tier only'). Sometimes this section may contain information that is not needed for your exam, but it is useful background knowledge and will help you in further study.

Each section contains a set of level-appropriate questions that allow you to check and apply your knowledge.

Look for:

> 'You will find out' boxes

> internet search terms (at the bottom of every page)

> 'Did you know?' and 'Remember' boxes.

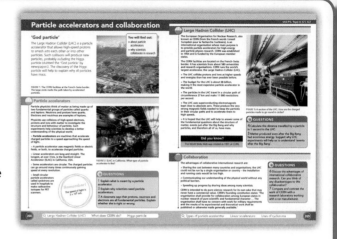

Unit introduction

Each Unit contains two Introductions – one at the start and the other midway through the Unit.

Link the science you will learn in the coming Unit with your existing scientific knowledge.

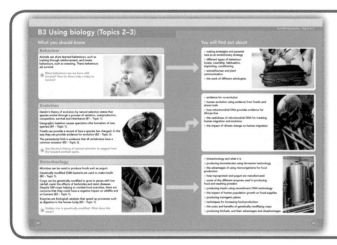

Unit checklists

Each Unit contains two graded Checklists – one midway through the Unit and the other at the end.

Summarise the key ideas that you have learnt so far and see what you need to know to progress. If there are any topics you find tricky, you can always recap them!

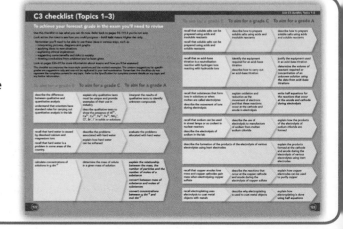

Exam-style questions

Every Unit contains practice exam-style questions for both Foundation and Higher tiers. There is a range of types of question and each is labelled with the Assessment Objective that it addresses.

There is a quick key to summarise the Assessment Objectives at the bottom of the page. A complete description of the Assessment Objectives – and how they apply to your written exam – can be found on pages 245–8 of this book and in Edexcel's Specifications.

Familiarise yourself with all the types of question that you might be asked.

Worked examples

Detailed worked examples with examiner comments show you how you can raise your grade. Here you will find tips on how to use accurate scientific vocabulary, avoid common exam errors and improve your Quality of Written Communication (QWC), and more. Any grades given in the worked example are target grades only. They are specific to the sample question and answer.

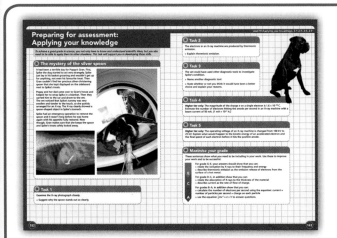

Preparing for assessment

Each Unit contains four Preparing for Assessment activities. These will help build the essential skills that you will need to succeed in your practical investigations and Controlled Assessment, and tackle the Assessment Objectives that appear throughout the Unit.

Each type of Preparing for Assessment activity builds different skills.

> Applying your knowledge: Look at a familiar scientific concept in a new context.

> Planning an investigation: Plan an investigation using handy tips to guide you along the way.

> Analysis and conclusions: Process data and draw conclusions from evidence. Use the hints to help you to achieve top marks.

Assessment skills

A dedicated section at the end of the book will guide you through your practical and written exams with advice on: the language used in exam papers; how best to approach a written exam; how to plan, carry out and evaluate an experiment; how to use maths to evaluate data, and much more.

B3 Using biology (Topic 1)

What you should know

Control systems

Hormones are chemicals produced by glands in the body and released into the blood. They help regulate the body's activities (B1 – Topic 2).

The body works to keep conditions stable or constant, e.g. maintaining body water content. This is called homeostasis (B1 – Topic 2).

Plasma in the blood carries dissolved waste products (B2 – Topic 3).

Sex cells are specialised for their purpose.

The menstrual cycle is a series of events where an egg is released and the uterus prepares for implantation of a fertilised egg.

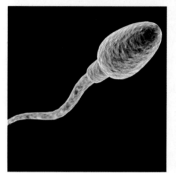

- What is the function of a sperm cell? Describe how and why it is specialised.

Inheritance

Humans have 23 pairs of chromosomes (B1 – Topic 1).

Genetic variation is inherited. Variation is a result of the way in which chromosomes pair up during fertilisation (B1 – Topic 1).

Genetic disorders such as cystic fibrosis can be inherited. Genetic diagrams can be used to predict the probability of inheritance (B1 – Topic 1).

Meiosis produces haploid sex cells (B2 – Topic 1).

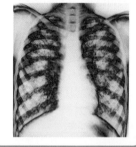

- A man and a woman are both carriers of cystic fibrosis. What is the probability they have a child with the illness?

Health

Pathogens are microbes which cause infectious diseases such as colds and malaria. They are known as vectors (B1 – Topic 3).

Microbes can be grown on agar plates.

Vaccination (immunisation) is used to prevent people from developing infectious diseases.

The immune system kills pathogens that enter the body. One way this is done is by white blood cells producing antibodies (B2 – Topic 3).

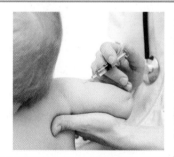

 What is a vaccine?

Plant control systems

Plants produce antibacterials that kill bacteria. Some of these chemicals can treat human diseases (B1 – Topic 3).

Farmers can use chemicals called pesticides to kill weeds and pests.

Plant hormones control plant growth. These hormones can be used in food production (B1 – Topic 2).

Genetically modified foods such as golden rice can provide solutions to problems in the human food supply (B2 – Topic 1).

 How does auxin control plant growth?

You will find out about

> the names of wastes produced by cell metabolism

> the structure of urinary the system

> the structure and function of the nephrons in the kidneys

> how antiduretic hormone (ADH) regulates the body's water content

> the treatment of kidney failure

> the hormonal control of the menstrual cycle

> the structure and functions of sex cells

> infertility treatments

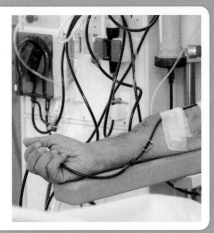

> how the sex of offspring is determined at fertilisation

> how sex-linked genetic disorders are inherited

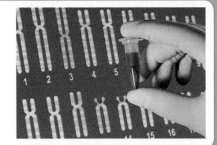

> Edward Jenner and the development of vaccines

> the process of immunisation, its risks and advantages

> the role of memory lymphocytes

> the production and use of monoclonal antibodies

> how bacterial populations grow

> Louis Pasteur and aseptic techniques

> conditions affecting the growth of microorganisms

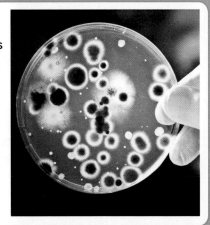

> the impact of pests and pathogens on the human food supply

> how plants defend themselves against attack

> photoperiodicity in plants

> circadian rhythms

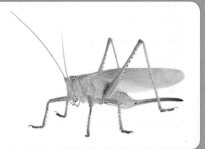

Removing wastes

You will find out:

> that cell metabolism produces wastes

> about the structure of the urinary system

> about the structure and function of the nephron

Insect waste

The waste removal tissues of many insects are called Malpighian tubules. The tubules are bathed in the blood filling the inside of the insect body. Wastes in the blood filter into the Malpighian tubules, are converted into uric acid and then removed through the gut and eventually, the insect's anus.

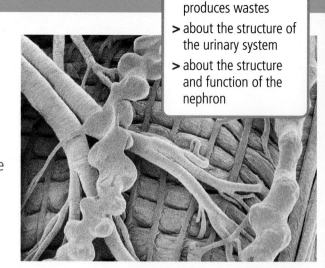

FIGURE 1: Malpighian tubules are slender tubules attached to the insect's gut. In this micrograph they are coloured orange.

Cell metabolism produces wastes

The term **metabolism** refers to all of the chemical reactions taking place in cells. Metabolic reactions break down compounds and form new ones. Some of the new compounds are waste substances and harmful if not removed from the body.

Waste substances produced by cell metabolism build up in the blood. The term **excretion** means their removal from the body.

> Water and carbon dioxide are waste products of aerobic respiration.

> **Urea** is a waste product produced when the liver breaks down excess amino acids.

> Carbon dioxide is excreted by gas exchange in the lungs.

> Water and urea are excreted in the urine.

The kidney is the main excretory organ in humans and other mammals. It also plays a part in **homeostasis** by regulating the amount of water and the concentration of salts and other useful substances in the blood.

Did you know?

The removal of solid waste (faeces) from the body is *not* an example of excretion – this is because the faeces are not produced by cell metabolism.

Remember!

Homeostasis is the maintaining of a stable internal environment, e.g. stable blood glucose content or body temperature.

QUESTIONS

1 Make a table to summarise the excretion of water, urea and carbon dioxide. Use these column headings:

Waste substance	Processes which make this waste substance	Where it is made	Where they are removed from

The urinary system

Urea produced by liver cells is removed in the liquid produced by the kidneys. The liquid is **urine**. It is temporarily stored in the **bladder** before being released from the body.

Figure 2 shows the **urinary system** – the kidneys, their blood supply and connection to the bladder.

Water and salts are needed for the cells of the body to work properly. The surplus which the body does not need is also removed in the urine. Some salts are also lost through the skin when we sweat.

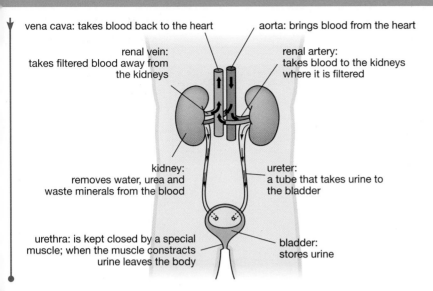

vena cava: takes blood back to the heart

aorta: brings blood from the heart

renal vein: takes filtered blood away from the kidneys

renal artery: takes blood to the kidneys where it is filtered

kidney: removes water, urea and waste minerals from the blood

ureter: a tube that takes urine to the bladder

urethra: is kept closed by a special muscle; when the muscle contracts urine leaves the body

bladder: stores urine

FIGURE 2: The urinary system.

QUESTIONS

2 Describe the function of
  a the renal vein
  b the kidneys
  c the bladder
in the urinary system.

3 Draw a flowchart describing the journey of a molecule of urea through the urinary system.

The nephron

Each kidney consists of about a million tiny tubules called **nephrons**. The nephron's functions are:

> filtration of soluble wastes from the blood

> reabsorption of useful substances back into the blood.

Filtration

Filtration takes place in the hollow shaped **Bowman's capsule** which surrounds a knot of capillary blood vessels called the **glomerulus**. The blood vessels branch from the renal artery. The high pressure of the arterial blood forces urea, glucose and other substances in solution from the blood through the thin walls of the capillary vessels and Bowman's capsule into the space within the capsule. Large molecules and blood cells remain in the blood.

Reabsorption

As the solution of substances travels from the Bowman's capsule through the rest of the nephron, glucose is reabsorbed in solution back into the blood through the walls of the **convoluted tubules**. Blood vessels carry away the glucose to the renal vein. Reabsorption of glucose is selective because urea is not reabsorbed. The blood passing to the renal vein is therefore clean of urea (and other wastes).

Water is reabsorbed back into the blood through the walls of the **loop of Henlé** and **collecting duct**. It is then carried away by blood vessels to the renal vein. The amount of water reabsorbed depends on how much the body needs. More water is absorbed if the body is dehydrated (short of water) than if its tissues are fully hydrated. The body's water balance is regulated by a hormone released from the brain. The process is called **osmoregulation**.

The liquid in the collecting duct is urine. Its composition is very different from when its journey started from the Bowman's capsule through the rest of the nephron. It trickles down the collecting duct to the **ureter** and eventually to the bladder, where it is temporarily stored before release from the body to the outside.

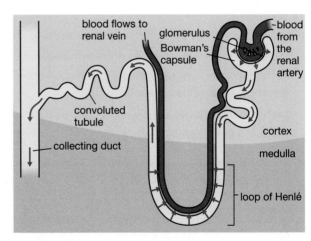

blood flows to renal vein

glomerulus

Bowman's capsule

blood from the renal artery

convoluted tubule

collecting duct

cortex

medulla

loop of Henlé

FIGURE 3: The nephron at work.

QUESTIONS

4 Name in order the structures through which a molecule of urea passes from the renal artery to the outside of the body.

5 Describe how the concentration of glucose, urea and water changes within fluids in the renal artery and vein, glomerulus, Bowman's capsule and bladder.

Helping the kidneys to function

Toxic sharks

The urea content of human blood is on average 14 mg/dm^3 blood while in shark's blood it is 750 mg/dm^3 blood. Inuits who eat shark make sure that they process the meat carefully to avoid being poisoned by this high urea content.

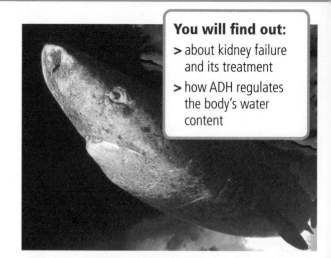

FIGURE 1: A Greenland shark's high blood urea content helps the fish to regulate the water content of its body in salty seawater.

Kidney failure

The presence of proteins in the urine is one of the symptoms of kidney failure. Other symptoms include drowsiness, nausea and swollen feet.

Short-term kidney failure can be caused by:

> infection

> blockage of a ureter.

These can usually be treated by antibiotics or surgery.

Long-term kidney failure can have many causes including:

> effects of unregulated diabetes

> high blood pressure

> tumours in the abdomen.

Controlling the amount of protein in the diet helps to reduce the amount of urea produced by the liver.

However as the person's kidney failure worsens, the urea content of their blood increases to life-threatening levels. The patient needs treatment before this happens.

QUESTIONS

1 List the symptoms of kidney failure.

2 Suggest why restricting the amount of protein in the diet is part of the treatment of a person with kidney failure.

Treatments for kidney failure

Dialysis

One treatment for failing kidneys is **dialysis**.

Blood from the person being treated is pumped to the dialysis machine. Inside the machine, the blood passes through tubes made of a permeable membrane. Urea diffuses from the blood in the tubes through the membrane into the liquid surrounding them. The blood cleared of urea then passes through a tube from the machine back into the person linked up to it.

Did you know?

The Visking tubing used in your biology experiments was originally designed for dialysis machines.

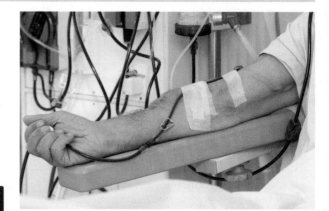

FIGURE 2: A person with kidney failure must use the kidney dialysis machine three times a week. Each treatment takes 3–4 hours.

> Blood containing urea passes from the person into the machine.

> The concentration of salts and sugars dissolved in the **dialysis fluid** is the same as their concentration in the blood. Urea diffuses from the blood in the tubes where it is in high concentration into the dialysis fluid where it is in low concentration.

> As urea diffuses from the blood into the dialysis fluid, the continuous stream of liquid carries it away. This maximises the rate of clearance of urea from the blood in the dialysis tubes.

> 'Clean' blood returns to the person.

Organ donation

Transplantation of a donated kidney gives a person with kidney failure freedom from a restricted diet and the routine of dialysis up to several times each week.

However, the supply of suitable donor kidneys is limited. Rejection of transplants is a risk, and drugs must be taken to combat this.

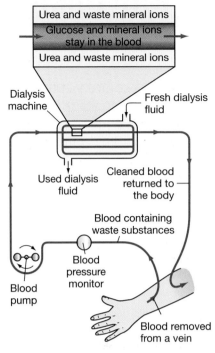

FIGURE 3: Inside a kidney dialysis machine. What is the function of the blood pump?

QUESTIONS

3 Suggest why urea diffuses out of the blood in the dialysis tubes but salts and sugars do not.

4 Explain why the continuous flow of dialysis fluid through the machine maximises the rate of clearance of urea from the blood.

5 Construct a table to show the benefits and drawbacks of kidney transplants and kidney dialysis.

Regulating water content (Higher tier only)

The **pituitary gland**, just below the brain, produces and releases a number of different **hormones** into the blood. One of the hormones is called **antidiuretic hormone (ADH)**. This hormone controls the reabsorption of water from the kidney back into the blood. This control mechanism is an example of **negative feedback**.

ADH: control by negative feedback

Receptor cells in the hypothalamus of the brain detect how much water is in the blood. Nerve impulses from the receptor cells pass to the pituitary gland which then releases more or less ADH depending on the water content of the blood. The process is self-adjusting and an example of homeostasis at work.

If there is an excess of water in the blood

> less ADH is released

> the walls of the collecting ducts of the nephrons become less permeable to water

> less water is reabsorbed back into the blood

> more water is removed in the urine from the body.

If there is too little water in the blood

> more ADH is released

> the walls of the collecting ducts of the nephrons become more permeable to water

> more water is reabsorbed back into the blood

> less water is removed in the urine from the body.

The water content of the blood therefore fluctuates and self-adjusts around a normal, fairly constant, value.

Did you know?

Water makes up about two-thirds of our body weight. It is taken into the body either directly by drinking or indirectly as part of food.

QUESTIONS

6 Explain how ADH keeps the water content of the body's tissues constant.

7 Explain why ADH is an example of a hormone controlled by negative feedback. Draw a diagram to illustrate your answer.

Transplant rejection   Antidiuretic hormone

Controlling the menstrual cycle

Hormone controlled

The human ovary contains tens of thousands of fluid-filled sacs called follicles. Each follicle contains an egg surrounded by cells enclosed within several layers of membrane. During a process called ovulation the eggs are released and are available for fertilisation.

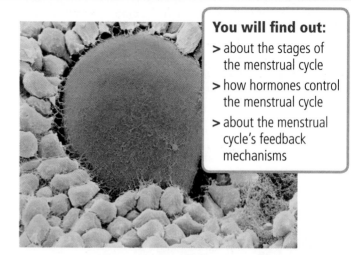

> **You will find out:**
> - > about the stages of the menstrual cycle
> - > how hormones control the menstrual cycle
> - > about the menstrual cycle's feedback mechanisms

FIGURE 1: A micrograph of an immature egg cell surrounded by smaller cells that nourish it while it develops. Where in the body is this egg found?

What is the menstrual cycle?

Between the ages of about 11 and 17 years, a girl's ovaries begin to release eggs, and her periods begin (**menstruation**). The event marks the beginning of **puberty**.

Figure 2 summarises the stages of the menstrual cycle.

> ### QUESTIONS
>
> **1** List the stages of the menstrual cycle.
>
> **2** What is meant by ovulation?

1. On the first day of the cycle, menstruation begins. The thick lining of the uterus breaks down and is lost through the vagina

2. One week into the cycle, the uterus lining is just starting to build up again. An egg is ripening in the ovary

Follicles each containing an egg begin to develop in one of the ovaries

3. Two weeks into the cycle, an egg is released from the ovary (ovulation). The lining of the uterus is soft and thick, ready to receive the egg if it is fertilised

4. Three weeks into the cycle, the egg has almost reached the uterus. If it hasn't been fertilised, it will die

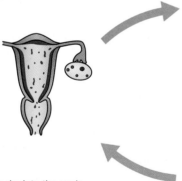

FIGURE 2: The menstrual cycle: the timing of events varies depending on the individual. Why is the menstrual cycle called a 'monthly' cycle?

Role of oestrogen and progesterone in the menstrual cycle

Different hormones control the menstrual cycle. **Oestrogen** and **progesterone** are produced by the ovaries and circulated in the bloodstream.

Oestrogen stimulates growth and repair of the uterus lining, and the development of follicles each containing an egg begin to develop in the ovaries.

As the concentration of oestrogen in the blood increases, the lining of the uterus thickens.

The concentration of progesterone increases just before ovulation, as the concentration of oestrogen falls. The hormone takes over the role of oestrogen. It maintains the thickness of the uterus lining.

If the egg is fertilised, then the pregnant woman does not menstruate. The embryo attaches to the thick spongy lining of the uterus. The blood flowing through the vessels of the lining supplies the embryo with food and oxygen and carry away its wastes.

High levels of blood progesterone continue during pregnancy. This prevents development of more follicles and the release of eggs. Ovulation stops.

QUESTIONS

3 Describe the of the hormones oestrogen and progesterone in the menstrual cycle.

4 Suggest why ovulation stops during pregnancy.

5 Explain why maintaining the thickness of the lining of the uterus is important when a woman becomes pregnant.

Hormones and feedback (Higher tier only)

As well as oestrogen and progesterone, **follicle stimulating hormone (FSH)** and **luteinising hormone (LH)**, released by the pituitary gland, control the menstrual cycle.

Days 1–7

> FSH released from the pituitary gland stimulates maturation of egg follicles.

> The maturation of the follicles stimulates oestrogen production which stimulates the growth and repair of the lining of the uterus and stimulates secretion of LH from the pituitary gland.

Days 8–14

> Continuing release of oestrogen stimulates release of even more LH.

> Progesterone is released before ovulation.

> A surge of LH stimulates the mature follicle to break open, triggering ovulation around day 14. The egg is released. The follicle empty of its egg is called the corpus luteum (yellow body).

Days 15–21

> The corpus luteum secretes progesterone, which maintains the lining of the uterus.

> Progesterone inhibits the secretion of FSH and LH, preventing the growth and development of more follicles.

Days 22–28

If the egg is not fertilised:

> The levels of oestrogen and progesterone drop, triggering the breakdown of the lining of the uterus. Menstruation begins. Low progesterone levels allow an increase in secretion of FSH from the pituitary gland.

> As the menstrual flow tapers off, secretion of FSH increases, marking the start of the next cycle. The next round of growth and development of follicles begins.

If the egg is fertilised:

> Progesterone levels remain high, maintaining the thickness of the lining of the uterus in preparation for pregnancy.

> Inhibition of FSH secretion continues, preventing growth and development of more follicles.

Negative feedback

The menstrual cycle is regulated by negative feedback:

> Negative feedback is the result of the increasing level of oestrogen before ovulation. It inhibits secretion of FSH.

> Similarly, the fall is progesterone towards the end of the cycle results in the pituitary gland releasing more FSH.

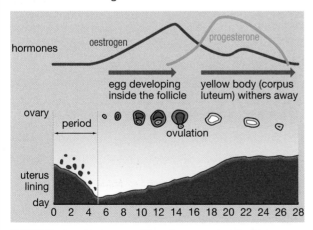

FIGURE 3: How hormones affect the menstrual cycle.

QUESTIONS

6 Explain the feedback mechanisms that regulate the menstrual cycle.

7 Draw a flow diagram to summarise the changes that happen during the menstrual cycle. Add a time scale down the side of your flowchart.

Sex cells and fertilisation

You will find out:
> about how eggs and sperm are adapted
> about fertilisation
> about infertility treatments

Life in a test-tube

Many couples long for a baby but for many reasons find it difficult to conceive. Fertility treatments, such as *in vitro* fertilisation, are now widely available but are still expensive. Fertility treatment available on the National Health Service in the UK varies from region to region, waiting lists can be very long and the eligibility criteria can also be different.

Fertility treatment is, however, a controversial subject. Some people believe that everyone should have access to fertility treatment; others believe that limited funds for healthcare should be directed at those who are ill.

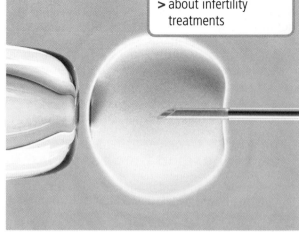

FIGURE 1: *In vitro* fertilisation. Some people are against fertility treatments as they feel the world is overpopulated, while others think it is a basic human right to have a child. What do you think?

Sex cells

> Male sex cells are called sperm.

> Female sex cells are called eggs.

> The term gametes refers to sperm and eggs.

> Each gamete contains one set of genetic material.

Sperm

> Millions of microscopic sperm are released with seminal fluid from the penis.

> A sperm cell is adapted to swim to and fertilise an egg.

> The sperm's tail lashes back and forth driving the sperm towards the egg.

> The lashings are powered by the energy released from the reactions that break down glucose. The reactions occur in the mitochondria of the middle section.

> The **acrosome** helps the sperm to penetrate the outer layers surrounding the egg.

> Sperm do not have food reserves.

Eggs

> An egg cell is bigger than a sperm.

> The egg's cytoplasm contains nutrients for the embryo that develops after fertilisation but before it attaches to the uterus wall.

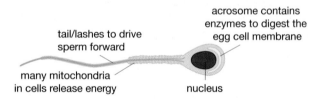

FIGURE 2: A human sperm cell. Why is it important?

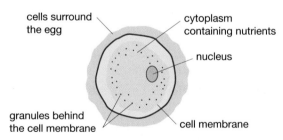

FIGURE 3: A human egg cell. How many sets of genetic material are contained in the nucleus.

QUESTIONS

1 Describe how sperm swim.

2 Suggest why eggs are larger than sperm.

3 Make a table to compare the structure and function of sperm and eggs.

Fertilisation

Sperm and egg cells are haploid and have a nucleus. They have only half the number of chromosomes of most of the other (diploid) cells of the body.

Fertilisation occurs when the sperm nucleus fuses with the egg nucleus. The haploid set of chromosomes in the nucleus of each cell combine, forming the nucleus of the now fertilised egg. The egg when it is fertilised is called a **zygote**.

Fertilisation restores the diploid state. The zygote has a full set of chromosomes inherited equally from the parents.

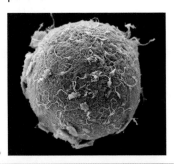

FIGURE 4: A coloured micrograph of sperm (blue) attempting to penetrate a human egg (brown). How does the sperm penetrate the egg?

> When a sperm reaches an egg, the acrosome at its pointed end releases enzymes. These break down the cells surrounding the egg, helping the sperm to penetrate it.

> After the head of the sperm makes contact with the cell membrane of the egg, its tail and middle section break off. The head enters the cytoplasm of the egg. A substance released by granules in the cytoplasm just behind the egg membrane seals the membrane. No more sperm cells can enter the egg.

> The nucleus of the sperm head is released and passes through the cytoplasm of the egg to the egg nucleus. The nucleus of the sperm and the egg nucleus fuse. A zygote is formed.

QUESTIONS

4 Define fertilisation.

5 Explain the statement 'fertilisation restores the diploid state'.

Treating infertility

Couples are usually thought to be infertile if they have regular sexual intercourse without contraception for 12 months without the woman becoming pregnant.

Male infertility

Normal semen contains over 20 million sperm cells/cm^3, more than 50% of which are healthy. A man's fertility is affected if his sperm count falls much below this figure.

Taking tablets containing testosterone (the hormone promoting sperm formation) can improve an infertile man's sperm count. Another solution is **insemination** of the woman with the semen from another man (donor).

Female infertility

A woman may be infertile because she cannot:

> release eggs naturally

> carry pregnancy to full term.

Insufficient FSH is one cause of infertility. Oestrogen inhibits the production of FSH by the pituitary gland. So taking a drug that makes the pituitary gland insensitive to oestrogen can raise FSH levels and improve fertility.

In vitro **fertilisation (IVF)** begins by treating the woman with hormones that bring on ovulation. The eggs produced are retrieved and prepared for fertilisation in a laboratory dish or test-tube (*in vitro* means 'in glass'). Sperm from her partner (or donor) are mixed with selected eggs. One or two of the embryos produced are placed in the woman's uterus.

Donor eggs come from a third-party donor. Otherwise, the method is the same as for IVF.

Surrogate mothers agree to carry a baby for an infertile couple and give the baby to the couple after giving birth. There are two alternatives: the surrogate's own egg is fertilised with the father-to-be's sperm using IVF or the surrogate mother carries the genetic child of the infertile couple conceived through IVF.

Advantages and disadvantages

Drug and IVF treatment allow couples to have a baby that carries their own genes. The disadvantages include the possible drug side-effects as well as the cost and availability of treatment.

Insemination using donor sperm can raise issues of paternity. Likewise, using donor eggs and surrogate mothers can create emotional issues relating to the biological parents as well as the practical issues of family medical history.

The storage and potential use of embryos also raises ethical questions.

QUESTIONS

6 Compare the advantages and disadvantages of treating female infertility with hormones and with donor eggs.

7 Evaluate the issues of medically treating an infertile woman who cannot conceive with IVF.

8 Discuss the ethical issues surrounding surrogacy.

Sex and sex-linked genetic disorders

Red, green and blue

Red–green colour blindness is a sex-linked recessive trait. The gene for red and green colour receptors is found on the X chromosome. As males have only one X chromosome (XY), while females have two (XX), it is more common in males than females, although females are often carriers.

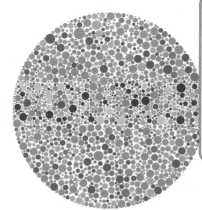

FIGURE 1: A colour-blindness test: can you see it?

Inheritance of sex

The **X chromosome** and **Y chromosome** are known as the sex chromosomes because they determine the sex of the individual.

Females have two X chromosomes and males have an X and a Y chromosome.

In a normal female one X chromosome becomes inactive and the other controls female development.

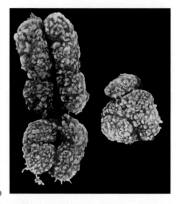

FIGURE 2: A coloured micrograph of human X and Y chromosomes as found in a male. How did the X and Y chromosomes get their names?

In the male, the Y chromosome causes the male genital system to develop.

> There are 23 pairs of chromosomes.

> The chromosomes in the first 22 pairs are similar in size and shape in both the man and the woman.

> The chromosomes of the 23rd pair (the sex chromosomes) are different.

> The larger chromosome is the X chromosome; the smaller chromosome is the Y chromosome.

QUESTIONS

1 How could you identify the sex of a person from their chromosomes?

2 Why is it important that the 23rd pair of chromosomes are different in men and women?

Genetics of sex

Since the body cells of a woman each carry two X chromosomes, during meiosis the egg cell produced can only carry an X chromosome. Each body cell of a man, however, carries an X chromosome and a Y chromosome, so during meiosis two types of sperm are produced: 50% carry an X chromosome and 50% carry a Y chromosome. Whether the egg is fertilised by a sperm carrying an X chromosome or a Y chromosome determines a baby's sex.

The birth of almost equal numbers of girls and boys is governed by the production of equal numbers of X and Y sperm at meiosis.

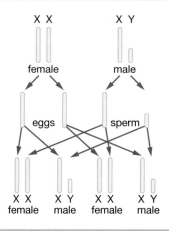

FIGURE 3: A genetic diagram showing how the sex of offspring is determined. What is the probability of a couple conceiving a girl?

Q Making a karyotype   Sex ratio   Sex-linked disorders

QUESTIONS

3 Explain why there is *almost* an equal number of births of baby girls and baby boys.

4 In reality there are *slightly* more boys born than girls. Suggest why, using the internet to help you.

Sex-linked disorders

Haemophilia

Haemophilia is a sex-linked genetic disorder that causes a person's blood not to clot properly. The person fails to produce a clotting agent because of a mutation in one of the **alleles** of the gene controlling its synthesis. The mutant allele is recessive and located on the X chromosome, which is why haemophilia is described as a sex-linked disorder.

A woman carrying the mutant allele on one of her X chromosomes does not suffer from haemophilia because the normal allele of the other X chromosome is dominant. The dominant allele hides the effect of its recessive mutant partner. Enough clotting factor is made for normal blood clotting to take place.

The woman is called a **carrier** because she has one recessive mutant allele on one of her X chromosomes. She is able to pass it on to her children. For a woman to have haemophilia she would have to have two recessive mutant alleles, one from each parent. Fortunately, the mutant allele is rare so this does not happen often.

The inheritance outcome probabilities for haemophilia are shown in Figures 4 and 5.

If a man inherits the recessive mutant allele for haemophilia on the X chromosome, there is no dominant allele on the Y chromosome to hide its effect. So the clotting factor is not produced and the man suffers from haemophilia.

Colour blindness

Another sex-linked disorder caused by a recessive mutant allele on the X chromosome is red–green **colour blindness**. Women with a single recessive allele on the X chromosome are carriers. They only have the disorder if they inherit two recessive alleles.

Red–green colour blindness is found in only 0.04% of women but in 8% of men.

Remember!
The outcomes shown in genetic diagrams represent probabilities, not necessarily the actual results.

QUESTIONS

5 Explain why women rarely suffer from sex-linked genetic disorders.

6 Use a genetic diagram to explain why red–green colour blindness affects more men than women.

7 Jane is a carrier of the haemophilia allele. None of her two sons or two daughters is affected by haemophilia. Explain why.

8 What is the probability of the offspring of a colour-blind man and a normal-visioned woman who carries the recessive colour-blindness gene inheriting the disorder? Express your results as ratios and percentages.

	Mother	
	X^h	X^H
X	$X^H X^h$	$X^H X^H$
Y	$X^h Y$	$X^H Y$

(Father on left axis; Children on right)

X^h represents the haemophilia-carrying chromosome and X^H represents a normal chromosome

FIGURE 4: The Punnett square shows the outcome possibilities for offspring of a haemophilia-carrier mother and a non-haemophiliac father. Express the probability of the children inheriting or carrying the disease as ratios and percentages.

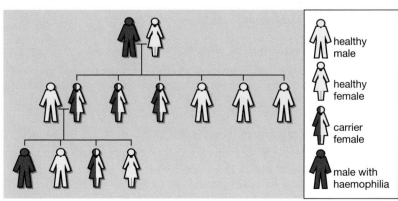

healthy male

healthy female

carrier female

male with haemophilia

FIGURE 5: A genetic diagram showing how haemophilia is passed on through a family. If the second-generation couple had another son, what is the probability of him having haemophilia?

Immunisation

You will find out:

> about Edward Jenner and vaccine development

> about immunisation

> about the role of memory lymphocytes

Eradication of a virus

Smallpox is caused by a virus. Fluid-filled pustules cover the body of someone with smallpox. Survivors are often left with a scarred and pitted skin. A global programme of vaccination helped to stamp out smallpox by 1977. The smallpox virus exists only in secure facilities in the USA and Russia. Some scientists have argued that these samples should be destroyed.

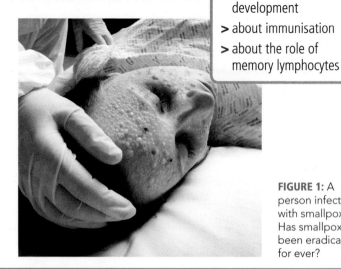

FIGURE 1: A person infected with smallpox. Has smallpox been eradicated for ever?

Vaccinations

Edward Jenner

> Smallpox is believed to have originated in the Middle East over 3000 years ago. Smallpox was a deadly disease and, until its eradication in 1979, killed over 30% of people it infected.

> Edward Jenner (1743–1823) was a country doctor who noticed that milkmaids who caught the mild disease **cowpox** from the cows they milked rarely caught the much more serious **smallpox**.

> Jenner tested his theory that people infected with cowpox were protected from smallpox.

> He deliberately infected several people with cowpox. The people soon developed cowpox but were not affected by smallpox.

> Next, he infected a boy who had just recovered from cowpox with pus from the pustules of someone with smallpox. His survival supported Jenner's theory.

> We now know that the virus causing cowpox is very similar to the smallpox virus.

> Jenner published his results in 1798. The work established **immunisation (vaccination)** as a powerful weapon in the fight against disease.

Risks and advantages of vaccination

> All vaccines have side-effects. For example, for every 500 000 immunisations of whooping cough vaccine, about 50 children experience a side-effect. Of these, less than seven suffer serious complications. Without immunisation, 20 000 children would be at risk of dying.

> If 80% of children are immunised, the population as a whole is protected from whooping cough. This is called the **herd effect**.

Following a scare of the vaccine's safety, the numbers of children immunised against whooping cough fell to 30% in 1975, well below the percentage needed for the herd effect. Outbreaks followed in 1977–9 and 1981–3. Gradually people's confidence in the vaccine was restored. By 1986 the numbers of children immunised had increased so that the herd effect meant that further outbreaks of whooping cough were prevented.

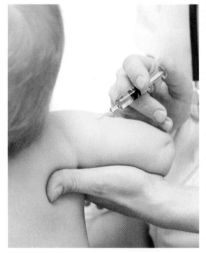

FIGURE 2: A baby being vaccinated. In the UK the immunisation of children starts in the first year of life.

QUESTIONS

1 Imagine the year is 1798. Write a letter describing Jenner's vaccination discovery and persuading a relative to have a cowpox vaccination.

2 Read through the data on whooping cough. Do you think the data shows that the advantages of vaccination outweigh the risks?

The immune response

Bacteria, viruses and other organisms that cause disease are called pathogens. The body recognises pathogens because their surfaces are covered in 'foreign' molecules. These are called **antigens**.

White blood cells called **lymphocytes** and **phagocytes** take action when the antigens are detected. They are part of the body's immune system; their actions are the **immune response**:

B-lymphocytes produce proteins called **antibodies**. These antibodies bind to antigens and begin to destroy the pathogens carrying them (see Figure 4). Phagocytes finish the job (see Figure 5).

Antigens also trigger the production of **memory lymphocytes**. These quickly produce antibodies again if they detect the same antigens at a later date.

A **vaccine** contains a pathogen that has been made harmless by killing it, weakening it or using only a part of it. An immunisation may be given by injection or as something to swallow.

The harmless antigens in the vaccine trigger the person's B-cells to produce antibodies and memory cells. When the harmful form of the pathogen infects the body, the memory cells quickly produce antibodies which destroy the pathogen. The vaccine has made the person immune to the particular pathogen and the disease it causes.

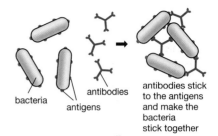

FIGURE 3: The immune response in action.

QUESTIONS

3 Describe what happens when B-lymphocytes detect antigen molecules.

4 Explain the difference between an antigen and an antibody.

5 Explain why we are not usually affected by the symptoms of infectious disease more than once in a lifetime.

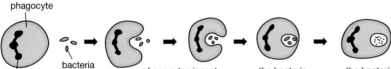

FIGURE 4: A phagocyte ingesting bacteria.

Immunological memory (Higher tier only)

The body's immune system takes some time for its B-lymphocytes to produce antibodies against a first-time infection. This is the **primary immune response**. We might feel ill for a few days and then recover.

For reccurring infections the reaction is much quicker. This is called the **secondary immune response**.

The memory lymphocyte cells left over as the result of the first-time exposure to antigen quickly divide on re-exposure to the same antigen.

The blood plasma concentration of antibodies increases very quickly. The immediate immune response often destroys the pathogen before it can multiply.

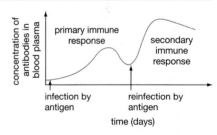

FIGURE 5: The graph shows how the concentration of antibodies in blood plasma varies in response to the first and subsequent infections by the same antigen.

QUESTIONS

6 Explain the difference between a primary immune response and a secondary immune response.

7 Explain the immune response in someone who has been vaccinated against chicken pox and is later re-exposed to the disease.

8 The flu virus continually changes its structure. Suggest why this means that we can get flu several times.

Monoclonal antibodies

You will find out:
> how monoclonal antibodies are produced
> how monoclonal antibodies are used

A magic bullet?

Researchers have discovered a monoclonal antibody that may be effective against avian (bird) flu and swine flu. Despite their names, these types of influenza can be fatal for humans and, although vaccines may be effective, they can take a long time to develop. It is thought that the monoclonal antibodies attack parts of the virus coat that is common to several strains of flu.

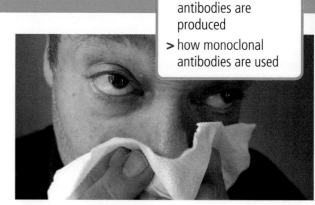

FIGURE 1: Could a flu epidemic be stopped in its tracks by monoclonal antibodies?

What are monoclonal antibodies? (Higher tier only)

B-lymphocytes produce millions of different antibodies in response to different antigens.

Each molecule of antigen usually has several regions, each of which triggers B-lymphocytes to produce antibodies specific to that region. This means that B-lymphocytes produce several antibody types in response to a particular antigen. The different types are a mixture and called **polyclonal antibodies**.

Successful use of antibodies often requires pure samples of a particular antibody that binds only to a particular antigen or part of an antigen. These antibodies are called **monoclonal antibodies**.

QUESTIONS

1 Explain the difference between monoclonal and polyclonal antibodies.

2 Explain the meaning of the phrase 'antibodies are specific'.

Hybridomas (Higher tier only)

Producing monoclonal antibodies in quantity from B-lymphocytes alone is impossible. The cells *cannot* divide. This problem is solved by fusing them with a cancerous B-cell called a **myeloma**. Myeloma cells *can* divide.

The fused cells are called **hybridomas**: they produce monoclonal antibodies *and* they divide.

Production technology

> A mouse is genetically engineered to produce human antibodies.

> The mouse is injected with the antigen that triggers production of the required antibody.

> If the immune response occurs, B-lymphocytes are removed.

> The lymphocytes are fused with myeloma cells grown in culture to produce hybridomas.

> Hybridomas are grown in culture and screened for antibodies specific to the antigen first injected into the mouse.

> The monoclonal antibodies are then extracted.

Once identified, the hybridomas can be kept more or less indefinitely growing in culture as a source of monoclonal antibodies that bind to the antigen in question (see Figure 2).

FIGURE 2: Producing monoclonal antibodies. Is it ethical to use mice to produce hybridomas?

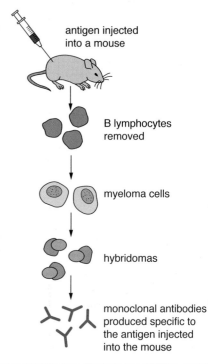

antigen injected into a mouse

B lymphocytes removed

myeloma cells

hybridomas

monoclonal antibodies produced specific to the antigen injected into the mouse

Did you know?

The ending '-oma' is often used for the rapidly growing cells of a tumour.

QUESTIONS

3 Explain why the discovery of hybridomas was a key step in the production of monoclonal antibodies.

4 Summarise the stages of monoclonal antibody production as a flow diagram.

Using monoclonal antibodies (Higher tier only)

Pregnancy testing

In the early stages of pregnancy a woman's urine contains the hormone **human chorionic gonadotropin (hCG)**. Its presence in urine is the basis of pregnancy test kits that use monoclonal antibodies.

A kit consists of a dipstick impregnated with antibodies. The stick is dipped into a sample of urine:

> any hCG molecules present in the urine will bind to the antibodies at the end of the dipstick and travel up the stick to meet other antibodies that also bind with hCG, to produce a colour change indicating the woman is pregnant.

> when there is no hCG in the urine, the antibodies diffuse along the stick and combine with another band of different antibodies to produce a colour change that indicates the woman is not pregnant.

Blood clots

Blood clots carry particular antigens. Specific monoclonal antibodies bind to the antigens. Markers on the antibodies enable doctors to locate the blood clots.

Diagnosis and treatment of cancer

Some types of cancer cell have different proteins at their surface compared with the surface proteins of healthy cells. The cancer cell proteins are antigens and they can trigger production of monoclonal antibodies that bind only to them. The monoclonal antibodies are combined with anti-cancer drugs, making it possible to deliver the drugs to the cancer cells only.

Advantages of using monoclonal antibodies

One of the problems with some cancer treatments, such as drugs and radiotherapy, is that healthy cells are often killed as well as the cancerous cells. As monoclonal antibodies are cancer-cell specific, healthy cells are unaffected. This means that side-effects to the patient that can result from losing healthy cells are reduced.

QUESTIONS

5 Explain how monoclonal antibodies are used to treat cancer.

6 Explain the biology behind using monoclonal antibodies in pregnancy testing kits.

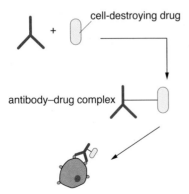
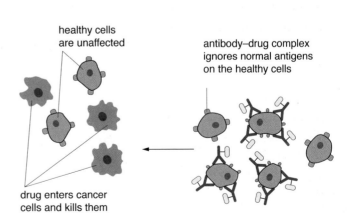

cell-destroying drug

antibody–drug complex

antibody–drug complex attaches to the abnormal antigens

healthy cells are unaffected

drug enters cancer cells and kills them

antibody–drug complex ignores normal antigens on the healthy cells

FIGURE 3: Monoclonal antibody–anti-cancer drug combinations target cancer cells.

Microorganism growth and infection

Filthy lucre

Figure 1 shows what happened after an old banknote was pressed on an agar gel plate containing a nutrient medium for 5 min and then removed. Bacteria and fungal spores started to grow on the plate. The photo shows the growth after 5 days.

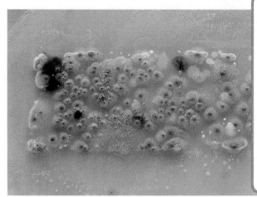

FIGURE 1: Banknotes have a wide variety of microorganisms on their surface. Why do you think it is a good idea to wash your hands after handling paper money?

Population growth

Laboratory studies show that populations of bacteria grow in a particular way. At first, the increase in the population is small.

However, as the population grows, so does the rate of increase. Think about it as a doubling: 2, 4, 8, 16, 32, 64, 128, 256, 512, 1024, … and so on.

> Each generation is double the size of the previous generation – the increase is **exponential**.

> Bacterial cells can divide every 20 minutes, producing a new generation.

> Starting with a single cell, 25 cycles of division produce more than a million descendant cells within 8–9 hours.

Exponential increase in numbers of a bacterial population occurs when conditions for growth are ideal. This exponential growth causes rapid development of infection.

Factors affecting bacterial growth include temperature, pH and the availability of resources such as nutrients and oxygen (depending on the species).

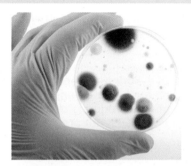

FIGURE 2: Imagine the first step of a bacterium dividing into two, and then the two bacteria dividing to create four cells. How many bacteria would there be after 12 steps?

QUESTIONS

1 Explain the difference between exponential increase and arithmetic increase. Use the internet to help you.

2 Why does the exponential growth of population of bacteria make the bacteria more dangerous to humans?

Growing microorganisms

The exponential growth of a bacterial population in culture does not continue indefinitely. Eventually it slows as the increasing population uses up the resources available to it.

It is possible to culture (grow) bacteria in Petri dishes on solid jelly-like agar or in test-tubes filled with a clear liquid broth. Agar and broth are **growing media**. Each contains the nutrients and other substances bacteria need to grow.

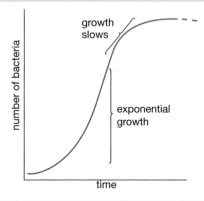

FIGURE 3: A population growth curve of bacteria in culture.

You can set up different experiments to investigate how changing conditions affect the rate of bacterial growth. For example, you could investigate the effect on bacterial growth of different:

> nutrient solutions, each containing nutrients in different proportions (constants: temperature and pH)

> temperature (constants: nutrients and pH)

> pH (constants: nutrients and temperature).

Make sure that you keep constant all conditions other than the one you're investigating.

Testing

You can test the growth of the bacterial population in each test-tube using a solution of **resazurin dye**. Substances produced by the bacteria cause the dye to change colour.

The faster the colour change, the faster the growth in numbers of bacteria.

Louis Pasteur and aseptic techniques

Louis Pasteur (1822–95) proved that bacteria made milk sour and turned the ethanol in wine into the ethanoic acid of vinegar.

What Pasteur did not know (nor did anyone else) was where the bacteria came from. Many people believed that 'bad' food made microorganisms and some thought microorganisms contaminated food and turned it 'bad'. Pasteur attempted to settle the question with his swan-necked flask experiments.

Pasteur put meat broth into glass flasks and heated the glass until he could pull out the necks into S-shaped curves. He then boiled the contents of the flasks to kill any microorganisms.

On cooling, the flasks' contents were not contaminated by microorganisms because the swan-necked design trapped them. As a result, the air reaching the meat broth was sterile, and the broth did not go bad.

When the flask was tilted, the microorganisms, attached to dust particles that had settled in the lower bend of the flask, fell into the meat broth and it soon turned bad.

Pasteur's ideas that microorganisms are killed by heat and that procedures preventing contamination are possible, are the basis of **aseptic techniques**. Aseptic means 'without sepsis', in other words, without the bacteria that cause disease or cause things to go bad.

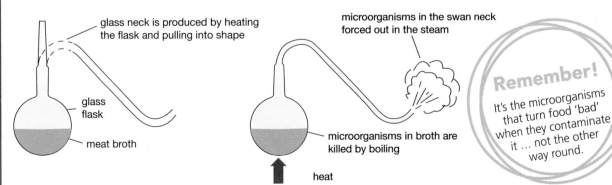

FIGURE 4: Pasteur's swan-necked flask experiments demonstrated that microorganisms are in the air.

Plants, defences and food supply

Biodiversity supplies new drugs

Scientists are hoping to devise new drugs that come from the substances that plants produce to defend themselves from attack by herbivores and pathogens.

FIGURE 1: The *Thonningia* flower is a traditional medicine used to treat kidney stones and ear infections. It is now being investigated as an antibacterial drug.

 ## Pests and pathogens

Pests are the plants, fungi and animals that destroy crops and livestock, or prevent land from being used for farming.

Their impact on human food supply can be devastating.

> Plant pests (**weeds**) compete with crop plants for soil, water, light and nutrients.

> Fungal pests cause disease. For example, **blight** is a disease of potatoes.

> Animal pests are mostly **herbivorous** insects. For example, cutworms chew off plants at soil level and locusts strip fields of crops.

> Insect pests spread plant diseases. As blackfly and greenfly suck the sap of plants, viruses pass through their mouthparts into the sap. The flow of sap transports the viruses round the plant.

In the UK, around 10–20% of crop production is lost to pests and pathogens, and growers spend millions on pesticides.

FIGURE 2: A farmer walks through a swarm of locusts in the desert near Keren, Ethiopia. State why locusts are a threat to human food supplies.

Did you know?

The Irish potato harvest failed between 1845 and 1849 because of blight. The majority of the population depended on potatoes as their main food supply.

More than a million people died of starvation. A further million escaped famine by emigrating, mainly to the USA. Within a few years the population of Ireland was halved.

○ QUESTIONS

1 Summarise the impact of pests on human food supply.

2 Describe the way blackfly and greenfly can pass on viruses to plants.

Plant defences

Plants can produce chemicals that kill, paralyse or deter their attackers.

> **Alkaloids** such as caffeine, nicotine and quinine, have different **pharmacological** effects, these include disrupting the transmission of nerve impulses causing paralysis, weakening cell structures or inhibiting protein synthesis.

Almost all produce a bitter taste which deters animals (including insect pests) from eating the plants.

> **Cyanogens** are stored in non-poisonous form in the vacuoles of plant cells. Eating breaks open the plant cells, releasing the cyanogens within.

Enzymes in the cytoplasm of the fragmented cells catalyse the conversion of the cyanogens to poisonous hydrogen cyanide which blocks cellular respiration. The animal eating the plant dies.

> **Phenolics** such as **tannins** and flavonoids make it difficult for herbivores to digest the plant material. The animals starve and die.

> **Terpenoids** such as taxol and citronella repel insects. You might burn citronella candles outdoors to keep insects away from barbecued food.

Costs and benefits to plants

Producing defensive chemicals costs plants in terms of resources and energy. Their benefits therefore must outweigh the costs. Survival of the plants is a measure of the chemicals' benefits. Plants reduce cost by:

> only producing defensive chemicals when under attack

> concentrating chemicals at the site of attack.

Did you know?

The word 'alkaloid' means imitation alkali because alkaloids contain nitrogen atoms making them bases. This is also why they taste bitter.

QUESTIONS

3 Explain why most of us do not like bitter-tasting substances.

4 Describe how plants prevent the cost of using their defences from killing them.

Pharmaceuticals

Many of the chemicals that plants produce to defend themselves affect the **metabolism** of the cells of the herbivores eating them. We can use these effects to produce **pharmaceuticals** that treat human diseases and relieve their symptoms.

Treating MRSA

Honey contains **antibacterials** and can be used to keep wounds clear of infection.

For example, trials show that Manuka honey stops the growth of methicillin-resistant *Staphylococcus aureus* (MRSA).

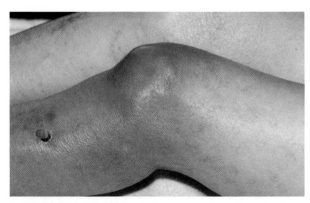

FIGURE 3: Septic arthritis of a knee joint caused by MRSA. How might new drugs help doctors to treat their patients?

Treating malaria

Malaria is a disease caused by the parasite *Plasmodium*, carried by mosquitoes. The parasites attack red blood cells and result in the infected person suffering flu-like symptoms and in severe cases coma and death.

It was found that quinine, from the bark and leaves of the *Cinchona* tree, could be used to treat malaria. The drug lowers body temperature and kills *Plasmodium* parasites.

Relieving pain

Aspirin is a derivative of salicylic acid, originally made from willow tree bark. It reduces:

> pain

> fever

> swelling in joints and other tissues

> the formation of blood clots.

QUESTIONS

5 Explain the meaning of 'active ingredient'.

6 Using the internet to help you, explain how traditional medicine has been used to develop important drugs.

Rhythms of life

You will find out:
> about photoperiodicity in plants
> about circadian rhythms

Synchronicity

Hamsters love to run in the play wheel in their pen. Their owners know, however, that their pet will only run in the wheel at a certain time of day. Their running time is so predictable you can set your watch by it. Why is this the case?

FIGURE 1: Running on time. What stimulus affects the hamster's behaviour?

What are rhythms?

Some environmental changes occur regularly and continuously: they have a rhythm and predictability – the changing seasons, for example. Organisms respond rhythmically in step with these predictable changes. For example, woodland plants respond to the seasonal changes in the intensity of light reaching the woodland floor.

The woodland cycle

> In woodland, winter/spring sunshine floods through bare branches, lighting up the woodland floor.

> As summer approaches, sprouting leaves filter the light. Less passes through to ground level.

> In high summer, the leaves are fully open and form a continuous **canopy**. Their dense layers are an effective light block. The woodland floor is dimly lit compared with spring time.

Plants of the woodland floor take advantage of the spring light shining through the bare branches. The increase in the hours of daylight and light intensity are the trigger for the **overwintering** seeds of different plant species to:

> *germinate* – the seeds sprout shoots and roots

> *grow* and mature into plants producing flowers

> *reproduce* and form new seeds.

These processes happen before the developing canopy reduces light levels.

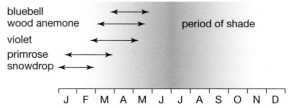

FIGURE 3: Plants of the woodland floor flower before the canopy is in full leaf. The arrows indicate the flowering season. Using this information, when was the photo in Figure 2 taken?

QUESTIONS

1 Using Figure 3, describe the sequence of flowering of the different plants of the woodland floor.

2 What is the advantage to woodland plants of flowering and reproducing before the canopy of leaves fully develops?

FIGURE 2: An ancient bluebell forest in Wales.

Photoperiodicity in plants

Figure 4 shows the seasonal changes in the amount of light reaching ground level in an oak wood in the UK. At the beginning of March there are 11 hours of daylight (11 light (L) and 13 dark (D)). This increases to 16 hours by the end of May (16L/8D).

The period of light/dark is called the **photoperiod**.

The ratio of the period of light to dark needed to cause flowering is called the **critical period**. The critical period for each plant species is different and accounts for the succession of woodland flowers before the leaf canopy is fully developed.

The flowering response of plants falls into three broad categories:

> long-day plants which flower in response to the long period of light of summer days

> short-day plants which flower in response to the shorter period of light of spring or autumn days

> day-neutral plants whose flowering is unaffected by the period of light.

Manipulating the photoperiod

So far we have described flowering times in terms of day length. However, the length of the dark period seems to be the critical factor.

Manipulating the photoperiod allows commercial plant growers to guarantee supplies of flowers out of season. For example, poinsettias and chrysanthemums make colourful displays at Christmas although the plants naturally flower in the autumn.

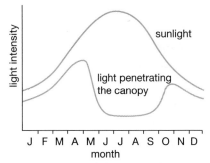

FIGURE 4: Seasonal changes in the amount of light inside an oak wood. The canopy is fully developed in June and July. What happens in October and November that increases the light passing through the canopy?

QUESTIONS

3 Look at Figure 3. Identify a short-day plant and a long-day plant and estimate their critical photoperiods.

4 Explain how light and dark affect flowering.

5 Suggest how poinsettias are made to flower at Christmas.

Circadian rhythms

Many biological rhythms approximate to a 24-hour (**circadian**) cycle.

Experiments show that circadian rhythms continue even when environmental conditions, such as light and temperature, stay constant. A rhythm that persists in this way is called **free running**.

The rhythm is driven from within cells and not by environmental changes. Nevertheless, environmental cues 'set' the clock so that the rhythms run 'on time'. Although free-running rhythms persist, they drift in the absence of cues. Supplying the cues resets the clocks and the rhythms return to the 'right time'.

Sleep is an example of a circadian rhythm. Jet lag or shift work can affect this.

What is a biological clock?

Scientists think that **biological clocks** within cells drive circadian rhythms. Quite how biological clocks work is not clear. Research suggests that switching genes 'on' and 'off' at the right time sets up a rhythm of transcription and protein synthesis, and is an important part of the process.

Many hormones and all enzymes are proteins. The rhythm of their secretion is often circadian, and supports the cycle of protein synthesis idea as a clock mechanism. For example, synthesis of the enzyme **alcohol dehydrogenase** peaks in most people in the late afternoon. The enzyme catalyses reactions which break down alcohol in the liver. Most people therefore are more tolerant of alcohol at around 5 pm than at other times of the day.

Did you know?

Some marmots were kept for long periods under constant temperatures and same day lengths. Despite the lack of external cues that winter was approaching, they started eating more food in the autumn, just as they do in nature, to prepare for hibernation.

QUESTIONS

6 Describe the features of circadian rhythms that are different from other types of rhythm.

7 Suggest the advantage of a circadian rhythm.

Preparing for assessment: Applying your knowledge

To achieve a good grade in science, you not only have to know and understand scientific ideas, but you also need to be able to apply them to other situations. This task will support you in developing these skills.

✳ New polio vaccine to save thousands of lives worldwide

It is the 1950s. Abi is 6 years old and lives in Chicago, America. She is going to be vaccinated against polio.

Polio is a disease that can be prevented but not cured. At this time, teams of scientists have just recently developed vaccines and polio is being virtually eradicated in North America and Europe.

At first Abi doesn't understand why she is at the doctors as she doesn't feel ill. Her mother explains though that polio is a horrible disease, leaving victims disabled, but that it is easy to prevent with a vaccine. A nurse puts a few drops of the vaccine on a sugar lump, which Abi then eats. She doesn't see how eating a sugar lump will stop her catching anything!

What happens is that the sugar lump dissolves in the mouth and stomach, and the polio vaccine, containing a harmless version of the polio virus, enters the bloodstream. The body's white blood cells respond. They start producing antibodies to attack the virus. Because this version of the virus cannot cause the disease, there is no risk to Abi. However, now she has antibodies ready and waiting if the harmful polio virus infects her in the future.

Having the vaccination meant that it was almost impossible for Abi to catch polio, even if the virus entered her body. Discuss in your group how the vaccination works.

✳ Task 1

> If Abi caught polio, why might it spread through her body?

> Why is it important to stop people catching polio?

Task 2

> Explain why, prior to vaccination, the body is unable to use its existing antibodies to deal with the polio virus.

 Task 3

> Vaccination involves putting a live but weakened virus into the body. How does the body recognise a virus?

> What would happen if the polio virus got into Abi's body after she had been vaccinated?

 Task 4

> Why do some people decide not to be vaccinated?

> What do you think about vaccination?

Task 5

> If Abi caught the polio virus after being vaccinated, what similarities and differences would you notice between blood tests straight after the vaccination and after the infection?

> Explain the secondary response you described above.

Maximise your grade

These sentences show what you need to include in your work to achieve each grade. Use them to improve your work and be more successful.

E
For grades F–E, your answers should show that you can:
> understand that microorganisms can produce substances that damage the body
> understand that our bodies provide ideal conditions for microorganisms to grow and multiply
> state the risks and advantages of immunisation
> describe what vaccines are.

C
For grades D–C, in addition, show that you can:
> explain how our immune systems, including white blood cells, defend us against disease
> explain how antibodies protect us from pathogens and also how they recognise and respond to organisms that have been encountered before.

A
For grades B–A, in addition, show that you can:
> evaluate the risks and advantages associated with immunisation
> describe how secondary response occurs.

Preparing for assessment: Planning an investigation

To achieve a good grade in science, you not only have to know and understand scientific ideas, but you need to be able to apply them to other situations and investigations. This task will support you in developing these skills.

✳ Investigating the growth of microorganisms

A student wanted to investigate the effect of different preservation processes on milk. She did this by investigating the growth of microorganisms.

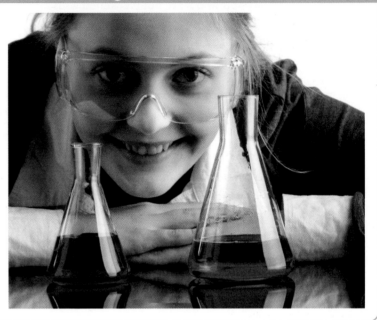

For her experiment, she used different types of milk such as pasteurised milk (skimmed, semi skimmed and full fat), long-life milk and raw milk.

The student's idea was to test for microbial growth in the different type of milk. She decided to use resazurin dye.

Resazurin is an indicator dye that is used to show the amount of oxygen in a liquid. When there is a high concentration of oxygen, resazurin is blue and as the oxygen concentration decreases it changes first to pink and then to colourless.

Planning

1. Suggest a hypothesis that the student could test.

2. Make a list of the variables that might affect the growth of microorganisms in milk. For each variable say how you are going to control it.

3. How are you going to measure the growth of the microorganisms?

4. Make a list of the equipment that is needed for the experiment.
Why is each piece of equipment needed?

5. How much data are you going to collect?

6. What risks are associated with microorganisms?
How can you minimise the risk?
How will you stop the risk of infection from the microorganisms?

7. Write down the step-by-step method you will use to collect your data.

> Think about what the microorgansims need for food and respiration.
> Remember the conditions for each milk should be identical apart from the different milk.

> What observations will you make? Explain clearly how you will know if the microorganisms are growing.
> You could carry out secondary research to help you.

> It might be useful to draw a labelled diagram to show how you will set up the equipment as well.

> Be precise here – how long and how often will you observe the milk? Will you repeat anything?

> Make a list of how you are at risk from infection.
> This is very important because infection from microorganisms could make people very ill.

> Use your answers from above. Make sure your method is clear and could be followed by someone else.

Results

1. Before you collect your data, use tasks 3 and 5 from the Planning section to draw a results table.

2. Which kind of graph is the best for the data you have planned to collect?

3. What information will you be able to take from your graph?
How will you know if the hypothesis is correct?

> Remember the table needs a title and each column needs a heading and units.

> Normally for numerical data that can be given decimal places you would use a line graph. For no numerical data or numerical data that can't be given decimal places you would use a bar chart.

Connections

How science works

> Collecting and analysing data.

> Working accurately and safely when collecting first-hand data.

> Planning to solve a scientific problem.

> Recalling, analysing, interpreting, applying and questioning scientific information or ideas.

> Planning an investigation using qualitative and quantitative approaches.

> Assessing and managing risks.

Maths in science

> Plot and draw graphs selecting appropriate scales for the axes.

B3 checklist (Topic 1)

To achieve your forecast grade in the exam you'll need to revise

Use this checklist to see what you can do now. Refer back to pages 10–29 if you're not sure.

Look across the rows to see how you could progress – *bold italic* means Higher tier only.

Remember you'll need to be able to use these ideas in various ways, such as:
> interpreting pictures, diagrams and graphs
> applying ideas to new situations
> explaining ethical implications
> suggesting some benefits and risks to society
> drawing conclusions from evidence you've been given.

Look at pages 230–52 for more information about exams and how you'll be assessed.

This checklist accompanies the exam-style questions and the worked examples. The content suggestions for specific grades are suggestions only and may not be replicated in your real examination. Remember, the checklists do not represent the complete content for any topic. Refer to the Specification for complete content details on any topic and any further information.

To aim for a grade E	To aim for a grade C	To aim for a grade A
state that cells produce wastes including carbon dioxide and urea recall that urea is produced from the breakdown of excess amino acids in the liver recall that wastes are removed from the blood by the kidneys and released from the body as urine	describe the structure of the urinary system	describe the structure of the nephron and how this relates to its functions of filtration and forming urine (osmoregulation)
describe what kidney failure is and identify its symptoms	explain the possible treatments of kidney failure including kidney transplants and dialysis	*explain how antidiuretic hormone (ADH) regulates the water content of the blood* *understand that production of ADH is controlled by a negative feedback mechanism*
recall that the menstrual cycle is controlled by the hormones oestrogen and progesterone describe the stages in the menstrual cycle	explain the events of the menstrual cycle, including ovulation and changes in the thickness of the uterus lining	*explain how the menstrual cycle is controlled by the hormones oestrogen, progesterone, FSH and LH, and a negative feedback mechanism*

To aim for a grade E

To aim for a grade C

To aim for a grade A

To aim for a grade E	To aim for a grade C	To aim for a grade A
explain how sperm and eggs are adapted to their functions	explain that egg and sperm cells are haploid and that fertilisation restores the diploid state	understand the advantages and disadvantages of infertility treatments
recall that the sex of a person is controlled by one pair of chromosomes, XX in a female and XY in a male	explain how the sex of offspring is determined at fertilisation, using a genetic diagram	explain, using probabilities, percentages and ratios, how sex-linked disorders are inherited
describe how the work of Edward Jenner contributed to the development of vaccines describe the risks and advantages of immunisation	explain the process of immunisation	*describe the role of memory lymphocytes*
recall the role of antibodies	explain the function of antibodies	*explain the production of monoclonal antibodies and how they are used*
describe the growth of bacterial populations	explain how microorganisms (bacteria) can be cultured in different growing media explain that different factors affect the growth of bacterial populations	describe the contributions of Louis Pasteur to the development of aseptic techniques
recall that plants defend themselves from attack by pests and pathogens recall the impact of pests and pathogens on human food supply	describe the ways in which plants use chemicals to defend themselves from attack	explain that some of the chemicals plants produce to defend themselves can be used to treat diseases or their symptoms
recall that life's processes are often cyclical	describe the importance of photoperiodicity in plants	explain that some of the rhythmic processes in living organisms are circadian

1 The nephron is the working unit of the kidney. The diagram represents its structure.

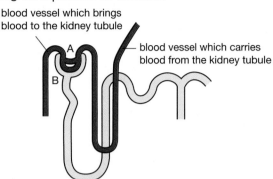

blood vessel which brings blood to the kidney tubule

blood vessel which carries blood from the kidney tubule

AO1 **a** Water is reabsorbed back into the blood through the walls of which structure?

A ☐ Convoluted tubules

B ☐ Collecting duct

C ☐ Bowman's capsule

D ☐ Loop of Henlé [1]

AO1 **b** Name the parts of the nephron labelled A and B. [2]

AO1 **c** Describe the flow of blood through the nephron. [2]

AO1 **d** Explain how the nephron is an essential part of the excretory system. [3]

[Total: 8]

2 Culture solutions supply bacteria with the nutrients that they need for growth.

Bordatella pertussis is a bacteria that causes whooping cough. The graph shows how the numbers of the bacteria *B. pertussis* increased when grown in a culture solution.

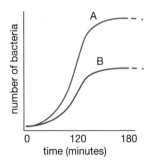

AO3 **a** Describe the trend shown in the graph by line A. [2]

AO2 **b** Explain why the growth of the bacterial population begins to slow after 150 minutes. [2]

AO1 AO2 **c** In this investigation, resazurin dye was used to track the rate of growth of the bacterial population.

Describe how the resazurin dye was used to track the rate of growth of the bacteria *B. pertussis*. [2]

AO2 AO3 **d** Using data from the graph, describe how ready access to nutrients could affect the rate at which *B. pertussis* develops in humans. [2]

[Total: 8]

3 Below is a diagram of an egg cell and a sperm cell (not to scale).

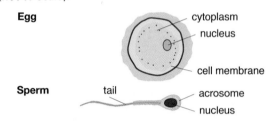

Egg — cytoplasm, nucleus, cell membrane

Sperm — tail, acrosome, nucleus

AO1 **a** The egg contains a large amount of cytoplasm. What is the function of the cytoplasm? [1]

AO1 **b** Explain the function of the sperm's tail. [1]

AO1 **c** Describe how the sperm penetrates the egg's cell membrane. [3]

AO2 **d** The diploid number of chromosomes in the nucleus of each human cell is 46. How many chromosomes does the sperm's nucleus contain? [1]

AO1 AO2 **e** Some couples cannot conceive naturally. This is often because the man or woman is infertile. Couples having difficulty conceiving can undergo fertility treatments such as *in vitro* fertilisation (IVF) and hormone treatments. Discuss the advantages and disadvantages of using IVF and hormones to treat infertility. [6]

[Total: 12]

4 Smallpox was a disease that was completely eradicated through immunisation by 1979. The vaccination was developed after Edward Jenner observed that milk maids had clear skin because they never contracted smallpox.

AO2 **a** What does the cowpox virus have in common with the smallpox virus that prevented the milk maids from contracting smallpox? [1]

AO1 **b** Explain how Edward Jenner developed the smallpox vaccine from his observations. [3]

AO1 **c** Describe two advantages and two risks associated with immunisation. [4]

[Total: 8]

Worked example

AO1 **a** State the pair of chromosomes that control sex in a female and in a male. [2]

Female: XX ✔

Male: XY ✔

AO2 **b** Across the world there are roughly 107 boys to 100 girls.

Explain, using a genetic cross diagram, why the numbers of girls and boys should be equal. [2]

✔	*X*	*Y*
X	*XX*	*XY*
X	*XX*	*XY*

There is a 1:1 chance of either a girl or a boy. ✔

AO3 **c** Haemophilia is an inherited genetic disease. It is carried on the sex chromosomes.

Rachel is a carrier for haemophilia, her chromosomes are X^hX^H, Ben does not have the disease. Draw a genetic diagram to find the probability that their child will have haemophilia. Let h = haemophilia, let H = normal. [3]

mother = X^HX^h father = X^HY^H ✘

✔	X^H	Y^H
X^H	X^HX^H – *normal girl*	$X^H Y^H$ – *normal boy*
X^h	X^HX^h – *carrier girl*	$X^h Y^H$ – *haemophiliac boy*

There is no chance of having a girl with haemophilia ✘

AO1 **d** Name one other genetic disorder which is sex linked. [1]

Sickle cell anaemia. ✘

[Total: 8]

How to raise your grade

Take note of the comments from examiners – these will help you to improve your grade.

A correct answer. This is a vital fact to remember in order to answer exam questions on how sex is determined.

This is a challenging question. The student has been awarded the first mark for a correctly drawn a Punnett square. They have then used their Punnett square to calculate the ratio of girls and boys born. This has gained them the second mark.

This is incorrect. Haemophilia is carried on the X chromosome only.

Despite getting the chromosomes wrong, the student has drawn their Punnett square correctly.

Incorrect. The question asks for the probability that their **child** will have haemophilia – not a **daughter**. The correct answer is 1 in 4 (or 1:4).

Always read the question carefully. Remember to always check what probability the question has asked for (probability, ratio or percentage).

No. Although this is a genetic disease, it is not carried on the sex chromosomes. A correct answer would be colour blindness.

This candidate scored 5 out of 8. The candidate showed a good understanding of how to use genetic cross diagrams but need to follow through on their written answers to make sure that they completely answered the question. The candidate could improve their grade by learning examples of sex-linked disorders and how to present the chromosomes for these disorders.

1 Kidneys are organs within the excretory system.

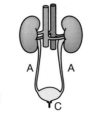

AO1 **a** Name the parts of the excretory system labelled A, B and C. [3]

AO1 **b** Describe how waste products are removed by the kidneys. [2]

c Patients with kidney failure can be treated with dialysis or organ transplants.

AO1 **i** Describe the process of kidney dialysis. [3]

AO2 **ii** If diabetes goes untreated, it can cause long-term kidney failure. Evaluate the benefits and drawbacks of treating kidney failure caused by diabetes with an organ transplant. [4]

[Total: 12]

2 The diagram shows the hormonal control of events during the menstrual cycle.

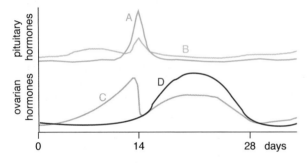

AO1 **a** Name the hormones labelled A–D. [4]

AO1 **b** Ovulation occurs on day 14. Explain why ovulation occurs, in terms of hormones. [2]

c The corpus luteum is formed from what is left of the follicle. If fertilisation occurs, the corpus luteum is not broken down.

AO1 **i** What hormone does the corpus luteum secrete? [1]

AO2 **ii** Suggest why it is important that the corpus luteum is not broken down if fertilisation occurs. [2]

AO1 **d** Using the evidence from the graph, explain
AO3 the menstrual cycle in terms of negative feedback. [3]

[Total: 12]

AO1 **3 a** Explain what is meant by the term 'monoclonal antibody'. [1]

AO2 **b** Describe the advantages of using monoclonal antibodies to treat pancreatic cancer. [3]

AO1 **c** Monoclonal antibodies can be produced in a
AO2 laboratory in large quantities and stored for future use. Describe the stages involved in producing monoclonal antibodies in the laboratory. You may use a diagram to help with your answer. [6]

[Total: 10]

4 Caroline carried out an investigation to test how three different activities – sitting, walking and dancing – affected the concentration of antidiuretic hormone (ADH) in volunteer's blood. Caroline carried out the same test on two different days. Her results are shown below.

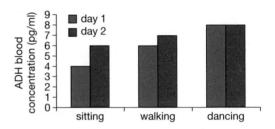

AO3 **a** Which activity made the volunteers sweat the most? Explain your answer. [3]

AO2 **b i** Calculate the difference in the concentration of ADH produced during sitting on day 1 and day 2. [1]

AO2 **ii** Suggest a reason for this difference. [1]

AO2 **iii** Suggest one way in which Caroline could improve the quality of her data. [1]

AO1 **c** Explain how ADH helps to maintain the body's
AO2 stable internal environment. [6]

[Total: 12]

5 Chrysanthemums are known as long day plants. They will only flower during the summer when the day length is longer than a critical period.

AO1 **a** What is meant by the term 'critical period'? [1]

AO1 **b** What is the name given to the physiological reaction of plants to the length of day? [1]

AO2 **c** Explain the benefit of this physiological reaction to chrysanthemums. [2]

AO1 **d** Discuss the importance of biological clocks to
AO2 plants and animals. [6]

[Total: 10]

✳ Worked example

The graph below shows the antibody response to two different pathogens A and B.

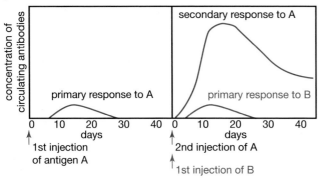

AO1 **a** What is the name of the part of the pathogen that the antibody binds to? [1]

  A antigen   B antibiotic
  C immunoglobulin   D lymphocyte

B. ✗

AO3 **b** Describe the differences between the primary and secondary response to A. [2]

The secondary response is much bigger and the primary response is much smaller. ✔ ✗

AO2 **c** Explain why the secondary response is different to the primary response. [3]

The body has seen the disease before and is better prepared because of the memory lymphocytes. ✔ When the body is infected with the same pathogen the memory lymphocytes multiply rapidly ✔ to produce B lymphocytes which make antibodies which fight the pathogen. ✔

AO3 **d** Why is the primary response to B similar to the primary response to A? [1]

Both show the body's first response to a pathogen. ✔

AO2 **e** How did Edward Jenner make use of the difference between the primary and secondary response? [3]

Edward Jenner was the first to vaccinate people against smallpox. ✔ He gave them cowpox which was similar to smallpox and so people had a primary response then if they got smallpox the secondary response would be enough to stop them becoming infected. ✗ ✗

[Total: 12]

This candidate scored 6 out of 10. They have a good understanding of how the body responds to an infection but lost marks by not expressing themselves carefully. They could improve their grade by revising scientific terminology and practising applying this terminology in exam questions.

How to raise your grade

Take note of the comments from examiners – these will help you to improve your grade.

Antigen is the correct answer. Be careful when reading multiple choice answers as they will often put words that look similar.

This is correct, but the question is worth 2 marks and saying the opposite of the first statement is not worth another mark. The second mark would be for saying the secondary response is also faster.

Make sure you use the word lymphocyte and not cell.

This is a strong answer. There are three separate pieces of information for the 3 marks. The candidate has communicated their answer clearly and logically.

Correct. Every new pathogen that infects the body will have a similar primary response.

You could also write immunise.

This isn't enough to gain the mark. The candidate should also state that smallpox and cowpox have the same antigens.

This isn't true. After vaccination people can still get infected, but the secondary response is bigger and faster, and so stops the infection making people sick. Always express yourself carefully.

B3 Using biology (Topics 2–3)

What you should know

Behaviour

Animals can show learned behaviours, such as training through reinforcement, and innate behaviours, such as sneezing. These behaviours aid survival.

 What behaviours are we born with (innate)? How do these help a baby to survive?

Evolution

Darwin's theory of evolution by natural selection states that species evolve through a process of variation, overproduction, competition, survival and inheritance (B1 – Topic 1).

Geographic isolation causes speciation (the formation of new species) (B1 – Topic 1).

Fossils can provide a record of how a species has changed. In this way they can provide evidence for evolution (B2 – Topic 3).

The pentadactyl limb is evidence that all vertebrates have a common ancestor (B2 – Topic 3).

 Use Darwin's theory of natural selection to suggest how the leopard evolved spots.

Biotechnology

Microbes can be used to produce foods such as yogurt.

Genetically modified (GM) bacteria are used to make insulin (B2 – Topic 1).

Crops can be genetically modified to grow in places with low rainfall, resist the effects of herbicides and resist diseases. Despite GM crops helping to combat food scarcities, there are concerns that they could have a negative impact on wildlife and on humans (B2 – Topic 1).

Enzymes are biological catalysts that speed up processes such as digestion in the human body (B2 – Topic 1).

 Golden rice is genetically modified. What does this mean?

You will find out about

> mating strategies and parental care as an evolutionary strategy

> different types of behaviour: innate, courtship, habituation, imprinting, conditioning

> animal/human and plant communication

> the work of different ethologists

> evidence for co-evolution

> human evolution using evidence from fossils and stone tools

> how mitochondrial DNA provides evidence for African Eve

> the usefulness of mitochondrial DNA for tracking human migration and evolution

> the impact of climate change on human migration

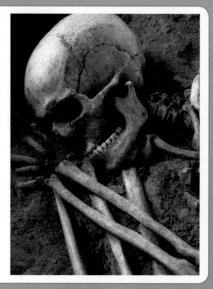

> biotechnology and what it is

> producing biomolecules using fermenter technology

> the advantages of using microorganisms for food production

> how mycoprotein and yogurt are manufactured

> some of the different enzymes used in producing food and washing powders

> producing insulin using recombinant DNA technology

> the impact of human population growth on food supplies

> producing transgenic plants

> techniques for increasing food production

> the costs and benefits of genetically modifying crops

> producing biofuels, and their advantages and disadvantages

Innate behaviour

Behavioural research

When Niko Tinbergen spent two weeks studying herring gull behaviour on the Dutch island of Terschelling in the 1940s, it was an important step in scientific research. His use of models to investigate the feeding mechanisms of chicks was a step forward in the study of behavioural biology and his innovative experiments have led the way to further studies in this area.

FIGURE 1: How does the herring gull chick obtain a meal?

You will find out:
> that innate behaviour is instinctive
> about investigating innate behaviour

What is innate behaviour?

> **Innate behaviour** is instinctive, automatic and follows a fixed pattern.

> Innate reactions are inherited from parents.

> For each particular stimulus triggering an innate reaction, the individual's response to it is the same.

> The faster an individual reacts, the better its chances of survival.

If you tickle the underside of a baby's foot, the baby will instinctively fan his or her toes. The baby's toe-fanning behaviour is innate, as is a baby grasping a finger or suckling its mother.

QUESTIONS

1 What is innate behaviour?

2 From where is innate behaviour inherited?

Releasing innate behaviour

Herring gulls

The Dutch ethologist Niko Tinbergen (1907–88) studied bird behaviour. He investigated the innate reaction of herring gull chicks to their parent's beak. The parental beak is yellow with an obvious red spot. Herring gull chicks peck at their parent's beak when they want food, and the red spot is pecked more frequently than other parts of the beak. Tinbergen found that the chick pecks the beak less when the spot is covered with a dab of yellow paint matching the colour of the parent's beak.

Tinbergen investigated the question of whether other colours would affect pecking behaviour by using model adult herring gull heads made of wood. The beak of each model head was painted yellow. Each beak except one had differently coloured spots, including red.

The model heads were shown to herring gull chicks. Chicks pecked the red-spotted model beak more often than the unspotted beak. The models with beaks spotted with other colours were pecked:

> more often than the unspotted beak

> but less often than the red-spotted beak.

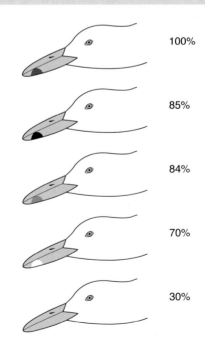

100%

85%

84%

70%

30%

FIGURE 2: Pecking response: percentage of herring gull chicks responding to model beaks, each spotted with a different colour. What conclusions can you draw?

Robins

Male robins are fiercely territorial. The red breast is a warning to rival males.

But does the sight of a rival release a robin's territorial behaviour or is the sight of a blob of red alone enough?

A simple experiment can demonstrate.

A model robin painted with a red breast will soon attract the attention of any male robin nearby. He will behave aggressively towards the model until it is removed.

Replace the model with a ball of cotton wool soaked in red ink and attached to a piece of wire, and the same male will react as aggressively to the cotton wool ball as if it were the model or even the real thing. His behaviour is automatic.

FIGURE 3: What makes the robin engage in aggressive behaviour?

QUESTIONS

3 Look at Figure 2. Summarise the pecking response of herring gull chicks to models of the herring gull beak, each with differently coloured spots.

4 Explain why a robin's aggressive response to a red-coloured model is an example of innate behaviour.

Using choice chambers

Choice chambers can be used to investigate innate behaviour.

You can use a **choice chamber** to investigate the innate responses of woodlice to dry/wet and light/dark conditions.

In dry conditions woodlice quickly lose water from the body and die. They need to find damp places to survive. When woodlice are in dry air, their walking activity increases to improve their chances of finding damp shelter. When they find a damp place their walking activity decreases.

Woodlice associate bright light with a lack of shelter and dry air. For this reason, their walking activity will also increase in brighter light.

Remember!
Innate behaviour is automatic.

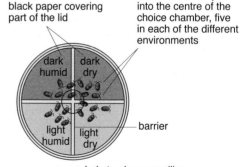

black paper covering part of the lid

20 woodlice are put into the centre of the choice chamber, five in each of the different environments

dark humid | dark dry
light humid | light dry

barrier

QUESTIONS

5 Look at Figure 4.

a State the different environments provided by the choice chamber.
b Explain how air humidity in the choice chamber is controlled.
c Explain why woodlice prefer a dark humid environment.

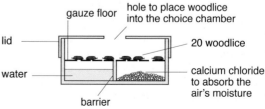

gauze floor

hole to place woodlice into the choice chamber

lid

water

20 woodlice

calcium chloride to absorb the air's moisture

barrier

FIGURE 4: Using a choice chamber: which conditions do you think woodlice would like the least?

Imprinting and habituation

You will find out:
> about imprinting
> about Konrad Lorenz
> about habituation

Learning who to trust

In 1973 the ethologist Konrad Lorenz shared a Nobel Prize with Niko Tinbergen and Karl von Frisch for their work on animal behaviour.

Like Tinbergen, Lorenz studied bird behaviour. In one of his experiments, he noted that jackdaws that had imprinted on him would seek his approval by bringing him fresh earthworms and would even try to place them in his ears!

FIGURE 1: What did Lorenz find out from his study of bird behaviour?

Follow the leader

Much of an animal's learning takes place as a result of its early experience of life. Ducklings and goslings (young geese) are ready to leave the nest a few hours after hatching. They follow the first moving thing that they see (usually their mother). This is called **imprinting**.

It doesn't even have to be a living creature. Experiments have shown that ducklings will follow a model duck or even a cardboard box, especially it it is the same colour as a female duck.

> In his studies, Lorenz made sure that he was the first thing the ducklings saw when they hatched.

> They responded to him as if he was their mother!

Imprinting **develops** early in an animal's life. This is called the **sensitive period**.

Imprinting will not occur outside the sensitive period. The sensitive period depends on the species. For example, it is the first 48 hours for a duckling or gosling, but between 3 and 10 weeks for dogs.

Imprinting on parents improves the chances of the young animals surviving because their parents protect them and supply them with food.

Imprinting can affect the social behaviour of adults. For example, goslings that have imprinted on ducks might attempt to court and mate with them later in life.

FIGURE 2: Greylag geese parent and its goslings. Does imprinting on their parent keep the goslings safer?

QUESTIONS

1 Suggest why imprinting is a type of learning.

2 What is the advantage of young animals imprinting on their parents?

3 State how you think Lorenz's research might help to protect endangered species.

Getting used to it

Birds can be a problem at airports because they can damage aircraft, for example by being sucked into their engines. Airport authorities are always on the lookout for ways of scaring birds away. Ideas that have been tried include putting models of hawks and owls around the airport and playing recordings of the distress calls of birds. At first these methods keep birds away from the airport. After a while, however, the birds learn that there is no danger from a model hawk or that a distress call does not mean there is a predator about. They start to come back to the airport where they pose a danger to aircraft once more.

This form of learning is called **habituation**. The birds get used to a stimulus, see no danger and no longer respond to the stimulus.

Investigating habituation

The snail's tentacles help it to test the direction in which it is moving. Each one contains touch-sensitive receptors. Touch its tentacles and a snail withdraws them into its head.

You can investigate habituation by repeatedly touching a snail's tentacles gently, using a clean glass rod. Table 1 gives you an idea of the results you might expect to get.

Notice that the more times the tentacles are touched the less the snail responds to the stimulus. It learns that there is nothing really in its way, so that eventually it doesn't change direction, despite repeated gentle touching of its tentacles.

TABLE 1: Investigating habituation in the snail.

Number of times tentacle touched	Time for tentacle to fully extend (s)	Tentacle withdrawal (%)	Angle of direction
1	47	100	10°
2	44	97	10°
3	36	89	7°
…	…	…	…
8	6	7	2°
9	5	6	1°
10	5	6	1°

FIGURE 3: How can we tell that this bird has become habituated to the scarecrow?

FIGURE 4: A garden snail (*Helix aspersa*) with extended tentacles. The snail is detecting vibrations caused by tapping the plastic rod held close to it. What effect might this have on the snail?

QUESTIONS

4 Explain the benefits of habituation.

5 Suggest a disadvantage of habituation.

6 Use the data in Table 1 to show that the snail has become habituated to touch.

Training and habituation

Imprinting and habituation are very important in animal training. Guide Dogs for the Blind have considered these behaviours in order to establish the most effective way of training their dogs. They found that keeping puppies with their mother and siblings up until they were 6 weeks old allowed the puppies time to be socialised with other dogs, so avoiding problems later in life.

At six weeks the puppies are put into private homes, which ensures that they have time to habituate by being exposed to many day-to-day situations, from vacuum cleaners to traffic noise. This then makes it easier for the puppies to start their proper guide dog training when they are about a year old.

QUESTIONS

7 Goslings are mobile soon after hatching, but puppies are helpless at birth. Suggest why early imprinting is more important for goslings than for pups.

8 Suggest why it may be more difficult to train an older dog.

9 Suggest why dog breeders must be careful that their puppies do not imprint on them.

FIGURE 5: Socialisation of a puppy helps to form the bond between a dog and its owner. Why is this useful for training dogs?

Conditioning

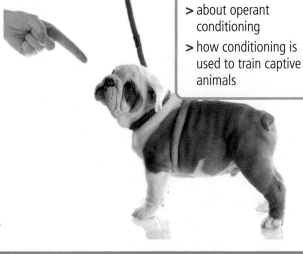

You will find out:
> about classical conditioning
> about operant conditioning
> how conditioning is used to train captive animals

Positive training methods

Rewarding a puppy for walking on a lead without pulling positively reinforces this behaviour in our 'best friend'. The puppy enjoys the rewards and will work hard to get them. The rewards are one way of conditioning the puppy to behave in the way its owner wants.

FIGURE 1: What is the benefit of conditioning the puppy's behaviour?

Learned behaviour

> When behaviour changes in the light of experience, we say that the behaviour is learned.

> For example, a kitten will only show interest in food when it sees the food, tastes it and eats it. Seeing food and tasting it are **primary stimuli**.

> Later the animal learns to associate non-food stimuli with food. For example, a move by its owner to where the food is kept. Non-food associations are **secondary stimuli**.

> The secondary stimulus is not directly linked to the primary stimulus but the association is learned. **Conditioning** refers to the cat's behaviour.

 QUESTIONS

1 Describe the difference between innate behaviour and learned behaviour.

2 What is the difference between primary stimuli and secondary stimuli?

FIGURE 2: From the cat's viewpoint, the link between owner and cupboard means food.

Conditioning

Classical conditioning

Ivan Pavlov (1849–1936) scientifically studied conditioned responses. He investigated the response of dogs to food and other non-food stimuli by measuring the amount of saliva they produced.

When he placed food in a dog's mouth Pavlov noticed that the flow of saliva increased.

Also he saw that the dog smelling his hand had the same effect. This was before food was placed in the dog's mouth. The dog's production of saliva increased even more when food followed Pavlov's personal smell.

After a time Pavlov's personal smell alone produced the same response in the dog as if it had been given food. The dog had learned to associate a non-food secondary stimulus (Pavlov's personal smell) with food.

FIGURE 3: What do you think is on this dog's mind?

Pavlov used the term 'conditioned' to describe the dog's response. **Classical conditioning** refers to the process.

Operant conditioning

Conditioning can also be the result of trial and error learning. Reward (getting the response right) or punishment (getting the response wrong) are key to this type of learning. The process is called **operant conditioning**.

We all experience operant conditioning, the promise of a treat for doing your homework, for example, and being banned from playing computer games for not tidying your room.

QUESTIONS

3 Explain the differences between classical conditioning and operant conditioning.

4 a Summarise the stages in Pavlov's experiment. Use the internet to help you.

b What conclusion can you draw from Pavlov's experiment?

5 Research the work of B.F. Skinner and his box. Explain what this can tell us about the learning behaviour of animals.

Training animals

Operant conditioning plays an important role in animal training:

> *Positive reinforcers* are events which the animal likes and which are provided immediately after the animal displays the wanted behaviour.

> *Negative reinforcers* are events which the animal dislikes and which are removed immediately after the animal displays the wanted behaviour. For example, pressure from a rider's leg is removed when the horse moves in the required direction.

Police horses

A trained police horse will not be startled or distracted by gunfire or crowds of noisy people, etc.

Positive reinforcers do not motivate horses as much as dogs. Negative reinforcers are more effective at conditioning their behaviour. For example, relaxing a restraint reinforces the wanted behaviour. Horse memory is long term. Once learned, wanted behaviour is retained for a very long time.

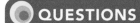

FIGURE 4: Training helps police horses remain calm in noisy situations.

Sniffer dogs

A dog's nose is extremely sensitive. A trained sniffer dog is around 2000 times better than humans at detecting smells. Sniffer dogs are trained to search for the smells given off by money, drugs, explosives, human remains and much else. They are used in a variety of roles including police work, search and rescue and by customs officers.

Dogs usually respond best to positive reinforcement, such as food, praise and stroking, and this help to condition their behaviour. A dog often lives in the family home strengthening the bond with its handler.

Dolphins

At the start of training a dolphin is taught to look above water at its trainer. This is called **stationing**. The dolphin is then able to follow its trainer's signals which are a cue for a particular behaviour. The behaviour is immediately reinforced by rewarding with food or praise. The rewards are a way of conditioning the dolphin's behaviour.

QUESTIONS

6 Explain the role of operant conditioning in training animals.

7 Explain why different types of reinforcers are used to train dogs and horses.

8 How could you investigate operant conditioning in animals?

9 Studies have shown that dolphins have distinct personalities, a sense of self and can think about the future. Comment on the ethical issues around using dolphins to research operant conditioning.

Courtship and mating strategies

Intra-species recognition

In some species of spiders the male is often smaller than the female. He uses courtship ritual to prevent her from eating him before mating.

For example, a male web-weaving spider sets up particular patterns of vibration in the female's web, signalling his intentions and that he is the same species as her.

FIGURE 1: Female and male black widow spiders. Unlike the deadly female, the much smaller male is not considered dangerous. Why is species recognition important?

 ## Courtship behaviour

What is courtship behaviour?

Finding and selecting a suitable mate is crucial to sexual reproduction. **Courtship behaviour** is the mechanism used by animals, usually the male, to attempt to attract and secure a mate.

Courtship behaviour:

> establishes territory

> drives away rival males

> through advertising an individual's qualities, attracts females.

> enables males and females to recognise individuals of the same species as potential partners

> helps to synchronise sexual behaviour between partners

> encourages parental care by individuals of species who look after their offspring.

The importance of courtship

Courtship behaviour can be illustrated by sticklebacks.

Once he has established his territory, the male stickleback builds a nest. His red belly and blue-rimmed eyes attract a female. He courts her with a form of water ballet called the **zigzag dance**. Eventually she enters the nest and lays her eggs. The male then releases sperm over them. The sperm fertilises the eggs which develop and eventually hatch into small fry (young fish).

If signals or the responses to them are inappropriate, then the sequence breaks down. Courtship behaviour stops … no courting, no sexual reproduction!

FIGURE 2: Sticklebacks in their nest.

QUESTIONS

1 Why do males and females of the same species court each other?

2 Identify the features of stickleback courtship behaviour.

3 Suggest two similarities between human and animal courtship.

Defining mating strategies

Sexual reproduction involves mating and the mixing of genes. The number of mates that an animal has depends on the social organisation of each species. Some species are **monogamous**, which means they mate with only one partner. Monogamy is most common among birds.

Many other species are **polygamous**, which means they mate with more than one partner. Polygamy usually means one male mates with several females, but in a few species one female may mate with several males.

Male animals make millions of sperm but, in most species, females make far fewer eggs. This means that males can ensure that their genes are widely spread by mating with as many females as possible. For a female it is more important that the male she mates with is healthy and is therefore likely to carry genes for healthy offspring.

In some species males fight to establish who has the right to mate with the females. The winner benefits by passing on his genes through as many females as possible (although, obviously, most males don't get to mate at all). The females benefit because they mate with the males with the 'best' genes.

QUESTIONS

4 What is meant by polygamy and monogamy?

5 Why is reproductive success measured in numbers of *surviving* offspring?

Different types of mating strategy

Mating strategies are often defined in terms of monogamy and polygamy. However other factors are:

> whether or not a pair bond forms

> if the bond forms, how long it lasts (for a breeding season, or a lifetime)

> how much each partner of a pair contributes to care of the young.

Even then, defining mating strategies is complicated by matings of supposedly monogamous males or females with opposite sex individuals other than the bonded partner. For example, DNA studies suggest that up to 30% of house wren chicks are not the genetic offspring of one of the supposed parents.

Monogamous pairing

The behaviour between a male and female sometimes forms bonds between the pair, helping to keep them together. Grey wolves are an example: the male and female usually mate for life. Cooperative hunting behaviour reinforces this **pair bonding**.

Monogamy often occurs in species where pair bonding helps to motivate cooperation between the male and female to raise their offspring. The male bird helps the female to incubate eggs and to feed the young after hatching. Most birds do not mate for life but for a season. Others, like doves, robins, or swans, may stay together over several seasons or even for life.

QUESTIONS

6 Describe the mating strategies that animals can have.

7 Explain pair bonding in paternal care.

Polygamous pairing

Red deer do *not* pair bond. Males move to where lush late summer grass provides mating areas. There is plenty of food for the females which gather in the mating areas. The males compete for the best mating areas. The males best able to defend the best areas mate with more females, they have several mates over a life time.

Polygamy occurs in species which do not form strong pair bonds between male and female. Only one parent is involved in raising offspring. In mammals, males are usually the absent parent because young develop within the female and are nursed by her. Female bears are likely to mate with more than one male bear over a season.

FIGURE 3: How do grey wolves strengthen the pair bond?

Parental care

Parenting

You may have a cat at home and have perhaps seen her carry her kittens by the scruff of the neck. This parenting behaviour is an evolutionary strategy that is seen in many cats and other animals.

FIGURE 1: A female cheetah carrying her cub. How does she know the best way to do this?

What is parental care?

Parental care can range from the very basic to the very complex.

> Many fish, amphibians and reptiles simply lay their eggs and leave them to hatch.

> Some species, however, look after their eggs until they hatch and may care for the young afterwards.

In birds and mammals parental behaviour is highly evolved.

> Most birds build nests and have to incubate their eggs, keeping them at the correct temperature until they hatch.

> Once the chicks have hatched they need to be fed.

> This takes so much parental time and effort that it is common for male birds to help.

> Males and females often share tasks such as incubating the eggs and bringing food for the chicks.

Parental behaviour is triggered by the behaviour in the young.

> Baby birds in the nest open their mouths wide and make 'begging' sounds. Parents respond by favouring the noisiest chick.

> The bigger chicks get more food than the smaller ones. From the parents' point of view this is good as it produces some fit offspring who are more likely to pass on their genes. The weaker chicks may die or be pushed from the nest by the others.

FIGURE 2: A Meadow pipit feeding a young cuckoo in its nest. Why does the parent care for what is obviously not its own chick?

Did you know?

The offspring of many species of invertebrate receive no parental care at all.

QUESTIONS

1 What is meant by paternal care?

2 What does incubate mean?

3 How do adult birds benefit when a smaller chick dies?

4 Do humans respond differently from birds to their noisiest children?

Q Types of parental care in animals

The implications of parental care

Feeding and protecting offspring are all part of parental care. It also includes helping offspring to learn how to interact with individuals of the same species, avoid predators, catch prey, and so on.

The extent to which parents care for their offspring influences the mating strategy of a species.

> Species where matings produce numerous offspring are usually polygamous. Parental care is minimal. For example, it only takes two offspring of fish such as cod to survive to adulthood for the cod population to remain stable. Cod do not care for their young.

> Species where matings produce relatively few offspring are usually monogamous and parental care of offspring is common.

Parental efforts, however, take time and energy and represent **parental investment** in the increased chances of survival of their offspring.

Parental care often involves risks. This is because caring for their young can make the parents more vulnerable to predator attack as they have to protect their babies. The parents may also be weakened themselves through finding it difficult to source sufficient food or in the case of nursing mothers be malnourished through milk production.

However despite the risks to parents, parental care which increases the survival chances of offspring also increases the chances of parental genes passing to the next generation. The selfish genetic interests of parents are perhaps what parental care is all about.

FIGURE 3: Human parental care carries on for many years. Here a farm worker keeps her baby close.

QUESTIONS

5 Compare the risks and benefits of parental care.

6 Explain why those species that produce numerous offspring each generation often exhibit little or no parental care.

Evolution of parental care

We can think of parental care as a successful evolutionary strategy. Earlier study has shown us that natural selection acts on variation within a species and is the mechanism of evolution. If variation depends on parental genes passing from generation to generation, then parental care maximises the chances of this happening. This is particularly so in species where parents produce relatively few offspring, and is probably why special behaviours for rearing young have evolved in mammals and birds.

In species where females each produce hundreds of thousands of eggs, only two offspring per pair of parents need survive for parental genes to transfer to the next generation. In fact, parental care in these circumstances would not be an advantage. Overpopulation would increase competition between individuals and lead to possible extinction.

QUESTIONS

7 In terms of evolutionary strategy, explain the advantage to cuckoos of laying eggs in the nests of other species of bird.

8 Identify *two* strategies which maximise the chances of parental genes passing from one generation to the next.

Animal communication

Trapped by smell

Many insects use chemical signals called pheromones to communicate with each other over many kilometres. Farmers can exploit this behaviour in pest insects to protect their crops. The photo shows a trap lined with codling moth pheromones on a sticky surface. The pheromones attract pests to the trap and away from the crop. This protects the apple orchard.

FIGURE 1: An apple orchard's insect pest trap. What are the advantages of using pheromones to attract pests to the trap?

Visual signals

What is animal communication?

Communication is a form of behaviour that influences the actions of other individuals.

Animals communicate with one another by releasing chemicals called **pheromones**, making sounds and giving visual signals.

Animal behaviour has evolved to ensure survival. By communicating, animals can better increase their chances of survival. For example:

> by establishing territorial rights to provide them with food and shelter

> by finding a mate to ensure that they can reproduce

> by warning members of their group of potential threat.

Facial expression

Pulling faces is a visual signal. It is a way of communicating our emotions to other people.

What do you think the woman in Figure 2 is portraying by her facial expressions?

Chimpanzees also pull faces. Their facial signals are similar to ours but there are differences. For example, chimpanzees grin more broadly than we do but we frown. The difference is due to differences in the shape of faces.

Also, some expressions can mean different things. Fear seems to be the emotion behind the full open mouth grin of a chimpanzee, not happiness.

FIGURE 2: What do these facial expressions say?

FIGURE 3: Happy or not? Chimpanzees' body language differs from our own.

Animal communication   Facial expressions   Body language

Body language

Your feelings and intentions are signalled by the way you hold yourself (posture). Sitting towards someone for example signals that you're probably interested in them; sitting sideways indicates you're not.

We often use our hands to send out signals, for example, waving good-bye and the clenched fist victory salute. These are gestures. However, gestures are cultural and should be used with caution when outside of your own country.

When your cat runs to greet you, its tail is held high. The raised tail signals welcome. A wagging tail signals annoyance. Loud yowling and an arched back mean anger. By contrast, when a dog wags its tail it is signalling happiness.

QUESTIONS

1 State two ways in which animals communicate.

2 Explain what the woman in the second picture in Figure 2 and the chimpanzee in Figure 3 are communicating. Are they communicating the same thing?

3 Describe the role of posture in animal-to-animal communication.

Sound signals

In most species of birds it is the male that sings, often to warn other males away from its territory and also to attract a female. This is partly connected with territorial singing: a large territory will provide plenty of food to feed chicks. In some species, however, males and females take it in turn to sing, this duetting behaviour helps to strengthen their bond.

Other animals use sounds to communicate:

> Many species of monkey communicate by sound as it is particularly useful in their forest habitat.

> Frogs often attract mates with characteristic calls.

> Whales make sounds called 'whale song', which is used for complex levels of communication.

QUESTIONS

4 Explain two functions of bird song.

FIGURE 4: A male blackbird. What is he hoping to achieve by singing?

Chemical signals

A male cheetah when urinating on a tree is also releasing pheromones at the same time.

The signal in the smell is understood by other male cheetahs to mean 'keep out of this territory as it belongs to another male'.

Male silk moths are attracted to a female silk moth because of a pheromone she releases. Male antennae are so sensitive to the pheromone that males detect the female producing it from several kilometres away. The female is signalling to males that she is ready to mate.

Once a male detects a female's pheromone trail, he follows its concentration gradient. This becomes stronger and stronger as the male approaches. Tracking the gradient enables the male to home in on the target of his attentions.

QUESTIONS

5 Explain the functions of pheromones.

6 Explain why only male silk moths respond to pheromones released by female silk moths and not to pheromones released by other moth species. Use the internet to help you.

FIGURE 5: How does a male cheetah mark its territory?

Plant communication and co-evolution

Potato surprises greenfly

Potato leaves are covered with 'hairs' that release a chemical when touched. The chemical is the same as the pheromone released by greenfly when stressed. When greenfly feeding on potato leaves touch the 'hairs' the chemical they release scares the greenfly away.

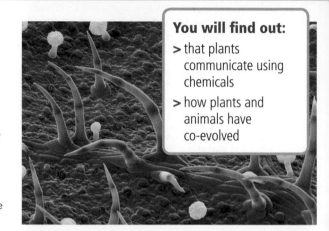

You will find out:
> that plants communicate using chemicals
> how plants and animals have co-evolved

FIGURE 1: A micrograph of a potato leaf surface. What is the role of these long, spiky growths (trichomes)?

Plant chemical use

Communication happens when messages from senders are understood by receivers. In the plant world:

> messages are molecules of different chemicals
> senders are the plants producing the chemicals
> receivers are other plants, animals, fungi or bacteria.

Receivers may interpret the meanings in messenger molecules as invitations, warnings or stress depending on the type of chemical released and the receiver.

Plant-to-animal communication

> Plants release chemicals in response to damage and other stress stimuli.

> Some of these chemicals attract parasites that in turn attack the organism that is damaging the plant.

> The message in the molecules is often quite specific. Only a particular receiver will understand it.

FIGURE 2: A caterpillar of a tobacco budworm moth on a flower. How does a wasp protect a plant?

An example of plant-to-animal communication is when tobacco budworm caterpillars feed on tobacco plants. The plants release a chemical into the air. Its molecules communicate the message: 'I'm being eaten by tobacco budworm caterpillars'.

A particular species of wasp will understand the messages and this triggers the following:

> This wasp lays its egg in tobacco budworm caterpillars.

> When the eggs hatch into grubs, they eat the insides of the caterpillars, killing them.

By communicating caterpillar attack to an understanding insect receiver, damage to the tobacco plant is reduced.

QUESTIONS

1 Define the terms:
   a senders, b receivers, c messages.

2 Explain how tobacco plants benefit from releasing chemicals.

Plant-to-plant communication

Some of the chemicals that plants produce and use for communication form vapours when released. These chemicals are volatile and they are called **volatile organic compounds (VOC)**. Once air-borne, these molecules quickly spread their messages far and wide.

Communication between same plant species

Ethene is a VOC that affects the growth of plants. In one study, tobacco plants were genetically engineered to be insensitive to ethene. As a result they grew more vigorously than their non-engineered neighbours.

Q Eavesdropping plants   Plant defences

Another study of tobacco plants showed that plants infected with a particular virus released a chemical that switched on defence genes in uninfected plants nearby. This resulted in fewer plants being infected with the virus and more plants survived.

The results of the described studies can be understood in terms of natural selection and evolution. Improved survival of individuals of one generation improves the chances of species reproduction and survival.

Communication between different plant species

Scientists have shown that VOCs released from the leaves of clipped sagebrush bushes reduces the damage to nearby wild tobacco plants by insects feeding on them. The sagebrush VOCs seem to increase the chemical defence levels in the tobacco plants, making them a less attractive food source to insects.

Other studies show that sagebrush VOCs also protect tomato plants. VOCs released by damaged lima bean plants have a similar effect on cucumbers.

FIGURE 3: Sagebrush: can one species of plant sound an alarm for another?

 QUESTIONS

3 Explain how plants communicate with one another.

4 Discuss this statement: 'Communication using VOCs between individual tobacco plants is the basis of species success.'

What is co-evolution? (Higher tier only)

In **co-evolution**, each species exerts selection pressures on the other, and benefits from the others' adaptations that evolve as a result. The evolution of flowers and the insects that pollinate them is an example.

Flowers and insects

Flowers enable plants to reproduce sexually. The parts of flowers **pollinated** by insects have adapted to attract the insects to them.

Adaptations include:

> *petals* that are brightly coloured, scented and secrete sugar-rich nectar

> *anthers* and stigmas that are positioned so that insects are likely to brush against them

> *pollen grains* that are large and sticky.

Adaptations of insects include:

> *antennae* that detect flower scent

> *eyes* that detect colour

> *body hairs* and other structures that collect pollen.

Both species benefit:

> the plant because the bee transfers its flowers' pollen to the stigmas of the flowers of a different plant

> the bee because it eats some of the pollen, and sucks up the sugar-rich nectar.

Plant defence and animal metabolism

Obviously plants cannot escape herbivores, but being eaten is a selection pressure that promotes the evolution of adaptations.

Different chemicals, produced by plants in response to the animals eating them, affect the animals' metabolism in different ways. For example:

> bitter tastes deter feeding

> changes in plant tissue make it less digestible

> poisons make animals sick and may even kill them.

These effects on metabolism are selection pressures that promote adaptations enabling herbivores to neutralise them. For example, milkweed produces poisonous chemicals that deter feeding. However, adaptations enable the metabolism of some insects (for example, monarch butterflies) to detoxify the milkweed's deterrents. The monarch accumulates the milkweed's poisons in its own tissues. This co-evolved adaptation with milkweed deters any potential predator from feeding on the butterfly.

QUESTIONS

5 How effective is the milkweed's 'poison adaptation'?

6 Explain why the co-evolution of plants and the insects that feed on them might be described as an 'arms race'.

Human evolution

You will find out:
> about the work of Goodall and Fossey
> about the fossil evidence for human evolution

Our bipedal ancestors

In 1978 Mary Leakey discovered footprints that had been preserved for 3.6 million years in damp volcanic ash that had set like cement. The find showed that our recent ancestors walked upright and were free striding.

FIGURE 1: Mary Leakey inspecting a trail of fossilised footprints in Tanzania. What was the significance of this find?

 ## Understanding early human behaviour

Because chimpanzees and gorillas are probably our closest living relatives, their social behaviours are sometimes used as models to help us understand our behaviour. Comparing these behaviours may also enable us to glimpse the behaviours of our early human ancestors.

Jane Goodall

An ethologist, Jane Goodall, studied chimpanzees in the wild in Tanzania and noticed the following:

> Chimpanzees use twigs as tools to help them find food. They place them into termite holes, then remove them covered with termites.

> Chimpanzees work together to hunt monkeys.

> Chimpanzees form social groups, find solutions to problems and so on.

> Males are larger than females and usually dominate them. In return, females and their young are protected and receive food.

Dian Fossey

In Rwanda, Dian Fossey saw that gorillas also form social groups and use tools, although less frequently.

Male gorillas are nearly twice as large as females. She observed that the more powerful a male is, the more a female wanted to mate with him, gaining protection for herself and her young.

● QUESTIONS

1 It was once thought that only humans used tools. How did Jane Goodall's work challenge this idea?

2 List the similarities and differences between the social behaviour of chimpanzees and humans.

 ## Fossil evidence

Fossil evidence suggests that our human ancestors probably diverged from chimpanzee ancestors about 5 mya (see Figure 2). The evolution of a large brain is an important trend in human evolution. So too is **bipedalism** (the ability to walk on two legs).

4.4 mya: Ardi

The fossil remains of a pre-human ancestor were discovered in 1992 in the Afar desert of Ethiopia. Dated to 4.4 mya and nicknamed Ardi, it is thought that the animal:

> was small brained

> walked upright on the ground

> could move among the branches of trees

> lacked the specialisation that chimpanzees have for hanging from branches, climbing vertically and knuckle walking

> had human-like teeth.

 Remember!
mya = million years ago and kya = thousand years ago.

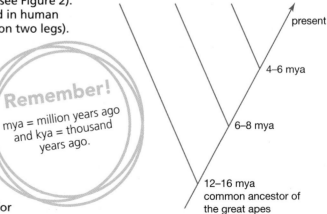

FIGURE 2: Humans and the great apes share a common ancestry. *Homo sapiens* (humans) appeared about 200 kya.

🔍 Ape behaviour   Trends in human evolution

3.2 mya: Lucy

In 1974 part of a fossil skeleton of a female nicknamed Lucy had been discovered. The evidence suggests that Lucy was shorter than Ardi, but like Ardi was small brained. However, her legs and feet were more human like, showing that she walked fully upright.

1.6 mya: Turkana boy

In 1984 Richard Leakey (the son of Mary Leakey) was part of the team that discovered an almost complete skeleton of a boy near Lake Turkana in northern Kenya. The fossilised remains were dated to 1.6 mya. Although not fully grown he was already 160 cm tall.

Turkana boy was much bigger brained than Ardi or Lucy. The fossil's long legs and narrow pelvis suggest that he might have been an even better walker than modern humans.

Remember!

Fossils are the remains or impressions of dead organisms usually preserved in sedimentary rocks.

FIGURE 3: A model of Lucy who lived 3.2 mya – more than a million years and 100 000 generations later than Ardi.

QUESTIONS

3 Explain why Ardi could not be a common ancestor of humans and chimpanzees.

4 Compare the similarities and differences between Ardi, Lucy and Turkana boy. Set out your answer as a table.

Bipedalism and brain size

Ardi (*Ardipithecus ramidus*) lived after the divergence from our most recent **common ancestor** shared with chimpanzees. However, she still gives clues as to what the ancestor looked like – and that was *not* chimplike. This probably means that the most recent common ancestor of humans and chimpanzees wasn't either.

The team who discovered Ardi also found many animal fossils and other specimens near to where they found her. The remains suggest that Ardi's habitat was moist woodland, very different from the region's present, hot and arid environment. So one theory is that climate change forced these early primates onto the savannah, where bipedalism rather than tree dwelling was an advantage.

So *Australopithecus afarensis* (Lucy) adapted to be able to walk more efficiently and use tools. Its brain started to develop in size, perhaps because better tools led to a better diet. A bigger brain allowing more complex and precise tool-making skills would give an advantage.

Similar, although less complete, fossil remains of Turkana (*Homo erectus*) have been found in Europe and Asia as well as Africa. It seems that *H. erectus* led the move of our near ancestors out of Africa. They did not reach the Americas. *Homo erectus* was similar to modern humans in size and stature and may possibly have had the ability to speak.

QUESTIONS

5 Describe the fossil evidence for the evolution of bipedalism.

6 Explain why the evolution of bipedalism in our ancestors came before an increase in brain size.

FIGURE 4: An artist's representation of *Homo erectus*. These creatures were thought to have used tools, lived in small groups and hunted together.

Stone tool technology

You will find out:
> how stone tools developed over time
> how stone tools can be dated

Making a stone tool

To make a stone tool a hammer stone is hit against a flint or quartzite core stone, producing sharp flakes. The flakes themselves can be used for cutting, or the core stone can be shaped by repeated flakings into a versatile tool. Such tools can be used for cutting meat and bone, scraping skins, chopping wood and digging.

FIGURE 1: A modern re-creation of making a stone tool. Tools such as this are thought to have been made by *Homo erectus*.

Stone tools developed over time

> A stone tool is an extension of the tool user's hands. It enables the user to do jobs that would not be possible without the tool: cutting up food, scraping skins and shaping wood, for example.

> The first simple step in making a stone tool is to strike flakes from a stone (the core) with another stone (the hammer).

> Chimpanzees will strike a stone and produce a flake. However, striking a series of flakes demands more ability driven by a greater intelligence. Each strike must be assessed to judge where best to next hit the core with the hammer to produce flakes best suited for the jobs to be done.

> An evolving brain is the link between stone tools and our near ancestors.

FIGURE 2: Re-creating stone tools in the manner of the oldest tools found at the Olduvai Gorge, Tanzania. Oldowan tools such as this were rounded rocks sharpened by blows that detached a flake, leaving a sharp edge.

QUESTIONS

1 What was the function of stone tools?

2 State how stone tools provide evidence for human evolution.

Different technologies

Oldowan

Oldowan refers to the earliest recorded stone tools from 2.6–1.5 mya. The oldest discovered so far come from Ethiopia. More recent examples have been found throughout Africa, south-east Asia (1.9 mya) and Europe (1.5 mya). Oldowan tools unearthed at Olduvai Gorge are relatively young.

> The distribution of Oldowan tools is global.

> The oldest specimens from Africa pre-date all of the other specimens in the world.

This evidence suggests that our early ancestors (probably *Homo erectus*) took their Oldowan technology with them as they migrated out of Africa and spread throughout the world.

Oldowan tools are flake tools. Figures 1 and 2 illustrate how our early ancestors probably produced them. Blows to one of the faces of the pebble shaped, palm-sized core stone produces flakes, each with a cutting edge of about 4 cm in length. The flakes are the tools.

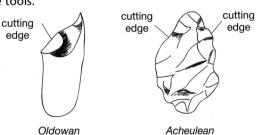

FIGURE 3: Oldowan and Acheulean tools compared. What differences can you see?

Acheulean

Acheulean tools were the result of a more sophisticated technology.

> Both sides of the core stone were struck to produce a cutting edge about 16 cm in length on the core itself – the core is **bifacial**.

> The core was the tool. Flakes as tools were no longer so highly prized.

> The tool was shaped and finished.

> Different types of tool were produced, each type designed for a particular job.

Mousterian and later

About 300 kya Acheulean technology was being replaced by the **Mousterian**. Before striking off flakes, Mousterian toolmakers first shaped the core into a stone prism. A few basic core shapes were then used to produce a variety of tools. The whole process was standardised into stages:

> basic core of stone

> roughly shaped core stone

> finished tool.

Types of tool included cutting tools, pointed tools designed to be tied to the end of a stick and scrapers for processing animal skins.

FIGURE 4: A timeline showing the different species of *Homo* associated with trends in developing tool technology from its beginnings to the emergence of modern humans.

QUESTIONS

3 Explain how the development of Mousterian tools from Oldowan tools supports the theory of human evolution.

4 Discuss the evidence that Oldowan tool technology probably originated in Africa.

Whose tools?

Late Oldowan is associated with *H. erectus* and the earlier *H. habilis*.

Later *H. erectus* developed Oldowan technology into the Acheulean but the two technologies overlapped in time and place.

In Europe, Mousterian tools are associated with later *H. neanderthalis*. However, elsewhere they were made by both neanderthals and early *H. sapiens* – humans in the modern sense.

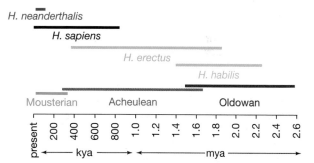

How are stone tools dated?

Scientists use different methods to date rocks.

> *Relative methods* indicate whether rocks are older or younger than something else. For example, provided the ground is undisturbed, the older stone tools are more deeply buried.

> *Absolute methods*, including **radiometric dating**, give a date to rocks within a range of years. Stone tools can be associated with rocks of known age, for example, sandwiched between two lava flows. So dating the rocks also dates the tools.

Radiometric dating depends on the known constant rate of decay of the **radioactive isotopes** in the rocks.

Half-life means the time taken for half of the radioactive element in a sample of rock to decay. Many radio-isotopes have half-lives that are too short to be useful for dating rocks, but potassium-40 decay has a suitable half-life. The decay product argon-40 is able to escape the liquid rock in a lava flow, but starts to accumulate when the rock solidifies. The age of the rock can be calculated by measuring the ratio of ^{40}Ar accumulated to ^{40}K remaining.

For example, if there are equal numbers of ^{40}K and ^{40}Ar atoms in a sample, it is one half-life old (1.3 billion years). If three-quarters of the ^{40}K has decayed, then two half lives have elapsed (2.6 billion years).

TABLE 1: Decay of isotopes of carbon and potassium.

Radioactive isotope	Half-life (years)	Decays to
Carbon-14 (^{14}C)	5730	Nitrogen-14 (^{14}N)
Potassium-40 (^{40}K)	1.3 billion	Argon-40 (^{40}Ar)

QUESTIONS

5 Explain the difference between relative methods and absolute methods of dating.

6 A piece of fossil bone contains one-quarter of its original amount of carbon-14. Use the half-life of this isotope to estimate the age of this fossil.

7 Explain why carbon dating is a suitable method to date fossilised wood about 30 000 years old.

Human migration

You will find out:
> the impact of climate on human behaviour
> why mitochondrial DNA is useful for tracking human migration and evolution
> that mitochondrial DNA provides evidence for African Eve

Neanderthals died out

Homo sapiens is the only living species of the *Homo* genus, the others being extinct. Some, including descendants of *H. erectus*, lived at the same time as *H. sapiens*. For example, *H. neanderthalis* survived as recently as 30 kya. However, our ancestors out-competed them all.

FIGURE 1: A model of a group of neanderthals during a burial ceremony. They buried their dead and looked after the infirm and the disabled.

Human migration and climate change

A drying and cooler climate in eastern Africa 2.5 mya meant that our tree-dwelling ancestors lost much of their food supply, as forests gave way to grassland. Individuals who could walk and run had an advantage over those adapted to tree-climbing.

Homo erectus emerged in the changed landscape: the first of the *Homo* genus to walk fully upright. *H. erectus* led the move of our near ancestors out of Africa, arriving in China and other parts of Asia about 0.6 mya. A separate migration reached central Europe about 0.7 mya.

 QUESTIONS

1 Suggest why climate change in eastern Africa 2.5 mya was probably selection pressure for walking on two legs.

Human migration: the sequence

Human migration out of Africa followed this sequence (Figure 2 shows the location of the numbered sequence):

1 *200 kya*: H. sapiens appears. Our ancestors spread through Africa over the next 100 000 years.

2 *85 kya*: out of Africa, a group and their descendants follow the coast of the Arabian Peninsula into India. Their descendants continue to follow the coast to Borneo and then to China.

3 *70 kya*: groups cross by boat from Timor into Australia, and from Borneo into New Guinea.

4 *50 kya*: groups move through the Middle East and into Europe.

5 *40 kya*: migrants from China move north and east through central Asia, and into Siberia.

6 *23 kya*: their descendants pass from Siberia across the Bering Strait into North America.

7 *15 kya*: migration continues southwards into South America.

Effect of climate change

Climate change made human migration easier or more difficult depending on date and location. For example, falls in the sea level due to the last ice age connected land masses that are separated today:

> 71 kya, on average sea levels were 90 metres below present levels, making the sea crossing to Australia and New Guinea realistic for migrants from Timor and Borneo (see **3** in Figure 2).

> 50 kya, lower sea levels allowed groups to move into the Middle East and Europe (see **4** in Figure 2).

> 18 kya, on average sea levels were more than 140 metres below present, so that land bridged the route from Siberia to North America (see **6** in Figure 2).

QUESTIONS

2 Explain the effects of the ice age on human populations and migration.

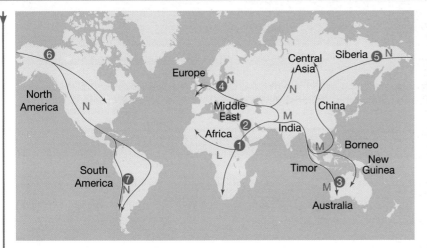

FIGURE 2: Human migration patterns out of Africa. The letters L, M and N refer to genetic markers described later.

FIGURE 3: A modern re-creation of an iron-age boat.

Mitochondrial DNA (Higher tier only)

When an egg is fertilised, only the sperm nucleus enters the cell. The rest of the sperm, including the mitochondria, is left behind.

Therefore, all of the **mitochondrial DNA (mtDNA)** inherited by offspring is contributed by mothers, and not fathers. Unlike nuclear DNA it does *not* recombine because of fertilisation, but follows a direct line of descent unchanged (except for mutations) from mother to offspring.

mtDNA is less likely to degrade over time than nuclear DNA. It can still be extracted from fossils tens of thousands of years old. This means that it is very abundant.

This is why mtDNA rather than nuclear DNA is used to trace human ancestry and migration.

Using mtDNA

mtDNA mutates about 20 times faster than nuclear DNA, and the mutations are key to tracing human ancestry and migration patterns. After several generations, each mutation becomes a **genetic marker** carried by most people in the region where it arose. Scientists can date the markers, since the age of fossils can be determined using radiometric techniques.

Markers appear fairly regularly because the mutation rate of mtDNA is fairly constant (one mutation roughly every 3500 years). Because mtDNA is *not* recombined, markers are not jumbled up but appear in sequence. The sequence is like a **molecular clock**. A marker appears every 3500 years, so the sequence of markers can be followed back in time.

Scientists can trace where and when each marker arose and hence find the migration patterns of our human ancestors. Ultimately, they identify our most recent *H. sapiens* common ancestor: **African Eve**.

Identifying Eve

Comparing the mtDNA sequences of people from different parts of the world identifies the number of markers in each population. The main markers are labelled L, M and N (see Figure 2):

> L is found predominantly in Africa.

> M and the markers that arose after it are found mainly in India, south-east Asia and indigenous Australians.

> N and the markers that arose after it predominate in Europe, central and north-east Asia, and the Americas.

The predominance of L in Africa and its relative rarity elsewhere suggest that L is the oldest mtDNA human marker. L almost certainly identifies African Eve.

Markers M and N are relatively rare in Africa. Also they appeared after L. This supports the idea that, as people outside of Africa mostly carry M or N (or the markers than appeared after them), all non-Africans therefore have their origins in Eve's descendants.

QUESTIONS

3 Explain why scientists prefer to use mtDNA rather than nuclear DNA to date the events of human migration.

4 Explain why the evidence from analysis of mtDNA favours the out of Africa hypothesis for human migration 85–15 kya.

Preparing for assessment: Applying your knowledge

To achieve a good grade in science, you not only have to know and understand scientific ideas, but you also need to be able to apply them to other situations. This task will support you in developing these skills.

✳ Mammals on the move

Ashley was watching a TV programme about wildlife. The broadcast was about the Serengeti National Park in Africa and showed animals called wildebeest. Ashley was fascinated by the odd appearance of the wildebeest, with their large heads, curved horns, big shoulders and spindly rear legs; then the programme explained that their journey is the biggest mammal migration in the world.

One reason for the wildebeest's migration is the need for fresh grazing areas – short grass is their preferred diet. They cannot go without water for more than a day or so. They have several predators, including hyena and lions. An adult wildebeest will live for up to 20 years. The females calve in May, giving birth to a single calf; they don't seek shelter but give birth surrounded by the herd. Most of the females in the herd give birth within two or three weeks of each other. The calf can stand and run within minutes of being born. Within a few days, it can run fast enough to keep up with the herd.

The wildebeest herd starts to migrate north soon after May and travels at a relentless pace through the day and night; many animals are lost, injured or even killed. In November the return journey south starts. Ashley was intrigued by the programme and could not understand why the wildebeest lived the way that they did. The young seemed to have a really rough time; they had to be up and on the move in a very short time and sometimes died before reaching adulthood.

Ashley thought that surely they would stand a better chance of survival if they were not all born at about the same time or, if the herd stayed in the same area for several months, until the calves were older and stronger? It made for an interesting bit of telly, and Ashley was so glad that humans didn't raise their young like that.

Task 1

> Why do wildebeest have to move on repeatedly?

> What type of behaviour is this?

Task 2

> Why do female wildebeest give birth in the middle of the grassy plain instead of finding a more sheltered place?

> Usually females give birth at around the same time. Why does this behaviour give an advantage in terms of survival?

Task 3

> Using the text, give possible examples of innate behaviour and imprinting.

> For each behaviour, state how it helps the wildebeest to survive.

Task 4

> Ashley found the mass migration a stunning sight, with a great number of animals relentlessly pressing on. They did not stop, even if some members of the herd were injured or left behind. Surely they would stand a better chance of survival if they cared more for each other? What do you think?

Task 5

> Explain, in terms of evolution, how the wildebeest's behaviour has helped the species to survive.

Maximise your grade

These sentences show what you need to include in your work to achieve each grade. Use them to improve your work and be more successful.

E
For grades G–E, your answers should:
> identify examples of innate behaviour and imprinting
> describe parental care.

C
For grades D–C, in addition show that you can:
> explain different behaviour in animals
> explain how the wildebeest's behaviour helps it to survive.

A
For grades B–A, in addition show that you can:
> explain the costs and benefits of parental care.

Biotechnology

You will find out:
> what biotechnology is
> about commercial uses of biotechnology

An essential nutrient

Vitamin C is a very important biomolecule. We depend on it for good health. The vitamin helps to bond the cells of our body together. Oranges, lemons and tomatoes are a rich source of vitamin C.

FIGURE 1: Citrus fruit contains vitamin C. Why is this an essential nutrient?

What is biotechnology?

The term **biotechnology** refers to the way scientists and engineers use plant cells, animal cells and microorganisms to produce useful **biomolecules** and then, perhaps, modify then chemically to make them even more useful.

A biomolecule is any molecule produced by a living organism. Vitamins, enzymes, and various sugars are examples.

The benefits of biotechnology have a long history. For thousands of years, humans have used microorganisms to produce food:

> *yeasts* to make wine, beer and bread

> *moulds* to flavour cheese

> *bacteria* to make yogurt, cheese and vinegar.

Many of the products of this traditional biotechnology are the result of **fermentation reactions**, that is reactions occurring in anaerobic or aerobic conditions that produce useful substances.

In the 1970s developments in genetic engineering marked the beginning of the modern era of biotechnology. New ways of using genes and manipulating cells opened up new opportunities.

FIGURE 2: The bark and leaves of willow trees contain salicin.

QUESTIONS

1 Name two examples of biomolecules.

2 What is meant by the phrase traditional biotechnology?

3 How is modern biotechnology different from traditional biotechnology?

Plant-based drugs

Drugs have been sourced from plants for thousands of years. They are examples of biomolecules. Even now more than 60% of the drugs used to treat disease come from plants.

Aspirin

People have long known that the liquid produced from stewing the bark and leaves of the willow tree in hot water relieves pain and reduces fever. The active ingredient in the liquid is **salicin**, and salicylic acid made from it is used to make an effective painkiller, **aspirin**.

Quinine

Chewing the bark and leaves of the *Cinchona* tree has long been known to be an effective treatment for malaria. Today we know that the active ingredient in the bark is **quinine**. It reduces fever and kills the parasite that causes malaria.

Taxol

In the late 1960s a substance called **taxol** was extracted from the bark of the Pacific yew tree. It killed cancer cells. By 1980 the structure of the taxol molecule had been worked out and its effect understood. Taxol stops cell division. It has an effect on healthy cells, but affects cancer cells even more.

So great was the demand for taxol that the Pacific yew tree soon became an endangered species. Fortunately the needle-like leaves of the European yew tree were found to be the source of a similar taxol-like substance. Since the tree quickly replaces its leaves, there is no risk of the European yew becoming endangered. Chemists modified the substance to form a semi-synthetic version of taxol called **paclitaxel**.

FIGURE 3: The bark of the Pacific yew tree was peeled and processed to provide taxol. Why was an alternative source sought?

QUESTIONS

4 Explain why aspirin is a biomolecule.

5 Suggest why the Pacific yew tree was in danger of becoming an endangered species.

Science in the service of medicine

Most drugs have unwanted side-effects on the user. Paclitaxel is no exception. Its **toxicity** produces side-effects including nausea, tingling in the hands and feet and other problems.

Paclitaxel may be combined with other substances which help to deliver the drug to where it is needed. The combination enables paclitaxel to have its effect on the cancer cells. However, many of the side-effects of treatment are linked to the chemistry of the substances paclitaxel is combined with. Recent research aims to alter this chemistry to reduce these unwanted effects. For example:

> DHA is short for a type of fatty acid easily absorbed by cancer cells. Paclitaxel combined with DHA is not toxic until it enters cancer cells. Then the bond between the DHA/paclitaxel combination breaks and paclitaxel does its work. Healthy cells are less likely to be affected.

> Combining paclitaxel with the amino acid glutamate is proving to be an effective treatment for people with cancer unresponsive to the action of paclitaxel on its own. Cancer cells take up more of the glutamate/paclitaxel combination than healthy cells, reducing side-effects.

> Monoclonal antibodies each combine with a specific type of cell. Chemists are designing drugs which combine paclitaxel with particular monoclonals that target specific types of cancer cell. Accurate targeting of cancer cells reduces the effects on healthy cells.

Did you know?

A leading cancer charity thinks that four out of 10 people in the UK will suffer from cancer during their lives.

FIGURE 4: Paclitaxel is delivered to the patient intravenously.

QUESTIONS

6 Explain the principle behind the different methods scientists are investigating to reduce the side-effects of paclitaxel combined with other substances.

7 Explain why biotechnology is useful.

Fermenters

You will find out:
> the conditions needed in fermenters
> how to investigate the growth of yeast

Cow power

Fermentation is a very versatile reaction. As well as its use in making alcohol and bread, it has a role in biogas production. Almost any organic material can be processed: waste paper, grass clippings, leftover food and even cow manure. The material is fed into digesters, which are sealed and sprayed with water vapour containing microorganisms. The microorganisms feed on the waste, producing biogas. The biogas is piped from the digester into a plant which then converts it into heat and electricity.

FIGURE 1: Dairy cows enjoying some grass. Are they four-legged fermenters?

A fermenter at home

> A **fermenter** is a container used to cultivate microorganisms for the production of biomolecules.

> Fermenters are used in waste treatment and for the production of antibiotics and of food (yogurt, cheese, soy sauce).

Making wine at home

Home winemaking is an example of fermentation technology on a small scale. On the opposite page you will see how the process is scaled up in industrial fermenters.

> Here, the microorganism is **yeast**.

> The **nutrient solution** is fruit juice (often grape).

> Enzymes in the yeast help sugar from the fruit juice break down into ethanol and carbon dioxide.

> The equipment is sterilised before the fruit juice and yeast are added.

> Each container is protected by an airlock. The lock allows the carbon dioxide to escape from the container. It also prevents unwanted microorganisms from contaminating the mixture and prevents air from entering.

> The container is kept in a warm place, such as near a radiator.

Remember!
A biomolecule is any molecule produced by a living organism.

FIGURE 2: Making wine at home. Why is it important that the equipment is sterilised?

QUESTIONS

1 List what you need to make homemade wine.

2 Describe two things that might happen if an airlock is not used in home winemaking.

3 Suggest how you could tell that the winemaking process has finished.

Investigating yeast

Yeasts are single-celled fungi. Different strains of yeast are used in baking and brewing. Yeast cells multiply by fermenting the sugars in cereals or fruit:

sugar (glucose) → ethanol + carbon dioxide

Did you know?

Brewing beer is probably the oldest human use for yeast, dating back to 9500 BC.

You can investigate the effect on the growth of yeast of different factors, such as pH, temperature, type of sugar, and species of yeast.

> Write down a hypothesis about your investigation.
> Next, identify the factors to be investigated.
> Design the experiment using the apparatus available in the laboratory.
> Work out how to measure the rate of the fermentation reactions, changing one factor at a time while keeping all other factors constant.

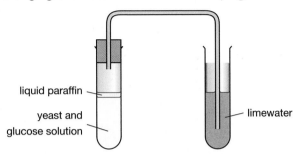

FIGURE 3: Small-scale fermentation set-up. Where is the ethanol and what do you predict will happen?

liquid paraffin
yeast and glucose solution
limewater

QUESTIONS

4 Design an experiment to investigate the effect of pH on the growth of yeast.

5 Different strains of yeast have different optimal fermentation temperatures. For example, the optimum temperature for dark beer yeasts is 12–18 °C, but for lager yeast is 8–12 °C. Suggest the effect on the fermentation if the temperature is

a too low
b too high.

Industrial-scale fermenters

Industrial fermenters may be 25 000 times bigger than the glass jars (demi-johns) used for home winemaking. But some of the conditions needed are the same in principle. Adjusting these conditions can affect microorganism growth rate.

> *Aseptic techniques* must be used. Superheated steam at 120 °C pumped through the fermenter and its pipelines kills microorganisms that might otherwise spoil the product.

> *Nutrients* are all the substances that microorganisms need to multiply and grow. They make up the culture medium. Commercially, microorganisms are cultured in a soup-like broth. The broth includes sugar and other carbohydrates as a source of energy, and mineral ions such as potassium, phosphate and nitrate.

> *pH* of the nutrient solution is controlled by adding acid or alkali to it. Optimum (best) pH depends on the microorganism cultured.

> *Oxygenation* of the nutrient solution is necessary for some fermentation processes. Sterile air is fed into the bottom of the fermenter through a perforated metal disc called a sparger. Air bubbles rise through the nutrient solution.

> *Agitation* of the nutrient solution ensures the even distribution of nutrients, microorganisms, gases in solution and heat throughout the fermenter. Motorised paddles stir the fermenter's contents.

> *Optimum temperature* is maintained by a cooling system. Heat released by the motorised paddles and fermentation reactions is quickly dispersed by cooling coils inside the fermenter or by a water jacket.

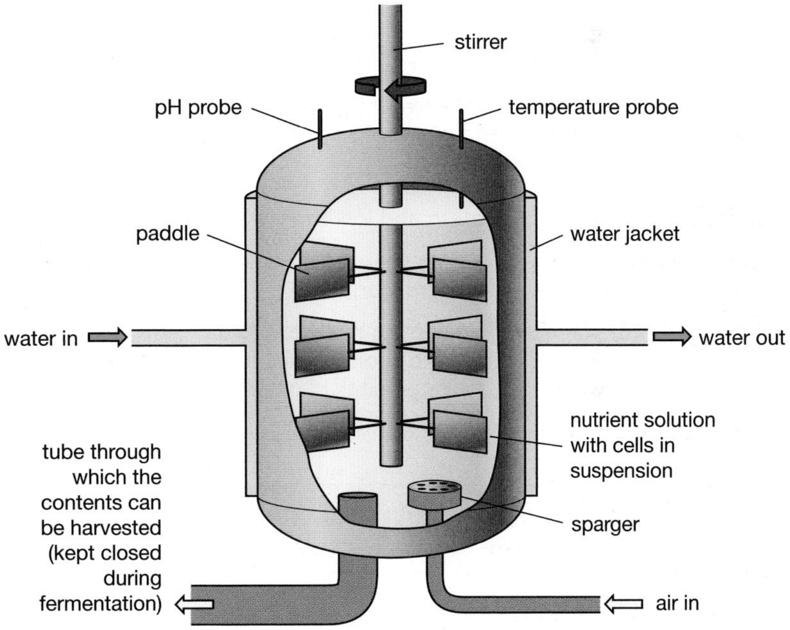

stirrer
pH probe
temperature probe
paddle
water jacket
water in
water out
nutrient solution with cells in suspension
sparger
tube through which the contents can be harvested (kept closed during fermentation)
air in

FIGURE 4: An industrial-scale fermenter.

QUESTIONS

6 Explain how a brewery maximises the yield of beer produced in its fermenters.

7 Suggest why air for oxygenation is fed into the bottom of the fermenter rather than the top.

Eating microorganisms

You will find out:

> about mycoprotein as a food

> how mycoprotein is manufactured

> about the advantages of using microorganisms for food

Edible bacteria

The bacterium *Spirulina maxima* grows in shallow water. People in Mexico make cakes of *Spirulina* and eat them. Commercial interest in *Spirulina* means the bacterium is being marketed as protein-rich health food.

FIGURE 1: Harvesting *Spirulina* on a farm. How do you think this will help feed people?

Mycoprotein

How can we produce enough food to feed the world's growing population? One option is to eat microorganisms produced by biotechnology. **Mycoprotein** is protein from fungus:

> The fungus *Fusarium sp.* is an example of a mycoprotein.

> It contains nearly 50% protein and less than 12% fat.

> It has a high vitamin and mineral content.

> Its nutritional value is equivalent to meat but with additional advantages. It has zero cholesterol and is high in fibre. Fibre in food helps peristalsis and a high level of blood cholesterol increases the risk of heart disease.

The commercial product called Quorn is mycoprotein. It looks rather like uncooked pastry dough. The addition of colours and flavours provides different food products such as burgers, sausages and pies.

The idea of eating mycoproteins is not new. During the First World War (1914–18), scientists helped to overcome food shortages when they discovered how to grow enough yeast to make food products.

Marmite, a commercial, savoury spread is made from yeast extract. Yeast left over from brewing beer is also used to make animal feed.

FIGURE 2: Quorn stir-fry with noodles. Quorn is often used as a meat substitute. Are there any advantages to this?

QUESTIONS

1 State why food made from *Fusarium sp.* might be described as healthy.

2 Give two uses for yeast left over from brewing beer.

FIGURE 3: Some people's favourite spread: Marmite on toast.

🔍 Spirulina   Mycoprotein

Microorganisms versus farming

What are the advantages of using microorganisms for food?

> Cell division in microorganisms occurs every 20–30 minutes, meaning that they double their mass within hours. The crops and livestock that we eat take weeks or months to grow.

> Microorganisms are easier to work with than crops and animals. Animals and crops can contract diseases or have difficult or unpredictable problems.

> Unlike crops, the production process is independent of the climate as it takes place in large fermentation tanks, takes up little space compared with a farm, and uses by-products from other industrial processes.

Did you know?

Yeast are single-celled fungi. Their name *Saccharomyces* means sugar fungi.

 QUESTIONS

3 Use the internet to help you describe the characteristics of *Fusarium sp.*

4 Describe four advantages of using microorganisms in food production.

Mycoprotein production

The microorganisms such as *Fusarium sp.*, used to produce mycoproteins, are grown in large quantities in huge fermenters. The fermenter is filled with nutrient solution that contains all of the substances microorganisms need to grow and multiply. Nutrients used to grow mycoprotein microorganisms are often by-products sourced from other industrial processes including:

> pulp from fruit processing

> agricultural waste (corn, wheat or rice starch, for example).

Mycoproteins are grown in fermenters in **continuous culture** for weeks at a time. Nutrients are replaced in the fermenter as they are used up, and temperature and pH are carefully controlled.

The conditions inside a fermenter are ideal for the rapid asexual reproduction of the microorganisms used to produce mycoproteins.

FIGURE 4: An industrial-scale fermenter. Why is it important that the factory is kept clean?

 QUESTIONS

5 Explain the process used to produce mycoprotein.

6 Mycoprotein food may not be acceptable to some people. How would you respond to someone who says that growing microorganisms as food is 'not natural'?

Making yogurt

You will find out:
> about making yogurt
> how to investigate factors affecting yogurt making

More than just sour milk

Milk is a useful food. Unfortunately it quickly turns sour. Keeping milk cool helps to keep it fresh, but even then only for a few days. Long before refrigerators, people preserved milk by turning it into other types of food, for example, yogurt.

FIGURE 1: Traditionally, yogurt used to be made in a skin bag. This is a modern-day factory for its production.

Making yogurt

All yogurt is produced in basically the same way. The process is:

> **Sterilised** milk (heating kills all of the bacteria in the milk) is thoroughly stirred and milk protein added.

> A starter culture of lactic acid bacteria is added to the still warm milk.

> The bacteria produce enzymes. The enzymes catalyse reactions that ferment the **lactose** to **lactic acid**. The milk becomes acidic and **coagulates** (solidifies). The milk has become raw yogurt.

> When cool, the yogurt may be flavoured or have fruit added to it. Natural yogurt has nothing added. The yogurt is placed into pots which are then sealed, and is then ready for distribution to shops.

FIGURE 2: Yogurt has gone from a useful way to store milk to a value-added mass consumer product. How do you think this affects yogurt's health benefits?

QUESTIONS

1 Outline the process used to make yogurt.

2 Explain why sterile milk is used to make yogurt.

Investigating yogurt making

To make yogurt you need milk and a starter culture of lactic acid bacteria. (The starter can be a spoonful of live natural yogurt.)

Enzymes produced by the bacteria **ferment** the lactose in milk, producing lactic acid.

Think about what factors might affect yogurt making, for example:

> *temperature*: different enzymes are active at different (optimum) temperatures

> *milk quality*: for example, skimmed, semi-skimmed, full fat (whole), full fat with milk powder, lactose-free milk.

Design the experiment using the apparatus available in the lab. Then work out how to test the quality of the yogurt produced, changing one factor at a time while keeping all other factors constant.

Using viscosity as a measure of quality, score the quality of the yogurt you've made: 1 (poor) – 5 (excellent). Before starting, you need a standard against which the yogurt made can be compared. Think what the standard might be: if you like thick yogurt then score 5, then use the apparatus in Figure 3 to work out the viscosity of your thick yogurt and compare this to the different yogurts that you have made.

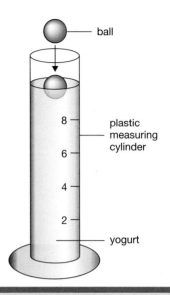

FIGURE 3: Measuring the viscosity of yogurt: record the time for a ball to sink to the bottom of a cylinder.

QUESTIONS

3 Why is it necessary to use *live* yogurt as a starter culture?

4 Design an experiment to investigate the effect of temperature on the production of yogurt.

Yogurt-making bacteria

The bacteria used to make yogurt are *Lactobacillus bulgaricus* and *Streptococcus thermophilus*. They do their work in anaerobic conditions which is why oxygen levels are kept low during yogurt manufacture. Their enzymes catalyse chemical reactions that ferment the lactose to lactic acid.

$$\text{lactose} \xrightarrow[\text{anaerobic conditions}]{\text{bacteria}} \text{lactic acid}$$

During fermentation, the numbers of bacteria increase. They consume more and more lactose, producing more and more lactic acid which lowers the pH of the milk (see Figure 4).

The *S. thermophilus* lowers the pH of the milk to 5.0 and *L. bulgaricus* lowers it further to about 4.5. The increasing concentration of lactic acid causes the milk to coagulate.

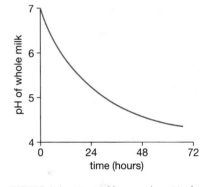

FIGURE 4: Lactic acid lowers the pH of milk over time. Where does the lactic acid come from?

QUESTIONS

5 Explain why yogurt is manufactured in anaerobic conditions.

6 Jo measured the pH of yogurt made from three different samples of milk over a period of 8 hours. Here are her results:

Time (hours)	0	1	2	3	4	5	6	7	8
Sample A pH	6.8	6.8	6.7	6.3	5.0	5.6	5.2	4.9	4.6
Sample B pH	6.8	6.8	6.8	6.8	6.8	6.8	6.8	6.8	6.8
Sample C pH	6.6	6.5	6.2	5.5	5.0	4.6	4.5	4.5	4.5

a Plot a graph of Jo's results.

b Is there an anomalous result – if so, which one?

c In which sample did the bacteria act more quickly?

d Suggest why this might have happened.

e Suggest a reason for sample B's results.

Did you know?

Lactose is a natural sugar found in milk. It is formed from galactose and glucose.

Q Yogurt history

Using enzyme technology

You will find out:
> about the use of enzyme technology
> how to investigate enzymes in food production

Honey production

Foraging bees add invertase and other enzymes to the nectar they collect. This helps to convert it to honey in the honeycomb. This is an example of enzyme technology in nature.

FIGURE 1: Honey bees entering a honeycomb.

Enzyme technology

Enzymes are useful industrial catalysts because:

> only a particular reaction is catalysed by an enzyme, making it easier to collect and purify the end product

> enzyme activity is high at moderate temperatures, saving energy costs

> only small amounts of enzyme are needed

> the enzyme is not used up in the reaction.

Enzymes are used in:

> food production

> detergents

> brewing

> pharmaceutical industry.

QUESTIONS

1 Why are enzymes useful industrial catalysts?

Useful enzymes

Chymosin and cheese

> **Chymosin** is an enzyme essential to cheese making.

> It catalyses reactions that cause the proteins in milk to coagulate and separate from the liquid.

> The liquid is called **whey**.

> The coagulated proteins form solid **curds** (raw cheese).

> Chymosin used to be obtained from the stomach tissue of slaughtered calves.

> Today most chymosin is made using genetically modified (GM) bacteria.

> GM-produced chymosin works in exactly the same way as the enzyme from calves. Because it contains fewer impurities it is more predictable.

FIGURE 2: A selection of hard and soft, full-fat and half-fat vegetarian cheeses. Vegetarian hard cheeses are manufactured with chymosin derived from a non-animal source. Soft cheeses are manufactured without the use of chymosin.

Invertase and sweets

Some sweets have a sticky, soft centre surrounded by chocolate. To make the soft centre manufacturers add invertase (sucrase) to a sucrose filling and store the mixture for several days at about 18 °C.

FIGURE 3: How does the manufacturer keep the sticky centre sticky?

> The enzyme catalyses the reaction which converts solid sucrose into liquid glucose and fructose:

$$\text{sucrose} \xrightarrow{\text{invertase}} \text{glucose + fructose}$$

> Invertase is produced by the yeast fungus called *Saccharomyces cerevisiae*.

QUESTIONS

2 Describe the role that enzyme technology plays in **a** cheesemaking **b** sweet manufacture.

3 Suggest why chymosin is produced naturally in the stomachs of young mammals.

4 Suggest why people working with biological washing products need protecting from the enzymes they contain.

5 Which type of enzyme would be effective in removing **a** blood or gravy stains and **b** grease marks?

Enzymes in washing powders

Biological washing powders contain enzymes:

> *proteases* break down proteins to amino acids

> *lipases* break down fats and oils to glycerol and fatty acids

> *carbohydrases* (such as amylase) break down polysaccharides (for example starch) into sugars.

Including enzymes in washing powders means that washing is most effective at low temperatures.

> Less energy is used to heat the water, saving costs and carbon emissions.

> The dye in coloured clothing is less likely to wash out of the fabric.

> The clothes are less likely to shrink.

The enzymes are sealed in capsules to protect them from the action of detergent powder. Encapsulation also protects the people who make washing powder.

Investigating enzymes

Immobilised enzymes

The industrial use of immobilised enzymes is particularly attractive because immobilisation protects the enzymes, helping them to resist changes in temperature and pH. This allows industrial processes to be designed to maximise the activity of enzymes without damaging them.

Immobilisation means that enzymes:

> are more easily recovered and reused

> do not contaminate the end product.

Immobilised lactase

Lactase catalyses the reaction that breaks down lactose sugar to glucose and galactose:

$$\text{lactose} \xrightarrow{\text{lactase}} \text{glucose + galactose}$$

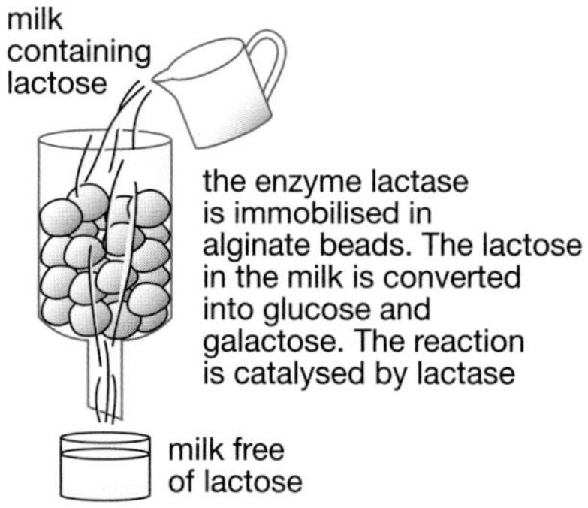

milk containing lactose

the enzyme lactase is immobilised in alginate beads. The lactose in the milk is converted into glucose and galactose. The reaction is catalysed by lactase

milk free of lactose

FIGURE 4: A method for producing lactose-free milk.

In some people, the cells lining the wall of the intestine do not produce lactase – they are **lactose intolerant**. Bacteria in the intestine feed on the undigested lactose, making these people feel unwell.

Milk contains lactose. People without lactase can still benefit from having milk in their diet if the lactose is removed. Figure 4 shows a method of producing lactose-free milk. Lactase is **immobilised** by bonding molecules of the enzyme to **alginate beads**. The beads are insoluble and unreactive.

Enzymes in food production

Food production depends on enzymes produced by different species of bacteria or fungi. For example, **glucose isomerase** is produced by the bacterium *Bacillus coagulans*. The enzyme converts glucose into fructose, which is sweeter. Fructose syrups are used to sweeten foods.

Different species of the bacterium *Acetobacter* produce **oxidase** enzymes used in vitamin C synthesis.

QUESTIONS

6 Suggest factors that would affect the production of fructose syrups.

7 Explain why some people are lactose intolerant.

8 Explain the advantages of immobilising the enzymes used as industrial catalysts.

Recombinant DNA technology

Human growth hormone

Some people's pituitary glands do not produce enough growth hormone and this affects their growth and development. Replacement growth hormone used to be obtained from corpses, but this led to some patients developing diseases. Recombinant DNA technology means that therapeutic growth hormone is now available and this is safe to use.

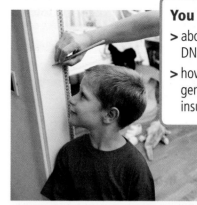

FIGURE 1: What can recombinant DNA technology be used for?

What is recombinant DNA? (Higher tier only)

Genes are sections of DNA. They carry information enabling cells to synthesise **proteins**. The information is encoded in the sequence of the **bases** of the gene. For example, the sequence CCG codes for the amino acid glycine.

Since the 1970s, scientists have been able to transfer useful genes from the cells of one type of organism to the cells of almost any other type: human to bacteria, for example. The host cells are the cells into which the genes are transferred. The organism with host cells is **genetically modified (GM)**.

To transfer a useful gene from one cell to another, the gene must be combined with another piece of DNA called a **vector**. Vectors can be viruses or **plasmids**. A plasmid is a circular piece of DNA found in bacteria. The combination of useful gene with vector DNA is called **recombinant DNA**. We say that the molecule has been **genetically engineered**.

Remember!

The bases are adenine (A), guanine (G), thymine (T) and cytosine (C).

QUESTIONS

1 Explain the difference between vectors and host cells.

2 What is meant by recombinant DNA?

Enzymes and DNA technology (Higher tier only)

Bacteriophages (phages for short) are viruses that infect bacteria with their genetic material. If the genetic material is DNA, then they infect the bacterial DNA and reprogramme it. Viral proteins are produced which assemble into new virus particles.

However, bacterial cells are not helpless victims to phage infection. They produce enzymes which cut up viral DNA into small pieces. This stops the viral DNA from inserting into the bacterial DNA. The enzymes are called **restriction enzymes**.

Many different types of restriction enzyme have been isolated from bacteria. An example is EcoRI from *Escherichia coli*.

Each type catalyses a particular reaction which cuts lengths of DNA into a mixture of fragments at points called the **recognition sites**. Each recognition site is a short sequence of bases specific to each restriction enzyme. For example, the recognition site for EcoRI is GAATTC.

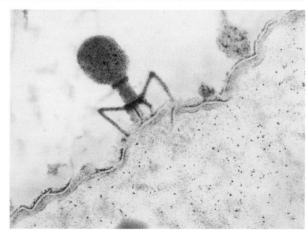

FIGURE 2: A micrograph of a phage (the red object with 'legs') binding to surface of a bacterial cell. The 'legs' of the phage's tail contract. The tail inserts the phage's genetic material into the cell (blue) like a hypodermic syringe.

Restriction enzymes can be used to cut out useful genes from longer lengths of DNA. The useful gene is identified from among the mixture of DNA fragments. It can then be inserted into a DNA vector, and the combination can then be transferred into a host cell.

Successful insertion depends on short, single-stranded lengths of exposed bases called **sticky ends**.

EcoRI does not cut at the same place within its recognition site. It cuts one strand of double-stranded DNA in one position, and the other strand in another position a few bases along the length of the molecule. We say that the cut is staggered (see Figure 3).

The same restriction enzyme is used to cut out a useful gene and the vector DNA into which it is to be inserted. The exposed bases of the sticky ends of the useful gene are sticky because they are **complementary** to the bases of the sticky ends of the vectors. **Ligase** enzymes catalyse the bonding process that repairs the DNA strands.

Not all restriction enzymes produce fragments of DNA with sticky ends. Sticky ends can be synthesised in the laboratory and joined to the DNA fragments.

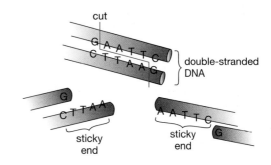

FIGURE 3: EcoRI is a restriction enzyme that creates sticky ends by cutting DNA at a specific place. What are sticky ends?

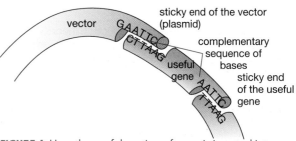

FIGURE 4: How the useful section of gene is inserted into the DNA vector.

QUESTIONS

3 Explain the importance of using the same restriction enzyme to cut out a useful gene and to cut open the plasmid vector.

Making genetically engineered insulin (Higher tier only)

A person with Type 1 diabetes needs to inject insulin to regulate the concentration of glucose in their blood as their pancreas does not produce enough insulin. Nowadays this insulin is obtained from GM bacteria.

To make genetically engineered insulin, the human insulin gene was cut from the chromosome carrying it and inserted into a plasmid vector. The vector carried the gene into the cells of the bacterium *E. coli*.

The GM bacteria now produce human insulin. The bacteria are cultured in a fermenter where they grow rapidly and the resulting insulin is removed for processing.

Human insulin was the first medicine made by genetic engineering.

QUESTIONS

4 Explain the meaning of the sentence, 'The human insulin gene can be synthesised in the laboratory.' Use the internet to help you.

5 Draw a flowchart to show the stages of producing genetically engineered human insulin.

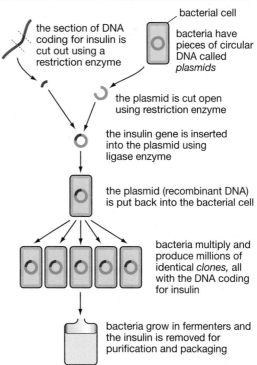

FIGURE 5: The process for making genetically engineered insulin. What is the role of ligase?

Producing transgenic plants

You will find out:
> about producing transgenic plants
> costs and benefits of genetic modification of crop plants
> about flavonoids in purple tomatoes
> about genes for insect resistance in crop plants

Anti-cancer plants?

Flavonoids are found only in plants. They give flowers and fruits their red, blue and purple colours. It is thought that they may help to prevent heart disease and some types of cancer.

FIGURE 1: What gives vegetables their bright colours?

Creating transgenic plants

Plants that have been genetically modified (GM) to create plants with beneficial characteristics obtained from the genes of other organisms are called **transgenic** plants.

Crops can be modified advantageously to:

> resist **herbicides**, so that insects can be killed but not the crop

> grow in places where rainfall is low

> resist the microorganisms causing crop diseases

> produce substances that kill their own insect pests.

There are concerns, however, that pests and diseases will develop a resistance to the modified crops.

GM technology allows us to improve the quality of food as well as the amount of it. The introduction of **flavonoids** in purple tomatoes is an example.

Scientists have isolated genes encoding flavonoids from snapdragon plants and inserted them into tomatoes. The result is modified purple tomatoes with nearly three times the flavonoid content of unmodified red tomatoes.

A study published in a scientific journal found that mice who ate the modified tomatoes lived longer and there are hopes that this 'superfood' will provide health benefits to humans. However, costly crops such as these are expensive to buy and are, in the short term at least, likely to be available only to wealthy consumers in developed countries.

Costs and benefits of GM crops

To feed the 6.7 billion people living in the world today, new approaches to producing more food are needed. This is particularly important in developing countries where harsh climate and poor soil can make growing crops difficult and food is sometimes in short supply.

A review by the UK government into the costs and benefits of GM crop cultivation over the next 10 years concluded that while there could be some advantages, any economic benefit is likely to be limited by the negative view of the public and retailers.

 QUESTION

1 What is a transgenic plant?

2 Explain the advantages of eating purple tomatoes in developed and developing countries.

Genetic modification of crops

A method of creating a transgenic plant is by using a common soil bacterium called *Agrobacterium tumefaciens* as a **vector**:

> *Agrobacterium*'s plasmid is called the *Ti* plasmid.

> *Ti* means 'tumour inducing'. It causes the cells of a plant infected with *Agrobacterium* to multiply more quickly than usual.

> A tumour-like mass of solid tissue (a **crown gall**) develops.

> The *Ti* plasmid is used as a vector for useful genes.

> The cells of the crown gall formed from genetically engineered *Agrobacterium* each contain the *Ti* plasmid with its useful gene.

> Small pieces of the crown gall can then be cultured and develop into small plants.

> The cells of each of these plants carry a genetically engineered *Ti* plasmid.

FIGURE 2: A crown gall growing on a chrysanthemum plant. What is a crown gall?

strand of plant DNA carrying the herbicide-resistance gene

bacterial cell

Agrobacterium tumefaciens bacteria have pieces of circular DNA called plasmid DNA

the DNA strand is cut using a restriction enzyme to isolate the herbicide-resistance gene

Ti plasmid DNA of *A. tumefaciens* is cut open with the same enzyme used to cut out the herbicide-resistance gene

the herbicide-resistance gene is inserted into the *Ti* plasmid DNA using ligase enzyme

the *Ti* plasmid DNA with the herbicide-resistance gene is put back into the *A. tumefaciens* cell

GM plantlets are resistant to herbicide and grow into mature plants

a plant infected with *A. tumefaciens* produces a crown gall. Its cells each contain a *Ti* plasmid DNA with the herbicide resistance gene in place. Small pieces are cut from the crown gall and cultured. Each grows into a plantlet. Each plantlet is a genetically modified version of the original

FIGURE 3: Genetically modifying crop plants with a herbicide resistance gene helps farmers to control weeds more efficiently.

QUESTIONS

3 Describe what happens when a plant becomes infected with *Agrobacterium tumefaciens*.

4 GM crops and GM food can stir up fierce debate in countries like the UK where there is enough food. Discuss whether the issues are the same for developing countries where food is in short supply.

Bacterial insecticides (Higher tier only)

Globally, 40% of the crops grown each year are damaged or eaten by insects. **Insecticides** are used to protect crops, however, they also kill other wildlife, are harmful to humans and costly to use.

The soil bacterium *Bacillus thuringiensis* produces a toxin called **Bt insecticidal crystal protein** (Bt ICP). The toxin kills a variety of insect pests. For example, it will attack the gut of a leaf-eating caterpillar. The caterpillar stops eating and dies. Bt ICP also kills the larvae of flies and beetles.

The gene from *B. thuringiensis* encoding Bt ICP is inserted into the *Ti* plasmid of *Agrobacterium*. Crop plants infected with the GM bacterium develop crown galls. Pieces of tissue cut from the galls are cultured and grown into plants that produce their own Bt ICP toxin. The plants are able to resist insect attack.

Advantages of Bt-modified crops

Bt ICP is selective: different versions of the toxin kill different insect species and only those species. This means that it is possible to target particular pest insects and not harm beneficial species. Also, Bt ICP is harmless to humans, other mammals, birds and fish.

Different studies suggest that growing Bt-modified crops can reduce the harmful impact of insecticides by up to 24%. The advantages arise because:

> the toxin is produced within the modified plants and only affects the insects feeding on them

> modified plants produce enough toxin to kill the insects feeding on them, replacing the need to use insecticides.

Disadvantages of Bt-modified crops

Other studies focus on the limitations of Bt-modified crops. Perhaps most important is the appearance of Bt-resistant strains of pest species. The development is an example of evolution in action. The population of any pest species will contain a few individuals resistant to the control measures taken against them. These individuals survive and produce offspring also with the resistance characteristic.

QUESTIONS

5 Draw a flow diagram to show how the gene encoding Bt ICP and the *Ti* plasmid of *Agrobacterium tumefaciens* are used in the culture of insect-resistant plants.

6 Discuss the significance of the appearance of Bt-resistant strains of pest species.

Q Flavonoids   Bt GM crops

Food security and production

Feed the world

Estimates suggest that more than nine billion people will be alive by mid-century. Providing enough food for the world's growing population is one of the major challenges of the 21st century. Unsurprisingly, making sure that there is enough food is at the top of the world's political agenda. Securing food supplies is an agreed aim. How to achieve that aim is another matter.

FIGURE 1: A woman sifts corn by hand in Africa. Why doesn't she just buy flour from a shop?

Securing the world's food supply

The world needs to produce enough food to feed an extra 90 million people each year for the foreseeable future. Yet there are limiting factors:

> a reduction in topsoil in which to grow crops because of soil erosion

> less groundwater to irrigate crops because of climate change.

The world's ecosystems continue to falter under the impact of human population growth.

QUESTIONS

1 If there were 6.7 billion people in 2010, calculate the percentage increase in the world's population by 2050.

2 Design a poster to show the requirements of achieving food security.

What is food security?

According to the World Health Organization, **food security** will only exist when everyone in the world is able to obtain enough food which is safe to eat and nutritionally balanced, making it possible to lead a healthy and active life.

Achieving food security depends on:

> farmers consistently growing enough food

> people having the means to obtain enough food

> people's knowledge of basic nutrition and healthy eating.

Remember!
Clean drinking water and proper sanitation is part of the meaning of food security as well.

Increasing food production

Because of advances in plant breeding, irrigation methods and the use of pesticides and fertilisers, farmers are producing more food than ever before.

Plant breeding programmes

Plant breeding programmes produce 'new crop' varieties with advantageous characteristics, such as high yield and insect resistance. Two varieties with desired characteristics are cross-bred to produce a new hybrid variety. The new variety is then reproduced asexually. High-yielding cereal plants absorb more nitrogen than other varieties. However, the tops of the plants are so heavy with grain that tall varieties can fall over. This makes it difficult to harvest the grain and the yield is reduced.

By cross-breeding tall, high-yielding plants with short plants, scientists have produced short, high-yielding varieties that do not fall over. This means that high-yielding varieties can be easily harvested.

Pest management strategies

Pests are the plants (weeds), fungi and animals (mostly insects) that destroy crops and livestock, or prevent land from being used for farming. Pesticides are the chemicals used to kill pests, and so assist in increasing crop yield.

While pesticides increase yields at a comparatively low cost, there are concerns that their residues may contaminant food supplies and harm the environment. Food agencies are encouraging farmers to use pest-resistant varieties of plants and to adopt natural methods of controlling pests, such as companion planting or the use of beneficial organisms, rather than using chemicals.

Genetic modification

Gene technology has made it possible to increase food production. For example, crop plants have been genetically modified to be resistant to herbicides, kill the insects eating them and grow where there is little rainfall.

Genetic modification produces plants with the desired characteristics more quickly than conventional breeding programmes.

Genetic modifications can also increase plant growth. For example, by transferring *Rhizobium* into cereal plants the genes responsible for controlling nitrogen fixation in the bacterium boosts grain production. Like peas, beans and other **leguminous** plants, GM-modified cereals in effect make their own fertiliser which improves their growth.

Despite the potential of these developments, opposition to using food produced from GM crops is widespread. Fears about damage to the environment and people's health have led some countries to ban growing GM crops.

QUESTIONS

3 Explain the advantage of breeding short, high-yielding varieties of cereal plant.

4 Suggest why the use of pesticides as part of an integrated pest management programme is to be preferred to using pesticides alone.

FIGURE 2: This researcher is working on a project to create 50 000 transgenic strains of rice. This research has developed strains of rice that have enhanced drought tolerance and fungal resistance.

Food supply versus demand

The graph in Figure 3 highlights the problem of how to achieve food security and feed all of us. Grain production may have nearly doubled in the past 40 years, but the amount available to each person as food has fallen.

There are a number of possible reasons for this including:

> the increasing demand for meat in newly prosperous developing countries means that grain is bought for animal feed

> the population growth means higher demand and higher prices

> the increasing production of biofuels means that arable land is given over to growing biofuels rather than crops.

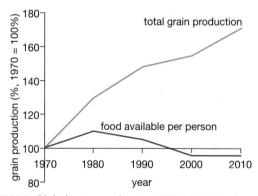

FIGURE 3: Global grain production 1970–2010. How has this growth in grain production been achieved?

QUESTIONS

5 Using Figure 3, explain the evidence suggesting that the chances of achieving food security in 2010 are less good than in 1980.

6 'Seventy per cent of all agricultural land is used for rearing farmed animals. Much of this is used to graze animals. However, a large proportion of land suitable for growing crops is used to produce feed for farmed animals.' Comment on how the views expressed here relate to food security.

Biofuels

You will find out:
> about producing biofuels
> about replacing fossil fuels with biofuels

Growing fuel

Brazil is the world's second largest producer of ethanol-based biofuel. Growing sugar cane is key to its production. Sugar cane is one of the most efficient photosynthesisers in the plant kingdom. It converts up to 2% of the sunlight energy it receives into biomass.

FIGURE 1: A sugar cane crop ready for harvesting.

What are biofuels?

The Sun floods the Earth with light energy. Plants trap light, using its energy to make sugar using photosynthesis.

> The term **biomass** refers to all of the organic material making up an organism's body.

> Biomass increases as the result of growth.

> Plants grow using the sugar produced by photosynthesis as a source of energy.

Plant biomass therefore represents a store of energy.

Producing biofuels

> **Biofuels** are produced from **renewable** organic materials such as plant biomass. Ethanol is an important biofuel.

> All fuels represent a store of energy. Burning fuel releases energy. Easy burning is an important feature of fuels.

> Ethanol burns easily and therefore has potential as a fuel.

> Ethanol is obtained by fermentation of sugar by yeast and then distillation.

> Biogas is a biofuel produced by the anaerobic fermentation of plant material and organic wastes. **Methane** is an example.

FIGURE 2: Sugar cane is used to produce ethanol. In the UK much of our sugar comes from sugar beet, rather than sugar cane. Why is that?

Did you know?

The USA is the world's largest producer of ethanol fuel. Maize provides most of the plant biomass for its production rather than sugar cane.

QUESTIONS

1 What is the link between plant biomass and biofuels?

2 Name two biofuels.

3 Suggest an advantage of biofuels.

Why use biofuels?

Fossil fuels

Burning fossil fuels produces gases that pollute the atmosphere. For example, sulfur dioxide and nitrogen oxides combine with water vapour to produce **acid rain**. Carbon dioxide is a **greenhouse gas** and may contribute to global warming. Also, fossil fuels are a non-renewable resource. Once used up they cannot be replaced.

Advantages of biofuels

The advantages of biofuels compared with fossil fuels are:

> *Supply*: biofuels are a renewable resource.

> *Clean burning*: burning biofuels do not produce sulfur dioxide and nitrogen oxides.

> *Conservation*: substituting fossil fuels with biofuels helps supplies of fossil fuels to last longer.

> *Greenhouse gases*: Their production uses the greenhouse gas carbon dioxide.

At first glance, burning biofuel seems to have far less impact on the environment than burning fossil fuel.

Disadvantages of biofuels

There is evidence that the expansion of biofuels would cause a reduction in food supply. This is because the land that is ideal for growing biofuel crops is also suitable for food crops.

Are biofuels neutral?

Burning fossil fuels or biofuel releases carbon dioxide.

It can be argued that the carbon dioxide released into the atmosphere by burning biofuels is only replacing the carbon dioxide absorbed during photosynthesis by the plants used to produce the biofuels in the first place.

In other words, biofuels are **carbon neutral**.

FIGURE 3: A price list in a Brazilian fuel station. *Álcool* is the word for ethanol. Sugar is an important crop in Brazil. Why do you think ethanol is a popular fuel choice in Brazil?

QUESTIONS

4 Explain the advantages of using biofuels compared with fossil fuels.

5 List the disadvantages of using biofuels, instead of fossil fuels.

6 Explain why biofuels might be described as carbon neutral.

Life cycle analysis

Life cycle analysis allows us to calculate the impact of human activity on the environment. In the case of producing ethanol-based fuel, the analysis lists the processes (the life cycle) of producing biofuel and the contribution each part of the process makes to the release of carbon dioxide.

Using the methods of life cycle analysis, recent research suggests that to produce 56 billion dm^3 of corn ethanol would require 140 million tonnes of grain, and 10.8 million more hectares of land to grow it. Even so, some scientists claim that burning the biofuels still releases the equivalent of less carbon dioxide compared with fossil fuels. However, other scientists using similar analyses claim that biofuels release more.

QUESTIONS

7 Explain the purpose of life cycle analysis.

8 Evaluate the advantages and disadvantages of replacing fossil fuels with biofuels.

FIGURE 4: This protestor is arguing that planting crops for biofuels, for rich people, will reduce the amount of farmland available for crops, to feed poorer people. Biofuels produce significantly more carbon dioxide than fossil fuels. Do you think biofuels are a good idea?

Preparing for assessment: Analysis and conclusions

To achieve a good grade in science, you not only have to know and understand scientific ideas, but you need to be able to apply them to other situations and investigations. This task will support you in developing these skills.

 ## Making lactose-free milk

Hypothesis

Alice read that cats and some people are lactose intolerant. As newborn mammals are fed on milk, all mammals start off with a working lactase enzyme, the enzyme that digests lactose. However as mammals get older the enzyme stops working and then they can only drink lactose-free milk.

Lactose-free milk has been treated with an immobilised lactase enzyme which turns the lactose into the simpler sugars glucose and galactose. As reactions happen faster at higher temperatures, Alice wanted to know the highest temperature that could be used for the reaction to happen.

Enzymes are biological catalysts and lactase is the enzyme that digests lactose. It catalyses the following reaction:

lactose → glucose + galactose

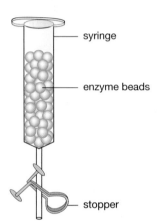

Method

First, enzyme beads are prepared. Lactase is mixed into liquid sodium alginate, then, using a pipette, this solution is dripped into calcium chloride which then solidifies the solution into hard, jelly-like beads.

The enzyme beads are placed into a large syringe with a rubber tube on the end. A stopper is clipped on the tube. Milk can then be poured into the syringe and left until all the lactose is digested. The final glucose concentration can be measured using a blood glucose monitor or glucose test strips. The enzyme beads are then reused.

To change the temperature, the milk and the enzyme beads were heated separately using a water bath at five different temperatures. They were then added together and left for 5 minutes. The milk was then tested to see how much glucose it contained. Untreated milk contains no glucose.

Alice knew that reactions happened faster at higher temperatures, so her hypothesis was the higher the temperature the faster the reaction and the more glucose will be produced.

Results

Alice's results are shown in the table.

Temperature (°C)	Glucose concentration after 5 min (mg/dm³)				
	Test 1	Test 2	Test 3	Test 4	Test 5
5	0	10	5	52	0
20	100	90	100	110	80
35	180	180	170	160	170
45	210	200	190	205	200
55	130	150	20	140	150
65	0	0	0	0	0

✳ Processing evidence

1. For each temperature calculate the average glucose concentration. Be careful and be sure to identify the anomalous result before you do the calculation.

2. Use the averages to plot a graph. Decide which graph you need to use to show the relationship between temperature and enzyme activity.

> Remember the mean can't have more decimal places than the numbers you used to calculate it.

> If your data can have decimal places you normally use a line graph, if having decimal places is impossible like counted data you use a bar chart.

✳ Stating conclusions

1. Using the graph, describe the relationship between temperature and enzyme activity.

2. Explain the relationship using your scientific knowledge.

> Describe the relationship qualitatively and quantitatively. This means that you should use the numbers on the graph, and describe the strength of the relationship.

> Use scientific language to explain the results. This will help to secure you Quality of Written Communication marks.

✳ Evaluating the method and conclusions

1. Do you agree with Alice's original hypothesis? What changes would you make?

2. Comment on the following sections of the method on how they might have affected the validity or repeatability of the method:

a stirring the enzyme into the sodium alginate

b reusing the enzyme beads

c repeating the readings of each temperature five times

d having the enzyme beads and the milk at the same temperature before adding them together.

3. Suggest how the method could be changed or extended to obtain extra evidence to increase the confidence with which you can draw a conclusion.

> Remember you can never prove a hypothesis – the data may support the whole of the hypothesis or just part of it.

> Make sure your suggestions relate to the original hypothesis and not a new one.

✳ Connections

How science works

> Collecting and analysing scientific data.

> Evaluating methods of data collection and considering their validity and reliability as evidence.

> Interpreting scientific information or ideas.

> Presenting information and drawing conclusions using appropriate language, conventions and ICT.

Maths in science

> Calculate arithmetic means.

> Plot and draw graphs.

> Extract and interpret information from charts, graphs and tables.

> Translate information between graphical and numeric forms.

> Provide answers to calculations to an appropriate number of significant figures.

B3 checklist (Topics 2 and 3)

To achieve your forecast grade in the exam you'll need to revise

Use this checklist to see what you can do now. Refer back to pages 42–81 if you're not sure.

Look across the rows to see how you could progress – **_bold italic_** means Higher tier only.

Remember you'll need to be able to use these ideas in various ways, such as:
> interpreting pictures, diagrams and graphs
> applying ideas to new situations
> explaining ethical implications
> suggesting some benefits and risks to society
> drawing conclusions from evidence you've been given.

Look at pages 230–52 for more information about exams and how you'll be assessed.

This checklist accompanies the exam-style questions and the worked examples. The content suggestions for specific grades are suggestions only and may not be replicated in your real examination. Remember, the checklists do not represent the complete content for any topic. Refer to the Specification for complete content details on any topic and any further information.

To aim for a grade E	To aim for a grade C	To aim for a grade A
recall that behaviour refers to the reactions of humans and other animals to their surroundings describe different types of behaviour: innate, courtship, habituation, imprinting, conditioning	explain different types of behaviour: innate, courtship, habituation, imprinting, conditioning describe the work of different ethologists helps to explain different types of behaviour	
describe types of parental care identify a link between mating strategy and parental care	explain that animals have different mating strategies that may (or may not) include parental care describe the costs and benefits of parental care	explain a range of mating strategies explain parental care as an evolutionary strategy
define communication in terms of behaviour that influences the action of other individuals describe the different signals used for communication	explain how animals use sound to communicate	explain how animals use pheromones to communicate
recall that plants can communicate with animals and other plants	explain how plants communicate with one another using chemicals	**_understand how plants and animals have co-evolved_**
describe the social behaviour of chimpanzees and gorillas as a basis for understanding human behaviour	describe and explain the fossil evidence for human evolution	analyse the link between bipedalism and brain size
recall what a stone tool is	describe how stone tools developed over time understand how stone tools can provide evidence for human evolution	explain how stone tools can be dated from the environment, including radiometric dating

To aim for a grade E	To aim for a grade C	To aim for a grade A
recall the fossil evidence for human evolution	explain the impact of climate change on human migration	*explain how mitochondrial DNA provides evidence for African Eve* *analyse the advantages of using mitochondrial DNA to track human migration and evolution*
describe what biotechnology is	describe how some biomolecules are useful as drugs to treat cancer and relieve pain describe the advantages of using microorganisms in food production	explain that producing biomolecules is an example of using science in the service of medicine
describe small-scale fermentation		explain the conditions used in industrial fermenters
state that mycoprotein is used to produce fungus-based foods	describe how mycoprotein is produced understand the advantages of using mycoprotein as a food source	
describe how yogurt is made	describe and investigate the factors that affect the production of yogurt	explain the bacterial fermentations that are the bases of yogurt making
recall that enzymes are used as catalysts in several industries	describe how enzyme technology is used to produce cheese, soft-centred sweets and biological washing powders	explain the advantages of using immobilised enzymes on an industrial scale
recall that genes can be transferred from cells of a particular species of organism into the cells of another species understand the costs and benefits of GM crop plants to producing food, including purple tomatoes	explain how *Agrobacterium tumefasciens* is used as a vector to produce transgenic plant	*explain recombinant DNA technology and its application in producing insulin and insect-resistant plants* *evaluate the advantages and disadvantages of Bt-modified crops*
define food security	explain how food production can be increased to improve food security	evaluate evidence that continuing growth of the human population undermines strategies to achieve food security
describe what biofuels are	discuss why biofuels are being developed and used in some countries	evaluate the advantages and disadvantages of using biofuels

1 The police use sniffer dogs to detect illegal drugs.

AO1 **a** Sniffer dogs are trained using operant conditioning. Read the sentences below. Which of them describes a similarity between operant and classical conditioning?

A ☐ Both involve the manipulation of reflexes

B ☐ Both involve reinforcing a specific behaviour with treats

C ☐ Both involve training animals to respond to a specific stimulus

D ☐ Both involve transferring a natural response onto a neutral stimulus [1]

AO2 **b** Suggest why it would not be suitable to train sniffer dogs by imprinting. [2]

AO2 **c** Suggest one animal, other than a sniffer dog, that humans train for a specific purpose. Describe how your chosen animal would be trained. [3]

[Total: 6]

2 The diagram shows that the great apes share a common ancestry.

orangutans gorillas chimpanzees

↗present

4–6 mya

6–8 mya

12–16 mya
common ancestor of
the great apes

AO2 **a** State with which great ape we share the most recent common ancestor. [1]

b Human fossils help us to track how humans have evolved from our common ancestor. Lucy, a skeleton fossil from *Autralopithocus afarensis*, is one hominid fossil.

AO1 **i** When was Lucy alive? [1]

AO1 **ii** How does Lucy provide evidence for human evolution? [2]

c

AO1 **i** Name two methods that could be used to date
AO2   these stone tools. [2]

AO3 **ii** Explain how these stone tools could be used as evidence for human evolution. [2]

AO2 **d** Humans are linked to chimpanzees by a common ancestor. Discuss why studying the social behaviour of chimpanzees can help to explain human behaviour. [6]

[Total: 14]

3 Fermenters are vessels used to cultivate microorganisms for the production of biomolecules.

AO1 **a** Name biomolecules that are manufactured using fermenters. [2]

AO1 **b** The contents of a fermenter warm up because of the heat released by which process?

A ☐ Oxygenation of the contents

B ☐ Sterilisation of the fermenter

C ☐ Fermentation reactions

D ☐ Stirring of the mixture [1]

AO1 **c** Explain why it is important that the fermenter agitates the solution of microorganisms. [1]

AO2 **d** Bagasse is the waste fibrous matter left after sugar cane production. It can be used in fermenters to make bioethanol.

What is the commercial benefit of producing bioethanol from bagasse? [1]

AO1 **e** Bioethanol is a renewable fuel. Discuss the
AO2   advantages and disadvantages of replacing fossil fuels with biofuels. [6]

[Total: 11]

4 The graph below shows how the concentration of lactic acid increases during the production of yogurt using bacteria.

concentration of lactic acid
time (hours)
0   6   12

AO3 **a** Describe the trend shown in the graph between 0 and 12 hours. [2]

AO3 **b** Explain the shape of the graph between 0 hours and 6 hours. [1]

AO2 **c** What will be the likely pH of the yogurt
AO3   produced at the end of the 12 hours? Give a reason for your answer. [2]

d Fungi can also be used in food production. For example, *Fusarium* is used to make mycoprotein.

AO1 **i** State the advantages of mycoprotein as a food source. [2]

AO1 **ii** Describe how *Fusarium* is used in the manufacture of mycoprotein. [3]

[Total: 10]

Summary of Assessment Objectives

AO1 recall the science   AO2 apply your knowledge   AO3 evaluate and analyse the evidence

Worked example

AO1 **a** Animals exhibit different kinds of behaviour. Use one of the terms below to complete the sentence.

Classical conditioning. describes the behaviour by which you avoid a stimulus at first but then accept it as you get used to it. ✗   [1]

A classical conditioning   C operant conditioning

B habituation   D imprinting

AO1 **b** The photograph below shows a male bird of paradise in the breeding season. His vividly coloured feathers are an important feature of his courting behaviour. Describe two features of his courtship behaviour which depend on the colour of his feathers. [2]

The colour of his feathers make him feel good about himself, frightens away other birds and makes him attractive to females.
✗ ✔

AO2 **c** Birds and mammals have developed special behaviours for looking after their young. These behaviours often disadvantage the parents in the short term by taking up a lot of time and energy. Explain in terms of evolutionary theory why this is a good strategy. [2]

Parental care improves the chances of offspring surviving. If offspring survive to become adults, they can then reproduce offspring themselves and pass on the parental genes.
So advantageous characteristics are passed on to future generations. ✔ ✔

AO1 **d**
AO2   A number of scientists have worked closely with animals to study their behaviour and to develop ideas about social behaviour. Describe how Dian Fossey and Jane Goodall have helped to develop ideas about social behaviour in primates. [4]

Dian Fossey worked with gorillas and discovered how gorilla groups form hierarchy's. Jane Goodall worked with monkeys and discovered they were used sticks as tools to catch termites. ✔ ✔ ✗ ✗

[Total: 9]

How to raise your grade

Take note of the comments from examiners – these will help you to improve your grade.

The correct answer is habituation. Both involve neutral stimuli, but habituation is becoming used to the stimulus so that it becomes neutral and classic conditioning is linking a reflex response with a previously neutral stimulus. Remember to learn these key terms carefully.

Be precise: only male birds are frightened away – scaring away female birds wouldn't be useful for courtship! The candidate could have also said that the brightly coloured feathers show that he is healthy.

This is a concise answer that uses the correct language and is explained well.

Be precise; Jane Goodall worked with chimpanzees. The answer is far too brief for a 4-mark question. They could have added:
> Chimpanzees work together to hunt monkeys.
> Males chimpanzees are usually dominant.
> Gorillas use tools (although less frequently than chimpanzees).
> The more powerful the male gorilla, the more a female wanted to mate with him.

This candidate scored 5 marks out of 9. They lost valuable marks through using imprecise language and not giving enough detail for the number of marks available. They could have improved their grade by checking their use of scientific terms and practising long-answer questions.

Exam-style questions: Higher

1 Evolution is the change in species over time. When two different species interact they often evolve together.

AO2 **a** The *Ophrys apifera* flower can communicate with the bee. State how the flower is communicating. [1]

AO2 **b** Above is a photo of the flower *O. apifera*. Suggest how *O. apifera* has co-evolved with bees. [2]

AO2 **c** Describe how *O. apifera* could communicate with other plants. [3]

AO1 **d** The relationship between *O. apifera* and the bee is mutually beneficial. Sometimes plants must defend themselves against a destructive relationship. Explain how plants have co-evolved with pests to develop defence mechanisms. [4]

[Total: 10]

2 Enzymes are biological catalysts that are used extensively in biotechnology. Chymosin is an enzyme which is used in the manufacturing of vegetarian cheese.

AO2 **a** Suggest why the manufacturers of vegetarian cheese grow chymosin in bacteria rather than take rennet from cows. [2]

AO1 **b** Describe how chymosin is used to produce vegetarian cheese. [3]

AO2 **c** Suggest one factor that the cheese manufacturers would need to monitor during production. [1]

AO1 **d** Enzymes also have a role in producing
AO2 genetically modified organisms. Enzymes are essential to the process of manufacturing insulin for people with Type 1 diabetes.

Describe how DNA technology is used to produce insulin. [6]

[Total: 12]

AO1 **3** **a** *Agrobacterium tumefaciens* is a soil bacterium that is often used to transfer genes into crop plants.

What characteristic of *A. tumefaciens* makes it a bacterium of choice for the transfer of genes into crop plants? [4]

AO3 **b** The bacterium *Bacillus thuringiensis* produces a toxin called insecticidal crystal protein (Bt ICP). The graph below shows the effect of introducing genes from *Bacillus thuringiensis* into crops on the number of oak feeding moths.

- ▉ modified to include Bt ICP
- ▢ treated with conventional insecticide

[Bar chart: y-axis "number of species present" from 0 to 30; x-axis years 2008, 2009, 2010, 2011. 2008: modified 18, treated 16; 2009: modified 10, treated 27; 2010: modified 18, treated 29; 2011: modified 15, treated 25.]

Describe the relationship between the number of moths present among crops modified to include Bt ICP and crops treated with conventional insecticide. [2]

AO3 **c** Explain the relationship shown by the bar chart. [2]

AO2 **d** Suggest how the bar chart would look if it included a bar for 'untreated' crops. [2]

AO1 **e** Insect-resistant crops could help combat
AO3 problems in the food supply in Africa. Compare the advantages of creating insect-resistance among crops by genetically modifying crops to include Bt ICP, with treating crops using conventional insecticides. Use evidence from the bar chart in your answer. [6]

[Total: 16]

4 By looking at ancient tools and fossils, Louis Leakey developed a theory that humans originated in Africa and migrated across the world.

AO1 **a** Describe how Leakey's discovery contributed to the overall evidence for human evolution. [2]

AO1 **b** Climate change was one cause of human migration. Explain why the Ice Age prompted human migration. [2]

AO3 **c** Human evolution was first studied by looking at the changing characteristics of fossils. We can now find more evidence of evolution by looking at DNA from the nucleus and mitochondria.

Discuss the advantages of using mitochondrial DNA compared to nuclear DNA as evidence for evolution. [6]

[Total: 10]

Summary of Assessment Objectives

| AO1 | recall the science | AO2 | apply your knowledge | AO3 | evaluate and analyse the evidence |

Worked example

AO2 **a** The diagram shows two examples of stone tools produced during the Oldowan and Acheulean periods of stone tool technology.

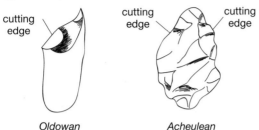

cutting edge

cutting edge   cutting edge

Oldowan   *Acheulean*

Suggest which tool is the oldest. Give a reason for your answer.   [2]

The Oldowan tool is probably more recent because it does the same job as the Acheulean tool but is simpler and wouldn't have taken as long to make. ✗ ✗

AO2 **b i** Carbon dating was used to date the axe head and its handle. Explain why the handle can be dated but the axe head can't.   [2]

The axe head will contain little carbon and therefore cannot be dated using carbon dating. The wooden handle contains a lot of carbon and can be dated using carbon dating. ✔

AO3 **ii** The radioactive isotope carbon-14 (^{14}C) breaks down to nitrogen-14 (^{14}N). Its half-life (the time taken for half of the ^{14}C in a sample to break down to ^{14}N) is 5730 years. The half-life of the radioactive isotope potassium 40 (^{40}K) is 1.3 billion years. A scientist excavated a stone axe head with its fossilised wooden handle nearby, and sent them to a laboratory for radiometric dating.

Explain why ^{40}K dating would not have been a suitable method, for dating the axe head and its handle.   [2]

The half-life of ^{40}K is too long. Not enough would have broken down to give an accurate date since the oldest known stone tool is about 1.6 million years old. ✔ ✔

AO3 **iii** A sample of the fossilised wooden handle contained 3.125% ^{14}C. Calculate the date of the handle and by implication the tool. Explain your working.   [3]

28,750 years old. ✔

[Total: 9]

How to raise your grade

Take note of the comments from examiners – these will help you to improve your grade.

This answer is incorrect. Tools become more complex over time. Two cutting edges are more efficient, so the Acheulean tool with one cutting edge is older.

To gain the extra mark say it has a lot of carbon because it is organic.

This is a good answer. It includes knowledge of the half life and the probable age of the tool.

A correct answer. However, the student has not shown their working.

If the sample contained 50% ^{14}C then it would be 5730 years old, if 25% ^{14}C then 11,460 years old, if 12.5% 17,190 years old and so on. Halving each time adds 5730 years to the date to the 3.125% ^{14}C contained in the sample.

This candidate scored 4 out of 9 for what is a challenging question. The candidate shows a detailed understanding of dating stone tools and their maths skills are strong. However, they lost valuable marks in part a by not applying their understanding fully, and in part **biii** by not showing their workings. They could have improved their grade reading the question carefully and checking their work to ensure they had fully answered the question.

C3 Chemistry in action (Topics 1–3)

What you should know

Qualitative analysis

Elements and compounds can be identified by their chemical and physical properties.

Ions can be detected by doing specific tests (C2 – Topic 2).

- Which would have the higher melting point, the ionic compound sodium chloride or the covalently bonded glucose?

Quantitative analysis

Formula masses can be calculated from a chemical formula (C2 – Topic 6).

Percentage composition can be calculated using the formula mass of a compound (C2 – Topic 6).

- What is the formula mass of sodium hydroxide (NaOH)?

Electrolytic processes

Anions have a negative charge and cations have a positive charge (C2 – Topic 2).

Molten ionic compounds or solutions of ionic compounds can conduct electrical current (C2 – Topic 2).

Electrolysis uses electrical energy to break down hydrochloric acid into hydrogen (C1 – Topic 3).

- What gas is produced at the anode when electrolysing water?

You will find out about

> the difference between qualitative and quantitative analysis

> qualitative tests for specific ions

> the use of qualitative tests to detect the presence of specific ions in industry

> calculating the concentrations of solutions

> hard water and the problems it can cause

> methods of treating hard water

> using moles in calculations to find masses and concentrations

> using excess reactants, filtration and evaporation to prepare a soluble salt from an acid and an insoluble reactant

> using titrations in the preparation of soluble salts from an acid and a soluble reactant

> using the results of titrations to calculate an unknown volume or concentration

> electrolytes and the reactions that occur at the cathode and anode

> writing half equations

> the industrial use of electrolysis to purify elements like sodium and copper

> the formation of products in electrolysis using inert electrodes and copper electrodes

> the process of electroplating

Testing for ions

You will find out:

> about the difference between qualitative and quantitative analysis

> about unique tests to identify ions

> how to identify certain ions

Identifying the unknown

The identification of unknown substances is essential in many jobs. For example, archaeologists analyse the remains of teeth from ancient burials or cremations, so that they can identify components of a person's diet and find out whether they had always lived in that area or had moved from elsewhere.

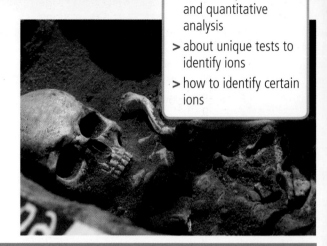

FIGURE 1: Can archaeologists find out where this person grew up and what they ate?

Types of analysis

To identify an unknown substance, a chemist can use:

> **qualitative analysis** – this tells us *which* ions are present in the compound

> **quantitative analysis** – this tells us *how much* of each ion is present.

We can identify some metal ions by their reaction in solution when mixed with sodium hydroxide (NaOH) solution in a test-tube. Many metal ions form insoluble precipitates of the hydroxides as shown in Table 1.

We can also use sodium hydroxide to identify compounds that contain the ammonium ion (NH_4^+):

> Ammonium compounds give off ammonia gas when mixed with sodium hydroxide solution and gently heated.

> The ammonia gas has a distinctive smell and turns moist red litmus paper blue.

TABLE 1: The reactions of some metal ions with sodium hydroxide.

Metal ion	Reaction with sodium hydroxide solution
Al^{3+}	White precipitate, redissolves in excess NaOH
Ca^{2+}	White precipitate
Cu^{2+}	Pale blue precipitate
Fe^{2+}	Grey–green precipitate
Fe^{3+}	Brown precipitate

Remember!

All sodium, potassium, ammonium and nitric compounds are soluble in water.

QUESTIONS

1 State the difference between qualitative analysis and quantitative analysis.

2 Describe how you would decide whether a compound contained iron (Fe^{2+}) or copper (Cu^{2+}) ions.

Analysis of ionic compounds

Qualitative analysis must use the *unique* properties or qualities of an ion to determine its presence. Tests that produced the same results for two or more ions would not allow chemists to find out which was present.

For instance, in Table 1 you can see that both aluminium and calcium ions produce a white precipitate when they react with sodium hydroxide solution. Adding more sodium hydroxide solution can help you to tell them apart:

> the aluminium hydroxide precipitate dissolves

> the calcium hydroxide precipitate does not dissolve.

Did you know?

Using modern analytical techniques, chemists can detect less than one millionth of a gram of a compound.

Q Qualitative chemistry   Quantitative chemistry

Cations

Ionic compounds are made up of positively charged ions (**cations**) and negatively charged ions (**anions**). To identify an unknown ionic compound both the cationic and anionic portions need to be identified.

Anions

We can identify chloride (Cl^-), bromide (Br^-) and iodide (I^-) ions using their reaction with silver nitrate dissolved in dilute nitric acid. All of these anions produce a silver halide precipitate with a characteristic colour. For example:

sodium + silver → sodium + silver
chloride + nitrate → nitrate + chloride
solution + solution → solution + precipitate

FIGURE 2: Which halide ion do each of these test-tubes contain?

Notice that the nitric acid does not take part in these reactions. However, it has to be present to ensure that only halide ions form the precipitates. (There are other insoluble silver compounds but they dissolve in nitric acid.)

TABLE 2: The reactions of some halogens with a solution of silver nitrate in aqueous nitric acid.

Anion	Reaction with silver nitrate in aqueous nitric acid
Cl^-	White precipitate
Br^-	Pale yellow precipitate
I^-	Yellow precipitate

QUESTIONS

3 Explain why the tests used by chemists in qualitative analysis need to produce unique results.

4 Explain how you would decide whether a compound contained aluminium, calcium or ammonium ions.

5 Prepare a flowchart to show how to identify chloride, bromide and iodide ions.

Ionic equations

Look again at the method above for identifying halides. In each case we are looking for a silver halide precipitate – formed from silver (Ag^+) ions and halide ions (Cl^-, Br^- or I^- ions). However, there will be other ions present, for example, H^+, NO_3^- and the metal ions from the metal halide. Ions that don't take part in a reaction are called **spectator ions**, and we do not need to include these in the equations we use to describe the reaction.

To show what happens when sodium bromide is added to an acidified solution of silver nitrate, we could write an equation:

$$NaBr \text{ (aq)} + AgNO_3 \text{ (aq)} \rightarrow AgBr \text{ (s)} + NaNO_3 \text{ (aq)}$$

We can write this as an **ionic equation**:

$$Na^+ \text{ (aq)} + Br^+ \text{ (aq)} + Ag^+ \text{ (aq)} + NO_3^- \text{ (aq)} \rightarrow AgBr \text{ (s)} + Na^+ \text{ (aq)} + NO_3^- \text{ (aq)}$$

But we can simplify this by including only those ions that are taking part:

$$Ag^+ \text{ (aq)} + Br^- \text{ (aq)} \rightarrow AgBr \text{ (s)}$$

QUESTIONS

6 Lead chloride ($PbCl_2$) forms as a precipitate when solutions of lead nitrate and sodium chloride are mixed. Write an ionic equation to show how lead chloride forms from its constituent ions. The formulae of the lead and chloride ions are Pb^{2+} + Cl^-, respectively.

Remember!
A halide is a salt containing a halogen ion.

Ions in industry

You will find out:
> about methods used to identify ions in unknown salts
> the uses of ion tests in industry

Looking for ions

Our water supply is tested to check that ions naturally present in the water (such as copper, iron and lead) are within safe limits and that the colour and taste of drinking water are acceptable.

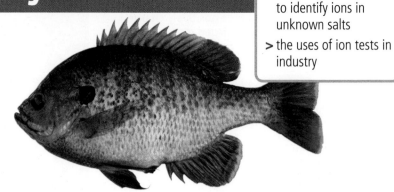

FIGURE 1: Scientists in the USA are using bluegill fish to monitor water quality. If pollutants are present, the fish change their breathing pattern and an alarm goes off. To protect the fish, they are replaced after 3 weeks with new, younger fish.

The presence of ions in blood and water

Testing for ions in blood

Chemists working in medical laboratories use chemical tests to look for specific ions in blood samples. This analysis helps in the diagnosis of medical conditions such as kidney, liver or bone disease.

For example, high levels of calcium in the blood can result from bone cancer, while low levels can indicate kidney failure. (However, there are many other causes of higher blood calcium levels.)

QUESTIONS

1 Why would chemists at water treatment facilities be interested in identifying the presence of metal ions in drinking water?

2 Explain why quantitative testing is used in medical diagnosis.

Tests for ions in water

The tests used by chemists to identify unknown substances can also be used to look for specific ions. Water treatment facilities check the purity of water by, for example:

> Measuring the concentration of metal ions such as copper which may find their way into the water system. These ions can come from many sources including fertilisers, animal feeds and algicides.

> Monitoring levels of chloride ions, which may enter the water system from natural sources such as weathering and seawater, or from sources such as industrial waste, fertilisers, road de-icing salts and landfill sites.

Water treatment facilities need to test for the presence of these ions and to take action if levels of a particular substance become too high.

Standard testing

Most chemical analysis labs have a standard set of rules to identify unknown substances. The rules set out a basic sequence of tests based on several factors. Two important factors are:

> how easy the tests are to carry out

> how hazardous the tests are (the safest test should be done first).

Imagine you are investigating a murder and suspect that the victim has been poisoned. For this you need the flowchart in Figure 3.

> You find some powder at the scene and decide to identify it.

> You carry out a flame test and find that the powder gives a blue–green flame.

> This shows that the powder contains copper ions.

> You add the powder to sodium hydroxide solution and get a pale blue precipitate.

> This confirms that the powder is a copper compound.

Next you need to identify which copper compound it is.

> You add dilute hydrochloric acid to the powder – no gas bubbles are produced, so the compound is not a carbonate.

> Next you add barium chloride ($BaCl_2$) dissolved in dilute hydrochloric acid (HCl) and see a white precipitate forming. This is the test for a sulfate.

> The suspect powder must be copper sulfate.

🔍 Laboratory protocol   Forensic chemistry

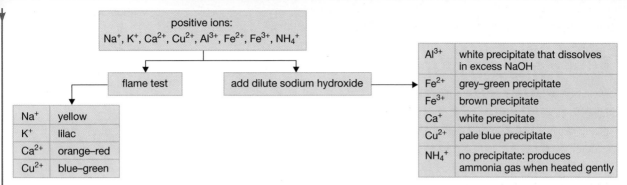

FIGURE 2: Flowchart to identify positive ions.

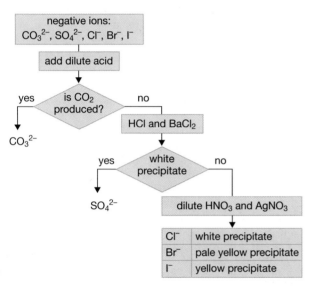

FIGURE 3: Flowchart to identify negative ions.

QUESTIONS

3 State two factors that help to determine the sequence of testing when identifying unknown ions.

4 Explain why the safest, easiest tests should be done first.

5 Name the ion that does not produce a coloured flame and produces a brown precipitate when mixed with sodium hydroxide (NaOH).

6 Name the ion that does not produce carbon dioxide (CO_2) when mixed with dilute acid and does not produce a white precipitate when mixed with hydrochloric acid (HCl) and barium chloride ($BaCl_2$), but produces a white precipitate when mixed with nitric acid (HNO_3) and silver nitrate ($AgNO_3$).

Semi-quantitative testing

It is possible to standardise a **qualitative** test to provide semi-**quantitative** data.

To create a standard calcium test, a reagent is added to solutions containing different *known* concentrations of calcium, forming precipitates. The limits of high, normal and low are defined, using an objective measure, such as the ability to read text through the precipitate. To test for calcium in urine, the same test is carried out and the precipitate formed can be compared with the standards to classify the calcium content as high, normal or low.

Remember!

Qualitative tests tell you what is there. Quantitative tests tell you how much is there.

TABLE 1: Example of a semi-quantitative determination for calcium levels in urine.

Calcium level	Amount of precipitate
Low	Black text can be seen and read through the precipitate
Medium	Black text can be seen but not read through the precipitate
High	Black text cannot be seen through the precipitate

QUESTIONS

7 Explain what is meant by semi-quantitative.

8 Hard water contains high levels of calcium ions. Describe a semi-quantitative test for hard water.

9 Look again at your answer to question 8. How would you ensure that your test is accurate and valid?

Hard water

You will find out:
> what causes hard water
> how hard water causes problems
> how hard water can be softened

Bubbles or no bubbles

You can use the lather test to find out how hard the water is. Carry out the test by shaking a water sample with measured amounts of soap flakes. Keep adding soap until a lasting lather is produced. With soft water not much soap will be needed. With very hard water more soap will be needed.

FIGURE 1: In soft water areas it can be a problem washing the lather off!

Hard and soft water

If the tap water in your area makes a lot of lather you probably live in a **soft water** area:

> The water does not contain many dissolved ions.

If the tap water in your area does not form lather easily you are probably in a **hard water** area:

> The water contains dissolved ions such as calcium and magnesium.

> The ions react with the soap and form a precipitate called a scum.

QUESTIONS

1 List two types of ion that are found in hard water.

2 Describe how scum is formed.

3 Design a leaflet to explain to householders why their water is hard.

If you keep using more and more soap, eventually all the ions will have reacted and lather will form. However, this makes washing much more expensive and the scum can make clothes and skin feel rough.

Formation of hard and soft water

Pure water is soft.

Rainwater is also soft. As rainwater falls it can **leach** out ions from the soil and rock it filters through. These ions can then enter the water supply.

If the rock contains calcium and magnesium, such as limestone and gypsum, then the water will be very hard.

If the water passes through rocks that do not contain calcium and magnesium then it can remain soft.

This is why some areas of the country are hard water areas and some are soft water areas.

Softening hard water

There are two types of hard water: **temporary hard water** and **permanent hard water**.

Temporary hardness

Temporary hardness is caused when calcium carbonate, such as in limestone, reacts with rain that contains carbon dioxide. The product is calcium hydrogen carbonate:

calcium carbonate + carbon dioxide + water → calcium hydrogen carbonate

Removing hardness in water by boiling
Boiling the water can remove temporary hardness. When the water is heated the reverse of the reaction above occurs:

calcium hydrogen carbonate → calcium carbonate + carbon dioxide + water

The calcium carbonate produced is a solid. This is the scale that forms in your kettle if you live in a temporary hard water area.

Sodium carbonate

Sodium carbonate can be also be used to remove temporary hardness. The sodium carbonate reacts to produce a precipitate of calcium carbonate. This removes the calcium ions from the water.

Permanent hard water

Permanent hardness is produced when calcium sulfate dissolves in water. Boiling the water will not remove the hardness. The two ways of softening water by removing permanent hardness are:

> using sodium carbonate (washing soda)

> using an **ion exchange column**.

Ion exchange resin

An ion exchange column contains **resin** with many granules that hold large amounts of sodium ions. As the hard water flows through the column the more strongly positively charged calcium ions and magnesium ions are attracted to the negatively charged granules and exchanged for sodium ions.

The ion exchange column can be recharged by flushing it through with concentrated sodium chloride solution.

Domestic water softeners work on this principle. In industry, ion exchange columns can be large and process millions of litres of water.

FIGURE 2: How an ion exchange column works.

QUESTIONS

4 Write a balanced equation to show how water is softened by boiling.

5 Describe the process that occurs in an ion exchange column.

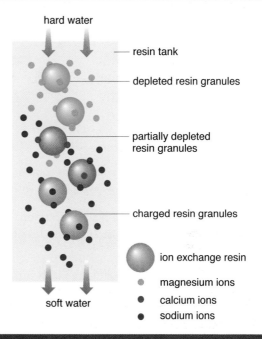

hard water

— resin tank

— depleted resin granules

— partially depleted resin granules

— charged resin granules

ion exchange resin

magnesium ions

calcium ions

sodium ions

soft water

Problems with hard water

As well as forming scum instead of lather, hard water causes other problems.

When water is heated some of the dissolved minerals can come out of solution and form an insoluble calcium precipitate, called scale or **limescale**. You may have seen scale on the heating element of your kettle if you live in a hard water area.

Scale can block pipes. Blocked pipes can cause pressure to build up and so the scale needs to be cleaned off or the equipment needs to be replaced.

Hard water scale also makes appliances less efficient. A 1 mm thick scale reduces the efficiency of heating pipes by 7%. If the scale gets to be 12 mm thick there is an added energy cost of 70%. Money and energy are lost in heating the scale.

Hard water can have some advantages. Some people prefer the taste of hard water. Also, in the brewing industry some water is artificially hardened to add flavour to the beer.

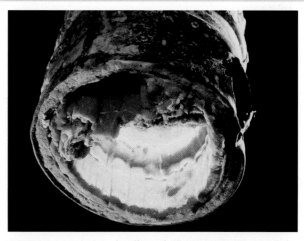

FIGURE 3: How has scale affected this water pipe?

Did you know?

It has been estimated that hard-water scale costs up to £1 billion per year to industry and households.

QUESTIONS

6 Draw a flowchart to explain how scale forms inside hot water pipes.

7 Explain how a build-up of scale can be both dangerous and expensive.

Measuring masses

Mole day

Mole day is an unofficial holiday to celebrate the unit we call the mole. One mole is the amount of substance that contains 6.02×10^{23} particles. Celebrations start at 6.02 am on 23 October, which is 6:02 10/23 in the American style of writing dates.

FIGURE 1: Perhaps you could arrange a science festival at your school to celebrate Mole day.

Concentrations of solutions

Many chemical reactions take place in solution.

> We sometimes dissolve substances in water before reacting them together.

> The substance is the **solute** and the water is the **solvent**.

> The amount of solute dissolved in a certain volume of solution is called its **concentration**.

To obtain a known concentration of a solution, dissolve a known mass of substance in a known volume of water. For example, 10 grams of sodium chloride dissolved in 100 cm³ of water will give a concentration of 10 g/100 cm³.

To standardise concentrations, we usually refer to a number of grams per dm³. These are shown as g/dm³ or g dm⁻³.

Therefore to convert 10 g 100 cm⁻³ into g dm⁻³, multiply both sides by 10, so 100 g/1000 cm³ is the same as 100 g dm⁻³.

Remember!
1 dm³ is almost exactly the same as a litre or 1000 cm³.

FIGURE 2: Dissolving copper sulfate in water. What information do you need to know to calculate the concentration?

QUESTIONS

1 Explain what is meant by the terms solute and solvent.

2 What is the concentration in g dm⁻³ if
   a 15 g of sodium chloride is dissolved in 100 cm³ of water?
   b 10 g is dissolved in 250 cm³?

3 How many grams of salt must be added to 2 dm³ of water to get a concentration of 20 g dm⁻³?

Mass of a solute

One way to determine the mass of solute in a solution is to evaporate the solvent (see Figure 3). The remaining solid is weighed to give the mass of the solute.

This method can be used in the lab when dealing with small amounts of product, but the same method is used in large-scale industrial processes like the production of sodium hydroxide.

QUESTIONS

4 Prepare an overall plan for carrying out the experiment shown in Figure 3.

5 How might you present any results from this experiment?

6 If 5 g of solid remained after evaporating the water from a 50 cm^3 salt solution, what was the original concentration of the solution in g dm^{-3}?

FIGURE 3: A watch glass containing sodium chloride solution is placed onto sand in a heat-proof dish. By applying heat to the sand rather than directly to the water, evaporation can be speeded up but boiling is avoided. What is left when the water evaporates from a salt solution?

Comparing masses (Higher tier only)

Amount can be measured in grams, numbers of particles, or number of moles of particles.

A word is often used to mean a specific number. If you are sent out to buy a dozen eggs then you would make sure you bought 12. Similarly, a decade is always 10 years, a century is always 100 years and a score of anything will always be 20.

In chemistry the word **mole** is used to mean a specific amount of substance.

The number of atoms in exactly 12 g of carbon is used as the standard. It has a fixed number of atoms in it, and this number is very large:

602 000 000 000 000 000 000 000 atoms, or 6.02 × 10^{23}

This is also known as Avogadro's number. One mole of any substance will have 6.02 × 10^{23} particles in it.

The mass of substance that contains as many atoms as there are in 12 g of carbon is called one mole.

So, the amount of substance is measured in moles.

FIGURE 4: A dozen of anything is always 12 and a pair is always 2.

FIGURE 5: How many atoms are there in the 12 g sample of carbon on the scale?

Did you know?

If I owned 1 mole's-worth of pound coins and shared it out with everybody in the world, I would still have enough left to make a tower of coins that would stretch from the Earth to the Sun and back!

QUESTIONS

7 What is meant by Avogadro's number?

8 Suggest why you might want to measure an amount in terms of number of particles or number of moles as well as in grams.

Mass, moles and concentrations

Supersaturation

Fizzy drinks are full of bubbles, that's what makes them fizzy. They are also examples of supersaturated solutions. This because the liquid is canned in conditions of increased pressure, which allows more carbon dioxide gas to be dissolved in the solution than would normally be the case.

You will find out:

> how to convert masses of substances into moles of particles, and vice versa

> how to convert concentration in $g\,dm^{-3}$ into $mol\,dm^{-3}$, and vice versa

FIGURE 1: When you open a can, the pressure on the liquid is reduced. What effect does this have on the dissolved gas in the can?

From masses to moles (Higher tier only)

The mass of one mole of a substance is the same as its relative atomic mass or relative formula mass.

It is easy to find the relative mass of the atoms of each element by looking at the periodic table.

Notice that each element has two numbers (see Figure 2):

> The upper number is the **relative atomic mass** (RAM).

> The lower number is the atomic number – this tells us the number of protons (and electrons) in each atom.

This tells us that if we want exactly 1 mole, 6.02×10^{23} atoms (**Avogadro's number**), of lithium we need 7 grams.

For 6.02×10^{23} particles of beryllium we would need 9 grams.

This shouldn't surprise you. After all, a dozen grapes is the same number as a dozen melons but the melons will have a much higher mass.

How to work out the amount of substance

To work out the mass of the substance you have, in grams, divide by the mass of one mole.

The answer to this simple sum is the number of moles that are present.

For example, calculate the amount of substance in 4.0 g of magnesium.

Amount of substance = 4.0/24 (the RAM of magnesium) = 0.017 moles.

Another example: I would like 3.0 moles of iodine atoms. What mass would this be?

Mass of iodine (in grams) = 3.0 × 127 (the RAM of iodine) = 381 g.

QUESTIONS

1 Explain why a mole of calcium atoms has a much greater mass than a mole of carbon atoms.

2 The formula for sodium sulfate is Na_2SO_4. Calculate the number of grams in a mole of sodium sulfate.

3 How many moles of molecules are there in

a 100 g of carbon dioxide (CO_2)
b 900 g of water?

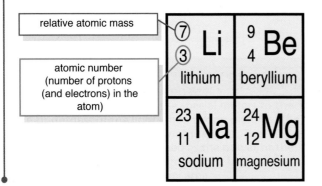

relative atomic mass

atomic number (number of protons (and electrons) in the atom)

⑦ ③ Li lithium	9 4 Be beryllium
23 11 Na sodium	24 12 Mg magnesium

FIGURE 2: It is easy to find the relative mass of the atoms of each element by looking at the periodic table. This section shows Li, Be, Na and Mg.

From moles to masses (Higher tier only)

Sometimes, we may want to know the mass of reactants required to form a certain mass of product. This can be found using the equation:

mass (g) = amount (mol) × molar mass (g)

The reaction below is between potassium and water:

potassium + water → potassium hydroxide + hydrogen

$$2K\ (s) + 2H_2O\ (l) \rightarrow 2KOH\ (aq) + H_2\ (g)$$

If we want to make 5.00 g of hydrogen gas, what mass of potassium is required? (Relative atomic mass data: H = 1, K = 39.)

> *Step 1*: Convert into an amount (in moles) any masses that are given.

Amount of hydrogen = 5.00/(2 × 1). (RAM of H_2) = 2.50 moles.

> *Step 2*: Using the equation, write down the amount of the substance that you are trying to find out.

Ratio of potassium to hydrogen is 2 : 1, so the amount of potassium needed is also 5 moles.

> *Step 3*: Convert the amount from step 2 into a mass.

Mass of potassium = 5 × 39 (RAM of K) = 195 g

QUESTIONS

4 The formula for iron (II) oxide is FeO. Calculate the mass of 3 moles of iron (II) oxide. Use a periodic table to look up the relative atomic masses.

5 The formula for copper sulfate $CuSO_4$. Calculate the mass of 0.5 moles of copper sulfate. Use a periodic table to look up the relative atomic mass.

Molar concentrations (Higher tier only)

We can also make up molar concentrations. For example, if we dissolve one mole of sodium chloride in 1 dm^3 of water we have a solution with concentration of 1 mol dm^{-3}. Note, adding two moles of a substance produces a two molar (2 mol dm^{-3}) solution and so on.

We know that a one molar solution of sodium chloride has 58.5 grams of solute per dm^3 of water. We can calculate that 100 cm^3 of water would contain one tenth as much sodium chloride. Our prediction would be that there would be 5.85 g of sodium chloride in the 100 cm^3 of solution.

Example

A solution is made by dissolving 5.85 g of sodium chloride in 100 cm^3 of water. What is the concentration of the solution in g dm^{-3} and mol dm^{-3}? (RAM data: Na = 23; Cl = 35.5):

> molar mass of NaCl = 23 + 35.5 = 58.5 g

> amount of NaCl used = 5.85/58.5 = 0.10 moles.

We therefore have 0.10 moles dissolved in 100 cm^3 of solution. This is the same concentration as 1.0 mol dm^{-3}, or:

$$\text{number of moles} = \frac{\text{volume of solution (}cm^3\text{)}}{1000} \times \text{concentration (in mol } dm^{-3})$$

> so $0.10 = \dfrac{100}{1000} \times \text{concentration (in mol } dm^{-3}) = 1.0$ mol dm^{-3}

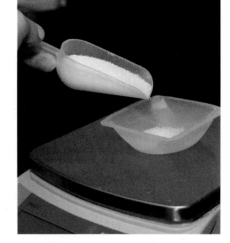

FIGURE 3: Careful measurement is an important part of chemistry.

QUESTIONS

6 Calculate how many grams of sodium chloride are present in 1 dm^3 of a 3 mol dm^{-3} solution.

7 Predict how many grams of sodium chloride you would expect to find if you evaporated 100 cm^3 of a 5 mol dm^{-3} solution of sodium chloride to dryness.

Salts from acids

You will find out:
> how to prepare soluble salts from acids

Important salts

Caves in some parts of the world are formed from salt. As water leaches through the soil it drips from the ceiling of the caves. The water then evaporates, leaving behind the salts in the form of stalactites.

FIGURE 1: These salt caves on Qeshm Island off the southern coast of Iran are several kilometres long and are thought to be the longest in the world.

What are salts?

Salts are ionic compounds. They are composed of positive cations and negative anions.

They form through chemical reactions between acids and other substances such as metals and **bases**. Bases include metal oxides and hydroxides.

Each acid makes its own salts:

> hydrochloric acid makes chlorides

> nitric acid makes nitrates

> sulfuric acid makes sulfates.

Salts can be either soluble or insoluble. Different salts can have many different colours. Insoluble salts formed from reactions in solution are called **precipitates**.

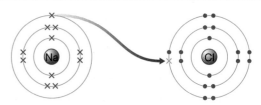

FIGURE 2: What is the salt formed here?

QUESTIONS

1 Name the two types of ion that combine to form salts.

2 List two types of substance that react with acids to form salts.

Preparing salts from an insoluble substance

Some bases, such as copper oxide, do not dissolve in water. They are insoluble.

To make the salt copper sulfate, copper oxide is added to sulfuric acid:

copper oxide + sulfuric acid $\rightarrow$ copper sulfate + water

$$CuO_{(s)} + H_2SO_{4(aq)} \rightarrow CuSO_{4(aq)} + H_2O_{(l)}$$

As copper oxide is added to the acid, copper sulfate and water will form. The copper oxide is added until no more will dissolve. This way we know that all of the acid has been used up. However, this means we have unused black copper oxide mixed in with the products we want. This extra is called an **excess** (see Figure 3, stage 1).

To remove the excess, filter the mixture. The insoluble, unused copper oxide will be held in the filter paper and the copper sulfate solution and water will pass through (see Figure 3, stage 2).

If a pure dry sample of copper sulfate is required, then the copper sulfate solution is left until the water has evaporated (see Figure 3, stage 3).

QUESTIONS

3 Explain why in the experiment above, the copper oxide has to be added in excess.

4 Describe how you would prepare a dry sample of copper chloride from copper oxide.

Stage 1 Mix the reactants and stir. Ensure the copper oxide is in excess

Stage 2 Filter off the excess copper oxide

Stage 3 Leave the filtrate to evaporate in an evaporating basin or crystallising dish

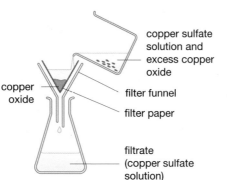

black copper oxide

aqueous sulfuric acid

excess copper oxide

copper sulfate solution and excess copper oxide

copper oxide

filter funnel

filter paper

filtrate (copper sulfate solution)

crystallising dish

copper sulfate solution

copper sulfate crystals

FIGURE 3: Apparatus for making copper sulfate from copper oxide and sulfuric acid. What safety precautions would you take to minimise the hazards in this experiment?

Preparing salts from a soluble substance

If both of the reactants are soluble then there is no point filtering the mixture after the reaction. All of the reactants and all of the products would simply pass through. This presents a problem if we wish to produce a pure sample of a salt from soluble reactants. How do we make sure that unused reactants are not present?

The answer is to make sure that the correct proportions of reactants are mixed, so they are all used up during the reaction. No excess is added. To do this we need to determine the exactly amount of soluble reactant that reacts with the acid. The most accurate way to do this is to use a **titration**. This process will be discussed in more detail on pages 104–5. After the reaction, only salt and water will remain.

A quicker, but less accurate, alternative to a titration is to use universal indicator paper.

For example, let us look at the preparation of sodium chloride salt from the alkali sodium hydroxide and hydrochloric acid. The reaction is:

sodium hydroxide + hydrochloric acid → sodium chloride + water

$$NaOH\ (aq)\quad +\quad HCl\ (aq)\quad \rightarrow\quad NaCl\ (aq)\quad +\ H_2O\ (l)$$

You can see that if too much acid or alkali was added it would mix with the products and stop us from obtaining a pure sample. To prevent this, the mixture is tested regularly with universal indicator paper. As the alkali is added, the paper turns from red (indicating acid) to green (indicating neutral). There should be no excess of acid or alkali. The solution remaining after the reaction comprises only the salt and water.

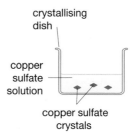

FIGURE 4: A universal indicator strip changes colour depending on the pH of the solution. What does the colour of the strip tell you about the solution?

Remember!
A reactant is a substance that is used up in a reaction, and a product is a substance that is made.

⊙ QUESTIONS

5 Explain why an indicator must be used when making a salt from an acid and an alkali such as sodium hydroxide.

6 Plan an experiment to make the salt zinc chloride using zinc oxide powder and hydrochloric acid.

🔍 Titration experiment

Acid–base titrations

You will find out:
> about acid–base titrations
> how to carry out an acid–base titration
> how to calculate the results of titrations

Neutralisation

Altering the pH of substances by adding either acid or alkali has many important uses. For example, acidic soil can be made less acid by adding an alkali such as lime. Farmers and gardeners do this to help them grow the desired crops or flowers.

FIGURE 1: Blueberries are tasty either fresh or cooked. They grow best in acidic soil.

What is happening during neutralisation?

An acid–base titration is a **neutralisation** reaction where hydrogen ions (H^+) from an acid react with hydroxide ions (OH^-) from an alkali.

A neutral solution has pH 7. Adding acid lowers the pH and adding alkali increases the pH.

Acids

Acids act as acids because they contain hydrogen that can readily form into hydrogen ions. For example, hydrochloric acid contains hydrogen and chloride ions:

$$HCl \rightleftharpoons H^+ + Cl^-$$

Alkalis

Alkalis act as alkalis because they contain hydroxide ions. For example, sodium hydroxide contains sodium and hydroxide ions:

$$NaOH \rightleftharpoons Na^+ + OH^-$$

Neutralisation

When neutralisation occurs, the hydrogen ions combine with hydroxide ions to form water. As you know, pure water is neutral.

$$H^+ + OH^- \rightarrow H_2O$$

The full equation for hydrochloric acid reacting with sodium hydroxide is:

$$\text{sodium hydroxide} + \text{hydrochloric acid} \rightarrow \text{sodium chloride} + \text{water}$$

$$NaOH\ (aq) + HCl\ (aq) \rightarrow NaCl\ (aq) + H_2O\ (l)$$

1	2	3	4	5	6	7	8	9	10

1 = strong acid, 7 = neutral, 10 = strong alkali

FIGURE 2: The range of colours of universal indicator.

QUESTIONS

1 Name the positive ion that has to be present in acids.

2 Name the negative ion that has to be present in alkalis.

3 Describe what you would see if alkali was added to a neutral solution containing universal indicator.

Using titrations

A **titration** is a process to find an unknown concentration of a reactant. The use of acid–base titrations depends on the key scientific principle of neutralisation.

To carry out a titration:

> A burette is filled with aqueous acid of known concentration and clamped above a clean conical flask (Figure 3). The initial volume is read.

> A pipette is used to deliver a known amount (usually 25.00 cm³) of alkali into the flask.

> A few drops of indicator are added to the alkali in the flask. (There are hundreds of indicators. Two of the most used are called methyl orange and phenolphthalein.)

> The burette tap is opened, allowing a slow stream of acid to run into the flask which is swirled continuously to mix the contents.

> As soon as the indicator changes from its colour in alkali to its colour in acid, the burette tap is closed. This is called the 'end point'. The volume of acid added is read from the burette.

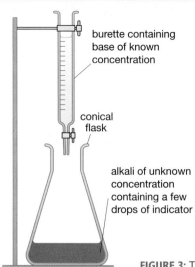

burette containing base of known concentration

conical flask

alkali of unknown concentration containing a few drops of indicator

FIGURE 3: Titration apparatus.

The titration is repeated several times and the average volume of acid added is calculated.

We now know exactly how much acid has to be added to the alkali to neutralise it. If the purpose is to produce a pure salt, then the reaction can be carried out again but without the indicator.

QUESTIONS

4 Explain the importance of the end point in a titration.

5 Predict what would happen to the mixture in the conical flask if excess acid was added from the burette.

6 Plan an acid–base titration to prepare lithium chloride from lithium hydroxide (LiOH) and hydrochloric acid (HCl).

Finding out the concentration and volume (Higher tier only)

We can use titrations to find out the concentration of an acid. To do this we need to have a known concentration of an alkali so we can carry out a neutralisation reaction. We can also do the reverse if it is the alkali that is of unknown concentration. It is usual to place the alkali in the flasks and the acid in the burette. This is to prevent the alkali attacking the ground glass of the burette tap and causing it to seize up.

The principle is straightforward. For instance, if we had 25 cm^3 of an acid and it required exactly 25 cm^3 of an alkali to neutralise it then we would know the

acid and alkali were of the same concentration. If we need 50 cm^3 of the alkali then the alkali must be half as concentrated. For example, the acid might be 2 mol dm^{-3} and the alkali might be 1 mol dm^{-3}.

Table 1 shows some results from an acid–base titration using sodium hydroxide and hydrochloric acid. Notice that the titration was carried out roughly at first to get an idea of when the experimenter had to start to reduce the addition of acid to one drop at a time. The titration was then done three times very carefully to make sure the results were as accurate as possible.

TABLE 1: Results from titration of 25.00 cm^3 of 0.100 mol dm^{-3} of aqueous sodium hydroxide (NaOH) against hydrochloric acid (HCl) of unknown concentration.

Volume of HCl (cm^3)	Experiment 1 (rough)	Experiment 2	Experiment 3	Experiment 4
Final volume	25.80	24.15	48.25	24.20
Initial volume	0.00	0.00	24.15	0.00
Volume used	25.80	24.15	24.10	24.20

To find the concentration of hydrochloric acid:

$$\text{average volume of HCl used} = \frac{24.15 + 24.10 + 24.20}{3} cm^3 = 24.15 \ cm^3$$

$$\text{volume of HCl} \times \begin{array}{c}\text{concentration}\\\text{of HCl}\end{array} = \begin{array}{c}\text{volume of}\\\text{NaOH}\end{array} \times \begin{array}{c}\text{concentration}\\\text{of NaOH}\end{array}$$

$$24.15 \ cm^3 \quad \times \quad \begin{array}{c}\text{concentration}\\\text{of HCl}\end{array} = \quad 25.00 \ cm^3 \quad \times \ 0.100 \ mol/dm^3$$

$$\text{concentration of HCl} = \frac{25.00 \ cm^3 \times 0.100 \ mol/dm^3}{3} = 0.104 \ mol/dm^3$$

Note that the calculation becomes more complicated if the acid used has more than one hydrogen atom, for example H_2SO_4.

QUESTIONS

7 Explain why the first titration is carried out quickly to obtain a rough result.

8 Calculate the concentration of an unknown acid if 25 cm^3 of it is neutralised by 100 cm^3 of a 1.00 mol dm^{-3} solution of sodium hydroxide.

9 What volume of 0.200 mol dm^{-3} NaOH would be needed to exactly neutralise 40.00 cm^3 of 0.150 mol dm^{-3} HNO_3?

Q Neutralisation reactions

Preparing for assessment: Planning an investigation

To achieve a good grade in science, you not only have to know and understand scientific ideas, but you also need to be able to apply them to other situations and investigations. This task will support you in developing these skills.

☀ Making the perfect pickle

Heather wanted to make a new type of pickle preserve. She knew that the type of vinegar used in a pickle is very important and the amount of ethanoic acid that was present in each vinegar affected both the strength of the taste and how well the contents of the pickle would be preserved. So Heather decided to investigate the concentration of ethanoic acid in a number of vinegars to help her decide which vinegar would be the best choice for her pickle.

Acid–base titrations can be used to determine the concentration of an acid using a base of known concentration. Using a pH indicator that shows neutral let Heather add the base until she could see that a neutral pH was reached. The volume and the concentration of the base, along with a balanced chemical equation, can then be used to work out the concentration of the acid.

☀ Useful information

When doing titrations, it is standard practice to repeat the titration until two matching results are achieved, that is two results that are within 0.1 cm³ of each other.

> Repeating the titration increases reliability.

Determining the end point for a titration is sometimes difficult. It may be useful to have a reference to compare results with. This can be made by preparing a neutral solution with the pH indicator in it to show what a neutral solution looks like.

> You could also use the internet to research similar experiments.

☀ Planning

1. Suggest a hypothesis that Heather could test.

2. Prepare a list of equipment needed to carry out a titration. Include a reason why each piece of equipment is needed.

> In titrations accuracy is extremely important. All measurements should be done as carefully as possible, so be sure to use the most accurate measuring tools available.

3. Draw and label a diagram to show how you will set up the equipment to carry out the titration.

> Correctly identifying all of the equipment needed before starting a lab procedure allows you to focus on the procedure and achieve accurate results.

4. How many tests will you carry out? Explain your answer.

> Think about control variables.

5. State all the possible errors that could occur during the experiment. How will you prevent these errors to ensure your results are accurate and precise?

> Remember, the key to good risk assessment is identifying all possible hazards and then reducing the risk that those hazards present through proper planning.

6. Prepare a risk assessment for an acid–base titration.

7. Write out a complete plan for the acid–base titration.

> Your plan should always indicate the data that will be collected and how that data will be analysed. Remember you could be assessed on your Quality of Written Communication so write your plan clearly.

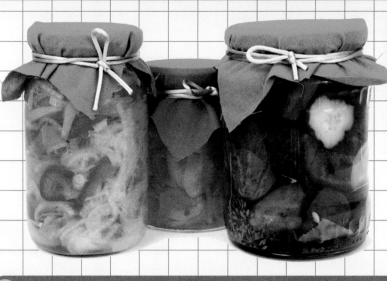

✳ Processing the data

1. Think about what data will be collected for each vinegar. Write a word equation for the reaction between sodium hydroxide and ethanoic acid.

Higher tier only: Write a balanced chemical equation for the reaction between sodium hydroxide and ethanoic acid.

2. Prepare a table to record the data for each vinegar. Heather performed the titration using 25 cm³ of vinegar and 0.50 mol dm⁻³ of sodium hydroxide. She produced the following results for the first vinegar tested:

When doing a titration it is important to record the start volume and the end volume on the burette. The volume used during the titration can then be calculated.

Burette readings (cm³)	Titration 1	Titration 2	Titration 3	Average of two matching values
Start point	50.0	31.1	50.0	
End point	31.1	12.4	31.3	
Titration volume				

3. The sodium hydroxide solution was made by dissolving 5.00 grams of sodium hydroxide in 250 cm³ of distilled water. What is the concentration of the solution in grams per cubic decimetre?

4. Calculate the titration values for each titration.

5. Calculate the average titration value for the two matching results.

Higher tier only: Calculate the concentration of the ethanoic acid based on the data from the titration.

To work out the concentration of the ethanoic acid, first determine the number of moles of sodium hydroxide in the titrated volume. Then, using the balanced chemical equation, convert the number of moles of sodium hydroxide to the number of moles of ethanoic acid. Once you've determined the number of moles of ethanoic acid you can determine the concentration by dividing the moles by the volume in dm³.

✳ Connections

How science works

> Collecting and analysing data.

> Planning to solve a scientific problem.

> Collecting data from secondary sources.

> Working accurately and safely when collecting first-hand data.

> Presenting information using appropriate language, conventions, symbols and tools.

Maths in science

> Carry out calculations.

> Calculate arithmetic means.

> Understand the use of direct proportions and simple ratios.

> Provide answers to calculations to an appropriate number of significant figures.

Electrolytes

You will find out:
> what electrolytes are
> about the movement of ions during electrolysis

Ionic solutions

Electrolytes are essential for our bodies to function properly as we require the correct balance of electrolytes (or ions in solution). This is to ensure, for example, our blood chemistry is at the right level, to allow our muscles to contract, or our nervous system to send and receive signals. The levels of electrolytes in the body can sometimes become too high or too low, perhaps because of excessive exercise, heat or illness. Isotonic or sports drinks can help to replace lost fluids and electrolytes.

FIGURE 1: Why might an isotonic drink be a good idea on a hot day?

Ions and charges

What are electrolytes?

Electrolytes are liquids that:

> contain ions (charged particles) that are free to move

> are often molten salts or salts dissolved in water

> conduct electricity.

Remember!
Positively charged ions are cations. Negatively charged ions are anions.

Salts are made up of positively charged ions and negatively charged ions. In a solid these ions are held firmly together by strong ionic bonds.

Heating a salt until it melts or becomes molten, makes these bonds break and the ions are free to move around. If instead, the salt is added to water, an ionic solution is formed. The ions are again free to move.

The mobility of ions in the molten salt or in a solution means that the molten salt and the salt solution will be able to conduct electricity.

Electrolysis

Electrolysis literally means splitting by electricity. Electrolysis is carried out in an electrolytic cell. An electrolytic cell is composed of:

> an **electrolyte** – a liquid containing ions, so it conducts electricity. This can be a metal compound or an acid

> two electrodes – pieces of metal (or sometimes graphite) that dip into the electrolyte to conduct the electricity in and out

> a d.c. electricity source – battery or rectified mains supply.

The anode is the electrode connected to the positive (+) electricity supply. The cathode is negative (–). When the current is switched on, reactions decompose the electrolyte.

Electrolysis allows an ionic compound to separate into its ions because:

> Positively charged cations migrate to the negatively charged cathode.

> Negatively charged anions migrate to the positively charged anode. This can be seen in Figure 2.

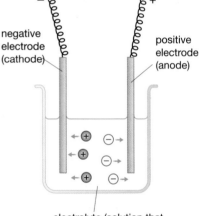

negative electrode (cathode)

positive electrode (anode)

electrolyte (solution that conducts electricity)

Key:
⊖ negative ion moves towards anode   ⊕ positive ion moves towards cathode

FIGURE 2: The movement of ions during electrolysis. What do you notice?

QUESTIONS

1 What is an electrolyte?

2 Name a common electrolyte.

3 Describe what happens to an ionic substance during electrolysis.

Uses of electrolysis

Most metals are extracted (smelted) by heating with carbon. This is the cheapest method and used for many important metals like iron and copper. However, metals that are more reactive than carbon (such as aluminium) cannot be extracted this way. Electrolysis is used for these reactive metals.

Electroplating

An electrolytic cell can be used to coat metal objects with another metal. This process is called electroplating. If, for example, copper is used as the cathode and placed in a solution containing silver ions, the silver ions will be attracted to the copper and form a layer of silver on its surface.

FIGURE 3: A rack of copper-plated sheets being removed from an electroplating bath.

◉ QUESTIONS

4 Explain why electrolysis is not used to extract all metals.

5 Briefly describe how electroplating uses electrolysis.

Strong and weak electrolytes

When sodium chloride dissolves in water, the ions readily interact with water owing to water's **dipole** nature. (Since oxygen has a higher electronegativity than hydrogen, the side of the molecule with the oxygen atom has a partial negative charge.)

The positively charged ions will be attracted to the partial negative charge of the oxygen in water molecules, while the negatively charged ions will be attracted to the partial positive charge of the hydrogen (see Figure 4). Because of these attractive forces the salt dissolves in water, forming an electrolyte.

The strength of an electrolyte depends on the amount of **dissociation** that occurs. Substances such as strong acids, strong bases and salts are classified as **strong electrolytes**. These substances dissociate almost completely in solution. Strong electrolytes are good conductors. **Weak electrolytes** such as ethanoic acid do not dissociate very much at all and are not good conductors.

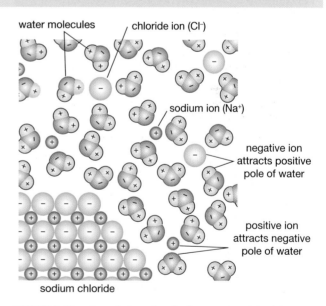

water molecules — chloride ion (Cl⁻)

sodium ion (Na⁺)

negative ion attracts positive pole of water

positive ion attracts negative pole of water

sodium chloride

FIGURE 4: The dissociation of an ionic compound, in this case sodium chloride, in water.

Did you know?

Svante Arrhenius (1859–1927) was one of the first scientists to suggest that electrolytes conduct electricity because they contain freely moving ions. Arrhenius also proposed the definition of acids as those substances that dissociate in water and increase the hydrogen ion concentration.

◉ QUESTIONS

6 Explain how the amount of dissociation affects conduction in electrolytes.

Oxidation and reduction

You will find out:
> about oxidation and reduction
> how to write half equations

Moving electrons

Electrons weigh only 9.1×10^{-31} kg, but their movement can destroy battleships and provide the energy to power every living thing on this planet. Oxidation and reduction may be the most important types of reaction in chemistry.

FIGURE 1: Oxidation is defined as the loss of electrons. What oxidation reactions can you see in this photo?

Losers and gainers

Oxidation is defined as the loss of electrons.
Reduction is defined as the gain of electrons.

Oxidation and reduction reactions always happen together. For example, if calcium reacts with oxygen in the air to form calcium oxide:

$$2Ca\ (s) + O_2\ (g) \rightarrow 2CaO\ (s)$$

> The calcium is oxidised.

> The oxygen is reduced.

> Each calcium atom gives two electrons to each oxygen atom.

Figure 2 shows what is happening at the atomic level.

Remember!
OIL RIG: Oxidation Is Loss, Reduction Is Gain

QUESTIONS

1 Write definitions for oxidation and reduction based on the transfer of electrons.

2 Suggest why oxidation–reduction reactions always happen together.

Did you know?

The reason chlorine is toxic is because of its strong oxidising properties.

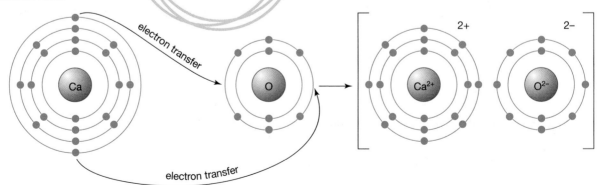

FIGURE 2: The transfer of electrons from calcium to oxygen is really what happens when oxidation occurs.

Electrolysis

We can now explain what happens during electrolysis in terms of moving electrons.

In electrolysis, the positively charged ions (cations) are attracted to the cathode, where they undergo reduction by gaining electrons.

The negatively charged ions (anions) are attracted to the anode, where they are oxidised by losing electrons.

For example, electrolysis of aqueous hydrochloric acid solution produces hydrogen and chlorine:

$$2HCl\ (aq) \rightarrow H_2\ (g) + Cl_2\ (g)$$

Notice that some oxidation reactions do not involve oxygen!

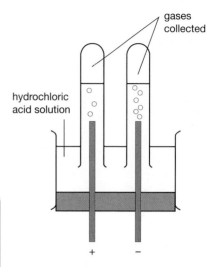

QUESTIONS

3 Explain why hydrogen is said to be reduced during the electrolysis of hydrochloric acid.

4 Draw a diagram to show the transfer of electrons during the electrolysis of hydrochloric acid.

FIGURE 3: What gases are collecting above the anode and above the cathode?

Half equations (Higher tier only)

In solution, hydrochloric acid ionises to H^+ and Cl^-. If we examine the reactions that are happening at the electrodes we can see the oxidation and reduction reactions occurring. The reduction occurs at the cathode:

$$2H^+ + 2e^- \rightarrow H_2 \text{ (cathode reaction)}$$

This type of equation is called a **half equation**, because it shows half of the overall oxidation–reduction reaction. The other half of the equation occurs at the anode where chloride ions are oxidised:

$$2Cl^- \rightarrow Cl_2 + 2e^- \text{ (anode reaction)}$$

Remember!

Half equations must be balanced with respect to both charges and actoms.

Oxidation state

Oxidation state is a useful concept when writing equations for **redox** reactions. Atoms have been oxidised when their oxidation state increases and reduced when their oxidation state decreases. Oxidation states are assigned following a set of rules:

> The oxidation state of atoms in uncombined elements is 0.

> Hydrogen in compounds always has an oxidation state of +1, except in metal hydrides.

> Oxygen in compounds usually has an oxidation state of −2.

> Ions have an oxidation state equal to the charge of the ion.

> The sum of the oxidation states of a neutral molecule is always 0.

QUESTIONS

5 Write two half equations to show the oxidation and reduction reactions that occur during the electrolysis of:

a water

b copper sulfate

c copper chloride.

6 Using the rules above, assign oxidation states for:

a hydrogen in water

b sodium ions

c chloride ions.

Manufacturing sodium

You will find out:
> about the manufacture of sodium by electrolysis
> about some of the uses of sodium

Excitable sodium

Sodium is a silvery, highly reactive metal. It is so reactive that it is never found as an element and so was not discovered until 1807. It has many uses in industry: in soap manufacture and paper-making, in fireworks and in the distinctive yellow street lights we see in towns and cities.

FIGURE 1: These lamps contain vaporised sodium that glows with a yellow light when energised. They are more efficient than ordinary lamps, producing more light from less energy.

Uses of sodium

Pure sodium is very useful, but it first must be extracted from its compounds.

Pure sodium can be produced by electrolysis of sodium chloride. Sodium is used:

> in sodium vapour street lamps

> as a coolant in nuclear reactors used to generate electricity. Sodium has a higher boiling point than water and is a much better conductor of heat, so is better suited to high-temperature situations such as inside a nuclear reactor.

FIGURE 2: The most common compound of sodium: sodium chloride or table salt. Which pure substances can be obtained from sodium chloride?

QUESTIONS

1 State one reason why sodium vapour lamps are so widely used as street lamps.

2 Explain why sodium is used as a coolant in nuclear reactors.

Electrolysis of molten sodium chloride

Pure sodium is produced using electrolysis. Instead of using an aqueous solution of sodium chloride, molten sodium chloride is used. This is because in an aqueous solution of sodium chloride the sodium would react with the hydroxide (OH$^-$) ions and produce sodium hydroxide. So, for sodium production molten sodium chloride must be used.

When an electrical current is applied to the electrodes in the electrolytic cell:

> The positively charged sodium ions are attracted to the cathode where they gain an electron.

> The sodium is reduced to form pure sodium metal.

> The sodium is has a low melting point and is in liquid form.

> The sodium metal is less dense than the liquid sodium chloride and floats to the surface where it is collected.

> At the anode, chlorine is losing an electron to be oxidised, forming chlorine gas.

> The chlorine gas bubbles up from the anode and is collected.

The sodium and chlorine gas never come in contact with each other. This would result in a violent explosion so extreme care must be taken when carrying out this process on an industrial scale.

The half equations for the electrolysis of sodium chloride clearly show the oxidation and reduction reactions:

> cathode: $2Na^+ + 2e^- \rightarrow 2Na$

> anode: $2Cl^- \rightarrow Cl_2 + 2e^-$

> full equation for the electrolysis of sodium chloride: $2Na^+ + 2Cl^- \rightarrow 2Na + Cl_2$

Did you know?

By using electrolysis, Humphrey Davy (1778–1829) discovered sodium and potassium in 1807, and magnesium, calcium, strontium and barium in 1808.

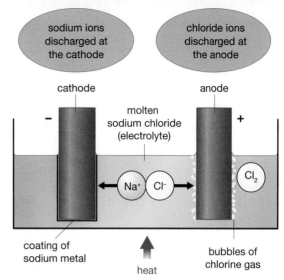

FIGURE 3: The commercial electrolysis of sodium. Suggest why heat is required for the electrolysis.

Remember!

An electrolyte must be an aqueous solution or molten, so that the ions are free to move.

QUESTIONS

3 Explain why ionic compounds used for electrolysis must be molten or in solution.

4 Describe the reactions that happen at the cathode and the anode during the electrolysis of molten sodium chloride.

5 List all the hazards for the electrolysis of sodium chloride. Describe the precautions you would take to minimise those risks.

Voltaic cells

In **voltaic cells**, or galvanic cells, a spontaneous electrochemical reaction can be used to generate electrical energy. In electrolytic cells, electrical energy is used to cause an electrochemical reaction. The discovery of electrolysis came as a result of voltaic cells.

If a piece of zinc is placed in a solution of copper sulfate, the zinc will slowly form a dark layer on its surface and the blue copper sulfate solution will fade to colourless. Examination of the zinc reveals that a thin layer of copper has formed on the surface and the solution now contains zinc ions. The zinc has displaced the copper from the solution and two electrons are displaced for each zinc atom to a copper atom:

$$Zn\ (s)\ +\ Cu^{2+}\ (aq)\ \rightarrow\ Zn^{2+}\ (aq) + Cu\ (s)$$

A voltaic cell harnesses this movement of electrons to generate an electric current.

In Figure 4 the right beaker contains a copper ion solution and a copper electrode. The left beaker has a solution of zinc ions and a zinc electrode. A salt bridge connects the two chambers. As you can see from the voltmeter, a current is produced. This type of electrochemical reaction is the basis of electrochemical cells commonly called batteries.

FIGURE 4: A voltaic cell. What does the reading on the large device show?

QUESTIONS

6 Describe the redox reaction when a piece of zinc is placed in a solution of copper sulfate.

Electrolysing sodium chloride solution

Hydrogen power

In the next few years we will probably need to replace the fossil fuels that run our cars and buses with other energy sources. One alternative is to use hydrogen: an almost unlimited supply of hydrogen could come from the electrolysis of seawater (effectively sodium chloride solution).

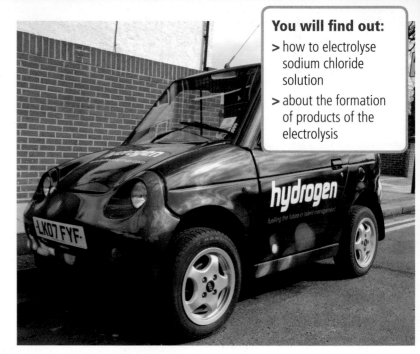

You will find out:
> how to electrolyse sodium chloride solution
> about the formation of products of the electrolysis

FIGURE 1: Will cars of the future run on hydrogen? Think of the arguments for and against using hydrogen as a fuel.

 ## Electrolysis in the lab

The electrolysis of sodium chloride solution can easily be done in the lab using the set-up shown in Figure 2:

> Use a concentrated solution of sodium chloride.

> Turn on the direct current power supply.

> Bubbles form at each electrode.

> The bubbles float up and are trapped in the test-tubes.

The gas collected over the anode is greenish in colour, does not relight a glowing splint and bleaches moist litmus paper. These results indicate chlorine gas.

The gas collected over the cathode is colourless and burns with a popping sound when exposed to a burning splint in air, indicating hydrogen.

The electrolysis of sodium chloride solution produces chlorine gas and hydrogen gas.

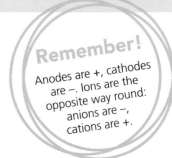

Remember!
Anodes are +, cathodes are −. Ions are the opposite way round: anions are −, cations are +.

QUESTIONS

1 Name the two gases produced by the electrolysis of sodium chloride solution.

2 Describe two tests that indicate the presence of chlorine gas.

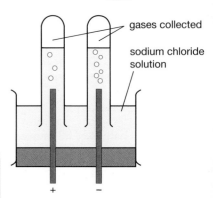

FIGURE 2: Laboratory set-up for the electrolysis of sodium chloride solution. What hazards are present in this experiment?

gases collected

sodium chloride solution

Q Cathode reactions   Anode reactions   Chlorine production

Thinking about the products

The formula for sodium chloride is NaCl. So in the electrolysis of sodium chloride solution, where has the hydrogen at the cathode come from?

The hydrogen must have come from the water in which the NaCl is dissolved. The formula for water is H_2O. The electrolysis has made the water molecules split up into H^+ ions and hydroxide (OH^-) ions.

Where is the sodium? It is still in solution. If the electrolyte solution is allowed to evaporate, the solid that remains will include sodium hydroxide.

QUESTIONS

3 Explain why sodium metal must be produced by the electrolysis of *molten* sodium chloride.

Explaining how the products form

Competing reactions

The electrolysis of molten sodium chloride produces sodium and chlorine gas. The electrolysis of aqueous sodium chloride produces hydrogen, chlorine and sodium hydroxide. The half equations for both situations make the difference clear. In the electrolysis of molten sodium chloride, sodium ions are reduced at the cathode and chloride ions are oxidised at the anode:

> cathode: $Na^+ + e^- \rightarrow Na$

> anode: $2Cl^- \rightarrow Cl_2 + 2e^-$

In the electrolysis of aqueous sodium chloride solution there are two competing reactions at the cathode:

> cathode: $Na^+ + e^- \rightarrow Na$

or

> cathode: $2H_2O + 2e^- \rightarrow H_2 + 2OH^-$

The water is more easily reduced, so the second reaction happens more readily than the first, producing hydrogen gas.

At the anode a similar situation occurs. The two competing reactions are:

> anode: $2Cl^- \rightarrow Cl_2 + 2e^-$

or

> anode: $2H_2O \rightarrow O_2 + 4H^+ + 4e^-$

These two reactions happen more or less equally readily. The concentration of sodium chloride determines the anode reaction:

> high concentration produces mostly chlorine

> low concentration produces oxygen and chlorine

> very low concentration produces mostly oxygen.

With this information it is clear why a concentrated solution of sodium chloride is required to produce chlorine.

Producing a potential difference

The electrolysis of sodium chloride solution with two competing reactions shows that some substances undergo redox reactions more easily than others. A spontaneous movement of electrons results in a potential difference in energy between the two electrodes. This potential difference can be measured in volts.

Remember!
Hydrogen (H_2), nitrogen (N_2), oxygen (O_2) and chlorine (Cl_2) are all diatomic gases. (They have two atoms per molecule.)

FIGURE 3: This factory in Cheshire is where brine is purified to remove impurities such as calcium and magnesium before it is used as a raw material in the chemical industry. Why is this process necessary?

QUESTIONS

4 Describe how the gas produced at the anode can be altered in the electrolysis of sodium chloride solution.

5 Discuss how the electrolysis of sodium chloride solution demonstrates that some substances oxidise more easily than others.

Products of electrolysis

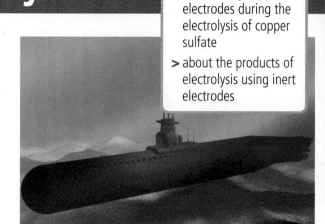

FIGURE 1: A nuclear submarine.

You will find out:
> about using copper electrodes during the electrolysis of copper sulfate
> about the products of electrolysis using inert electrodes

Breathing underwater

Nuclear submarines can stay underwater for a very long time as nuclear-powered engines do not need to refuel. However, their crews need oxygen and this is provided by the electrolysis of seawater. With plenty of seawater and plenty of electricity generated by nuclear power, oxygen supply is not a problem.

Electrolysis using copper electrodes

The electrolysis of copper sulfate solution can easily be done in the lab using the set-up shown in Figure 2:

> Before setting up the experiment, the two copper electrodes are weighed accurately.

> Copper sulfate is used as the electrolyte. The power is switched on and adjusted to deliver a small current.

> After running for about half an hour, the power is switched off and the electrodes are removed, carefully washed, dried and reweighed.

> The anode has lost mass and the cathode has gained mass.

> At the anode, copper atoms have been oxidised to copper (Cu^{2+}) ions and gone into solution.

> At the cathode, copper (Cu^{2+}) ions from solution have been reduced to form copper atoms which have coated the cathode.

> This is why the anode has lost mass and the cathode has gained mass.

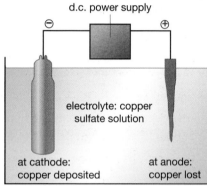

FIGURE 2: Electrolytic cell showing the movement of copper from the anode to the cathode.

d.c. power supply

electrolyte: copper sulfate solution

at cathode: copper deposited

at anode: copper lost

QUESTIONS

1 Explain why it is important to know the mass of the electrodes before doing this experiment.

2 Describe how you would make sure your investigation produces accurate data.

Electrolysis using inert electrodes

Above we looked at the electrolysis of copper sulfate solution using copper electrodes. If the electrodes are changed to inert electrodes the results change. (Most inert electrodes are made of graphite.)

Inert electrodes are usually used in electrolysis.

Electrolysis of copper sulfate solution

In the electrolysis of copper sulfate solution using inert electrodes, the copper ions is reduced at the cathode and oxygen is produced at the anode by the oxidation of water.

This reaction produces copper metal and oxygen. The blue colour fades as copper ions are removed from solution and replaced by colourless hydrogen ions. At the end, dilute sulfuric acid is left.

Electrolysis of copper chloride solution

Electrolysis of a copper chloride solution produces copper and chlorine gas. Copper ions are reduced at the cathode and chloride ions are oxidised at the anode.

Electrolysis of sodium sulfate solution

This is an interesting case. Because it is easier to reduce the water than the sodium ions and easier to oxidise the water than the sulfate ions, this reaction produces hydrogen and oxygen. The sodium sulfate remains unchanged by the electrolysis.

Electrolysis of lead bromide

The electrolysis of molten lead bromide produces lead metal and bromine gas. The lead ions are reduced at the cathode and the bromide ions are oxidised at the anode.

In general, predicting the products at the cathode depends on the reactivity series.

> If the metal is more reactive than hydrogen then hydrogen will be formed.

> If the metal is less reactive than hydrogen then the metal will be formed.

Predicting the products at the anode is not as straightforward. Generally, the most electronegative element will be produced so if a halogen is present then that will be the product.

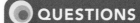

QUESTIONS

3 Explain why inert electrodes are used in most electrolysis experiments.

4 Explain what processes always occur at the cathode and anode in an electrolytic cell.

5 Construct a table to show what is being oxidised and what is being reduced for each of the reactions in this section. Use these words as headings: electrolyte, oxidised, reduced.

Electrolysis reactions (Higher tier only)

Half equations

The half equations for the reactions described in 'Electrolysis using inert electrodes' are as follows:

> the electrolysis of copper sulfate solution:

cathode: $Cu^{2+} + 2e^- \rightarrow Cu$

anode: $2H_2O \rightarrow O_2 + 4H^+ + 4e^-$

> the electrolysis of copper chloride solution:

cathode: $Cu^{2+} + 2e^- \rightarrow Cu$

anode: $2Cl^- \rightarrow Cl_2 + 2e^-$

> the electrolysis of sodium sulfate solution:

cathode: $2H_2O + 2e^- \rightarrow H_2 + 2OH^-$

anode: $2H_2O \rightarrow O_2 + 4H^+ + 4e^-$

> the electrolysis of lead bromide:

cathode: $Pb^{2+} + 2e^- \rightarrow Pb$

anode: $2Br^- \rightarrow Br_2 + 2e^-$

Agents of change

If you place a piece of zinc in a solution of copper sulfate, the zinc becomes coated in copper. This shows that some substances have the ability to oxidise others and leads to the concept of oxidising and reducing agents. An **oxidising agent** is a substance that has the ability to take electrons from the other substance. A **reducing agent** is a substance that easily loses its electrons to other substances. When the zinc is placed in a copper sulfate solution, the zinc atoms on the surface of the piece are oxidised, losing electrons to the copper ions, and the copper ions are reduced. This makes the copper ions the oxidising agent and zinc the reducing agent.

Remember!
Products of electrolysis can be affected by the electrodes used, the state and concentration of the electrolyte.

FIGURE 3: Copper sulfate solution and a piece of zinc foil. What will happen here?

QUESTIONS

6 Draw the half equations for the electrolysis of

a potassium chloride

b magnesium chloride.

7 Describe oxidising agents and reducing agents.

Industrial electrochemistry

You will find out:
> about the purification of copper using electrolysis
> about using electroplating in the treatment of metal objects

More than just shiny

Chrome is short for chromium, although solid chromium itself is never used. Chrome is a thin layer of chromium applied to an object, usually made of steel. This thin layer is called a plating. Chrome plating produces a shine with a mirror finish that is protective and attractive.

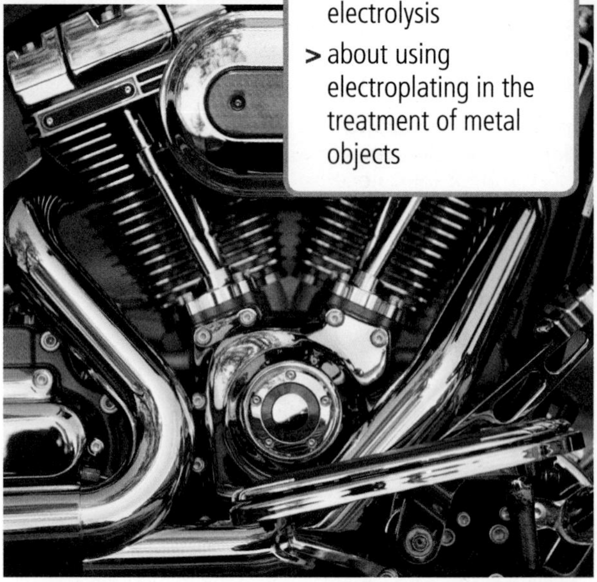

FIGURE 1: Chrome plating is often used on motorbikes. Why is this?

Purification of copper

Copper metal, when extracted from copper ore, is only about 95% pure. The final purification is done using electrolysis:

> The anodes are made from the impure copper.

> The cathodes are made from pure copper.

The anode and cathode are connected to a d.c. power supply. The anode is connected to the positive, and the cathode is connected to the negative.

> The electrolyte is usually copper sulfate solution.

> The copper in the anode is oxidised and goes into solution as copper ions.

> The copper ions are then reduced at the cathode and deposited as pure copper.

> The cathodes can then be removed and melted down to produce pure copper.

FIGURE 2: Electrolytic cell for the purification of copper. Where do the oxidation and reduction reactions occur?

QUESTIONS

1 Describe the movement of ions during the electrolysis of copper.

2 Suggest why only the final stage of the purification of copper is done using electrolysis.

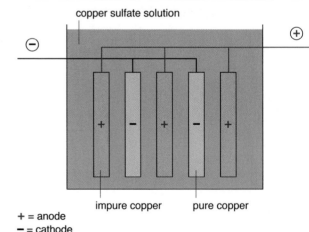

copper sulfate solution

impure copper   pure copper

+ = anode
− = cathode

Electroplating

Objects can be plated with another metal if they are used as the cathode in an electrolytic cell. This is called **electroplating**. For example, to nickel-plate a piece of iron:

> Iron is used as the cathode.

> Nickel is used as the anode.

> The electrolyte is a solution of nickel sulfate.

> The iron will be covered by a thin layer of nickel.

Q Copper refining   Chrome plating   DNA fingerprinting

Since nickel is more resistant to corrosion than iron, the iron object will be protected and will not easily corrode.

In silver plating the same process is used. The object to be plated is made the cathode. The anode is pure silver. The electrolyte is a solution containing silver ions (such as silver nitrate).

Silver is oxidised at the anode and the silver ions dissolve into the electrolyte solution. The silver ions are then reduced at the cathode and plate the metal object, improving its appearance.

FIGURE 3: Why have these dishes been silver-plated?

Remember!

Oxidation takes place at the cathode. Reduction takes place at the anode.

QUESTIONS

3 State two advantages of electroplating metals.

4 Explain why the object to be plated is made at the cathode.

The reactions as equations

Copper purification equations

The purification of copper using electrolysis shown in Figure 2 can be represented by the following reactions:

$$Cu\ (s) \rightarrow Cu^{2+}\ (aq) + 2e^-$$

$$Cu^{2+}\ (aq) + 2e^- \rightarrow Cu\ (s)$$

Electroplating reaction equations

The reactions for electroplating are similar to those that occur in any electrolytic cell.

For silver plating, the reactions are:

> cathode: $Ag^+ + e^- \rightarrow Ag$

> anode: $Ag \rightarrow Ag^+ + e^-$

In nickel plating, the nickel anode is oxidised to produce nickel ions that dissolve in the electrolyte solution. Nickel sulfate is used as the electrolyte:

> cathode: $Ni^{2+} + 2e^- \rightarrow Ni$

> anode: $Ni \rightarrow Ni^{2+} + 2e^-$

So, the nickel is removed from the anode by oxidation to nickel ions, which are reduced and plated onto the cathode.

Did you know?

Electrophoresis is a method, like electrolysis, for separating compounds. It is used in DNA fingerprinting.

FIGURE 4: A galvanised watering can. Why not just have a steel one?

QUESTIONS

5 Look at the two half equations for the purification of copper. What do they suggest about the amount of copper lost and gained?

6 Look up the chemical symbol for gold. Write the half equations for gold plating.

7 Iron and steel tools are sometimes galvanised by electroplating with zinc. Explain how this process can increase the lifetime of a steel toolbox.

Preparing for assessment: Applying your knowledge

To achieve a good grade in science, you not only have to know and understand scientific ideas, but you also need to be able to apply them to other situations. This task will support you in developing these skills.

✳ Make it shine!

Everyone likes to see bright and shiny objects. At first people used precious metals to make beautiful objects, as the metals could be polished and made shiny. Unfortunately these metals, such as gold and silver, are usually expensive, so people invented ways of coating cheaper metals with the bright, shiny and expensive ones.

One method was known as Sheffield Plate. It was made by melting a thin layer of silver metal onto a cheaper metal such as copper, then making the object from the sheet of combined metal. Unfortunately, lots of polishing eventually caused the copper to show.

Today electroplating is used to make objects shiny. It can make metal objects rust-proof, shiny and good to look at.

To make shiny chromium-plated motorcycle handlebars (and other parts of the bike), the handlebars are first made from mild steel (a type of iron).

> The mild steel handlebars are connected to the negative side of an electric circuit becoming the negative electrode, and placed into a hot solution of chromium sulfate.

> An electric current is passed into the solution. The electric current provides a flow of electrons that cause a thin layer of chromium to cover the handlebars.

> The positive electrode of the circuit is often made from chromium. This dissolves into the solution, maintaining the concentration of chromium ions in the solution.

The electroplating process removes the Cr^{3+} ions from the solution by giving each ion three electrons. The ion becomes a chromium atom and sticks to the negative electrode which is the handlebar.

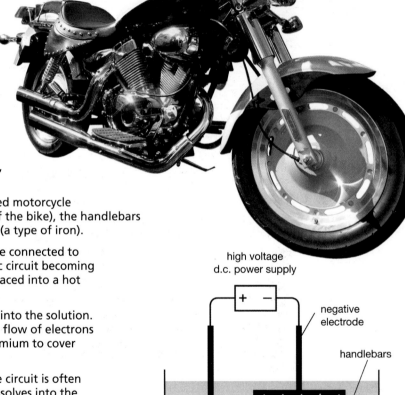

high voltage
d.c. power supply

negative electrode

handlebars

chromium positive electrode

hot chromium sulfate solution

Task 1

> Explain why it is necessary for chromium sulfate to be a solution.

> Use diagrams to suggest the structure of solid chromium sulfate and also how the ions are in the solution. You could represent sulfate ions using a circle with 'SO_4^{2-}' inside and chromium ions as 'Cr^{3+}'.

 Task 2

At the negative electrode, a process called reduction is happening.

> Explain what is meant by reduction in terms of electron transfer.

 Task 3

> Draw diagrams to show what happens to the chromium ions at the negative electrode.

Higher tier only: Use a half equation to represent the reaction.

 Task 4

> Explain why the positive electrode of the circuit is made from chromium metal.

> Draw a diagram to show what happens at the positive electrode.

Higher tier only: Use a half equation to represent the reaction.

 Task 5

When solutions of sodium chloride are electrolysed, the negative electrode does not get covered in sodium metal; instead, hydrogen gas is produced.

> Explain why the more reactive sodium cannot be electroplated in this way.

> What happens to the sodium ions?

 Maximise your grade

These sentences show what you need to include in your work to achieve each grade. Use them to improve your work and be more successful.

E

For grade G–E, your answer should show that you can:
> recall electroplating is using electrolysis to coat metal objects with metals
> recall that substances form ions in solution or when molten
> describe the movement of ions during electrolysis.

C

For grade D–C, in addition show that you can:
> describe why electroplating is used to coat metal objects
> explain oxidation and reduction as the movement of electrons
> briefly explain how products form at the cathode and anode.

A

For grade B–A, in addition show that you can:
> explain how electroplating can be done
> explain in detail the products formed at the cathode and anode during electrolysis of various electrolytes
> write half equations for the reactions that happen at the cathode and anode.

C3 checklist (Topics 1–3)

To achieve your forecast grade in the exam you'll need to revise

Use this checklist to see what you can do now. Refer back to pages 92–119 if you're not sure.

Look across the rows to see how you could progress – **bold italic** means Higher tier only.

Remember you'll need to be able to use these ideas in various ways, such as:
> interpreting pictures, diagrams and graphs
> applying ideas to new situations
> explaining ethical implications
> suggesting some benefits and risks to society
> drawing conclusions from evidence you've been given.

Look at pages 236–59 for more information about exams and how you'll be assessed.

This checklist accompanies the exam-style questions and the worked examples. The content suggestions for specific grades are suggestions only and may not be replicated in your real examination. Remember, the checklists do not represent the complete content for any topic. Refer to the Specification for complete content details on any topic and any further information.

To aim for a grade E	To aim for a grade C	To aim for a grade A
describe the difference between qualitative and quantitative analysis understand that scientists have standard rules for carrying out quantitative analysis in the lab	explain why qualitative tests must be unique and provide examples of their use in industry describe and interpret qualitative tests to show the presence of Al^{3+}, Ca^{2+}, Cu^{2+}, Fe^{2+}, Fe^{3+}, NH_4^+, Cl^-, Br^-, I^- in solids or solutions	interpret the results of qualitative tests to identify unknown compounds
recall that hard water is caused by dissolved calcium and magnesium ions recall that hard water is a problem in some areas of the country	describe the problems associated with hard water explain how hard water can be softened	evaluate the problems associated with hard water
calculate concentrations of solutions in g dm^{-3}	determine the mass of solute in a given mass of solution	*explain the relationship between the mass, the number of particles and the number of moles of a substance* *convert between mass of substance and moles of substances* *convert concentrations between g dm^{-3} and mol dm^{-3}*

To aim for a grade E   To aim for a grade C   To aim for a grade A

To aim for a grade E	To aim for a grade C	To aim for a grade A
recall that soluble salts can be prepared using acids and insoluble reactants recall that soluble salts can be prepared using acids and soluble reactants	describe how to prepare soluble salts using acids and insoluble reactants	describe how to prepare soluble salts using acids and soluble reactants
recall that an acid–base titration is a neutralisation reaction with hydrogen ions reacting with hydroxide ions	identify the equipment required for an acid–base titration describe how to carry out an acid–base titration	justify the equipment used in an acid–base titration *determine the volume of reactant required or concentration of an unknown solution using the data from acid–base titrations*
recall that substances that form ions in solutions or when molten are called electrolytes describe the movement of ions during electrolysis	explain oxidation and reduction as the movement of electrons and that these reactions occur at the cathode and anode in electrolysis	*write half equations for the reactions that occur at the anode and cathode during electrolysis*
recall that sodium can be used in street lamps or as coolant in nuclear reactors describe the electrolysis of sodium in the lab	describe the use of electrolysis in the manufacture of sodium from molten sodium chloride	explain how the products of the electrolysis of sodium chloride are formed
describe the formation of the products of the electrolysis of various electrolytes using inert electrodes		explain the products formed at the cathode and anode during the electrolysis of various electrolytes using inert electrodes
recall that copper anodes lose mass and copper cathodes gain mass when electrolysing copper sulfate	describe the reactions that occur at the copper cathode and anode during the electrolysis of copper sulfate	explain how copper electrodes can be used to purify copper
recall that electroplating uses electrolysis to coat metal objects with metals	describe why electroplating is used to coat metal objects	explain how electroplating is done **using half equations**

1 Qualitative and quantitative analysis are an important part of chemistry.

AO1 **a** Qualitative testing is used to detect hard water. Hard water is caused by dissolved …

    A ☐ hydrogen ions
    B ☐ calcium and magnesium ions
    C ☐ sodium and chloride ions
    D ☐ hydroxide ions   [1]

AO1 **b** State one other use of qualitative testing in industry.   [1]

AO1 **c** Sodium hydroxide can be used as a qualitative test to detect certain ions.
Copy and complete the table below by describing what you would expect to see when sodium hydroxide solution is added to a solution containing each of the ions.

Ion	Reaction with sodium hydroxide
Al^{3+}	
Ca^{2+}	
Fe^{2+}	

    [3]

AO2 **d** Chemists deduced that a 250 cm³ water sample contained 0.8 grams of calcium ions. Calculate the concentration of calcium in grams per cubic decimetre (g dm^{-3}).   [3]
    [Total: 8]

2 a An acid–base titration was used to determine the concentration of hydrochloric acid.

AO1 **i** What kind of reaction occurs during an acid–base titration?   [1]

AO2 **ii** Write the word equation for the reaction between sodium hydroxide and hydrochloric acid.   [2]

AO2 **b** Explain the purpose of using a burette during a titration.   [1]

AO2 **c** Titration can also be used to prepare salts. Describe how titration would be used to prepare sodium chloride.   [3]

AO2 **d** Describe how the mass of sodium chloride would be determined after titration.   [2]
    [Total: 9]

3 Electrolytes are important substances in both chemistry and biology.

AO1 **a** An electrolyte is a substance that …

    A ☐ produces electricity
    B ☐ absorbs electrical current
    C ☐ produces ions in solution
    D ☐ glows when electrified   [1]

AO1 **b** Sodium is produced using electrolysis of molten sodium chloride. State two uses of sodium.   [2]

inert cathode   inert anode

AO2 **c** The diagram above shows an electrolytic cell. Describe how the ions would move in the solution of the electrolytic cell.   [2]

AO2 **d** Explain what happens to the positive and negative ions at the electrodes in the electrolytic cell in the diagram.   [2]
    [Total: 7]

4 Sharon was investigating how pure copper is produced by electrolysis. She passed electricity through copper sulfate solution using copper electrodes. Sharon repeated her experiment three times. Each time she passed the current through the solution for a different length of time, and each time she measured the mass of the cathode and anode before and after calculating the change in mass.

Sharon's results:

Experiment	Time current passed through solution (min)	Increase in mass of cathode (g)	Decrease in mass of anode (g)
1	10	0.05	0.06
2	20	0.11	0.13
3	30	0.16	0.18

AO2 **a** Name two variables Sharon had to control to make her experiment a fair test.   [2]

AO3 **b** What conclusion can Sharon make from her experiment?   [2]

AO3 **c** Use ideas about copper atoms and copper ions to explain:

    i why the cathode increased in mass
    ii why the anode decreased in mass.   [4]

AO3 **d** Suggest why the increase in mass of the cathode is not the same as the decrease in mass of the anode.   [2]
    [Total: 10]

⚫ Worked example

Mia and Tom are thinking about installing a water softener in their home. They have problems with chalky limescale deposits in their washing machine and kettle and think their fuel bills are high.

AO1 **a** What is the chemical name for limescale? [1]

Calcium carbonate. ✔

AO2 **b** Mia thinks they have temporary hard water. What is her evidence for this? [2]

The limescale deposits. ✔ ✘

AO2 **c** Suggest how temporary hard water can increase fuel bills. [2]

Limescale coats the insides of pipes so you use more electricity to heat them up. ✘ ✘

d Domestic water softeners contain an ion exchange resin which removes dissolved calcium and magnesium ions from hard water.

AO1 **i** Explain how the ion exchange resin softens hard water. [2]

It contains hydrogin ions on the beads. These are swapped for calcium and magnesium when water runs through so the water coming out of the filter has hydrogin ions and no calcium or magnesium ions. ✔ ✔

AO2 **ii** What chemical test could you use to check whether there were any calcium ions in water that had passed through an ion exchange resin? [3]

You could add sodium hydroxide. A white precipitate is the test. ✔ ✔ ✘

[Total: 10]

This candidate scored 6 marks out of a possible 10. Their answers reveal a good knowledge of hard and soft water, but a lack of a good exam technique such as: noting the number of marks per question and making at least that number of points in the answer; taking care with spelling and grammar; reading the question carefully and asking what information the examiner is testing.

How to raise your grade

Take note of the comments from examiners – these will help you to improve your grade.

This is the correct answer. Make sure you know the difference between the chemical name for limescale and the chemical names for the compounds dissolved in hard water.

Limescale deposits are part of the evidence and earns 1 mark, but the answer needs to connect them with temporary hard water. There are 2 marks for this question and one piece of information was given.

The extra fuel is used by appliances that heat up water. The calcium carbonate deposit coats the insides of the appliance and is a poor conductor of heat. More energy is needed to heat up the water. The answer is along the right lines, but not accurate enough to earn any marks.

The candidate understands how ion exchange resins work and has made enough points to gain 2 marks. Take care with spelling and grammar. Avoid using 'it' if there is likely to be any confusion about what you are referring to and check the spelling: *hydrogen* not *hydrogin*!

The candidate knows the test but lost marks for lack of detail.

1 Chemists use both quantitative and qualitative testing.

AO1 **a** Bill wants to test for the presence of copper ions (Cu^{2+}) in an unknown solution. What reagent should he use?

  A ☐ sodium hydroxide
  B ☐ dilute nitric acid and silver nitrate
  C ☐ bromine water
  D ☐ chlorine water [1]

AO2 **b** Bill concluded that the solution was copper sulfate. He evaporated 25 cm^3 of a copper sulfate solution and was left with 2.0 grams of copper sulfate. Calculate the concentration of the solution in grams per cubic decimetre ($g\ dm^{-3}$). [3]

AO2 **c** The relative formula mass of copper sulfate is 160. What is the concentration in $g\ dm^{-3}$ of Bill's solution? [3]

AO2 **d** Copper sulfate can be prepared in the lab by reacting copper oxide with hot sulfuric acid. Copper oxide is an insoluble reagent. Describe the process used to make copper sulfate. [3]
[Total: 10]

2 Amanda works for a company that recycles ion exchange resins. Some are recharged by passing through dilute hydrochloric acid. Amanda is using an acid–base titration to find the concentration of a batch of waste hydrochloric acid from the recycling process using sodium hydrogen carbonate as the base.

AO1 **a** What two ions react during an acid–base reaction? [2]

AO2 **b** Write a balanced equation for the reaction between sodium hydrogen carbonate ($NaHCO_3$) and hydrochloric acid (HCl). [2]

AO2 **c** Amanda wanted to make 250 cm^3 of 0.50 $mol\ dm^{-3}$ sodium hydrogen carbonate solution. The relative formula mass of sodium hydrogen carbonate is 84.
How many grams of sodium hydrogen carbonate does Amanda need to weigh out? [3]

AO3 **d** Amanda used her sodium hydrogen carbonate solution to determine the concentration of a sample of hydrochloric acid. She titrated 25.0 cm^3 samples of the acid and recorded the following results.

	Trial	Titration 1	Titration 2
Volume of sodium hydrogen carbonate used (cm^3)	17.3	17.2	17.2

Amanda calculated the concentration of the hydrochloric acid as 0.344 $mol\ dm^{-3}$. Evaluate her conclusion. [3]
[Total: 10]

3 Sophie is investigating the electrolysis of copper sulfate solution using graphite electrodes. She uses this apparatus.

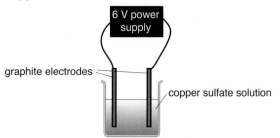

6 V power supply

graphite electrodes

copper sulfate solution

After a few minutes, a copper deposit formed on the cathode and a gas was given off at the anode.

AO1 **a** Name the ions present in the copper sulfate solution. [2]

AO2 **b** Write half equations for the reactions occurring at the cathode and anode. [2]

AO3 **c** Explain why:

  i the contents of the beaker became paler [2]

  ii its pH decreased. [2]

AO2 **d** Sophie adapts her apparatus so that she can purify a piece of copper metal. What changes must she make? [2]
[Total: 10]

4 Sodium is used as a coolant in nuclear reactors. It is produced industrially by electrolysis.

AO2 **a** Solid sodium chloride does not conduct electricity, but molten sodium chloride does. Explain why. [2]

AO2 **b** In the electrolysis of molten sodium chloride, a gas is produced at the anode.

  i Name the gas produced. [1]

  ii Write the equation to show its formation. [2]

AO2 **c** Explain how sodium is produced by the electrolysis of molten sodium chloride. [6]
[Total: 11]

Summary of Assessment Objectives

AO1 recall the science   AO2 apply your knowledge   AO3 evaluate and analyse the evidence

Worked example

1 Chemists working for the Environment Agency need to be able to measure the amount of calcium ions present in water supplies.

AO2 **a** Describe a test that the Environment Agency might perform to determine if there are calcium ions in your drinking water. [2]

Add a couple of drops of sodium hydroxide to a small amount of drinking water. If calcium ions present, a white precipitate will form. ✔ ✔

AO2 **b** Explain why consumers would be interested in knowing if calcium ions were present in their drinking water. [2]

Calcium is responsible for hard water. ✔ ✘

AO2 **c** Adam analysed a sample of drinking water, and found the concentration of calcium ions to be 0.005 mol dm⁻³. What is a mole? [1]

A mole of a substance contains the relative formula mass in grams. ✔

AO2 **d i** How many moles of calcium ions are there in 200 cm³ of a water sample? [2]

0.005 × 200 = 1.00 mole. ✔ ✘

AO3 **ii** The table shows how the amount of calcium ions in a water sample relates to its hardness.

Hardness of water	Concentration of calcium ions (g dm⁻³)
Soft	0 to 0.060
Moderately hard	0.061 to 0.120
Hard	0.121 to 0.180
Very hard	>0.181

Describe the level of hardness in the water sample. Explain your answer. [4]

Hardness: *It is very hard.* ✔ ✔ ✔

Reason: *Concentration = 0.005 × 40 = 0.2.*

[Total: 11]

This candidate scored 8 marks out of a possible 11. The candidate could have improved their grade by checking their calculations carefully and ensuring they had enough information for the number of marks available.

How to raise your grade

Take note of the comments from examiners – these will help you to improve your grade.

Full marks awarded. The answer is clear and explains a positive test result.

The candidate received a mark for correctly identifying calcium as a cause of hard water, but could have received the second mark for explaining that hard water can damage pipes or prevent soap from lathering properly.

The answer is a clear definition of the term mole.

The candidate should have multiplied 0.005 by 200/1000, because they need the number of moles in 200 cm³ of the sample. However, because the working is shown, the candidate gains credit for getting the rest of the calculation right, including the follow-through answer.

The candidate knows how to convert concentrations in mol dm⁻³ to g dm⁻³ to determine the concentration of calcium ions and so the level of hardness. The answer could be improved by including the correct units. The interpretation of the data is correct.

C3 Chemistry in action (Topics 4–5)

What you should know

Gases and commercial chemistry

Some elements and compounds exist as gases at room temperature.

Nitrates and phosphates from fertilisers can be washed into rivers, causing eutrophication (B1 – Topic 3).

Gases have low densities.

Changing the temperature of a reaction and using a catalyst can change the rate of reaction (C2 – Topic 5).

The yield of a reaction is the mass of a product obtained in the reaction. Industrial chemists work to find a reaction that produces a high yield in a suitable time (C2 – Topic 6).

 Explain why gases have low densities.

Organic chemistry

Hydrocarbons are molecules that are composed of carbon and hydrogen.

Alkanes are hydrocarbons that do not have any carbon–carbon double bonds (C1 – Topic 5).

Alkenes are hydrocarbons that contain carbon–carbon double bonds (C1 – Topic 5).

Ethanol can be used as a biofuel. It can be obtained by processing sugar beet or sugar cane (C1 – Topic 5).

 Why are alkanes less reactive than alkenes?

You will find out about

> the use of molar volumes to calculate amounts of gases

> the production of nitrogenous fertilisers

> the environmental effects of the over-use of fertilisers

> the Haber process

> dynamic equilibrium

> the effects of changes of temperature and pressure on reaching equilibrium

> using temperature, pressure and a catalyst to produce an acceptable yield in an acceptable time

> obtaining ethanol by fermentation and reacting ethene with steam

> choosing the best method for manufacturing ethanol

> the harmful effects of ethanol in alcoholic drinks

> the formation of ethene by dehydration

> the names and structures of simple alkanes, alkenes, alcohols and carboxylic acids

> the production and usage of ethanoic acid

> the esters ethyl ethanoate, polyester, oil and fats

> the uses of esters

> how soaps are produced and how they remove dirt

> catalytic hydrogenation

Volumes of gases

You will find out:
> about molar volumes
> how to use molar volumes in calculations
> how to use Avogadro's law in calculations

Reactions with gases

In the early 19th century the latest technology was lighter-than-air balloon flight. In an attempt to better understand and control the balloons some of the greatest minds in chemistry turned to the behaviour of gases.

FIGURE 1: Modern hot-air balloons. How much did the early pioneers of balloon flight understand about gases?

How much gas? (Higher tier only)

When solid or liquid reactants are mixed, it is usually very easy to see the reaction and do the calculations based on mass or concentrations. How do chemists deal with the reactions of gases?

Among the early chemists studying gases was Amedeo Avogadro (1776–1856). He formulated what is now called **Avogadro's law**. Avogadro's law states that equal volumes of all gases have equal numbers of molecules at the same temperature and pressure.

Since equal volumes contain an equal number of molecules, we can replace the coefficients in chemical equations with volumes:

$$2H_2 \text{ (g)} \quad + \quad O_2 \text{ (g)} \quad \rightarrow \quad 2H_2O \text{ (g)}$$

| 2 volumes of H$_2$ | + | 1 volume of oxygen | → | 2 volumes of water |

This provides a gas volume ratio of the reactions (hydrogen and oxygen) to products (water), when measured at the same temperature and pressure, of:

$$2 : 1 : 2$$

Therefore, 10 cm^3 of hydrogen would require half as much oxygen (5 cm^3) to react completely and produce 10 cm^3 of water vapour.

Molar volume

The **molar volume** of a gas is the volume of gas that contains 1 mole of that gas and is 24 dm^3 at room temperature (20 °C) and atmospheric pressure.

QUESTIONS

1 If 24 dm^3 contains 1 mole of CO_2, what volume would contain 3 moles of CO_2 at the same pressure and temperature?

2 The reaction of carbon monoxide with oxygen is $2CO + O_2 \rightarrow 2CO_2$. If 2 dm^3 of CO reacts with 1 dm^3 of oxygen, what volume of CO_2 is produced?

3 The colourless gas nitrogen (II) oxide, NO, reacts with oxygen, O_2, to form the brown gas nitrogen (IV) oxide. The equation is:

$$2NO \text{ (g)} + O_2 \text{ (g)} \rightarrow 2NO_2 \text{ (g)}$$

In an experiment using this reaction 600 cm^3 of NO_2 was produced. Calculate the volumes of NO and O_2 from which this amount of gas was obtained assuming the temperature and pressure didn't change.

Avogadro's law   Robert Boyle   Jacques Charles

Calculating volumes of gases in reactions (Higher tier only)

When calculating reacting masses for reactions, it is necessary to convert masses to moles, carry out the molar conversions and then convert moles back into masses.

When gases are involved in reactions, we can work with volumes of gases rather than masses.

For instance, what volume of oxygen would be required to completely oxidise 6.7 g of magnesium at room temperature and 1 atmosphere of pressure?

The equation of the reactions is:

$$2Mg\ (s) + O_2\ (g) \rightarrow 2MgO\ (s)$$

The coefficients are replaced with moles:

2 moles of Mg react with 1 mole of O_2

This means that:

1 mole of Mg reacts with 0.5 mole of O_2

Therefore

$\dfrac{6.7}{24}$ mole of Mg reacts with $0.5 \times \dfrac{6.7}{24}$ mole of O_2

$0.5 \times \dfrac{6.7}{24}$ mole of O_2 occupy $0.5 \times \dfrac{6.7}{24} \times 24\ dm^3 = 3.35\ dm^3$

Hence, 3.35 dm^3 of oxygen would be needed to oxidise 6.7 g of magnesium.

Remember!

A mole of any gas at room temperature and atmospheric pressure has a volume of about 24 dm^3.

FIGURE 2: Many reactions occur between gases or between gases and solids. In this case magnesium reacts with oxygen. What is formed?

QUESTIONS

4 Lithium hydroxide (LiOH) is used aboard the International Space Station to react with exhaled carbon dioxide to produce lithium carbonate (Li_2CO_3) and water. Write a balanced chemical equation for this reaction.

5 Calculate the volume of carbon dioxide that would react with 1000 g of lithium hydroxide.

6 What volume of oxygen, measured at room temperature and pressure, could be obtained by heating 101 g of potassium nitrate (KNO_3)? The equation for the reaction is:

$$2KNO_3\ (s) \rightarrow 2KNO_2\ (g) + O_2\ (g)$$

Fertilisers

You will find out:
> about the production and use of nitrogenous fertilisers
> about the environmental consequences of the over-use of fertilisers

Feeding the world

There are over seven billion people on Earth. In order to grow enough food to feed everybody we must maximise our food production. Plants require nitrogen to grow and although it is the most common gas in our atmosphere they cannot use this nitrogen; it must be provided in another form.

FIGURE 1: How will farmers in the developing world increase the yield of their crops?

Source of nitrogen

> All plants need nitrogen to grow.

> Most **nitrogenous fertilisers** promote plant growth. They are manufactured from **ammonia**.

> In 1908, a German chemist, Fritz Haber, discovered how to produce ammonia in the lab.

> The reaction of nitrogen and hydrogen to produce ammonia is known as the **Haber process**:

nitrogen + hydrogen → ammonia

> The ammonia produced by the Haber process can be used to make compounds such as nitrogenous fertilisers.

Did you know?

For many years, natural fertilisers (mainly from animal waste) were used to increase the nitrogen content of the soil. But by the end of the 19th century more fertilisers were needed than could be produced naturally. Chemists around the world began to look for a way to produce artificial fertilisers.

QUESTIONS

1 Which compound is used in the production of many nitrogenous fertilisers?

2 Explain what a nitrogenous fertiliser is.

FIGURE 2: What is the vital ingredient here that promotes plant growth?

Crop rotation   Denitrification

Too much of a good thing

Haber's process meant that cheap nitrogenous fertilisers became more readily available. A farmer might be tempted to use too much fertiliser on his land and let the excess wash away in the rain. The run-off ends up in rivers and lakes.

The high level of nitrogen leads to the increased growth of aquatic (water) plants. The plants eventually die. Bacteria then decompose the dead plants, using up most of the oxygen in the water. This means that other organisms (including fish) do not have enough oxygen and may die. The process is called **eutrophication**.

QUESTIONS

3 Describe the chain of events that leads from the over-use of nitrogenous fertilisers to the death of fish in rivers next to farmland.

4 Make a table listing the advantages and disadvantages of using fertilisers.

Another problem with over-use of nitrogenous fertilisers is the presence of nitrates in drinking water. Nitrates interfere with the haemoglobin in red blood cells and prevent them from carrying oxygen. This is particularly harmful for babies and small children.

FIGURE 3: How has the over-use of fertilisers affected this canal?

The balance of nitrogen

All the nitrogen on planet Earth must be recycled and reused in the **nitrogen cycle**.

The main source of nitrogen is the atmosphere. Some plants (such as legumes; peas and beans), in association with bacteria, can take nitrogen from the atmosphere and incorporate it in organic compounds through **nitrogen fixation**.

The plants use these nitrogen compounds for their own growth. Animals can use the nitrogen in the organic compounds of the plants when they eat the plants. The animals and plants return the nitrogen to the soil through animal waste and when they die and decompose. Plants use some of this nitrogen in the soil and some is returned to the atmosphere as nitrogen gas produced during decomposition of the plants and animals.

With the development of the Haber process we are able to change the amount of nitrogen available for plant growth. This affects the balance of the nitrogen cycle. We must learn to use the advantages that chemistry gives us responsibly.

QUESTIONS

5 'The Haber process has altered the balance of nitrogen in the environment.' Use your knowledge of the nitrogen cycle to evaluate this statement.

You will not need to know the details of the nitrogen cycle for your C3 exam.

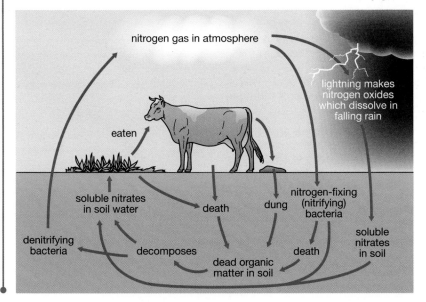

FIGURE 4: Can human actions affect the nitrogen cycle?

Dynamic equilibrium

You will find out:
> about reversible reactions
> about dynamic equilibrium and factors that affect it
> how chemists maximise yield with reversible reactions

What is best?

Determining the best conditions for any reaction can be difficult. The problem is even more difficult when trying to balance two reactions at once.

FIGURE 1: Finding the right balance can be difficult.

Back and forth

We are used to chemical reactions going in one direction only. Reactants yield products:

$$A + B \rightarrow AB$$

But many reactions are reversible. **Reversible reactions** proceed in both directions at the same time. That is, reactants react to produce products, but some of the products decompose to produce the reactants again:

$$A + B \rightleftharpoons AB$$

The double-headed arrow shows the reaction is reversible.

The Haber process is an example of a reversible reaction. Nitrogen (from the air) and hydrogen (from natural gas) react to form ammonia, but at the same time, ammonia changes back to nitrogen and hydrogen:

$$
\begin{array}{ccccc}
\text{nitrogen} & + & \text{hydrogen} & \rightleftharpoons & \text{ammonia} \\
N_2\,(g) & + & 3H_2\,(g) & \rightleftharpoons & 2NH_3\,(g)
\end{array}
$$

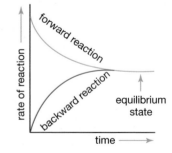

FIGURE 2: Is cooking an egg a reversible reaction?

QUESTIONS

1 Define the term reversible reaction.

2 Why is the Haber process an example of a reversible reaction?

Dynamic equilibrium (Higher tier only)

In a reversible reaction the reaction proceeds in the usual way, producing the products on the right-hand side of the equation. However, as the amount of product increases, the probability of the product decomposing increases. Eventually, a state of stability will occur. This stable state is called **dynamic equilibrium**. The reaction is proceeding in both directions at exactly the same rate.

For every reaction between A and B to produce AB there is an AB that is decomposing to form A and B. The term 'dynamic' is used because, although at equilibrium in, for example, the Haber process, the concentrations of hydrogen, nitrogen and ammonia do not change, both forward and reverse reactions are still taking place but at different rates.

A consequence of this is that at equilibrium the amount of reactants and products remains unchanged.

FIGURE 3: In dynamic equilibrium the forward and reverse reactions are happening at the same rate.

Changing factors

Through investigation, chemists discovered that this state of equilibrium could be shifted, by changing the reaction conditions and the amount of reactants and products present at equilibrium.

Reversible reactions   Le Chatelier's principle   Haber process

Two factors that can be used to shift the balance of dynamic equilibrium are temperature and pressure. Pressure only affects those reactions that take place in the gaseous phase. By understanding the effect of these two factors, the balance of a reversible reaction can be shifted to produce the highest percentage yield.

> *Temperature.* Increased temperature increases the rate of reaction. In reversible reactions we need to consider each reaction separately to understand how changes in temperature will affect the overall reaction. All reactions are either endothermic (take in energy) or exothermic (give off energy). Endothermic reactions are favoured by an increase in temperature and exothermic by a decrease.

> *Pressure.* When considering the effect of pressure we need to consider the number of moles of gas on each side of the chemical equation. An increase in pressure shifts the balance of the reaction to the side with the lower number of moles of gas.

Catalysts

Catalysts do not affect the balance of equilibrium. The rates of both the forward and reverse reactions are affected equally. Catalysts do, however, by lowering the activation energy (the energy required to get a reaction started), reduce the time required to reach equilibrium.

 QUESTIONS

3 Describe what is meant by dynamic equilibrium.

4 Describe the effect of increasing the temperature of a reversible reaction.

5 Explain what effect increasing the pressure has on a reversible reaction.

Equilibrium and the Haber process (Higher tier only)

In industrial processes, such as the Haber process, it is important that an acceptable yield of product, in this case ammonia, can be produced in an acceptable time. Balancing temperature, pressure and the use of catalysts can achieve this (see Figure 4).

Temperature

The forward reaction is exothermic, so any increase in temperature would favour the reverse reaction. In Figure 5 you can see that reducing the temperature from 500 to 200 °C increases the yield from 30% to 90%. Although lowering the temperature increases the final yield of ammonia, it also reduces the rate at which equilibrium is reached. So a compromise temperature of 400–450 °C is used.

Pressure

From the chemical equation we see that there are 4 moles of gas on the reactant side and 2 moles on the product side. This means that the forward reaction is favoured by an increase in pressure, producing a higher yield of ammonia.

Although increasing the pressure increases the final yield of ammonia, high pressures are expensive to produce, and difficult and dangerous to manage. So a compromise pressure of about 200 atmospheres is used.

Catalyst

At 400–450 °C and 200 atmospheres' pressure it takes a long while for the gas mixture to reach equilibrium. To reduce the time needed for equilibrium to be reached, an iron catalyst is used.

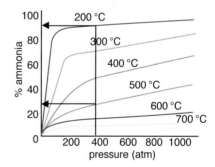

FIGURE 5: The effects of temperature and pressure on the percentage yield for the Haber process.

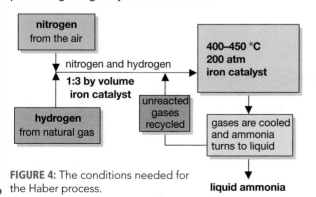

FIGURE 4: The conditions needed for the Haber process.

 QUESTIONS

6 Explain why low temperature and high pressure produce the highest percentage yield for the Haber process.

7 The use of a catalyst does not affect the yield. Explain why a catalyst is used in the Haber process.

Preparing for assessment: Analysis and conclusions

To achieve a good grade in science, you not only have to know and understand scientific ideas, but you also need to be able to apply them to other situations and investigations. This task will support you in developing these skills.

 Task

> Test the hypothesis that the molar volume of a gas is 24 dm³ at room temperature and pressure.

 Context

The Mars rover balloons being tested on Earth.

When NASA's Mars rovers *Spirit* and *Opportunity* landed on the surface of Mars the impact was softened by large air bags that needed to be inflated just before landing. Making sure that the air bags were properly inflated required a clear understanding of the relationship between the amount of gas, the volume, and the pressure and temperature.

Method and results

Dry ice is solid carbon dioxide. It has an unusual property in that it sublimates. This means it goes directly from a solid to a gas with no liquid phase.

A measured mass of dry ice was placed in a balloon and allowed to sublime. The volume of the balloon was then measured.

The results are shown in the table below:

Trial number	Starting volume of the balloon (dm³)	Ending volume of the balloon (dm³)	Mass of CO_2 (g)
1	0.005	2.80	5.05
2	0.005	2.80	5.10
3	0.005	3.01	5.50

Processing the results

1. Draw up a table to display the change in volume and the number of moles of carbon dioxide for each trial.

2. Calculate the number of moles that would be required to fill 24 dm³.

3. Average the results for the number of moles required to fill 24 dm³.

To determine the number of moles required to fill 24 dm³ you will need to set up the equality of:

$$\frac{\text{moles of } CO_2}{\text{change in volume}} = \frac{\text{unknown number of moles}}{24 \text{ dm}^3}$$

Why would you take the average?

Stating conclusions

1. Compare your result to the reference number of 1 molar volume is 24 dm³. How close was the experimental answer to the reference answer?

2. Does your experimental answer support the hypothesis that a molar volume is 24 dm³?

Be precise to gain Quality of Written Communication marks.

Are there any anomalies that need to be taken into account? How will you deal with these?

You should state clearly using the correct scientific language, ideas, mathematical language and data (to gain Quality of Written Communication marks) whether your results support or refute the hypothesis.

Evaluating the results and conclusions

1. Calculate the percentage error in your result.

2. Describe how you could reduce the percentage error in the experiment.

3. List the strengths of the method.

4. How could the method be improved?

5. Is your conclusion accurate and well supported by evidence?

6. Suggest how you could improve and extend the evidence to provide stronger support for your conclusion.

Subtract your result from the reference value, divide by the reference value, and multiply by 100.

Consider the weaknesses in the method and any errors caused by the instruments used.

How did these help obtain accurate data?

Any changes to the method should produce better quality evidence and reduce anomalies.

Consider how you could collect more reliable data from primary and secondary sources.

Connections

How Science Works

> Collecting and analysing data.

> Interpreting data to provide evidence for testing ideas and developing theories.

> Analysing and questioning scientific ideas.

> Working accurately and safely when collecting data

> Evaluating methods of data collection.

> Presenting information using appropriate language, conventions and symbols.

Maths in Science

> Carry out calculations.

> Calculate arithmetic means.

> Understand and use direct proportion and simple ratios.

> Substitute numerical values into equations.

Ethanol production

You will find out:
> about the production of ethanol
> about the distillation of ethanol

Fermentation

Throughout history fermentation has been used as a means of producing ethanol in alcoholic drinks. It was thought so important to the people of Finland that their 2000-year-old epic poem devotes 400 lines to the making of beer, compared with only 200 lines for the creation of the Earth!

FIGURE 1: Beer is one of the world's oldest prepared beverages, possibly dating back to when cereal was first farmed.

Fermentation

> The term **fermentation** refers to a natural process carried out by yeast and other microorganisms.

> Fermentation of carbohydrates (such as glucose) produces ethanol.

> The yeast contains enzymes that allow this reaction to occur.

> The yeast produces ethanol as a by-product of **anaerobic respiration**:

glucose $\rightarrow$ ethanol + carbon dioxide + energy

$C_6H_{12}O_6$ (aq) $\rightarrow$ $2CH_3CH_2OH$ (aq) + $2CO_2$ (g) + energy

> The mixture needs to be kept warm (between 15 and 27 °C) and in anaerobic conditions. The reaction rate is too slow at temperatures below 15 °C but temperatures above 27 °C kill the yeast.

You can prepare a solution of ethanol by fermentation as shown in Figure 2. Place the experiment in a warm place and observe it for several days.

Remember!
Anaerobic means without oxygen.

QUESTIONS

1 What does yeast contain that makes fermentation possible?

2 Suggest why there is a layer of paraffin above the carbohydrate and yeast solution in the set-up for fermentation.

3 Write an outline of an experiment to produce ethanol through fermentation.

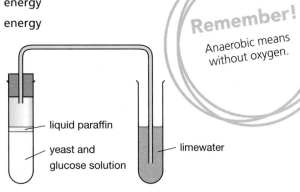

liquid paraffin

yeast and glucose solution

limewater

FIGURE 2: Small-scale fermentation set-up. Where is the ethanol? What do you predict will happen to the limewater?

Distillation

Fermentation produces a solution of up to 14% alcohol. High concentrations of ethanol are toxic and will kill the yeast.

If we need concentrations higher than 21%, we must use **fractional distillation**.

> The mixture produced by the fermentation of yeast and carbohydrate contains dead yeast cells and water as well as ethanol.

> After filtering, the mixture is heated as shown in Figure 3.

> Ethanol boils at 78 °C so it distills over, leaving most of the water behind in the flask.

> The ethanol is condensed and collected in the beaker.

Louis Pasteur   Biofuels

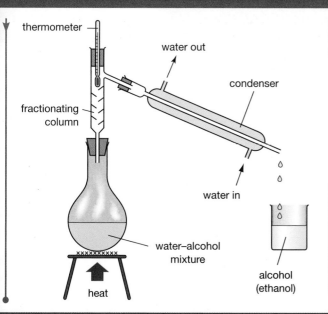

thermometer

water out

condenser

fractionating
column

water in

water–alcohol
mixture

heat

alcohol
(ethanol)

FIGURE 3: How does
this apparatus
produce ethanol?

QUESTIONS

4 Suggest why a thermometer is placed at the point where the vapour leaves the column.

5 Write a plan to produce ethanol with a concentration of 25%.

Ethanol from fermentation versus ethanol from ethene (Higher tier only)

While approximately 90% of all ethanol is produced by fermentation, it is also possible to make ethanol from ethene.

So, what determines the method used? Three important factors are as follows:

> the availability of raw materials

> the quality of product

> the use to which the alcohol is to be put.

Raw materials

Most fermented ethanol is produced from the juice of sugar cane or sugar beets, a renewable resource. These crops can be grown almost anywhere so are readily available.

Ethene is produced by cracking long-chain hydrocarbons (from crude oil) and is a non-renewable resource.

Ethene gas is mixed with steam to produce ethanol:

$$ethene \ + \ water \ \rightleftharpoons \ ethanol$$
$$C_2H_4 \text{ (g)} \ + \ H_2O \text{ (g)} \ \rightleftharpoons \ CH_3CH_2OH \text{ (g)}$$

Product quality

Ethanol produced from ethene is very pure and requires almost no treatment after production, whereas ethanol from fermentation has to be purified by fractional distillation.

Use

Wines contain up to 14% alcohol and so are produced by fermentation alone. Their tastes and smells result from the many compounds in the grapes used to make them.

Chemists often need pure alcohol for use both as a solvent and as a chemical raw material, and so they often use pure alcohol made from ethene.

Taking these factors into account, it is clear that the relatively cheap, readily available renewable aspect of ethanol fermentation outweighs the extra purification required in the majority of ethanol production.

Reversible reactions revisited

The formation of ethanol by reacting ethene with steam is another reversible reaction. The forward reaction is exothermic so is favoured by low temperatures. The temperature of 300 °C is a compromise, as at lower temperatures the reaction is too slow. The forward reaction is favoured by increased pressure because two moles of gas change into one:

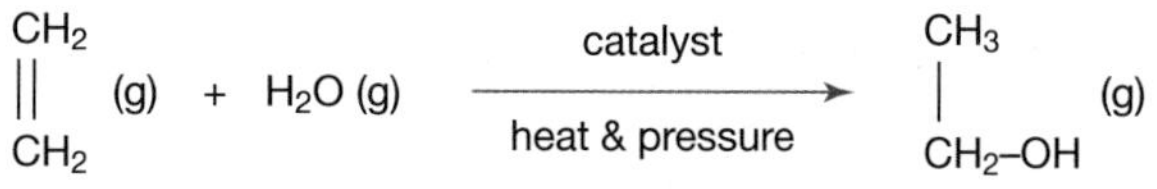

$$\underset{CH_2}{\overset{CH_2}{\|}} \text{ (g)} \ + \ H_2O \text{ (g)} \ \xrightarrow[\text{heat \& pressure}]{\text{catalyst}} \ \underset{CH_2-OH}{\overset{CH_3}{|}} \text{ (g)}$$

FIGURE 4: This reaction typically takes place at 300 °C and 60–70 atmospheres pressure in the presence of a catalyst.

QUESTIONS

6 Describe two factors that determine the method used to produce ethanol.

7 Explain why 90% of all ethanol produced is made by fermentation.

8 Explain, with reference to the molar ratio, why high pressure is used in the reaction of ethene and steam.

Alcohol and society

You will find out:
> about the alcohol content in different drinks
> about the social issues and harmful effects associated with drinking alcohol
> about the uses of ethanoic acid

The true cost of alcohol

In 2007 more than 860 000 hospital admissions were alcohol related. It is estimated that £2.7 billion was spent by the NHS in England on treating alcohol-related illnesses.

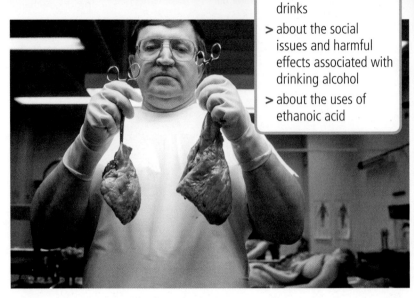

FIGURE 1: The heart on the left is a healthy specimen from a normal person while the heart on the right is from an alcoholic. Excessive and/or binge drinking causes the heart to become enlarged and weakened through stress, a condition known as alcoholic cardiomyopathy.

Alcohol content

Alcoholic drinks contain different percentages of alcohol, or ethanol. This is due to the different types of yeast used in their fermentation, distillation, or the addition of more alcohol (for example, to fortify wine).

Table 1 shows the percentage of alcohol in different alcoholic drinks. The amounts are given as **alcohol by volume** (ABV), which is the percentage measured by volume, not weight.

Did you know?

There are many alcohols, but the correct name for the alcohol that people drink is ethanol.

TABLE 1: Amount of alcohol in drinks.

Type of drink	Typical percentage alcohol (ABV)	Quantity of alcohol (cm³) in a typical serving (cm³)
Beer	4.0	11.4 in 285 (half pint)
Wine	11.5	14.5 in 125 (glass)
Fortified wine (sherry)	16.7	10.0 in 60 (small glass)
Spirits	38.0	11.4 in 30 (roughly pub measure)

As you can see in Table 1, all of the drinks have approximately the same amount of alcohol per serving. This is what the government uses as a unit of alcohol. The recommended maximum daily limit is 3–4 units per day for men and 2–3 units per day for women.

FIGURE 2: What is the volume of alcohol in this bottle of wine?

Consequences of misuse

The effects of the misuse of alcohol include both health and social issues. The health problems associated with the misuse of alcohol include:

> liver and cardiovascular disease

> psychological problems such as depression.

Social problems include:

> antisocial behaviour (such as violence) from intoxicated people

> a strain on the emergency services, which must help intoxicated people who are ill or have bad accidents

> reduced abilities of workers who consume too much alcohol

> death and injury caused by drink driving.

Ethanoic acid

Sometimes ethanol in opened bottles of beer or wine can 'go off'. The sour taste is due to the formation of ethanoic acid by the action of bacteria. The bacteria oxidise the ethanol to form ethanoic acid:

$$\text{ethanol} + \text{oxygen} \rightarrow \text{ethanoic acid} + \text{water}$$
$$CH_3CH_2OH\ (aq) + O_2\ (g) \rightarrow CH_3CO_2H\ (aq) + H_2O\ (l)$$

We can encourage the formation of ethanoic acid for use as vinegar. Vinegar (such as the malt vinegar we have with fish and chips) can be used as flavouring or for **pickling** (used to preserve food).

Pickling works because ethanoic acid lowers the pH, which prevents bacteria from growing. Most bacteria require a neutral pH to survive.

QUESTIONS

5 Explain why beer and wine can 'go off'.

6 Explain how pickling is used to preserve food.

FIGURE 3: Pickled onions: tasty and an age-old method of preservation.

Breathalysers

Breathalysers work by detecting ethanol in the breath of someone who has been drinking. Ethanol is readily absorbed into the bloodstream. As the blood circulates through the lungs, the ethanol concentration in the blood is higher than the ethanol concentration in the alveoli. The ethanol diffuses into the air in the lungs and is exhaled.

One type of breathalyser contains a reddish-orange chemical called potassium dichromate as well as sulfuric acid and silver nitrate. Any ethanol in the breath reacts with the potassium dichromate, changing it to green chromium sulfate (other products are potassium sulfate, acetic acid and water; the silver nitrate acts as a catalyst). The intensity of the green colour of the chromium sulfate indicates the blood alcohol concentration.

FIGURE 4: A breathalyser uses the oxidation of ethanol to measure blood alcohol levels.

QUESTIONS

7 Explain how a breathalyser can be used to detect ethanol in a person's blood.

Homologous series

You will find out:
> about homologous series
> how to name simple organic compounds
> how to draw the structure of simple organic compounds

Winter camping

Butane is part of a homologous series. It is often used as a fuel when camping, but in very cold weather it does not vaporise and is useless. So winter campers have to use a mixture of propane and butane.

FIGURE 1: Cold weather camping. Why is a mixture of propane and butane better than just butane? Why not use butane on its own?

Alkanes

A **homologous series** is a group of compounds that:

> have the same general formula

> show a gradual variation in physical properties like boiling points

> have similar chemical properties.

The simplest hydrocarbon is methane, a single carbon atom with four hydrogen atoms bonded to it. Methane is the first compound in the homologous series known as **alkanes**. If another carbon atom and two more hydrogen atoms are added, ethane is produced.

The formula for alkanes can be generalised as C_nH_{2n+2}. For example, for one carbon atom, $n = 1$, so

$$
\begin{aligned}
& 2n + 2 \\
=\ & (2 \times 1) + 2 \\
=\ & 2 + 2 \\
=\ & 4
\end{aligned}
$$

giving the formula CH_4.

TABLE 1: The first four alkanes.

Name	Formula	Structure	Boiling point (°C)
Methane	CH_4	H–C–H (with H above and below)	−164
Ethane	C_2H_6	H–C–C–H (with H's)	−89
Propane	C_3H_8	H–C–C–C–H (with H's)	−42
Butane	C_4H_{10}	H–C–C–C–C–H (with H's)	−0.5

Remember!
The prefixes for the first four hydrocarbons are meth-, eth-, prop- and but-.

FIGURE 2: At this liquefied natural gas (LNG) plant in the east of Russia, natural gas (which is mostly methane) is cooled within these huge chambers until it is in liquid form. Why is natural gas liquefied?

◉ QUESTIONS

1 State two characteristics shared by compounds in a homologous series.

Alkenes

Another homologous series is the **alkenes**. Alkenes are hydrocarbons with a double covalent bond between two adjacent carbon atoms.

The formula for alkenes can be generalised as C_nH_{2n}. As with alkanes, the boiling point increases as the hydrocarbon chain gets longer.

This is because the forces between molecules (the intermolecular forces) get stronger as the chain length increases.

TABLE 2: The first three alkenes.

Name	Formula	Structure	Boiling point (°C)
Ethene	C_2H_4		−104
Propene	C_3H_6		−48
Butene	C_4H_8		−6

QUESTIONS

2 Describe the difference between alkanes and alkenes.

3 Show that the formula for alkenes is C_nH_{2n}, using ethene and propene as examples.

Functional groups (Higher tier only)

A **functional group** is an atom or groups of atoms that replaces a hydrogen atom in a hydrocarbon chain. One of the simplest functional groups is the **hydroxyl group** (–OH). Hydrocarbons that have a hydroxyl group attached are called alcohols.

TABLE 3: The first three members of the alcohol homologous series.

Name	Formula	Structure	Boiling point (°C)
Methanol	CH_3OH		65.0
Ethanol	C_2H_5OH		78.6
Propanol	C_3H_7OH		97.5

QUESTIONS

4 Suggest a general formula to describe hydroxyls and carboxyls.

5 Predict the formula and structure of butanoic acid.

6 Explain why ethanol is soluble in water.

Another functional group is the **carboxyl group** (–COOH). These compounds are called carboxylic acids – they are acids because the hydrogen easily ionises in solution, increasing the hydrogen ion concentration.

TABLE 4: The first three carboxylic acids.

Name	Formula	Structure	Boiling point (°C)
Methanoic acid	HCOOH		100.7
Ethanoic acid	CH_3COOH		118.0
Propanoic acid	C_2H_5COOH		141.0

Properties of alcohols

All members of a homologous series show a gradual variation in physical properties. Short-chain alcohols are completely soluble in water. This is due to the interaction of the hydroxyl group with the water molecules.

Alcohols become less soluble as the length of the chain increases. This is because their hydrocarbon chains cannot form intermolecular bonds with water molecules.

Ethene, ethanol and ethanoic acid

Natural gas?

As well as by industrial methods, ethene is produced naturally by fruits such as apples, bananas and melons. It has an effect on the ripening of a fruit.

FIGURE 1: To make green tomatoes ripen more quickly, try putting them in a paper bag with an ethene-producing banana.

 Reactions of carboxylic acids

Ethanoic acid is a typical **acid**.

> It is a weak acid, with a pH of about 4, turning litmus paper pink and universal indicator orange.

> Acids react with metals, producing metal salts and hydrogen gas. Ethanoic acid will react with the more reactive metals of groups 1 and 2. For example:

ethanoic acid + magnesium → magnesium ethanoate + hydrogen

With the less reactive metals this reaction is so slow that it appears not to happen.

> Acids react with bases to produce a salt and water. For example:

ethanoic acid + sodium hydroxide → sodium ethanoate + water

> Acids react with carbonates to produce salt, carbon dioxide and water. For example:

ethanoic acid + sodium carbonate → sodium ethanoate + carbon dioxide + water

Did you know?

Many carboxylic acids occur naturally. Methanoic acid ($HCOOH$) is in red ant stings. Ethanoic acid (CH_3COOH) is in vinegar. Ethanedioic ($(COOH)_2$) is the poison in rhubarb leaves. Butanoic acid ($CH_3CH_2CH_2COOH$) is one of the substances which makes sweat smelly.

QUESTIONS

1 Describe two ways in which ethanoic acid is a typical acid.

2 Write a word equation for the reaction between ethanoic acid and calcium carbonate.

3 Write a balanced equation for the reaction between ethanoic acid and lithium hydroxide.

You will find out:
> about the properties of acids
> how ethanoic acid is used to make esters
> about using ethanol to make ethene

Esterification

Another important group of compounds is the **esters**. Esters are the product of the reaction, called **esterification**, between an alcohol and a carboxylic acid.

The hydroxyl group (–OH) of an alcohol reacts with the carboxyl group (–COOH) of a carboxylic acid. We can see this process using ethanol and ethanoic acid:

ethanol + ethanoic acid → ethyl ethanoate + water

The organic product of this reaction is an ester called ethyl ethanoate.

The rules for naming compounds say that the alcohol is named first adding the -yl suffix and the carboxyl portion is named second using the -oate suffix.

 QUESTIONS

4 Describe the process of esterification.

FIGURE 2: Glow-in-the-dark bracelets contain a mixture of an oxalate ester, a fluorescent dye and a glass vial containing an activator (hydrogen peroxide). By squeezing and breaking the glass, the activator mixes with the ester and, through a series of chemical reactions, makes the fluorescent dye emit light. When light is produced through a chemical reaction, it is called chemiluminescence. The colour of the emitted light depends on the dye used. The same principle is used in the glow sticks used by the emergency services. Why are glow sticks suitable for use in emergency situations?

Explaining esterification and dehydration (Higher tier only)

Explaining esterification

As we have seen, esters are formed from an acid and an alcohol. This is a **condensation reaction** as a molecule of water is removed when the ester is formed. This can be seen in the reaction between ethanol and ethanoic acid to form ethyl ethanoate:

$$CH_3COOH \text{ (l)} + CH_3CH_2OH \text{ (l)} \rightarrow CH_3COOCH_2CH_3 \text{ (aq)} + H_2O \text{ (l)}$$

The condensation reaction that produces esters occurs very slowly at room temperature. The addition of a small amount of sulfuric acid acts as a catalyst. The reaction is also reversible. When making esters in the lab this is usually not too significant and small amounts of esters can easily be made.

In an industrial setting the reversible nature of the reaction can reduce the percentage yield dramatically. In the industrial production of esters, drying agents are used to remove the water. This causes a shift in the equilibrium to the right, increasing the percentage yield.

Dehydration

Ethene is an extremely useful organic compound. Most ethene is made by cracking long-chain hydrocarbons obtained from crude oil. However, ethene can also be produced by dehydrating ethanol. Dehydration is literally the removal of water from the molecule:

In this reaction ethanol is vaporised and passed over a hot aluminium oxide catalyst to produce ethene.

QUESTIONS

5 Explain why drying agents are used in the industrial production of esters.

6 Explain why converting ethanol into ethene is described as dehydration.

Esters

You will find out:
> the uses of esters
> about the recycling of esters

Flavourings

Many sweets contain flavours arising from the family of chemicals called esters. For example, there are over 50 kinds of jelly bean, and some 'special editions' have flavours such as pencil shavings, black pepper and centipede. Esters help to create these flavours.

FIGURE 1: Jelly beans: turning sugar, esters and colouring into a sweet.

Food and perfume

Complex mixtures of natural esters give fruits their 'fruity' smells. Synthetic esters also smell pleasant, so we use them to produce artificial odours and flavours.

> Perfumes are created by blending mixtures of natural esters.

> The fruit flavour in sweets and manufactured foods is often a synthetic ester.

> Other 'smelly' uses include cosmetics and air-fresheners.

Esters are also useful solvents. One of the most important is ethyl ethanoate, used for paints, varnishes, inks and for decaffeinating tea and coffee.

Did you know?

Chemists make esters by reacting acids with alcohols. The general equation is:

$$RCOOH + R'OH \rightarrow RCOOR' + H_2O$$
$$\text{acid} + \text{alcohol} \rightarrow \text{ester} + \text{water}$$

R and R' stand for alkyl (hydrocarbon) groups, such as CH_3, C_2H_5 or C_4H_9.

R and R' may be the same or different and this gives lots of combinations. Two acids and three alcohols can give 2×3 different esters. For example:

	HCOOH	CH_3COOH
CH_3OH	$HCOOCH_3$	CH_3COOCH_3
CH_2H_5OH	$HCOOC_2H_5$	$CH_3COOC_2H_5$
C_4H_9OH	$HCOOC_4H_9$	$CH_3COOC_4H_9$

FIGURE 2: Many fruits produce esters naturally.

QUESTIONS

1 Give three uses for esters.

2 Prepare a pamphlet to advertise your own ester-based food, perfume or cosmetic product. List the ingredients that you might include and why they might make the product attractive.

🔍 Polyesters   Recycling polyesters

Use of esters in plastics and fabrics

Many organic compounds can be made into substances with large, long-chain molecules, called polymers. **Polyester** is a polymer made by linking together many ester molecules. Polyester is used to make fibres for fabrics, or formed into sheets for the production of plastics. About 30% of the world's production of polyester is used for making bottles, where it is usually labelled as PET (short for polyethylene terephthalate).

One advantage of polyesters is that they are easily recycled. One of the main uses of recycled polyesters is the production of fleece. Fleece is a synthetic fibre made by heating chips of polyesters and drawing them into fibres.

Polyester fleece is widely used for clothing because it can easily be dyed to make a wide range of colours and does not absorb water, so it dries quickly.

FIGURE 3: Why is PET a good material for making drink containers?

QUESTIONS

3 Explain why polyesters are so important in today's society.

Fats and oils

Fats and oils are naturally occurring esters used by organisms to store energy. They are made up of large molecules that are built around a common base molecule called glycerol.

Glycerol is similar to a propane molecule with a hydroxyl group attached to each of the carbons.

Fats are formed when a glycerol molecule reacts with three carboxylic acid molecules.

These carboxylic acids are long hydrocarbon chains (10–30 carbons) with a carboxyl group on one end of the chain. The **glycerol** molecule plus the three (**tri-**) acids give the alternative name for these fats – **triglyceride**s.

QUESTIONS

4 State three different substances that contain esters.

5 A friend tells you that a fat cannot be an ester because it does not smell fruity. Develop an argument to support or refute her statement.

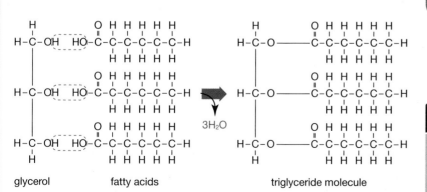

glycerol   fatty acids   triglyceride molecule

FIGURE 4: Is this formation of a fat an esterification reaction?

Did you know?

Glycerol is the traditional name for the alcohol we now call propan-1,2,3-triol. The new name tells us much more about its structure.

Q Triglyceride

Fats, oils and soaps

Soap and water

Hundreds, maybe thousands, of years ago, our ancestors would extract sodium hydroxide from wood ash using rainwater and boil it in animal fat to make soap.

You will find out:
> about fats and oils
> about the production and properties of soaps
> about the hydrogenation of unsaturated carboxylic acids

FIGURE 1: How can something like wood ash be used to clean things?

Making soap

Fats and oils

Fats and oils are naturally occurring esters. They are used for making soap. Different fats and oils give the soap different qualities. For example, soap made from olive oil is very moisturising, coconut oil soap gives a good lather, and soap made from lard is very economical!

Process of making soap

> Boiling alkali reacts with oils and fats to produce soap and glycerine.

> Adding hot brine dissolves out glycerine and impurities, leaving molten soap.

> The soap is cooled, coloured, perfumed and made into tablets, powder or flakes.

Fats and oils can be converted to soap by reversing the esterification reaction.

> By boiling fats or oils with a solution of concentrated alkali such as sodium hydroxide or potassium hydroxide, the ester bonds are broken, producing glycerol and soaps.

> Soaps are sodium or potassium salts of long carbon chain carboxylic acids.

The process is called **saponification**.

Soap-making still follows the same basic process used by our ancestors.

> The alkali is sodium hydroxide solution, made by electrolysing salt solution.

> Vegetable oils (for example, palm oil) are used, as well as animal fats. They contain similar chemicals.

Olive Oil Soap

FIGURE 2: Did you know you can even find soap made from emu oil?

QUESTIONS

1 Describe the conditions used to make soap from fats and oils.

Cleaning action of soaps (Higher tier only)

Soaps remove oil and grease because of the shape of the soap molecule. The molecules are so long that the ends have different properties.

> The carboxyl end of the molecule is polar and is attracted to other polar molecules, like water molecules, and is called **hydrophilic**. It dissolves in water.

> The long hydrocarbon chains are non-polar, that is they have no distinct charge associated with them.

The long hydrocarbon chain is not attracted to water and is called **hydrophobic**. It dissolves in grease and dirt.

When soap solution is mixed with oil or grease, the hydrophobic hydrocarbon chains are attracted to the drops of oil or greese. When the soap is rinsed away, the hydrophilic carboxyl 'heads' of the soap molecules are attracted to the water and take the oil or grease attracted to their hydrocarbon 'tails' with them.

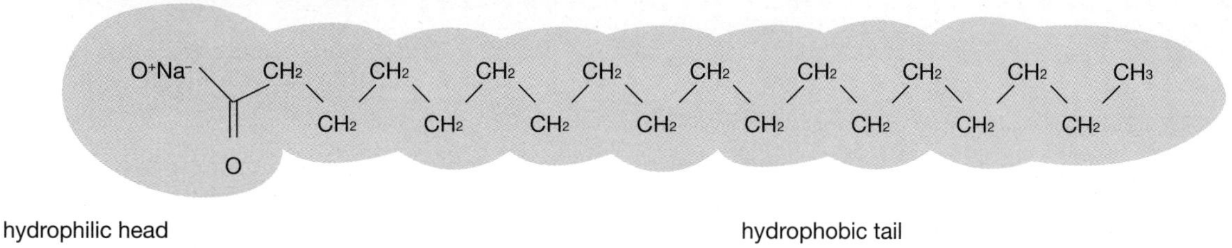

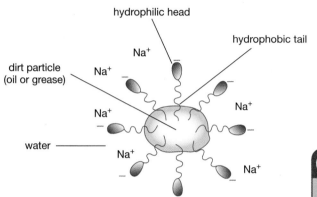

hydrophilic head   hydrophobic tail

FIGURE 3: The structure of a soap molecule showing the hydrophilic and hydrophobic regions.

hydrophilic head

hydrophobic tail

dirt particle (oil or grease)

water

FIGURE 4: How soap washes away dirt and grease.

Remember!
Hydrophilic means water loving. Hydrophobic means water fearing.

QUESTIONS

2 Design a leaflet or poster to show how soaps remove dirt and grease.

Manufacturing margarine (Higher tier only)

Fats are normally solid at room temperature but oils are liquid. This is due to the molecular structure of the carboxylic acid chains. Fats contain **saturated carboxylic acids,** while oils contain mainly **unsaturated carboxylic acids.** Saturated carboxylic acids have no carbon–carbon double bonds in the hydrocarbon chain. Unsaturated carboxylic acids contain at least one carbon–carbon double bond.

Because of the double bond, the carboxylic acid chain is bent. This bending reduces the intermolecular attraction between individual molecules. The reduced attraction means that the molecules are free to move around, making the unsaturated fats liquid at lower temperatures. Saturated fats become liquid at higher temperatures.

Hydrogenation of unsaturated carboxylic acids makes them saturated. Hydrogenation involves using a catalyst to add hydrogen to the carbon–carbon double bonds of unsaturated carboxylic acids. This has the effect of straightening out the hydrocarbon chains of the carboxylic acids and allowing more intermolecular attraction. The increased attraction between the molecules causes the fats to be solid at room temperature. This is how vegetable oil is solidified to make margarine.

FIGURE 6: Margarine or butter?

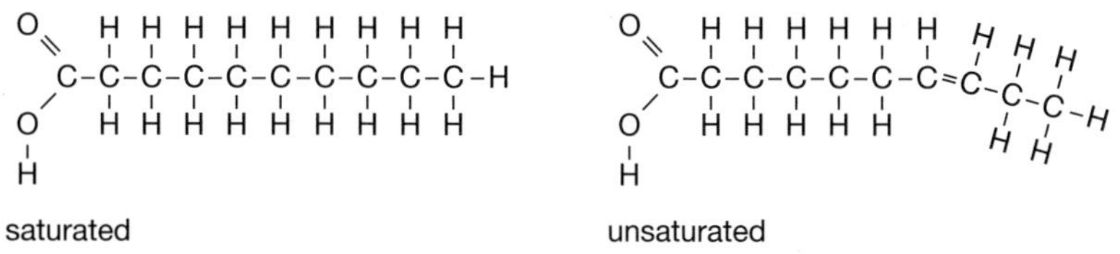

saturated

unsaturated

FIGURE 5: How does the double bond affect the shape of an unsaturated carboxylic acid?

QUESTIONS

3 Describe the difference between saturated and unsaturated carboxylic acids.

4 Explain how margarine is manufactured.

Preparing for assessment: Applying your knowledge

To achieve a good grade in science, you not only have to know and understand scientific ideas, but you also need to be able to apply them to other situations. This task will support you in developing these skills.

❉ Soap for Christmas

Christina and Bobby decided that they wanted to try to make their Christmas presents this year and thought that hand-made soap would be an ideal gift. They planned to use natural ingredients as much as possible.

Christina found a book in the library and they set to work to gather together everything that they needed.

First, they collected cooled wood ash from their wood-burning stove, and placed the ash in a barrel with rainwater. After three days they carefully drained off the liquid from the barrel into a container and added a chicken feather. Nothing happened to the feather, so they returned the liquid back into the barrel and after another two days they tried again.

This time the feather dissolved, indicating that the liquid had become lye-water (sodium hydroxide solution) and was at the correct strength to be used in soap-making.

Soap-making needs the lye-water to be mixed with a fat or an oil. Christina and Bobby decided to use lard from their local butcher. They melted the lard and cleaned it a number of times by boiling it with water and then straining. When the fat from the lard was clear, they mixed this with plum kernel oil made from the fruit in their orchard to add colour, fragrance and texture.

When the lye-water was added to the pot of heated oils, Bobby had to stir and stir until eventually the mixture thickened and turned creamy. Then the mixture was turned into moulds, covered and left to harden.

❉ Task 1

The chicken feather dissolved when the lye-water was at the correct strength.

> Why was this important?

> If a pH indicator was added to the lye-water, what would it show?

> Why do you think it is important to use rainwater rather than tap water?

Task 2

When working with the lye-water, Christina and Bobby made sure that they put on protective clothing and wore safety glasses.

> Why was this?

> What other safety precautions would you recommend?

 Task 3

Christina and Bobby could have used other fats or oils besides lard and plum kernel oil to make their soap.

> Suggest two other fats or oils that could have been used.

> Describe the structure of lard and plum kernel oil.

 Task 4

The recipe for the soap requires the lye-water to be mixed with an oil or a fat.

> Explain what happens when the two substances are combined.

> Why did Bobby have to stir the mixture for such a long time?

 Task 5

Bobby put some used engine oil on to his hands and then applied the soap to see if the hand-made soap would work. The soap made a good lather and the oil washed away in the warm water.

> Explain how the soap worked to clean the oil from Bobby's hands.

Maximise your grade

These sentences show what you need to include in your work to achieve each grade. Use them to improve your work and be more successful.

E

For grades G–E, your answers should show that you can:
> recall that oils and fats are esters
> state that oils and fats can be mixed with alkali solutions to produce soaps.

C

For grades D–C, in addition, show that you can:
> describe how esters can be mixed with concentrated alkali solutions to produce soaps

A

For grades B–A, in addition, show that you can:
> describe the structure of fats and oils.
> explain how soap removes dirt or grease, including the part played by the structure of the soap molecule.

C3 checklist (Topics 4–5)

To achieve your forecast grade in the exam you'll need to revise

Use this checklist to see what you can do now. Refer back to pages 130–49 if you're not sure.

Look across the rows to see how you could progress – **_bold italic_** means Higher tier only.

Remember you'll need to be able to use these ideas in various ways, such as:
> interpreting pictures, diagrams and graphs
> applying ideas to new situations
> explaining ethical implications
> suggesting some benefits and risks to society
> drawing conclusions from evidence you've been given.

Look at pages 236–59 for more information about exams and how you'll be assessed.

This checklist accompanies the exam-style questions and the worked examples. The content suggestions for specific grades are suggestions only and may not be replicated in your real examination. Remember, the checklists do not represent the complete content for any topic. Refer to the Specification for complete content details on any topic and any further information.

To aim for a grade E	To aim for a grade C	To aim for a grade A
		use molar volumes and balanced equations to calculate reacting masses and volumes for chemical reactions
		apply Avogadro's law to calculate volumes of gases involved in chemical equations
		recall that the molar volume of a gas at room temperature and atmospheric pressure is 24 dm³
recall that ammonia is used to produce nitrogenous fertilisers	describe some of the environmental effects of the over-use of nitrogenous fertilisers	explain the environmental effects of the over-use of nitrogenous fertilisers
recall that some reactions, such as the Haber process, are reversible		**_explain the effect of changes in pressure and temperature and catalysts on the position and rate of reaching a dynamic equilibrium_**
		explain how industrial chemists use their knowledge of dynamic equilibrium to produce maximum yields in an acceptable time

To aim for a grade E   To aim for a grade C   To aim for a grade A

To aim for a grade E	To aim for a grade C	To aim for a grade A
recall that ethanol is produced by fermentation	describe the conditions required for the production of alcohol using fermentation	*explain how ethanol can also be prepared by reacting ethene with steam and that this a reversible reaction* *evaluate the best method for producing ethanol*

recall that ethanol is used in the production of alcoholic drinks

recall that different alcoholic drinks contain different amounts of ethanol

describe some of the negative effects of ethanol in alcoholic drinks

To aim for a grade E	To aim for a grade C	To aim for a grade A
recall that ethanoic acid can be produced by the oxidation of ethanol	describe the production and uses of vinegar describe the characteristics of typical acids as exemplified by ethanoic acid	
recall that a homologous series is a group of compounds with the same general formula and similar chemical and physical properties	name, write the formulae and draw the structure of the first four alkanes and the first three alkenes	*name, write the formulae and draw the structure of the first three alcohols and the first three carboxylic acids* *explain that the dehydration of ethanol results in the formation of ethene*
recall that oils and fats are esters describe some of the uses of esters such as ethyl ethanoate and polyester	describe the reaction of ethanoic acid and ethanol to form esters and polyesters	*write the equation and formula for the production of ethyl ethanoate from ethanol and ethanoic acid*
describe how esters can be boiled with concentrated alkali solutions to produce soaps		*explain the cleaning action of soaps* *explain how the hydrogenation of the carbon–carbon double bond can solidify liquid oils*

153

1 Jed grows soft fruit and uses artificial fertiliser to improve the yield. His fertiliser contains ammonium sulfate. Ammonium sulfate is manufactured from ammonia gas.

AO1 **a** The two elements used to manufacture ammonia gas are …

- A ☐ argon and nitrogen
- B ☐ nitrogen and oxygen
- C ☐ hydrogen and nitrogen
- D ☐ hydrogen and argon [1]

AO1 **b** The reaction used to make ammonia is reversible. What does this mean? [1]

AO2 **c** Copy and complete the word equation to show how ammonia is used to make ammonium sulfate

ammonia + ... → .... [1]

AO2 **d** Which element in ammonium sulfate is a major requirement for healthy plant growth? [1]

AO2 **e** Jed's neighbour is complaining that fish are dying in his river. He blames Jed for using too much fertiliser. Explain why the overuse of fertiliser can be blamed for the fish dying. [6]

[Total: 10]

2 Propane and butane are both used as fuels in bottled gas for cooking and camping.

AO1 **a** **i** Name the homologous series that propane and butane belong to. [1]

AO1 **ii** What is the general formula for this series of compounds? [1]

b The structural formula for propane is:

$$H-\overset{\displaystyle H}{\underset{\displaystyle H}{C}}-\overset{\displaystyle H}{\underset{\displaystyle H}{C}}-\overset{\displaystyle H}{\underset{\displaystyle H}{C}}-H$$

AO2 **i** What is its molecular formula? [1]

AO2 **ii** A molecule of butane contains four carbon atoms. Draw its full structural formula. [1]

c The table shows the boiling points of the first six compounds in this family.

Compound	Boiling point (°C)
Methane	−161
Ethane	−88
Propane	−42
Butane	0
Pentane	36
Hexane	69

AO3 **i** Which compounds will be liquid at room temperature (20 °C)? [2]

AO3 **ii** Describe the relationship between the number of carbon atoms in the compound and the boiling point. [2]

[Total: 8]

3 Dan makes homemade wine as a hobby. He uses fruit, such as grapes, water, sugar and yeast.

AO1 **a** **i** Why does Dan add yeast to the mixture? [2]

AO1 **ii** Name the alcohol that should be present in Dan's wine. [1]

b Occasionally, a batch of Dan's wine turns sour and is not drinkable.

AO2 **i** Which compound is making Dan's wine sour? [1]

AO2 **ii** Explain why Dan's wine turned sour. [2]

AO2 **c** Dan's wine contains about 10% alcohol. The local whisky distillery produces drinks containing 40% alcohol. Explain how they increase the percentage of alcohol. [6]

[Total: 12]

4 Harry works as a lab technician. The labels have fallen off two of his chemical bottles. They each contain a colourless liquid. The labels say *ethanol* and *ethanoic acid*. Harry carries out two tests on the liquids. The table shows his results.

Liquid	Test and results	
	Adding sodium carbonate solution	Adding magnesium metal
1	No change	No change
2	Fizzes, gas turns limewater milky	Fizzes, gas 'pops' with a lighted splint

AO3 **a** **i** Which liquid is ethanoic acid? [1]

AO3 **ii** What is the evidence for this conclusion? [2]

AO2 **iii** Describe a simpler test that Harry could have used to distinguish between the liquids. [2]

AO2 **b** Harry is using the two liquids to prepare an ester.

i Name the ester he will make. [1]

ii How will Harry be able to detect the ester? [2]

[Total: 8]

Summary of Assessment Objectives

AO1 recall the science   AO2 apply your knowledge   AO3 evaluate and analyse the evidence

✳ Worked example

Sue works in a cosmetic factory. She is showing visitors how they make soft soap and hard soap. Sue uses potassium hydroxide and vegetable oil to make soft soap and sodium hydroxide and vegetable oil to make hard soap.

How to raise your grade

Take note of the comments from examiners – these will help you to improve your grade.

AO1 **a** What type of compounds are potassium hydroxide and sodium hydroxide? [1]

Alkalis. ✔

> This is the correct answer and gains 1 mark. Remember that group 1 hydroxides are soluble and called alkalis.

AO2 **b** Oil molecules break down when boiled with concentrated potassium hydroxide solution. Sue says this is reversing the process of reacting an alcohol with a carboxylic acid. Explain Sue's conclusion. [2]

Alcohol and carboxylic acids make esters and soap is an ester. ✔ ✘

> The first mark is for realising that an alcohol and a carboxylic acid react together to make an ester. To get the second mark, the candidate needed to explain that vegetable oils are also esters, but are broken down in the soap-making process.

AO2 **c** Name two safety hazards Sue needs to manage when making soap. [2]

Potassium hydroxide is an alkali. The ingredients need to boil and can spit and cause burns. ✘ ✔

> The statement about potassium hydroxide is correct, but the hazard is not described as corrosive. The second hazard is explained well.

AO2 **d** Before the soap is packaged, esters and colourings are added.

i Why are esters added to the soap? [1]

To make them smell nice. ✔

> This is a correct answer. Esters are often used as perfumes.

ii Suggest why Sue doesn't add the esters to the soap mixture when it is still hot. [2]

Because it may spit. ✘ ✘

[Total: 8]

> The correct answer is because esters have low boiling points (that's why you can smell them) and will evaporate in the hot soap mixture.

> The candidate scores 4 marks out of a possible 8. Knowing that vegetable oils are esters and working out that esters must have low boiling points would have gained extra marks. The candidate could have also improved their grade by reading the questions thoroughly and answering what is required.

Exam-style questions: Higher

1 Ammonia is manufactured in the Haber process from nitrogen gas and hydrogen gas. A temperature of 450 °C, a pressure of 200 atmospheres and an iron catalyst are used. The reaction is:

$$N_2 (g) + 3H_2 (g) \rightleftharpoons 2NH_3 (g)$$

AO1 **a** This is a reversible reaction. What is happening when a dynamic equilibrium is reached? [2]

b In the Haber process, the forward reaction to make ammonia is exothermic. The graph shows how the percentage yield of ammonia varies with temperature.

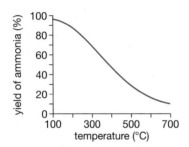

AO3 **i** What is the percentage yield at 450 °C? [1]

AO3 **ii** Describe the relationship between the percentage yield and the temperature. [2]

AO2 **iii** Explain why ammonia is manufactured at 450 °C, even though a lower temperature would give a higher yield. [2]

AO2 **c** Pressures of 200 atmospheres are used in the Haber process. Why do higher pressures increase the yield of ammonia? [2]

AO2 **d** Explain how the catalyst affects:

i the position of the equilibrium

ii the time taken to reach equilibrium. [4]

AO3 **e** The ammonia produced needs to be separated from the unreacted gases. Use the information in the table to explain how the ammonia is removed.

Substance	Boiling point (°C)
Ammonia	−33
Hydrogen	−253
Nitrogen	−196

[3]
[Total: 16]

2 Ethanol can be manufactured from ethene gas or from carbohydrates in biomass. Producing ethanol from ethene uses a catalyst, a pressure of 60–70 atmospheres and a temperature of 300 °C. The equation is:

$$C_2H_4 (g) + H_2O (g) \rightarrow C_2H_5OH (g)$$

The reaction to produce ethanol is exothermic.

AO2 **a** **i** Explain why a high pressure is used. [2]

ii Suggest why 300 °C is described as a compromise temperature. [4]

AO2 **b** **i** What volume of steam do manufacturers need to mix with 50 dm³ ethene gas? [3]

ii What is the maximum volume of gaseous ethanol they can make? [3]

iii Explain why they are unlikely to make this volume of ethanol. [2]

AO3 **c** The method chosen to produce ethanol depends on many factors. The table shows some of them.

	Fermentation of carbohydrates	Reacting ethene with steam
Type of process	Made in batches, inefficient	Made continuously by passing reactants over the catalyst
Reaction rates	Very slow	Very quick
Quality of ethanol	Very impure	Very pure
Conditions	40 °C, normal pressure	High temperature and pressure
Use of resources	Uses renewable biomass	Uses a finite resource, crude oil

You are working for a company that produces ethanol for use in industry.

Evaluate which is the best method to use to produce ethanol. [6]
[Total: 20]

Summary of Assessment Objectives

156   AO1 recall the science   AO2 apply your knowledge   AO3 evaluate and analyse the evidence

Worked example

Ammonium sulfate is manufactured from ammonia gas and sulfuric acid. It is used as a fertiliser to improve plant growth. The reaction is:

$$2NH_3 \text{ (g)} + H_2SO_4 \text{ (aq)} \rightarrow (NH_4)_2SO_4 \text{ (aq)}$$

The manufacturer is using 9.8 kg of sulfuric acid. (All carried out at room temperature and pressure.)

AO2 **a** What volume of ammonia gas is needed to react completely? (One mole of gas occupies 24 dm^3 at room temperature and atmospheric pressure.) [4]

9.8 kg = 9800 g

Relative formula mass of sulfuric acid = 2 + 32 + 64 = 98. ✔

Moles of H_2SO_4 = $\dfrac{9800}{98}$ = 100. ✔

Volume of NH_3 = 100 × 24. ✖

= 2400 dm^3 ✔ (follow through mark given)

AO2 **b** If the manufacturer only uses 1800 dm^3 of ammonia gas, what mass of ammonium sulfate can he make? [4]

Moles of ammonia = $\dfrac{1800}{24}$ = 75. ✔

75 moles of ammonia produce 37.5 moles of ammonium sulfate. ✔

Relative formula mass $(NH_4)_2SO_4$ = 28 + 8 + 32 + 64 = 132 g. ✔

Mass = 37.5 × 132 = 4950. g ✔

[Total: 8]

How to raise your grade

Take note of the comments from examiners – these will help you to improve your grade.

The candidate has used the correct method to answer this question, but has made an error. They have not realised that 1 mole of sulfuric acid reacts with 2 moles of ammonia, or 100 moles of sulfuric acid react with 200 moles of ammonia. The volume of ammonia should be 200 × 24 = 4800. Be aware of the units used for mass. Relative formula masses are in grams. If the question uses kilograms, you need to convert them to grams.

This is a good answer and is correct. The candidate scores maximum marks. This time, they have realised that 2 moles of ammonia are needed to make 1 mole of ammonium sulfate. When answering questions involving calculations, check that you have used the correct units throughout. Look for information in the question. You will be given everything you need to answer the question successfully. Generally, exam questions at GCSE do not involve complicated numbers. If your calculator is showing a string of decimal places, check to see if you have made an error.

The candidate scored 7 out of a possible 8 marks. This is an excellent mark and should contribute towards the highest grade. The candidate has revised thoroughly and shown a very good understanding of calculations based on gas volumes and masses.

P3 Applications of physics (Topics 1–2)

What you should know

Electromagnetic waves

Radiation can transfer some or all of its energy to the atoms of the material it passes through (P1 – Topic 2).

Light is an electromagnetic wave (P1 – Topic 2).

A converging lens has a focal length and can be used to form real and virtual images (P1 – Topic 1).

All waves transfer energy, and can be reflected and refracted (P1 – Topic 1).

Ultrasound is used for foetal scanning (P1 – Topic 3).

Total internal reflection happens when the angle of incidence is greater than the critical angle. It has an application in optical fibres.

Humans have a complex eye. Light passes through the cornea and the lens and is focused on the light-sensitive cells of the retina, which signals images to the brain.

 Name two waves with frequencies greater than that of ultraviolet.

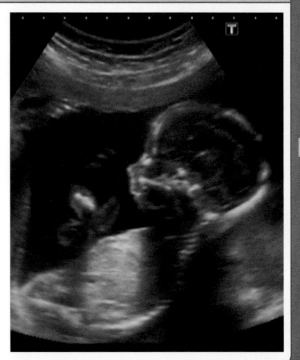

X-rays and energy

The flow of charge is given by the equation: charge = current × time.
It is measured in coulombs (C) (P2 – Topic 1).

Potential difference is the energy transferred per unit charge and is measured in volts (V) (P2 – Topic 2).

A moving object has kinetic energy given by the equation: $KE = \frac{1}{2} mv^2$ (P2 – Topic 4).

Infrared waves and X-rays are forms of electromagnetic radiation. They can harm the body's cells but if used in a controlled way, have important applications in medicine (P1 – Topic 2).

 List two applications of X-rays.

You will find out about

> intensity of radiation and the equation:

$$\text{intensity} = \frac{\text{power of incident radiation}}{\text{area}} \left(I = \frac{P}{A} \right)$$

> the properties of converging and diverging lenses

> the power of lenses and the equation:
power = 1/focal length

> the lens equation:

$$\frac{1}{\text{focal length}} = \frac{1}{\text{object distance}} + \frac{1}{\text{image distance}} \left(\frac{1}{f} = \frac{1}{u} + \frac{1}{v} \right)$$

> the key features of the eye

> eye defects

> using lenses and laser correction to treat short and long sight

> refraction, reflection and total internal reflection

> optical fibres

> the use of ultrasound in diagnosis and treatment

> X-rays and how they are produced by an X-ray tube

> the size of electric current in an X-ray tube

> the equations:
current = number of charged particles per second × charge on each particle ($I = N \times q$)
kinetic energy = charge on electron × accelerating potential difference
($KE = \frac{1}{2} mv^2 = e \times V$)

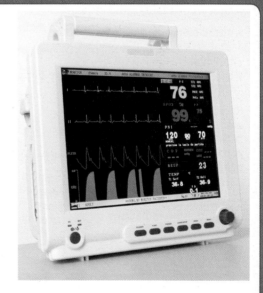

> the absorption of X-rays by matter

> the inverse square law for electromagnetic waves

> CAT scanners and fluoroscopes

> the use of X-rays for treatment and diagnosis

> ECGs and the action of the heart

> the equation: $\text{frequency} = \dfrac{1}{\text{time period}} \left(f = \dfrac{1}{T} \right)$

> the use of pacemakers

> pulse oximetry

Intensity of radiation

You will find out:

> about the term 'radiation'

> about intensity of radiation

> how to calculate the intensity of radiation

Intense lasers

Some surgeons use intense lasers to cut through soft tissues. The laser light has low power but its beam is concentrated on a very small area. A laser is an excellent alternative to a scalpel; it seals blood vessels and prevents bleeding during surgery.

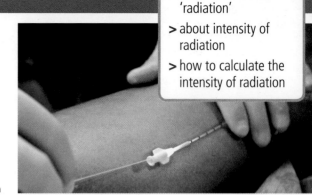

FIGURE 1: Laser surgery. What is the benefit of using lasers in this way?

Radiation

Physicists use the term **radiation** to describe any form of energy that originates from a source, including waves and particles.

Some radiations ionise the atoms of the matter through which they travel; these are referred to as *ionising radiations*.

Here are some examples of radiations that are part of the electromagnetic spectrum (the higher frequency waves shown in colour are ionising radiations):

> radio waves from a transmitter

> microwaves from a mobile phone

> infrared radiation from a heater

> light from a table lamp or laser

> ultraviolet radiation from the Sun

> X-rays from an X-ray machine used in a hospital

> gamma radiation from radioactive cobalt-60 used in hospitals for treatment of cancer.

Radioactive sources also emit alpha particles and beta particles. These particles have kinetic energy and they too are ionising radiations.

You will find out more about ionising radiations and their use in CAT scans on pages 174–5.

Remember!

All ionising radiations strip electrons off neutral atoms. This leaves positive ions and electrons.

Ultrasound is high-frequency sound that we cannot hear. Ultrasound is used in hospitals for ultrasound scans. Ultrasound cannot ionise atoms; it is an example of *non-ionising radiation*.

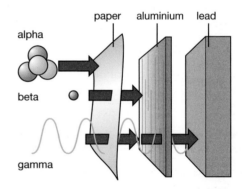

FIGURE 2: Different types of ionising radiation. Alpha particles are easily stopped but cause a lot of ionisation on the way. Beta radiation is more penetrating than alpha radiation and causes less ionisation. Gamma rays consist of high-energy electromagnetic rays, which are very difficult to stop even with thick lead or concrete and cause least ionisation.

QUESTIONS

1 List five ionising radiations.

2 State one similarity and one difference between ultrasound and ultraviolet radiation.

Intensity?

Sometimes photographers use special meters to check the brightness of the light when taking pictures. The meters measure the **intensity** of the light. The intensity of radiation is defined as the power of the radiation per unit area. The intensity is higher when the power is spread over a tiny area.

The intensity of radiation at a point some distance away from a source:

> decreases with distance from the source

> depends on the medium through which it travels.

For example, the intensity of light from a street light at night will decrease as you move further from the street light. Also, the intensity will be lower when it is foggy. This is because light is scattered or absorbed when travelling through fog.

QUESTIONS

3 Show that intensity has the unit W/m².

4 Figure 3 shows light passing through a converging lens. Explain how the intensity of light changes from **A** to **B**.

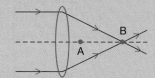

FIGURE 3: Light passing through a converging lens.

FIGURE 4: What does the photographer's meter measure?

What affects intensity? (Higher tier only)

Calculating intensity

Intensity of radiation is the power of the radiation per unit area:

$$\text{intensity} = \frac{\text{power of incident radiation}}{\text{area}} \quad \text{or} \quad I = \frac{P}{A}$$

where I is the intensity, P is the power of the radiation and A is the area. Intensity is measured in watts per square metre (W/m² or W m⁻²).

Let us calculate the intensity of a laser beam of power 1.5 W and radius 1.0 mm.

> *Step 1*: calculate the area A of the beam in square metres (m²):

$A = \pi r^2; \quad A = \pi \times 0.001^2 = 3.14 \times 10^{-6} \text{ m}^2$

> *Step 2*: calculate the intensity I of the beam.

$I = \frac{P}{A}; \quad I = \frac{1.5}{3.14 \times 10^{-6}} = 4.8 \times 10^5 \text{ W/m}^2$

The intensity of the laser beam is 4800 W/m².

Factors affecting intensity

Figure 5 shows radiation spreading uniformly from a source (e.g. light bulb). The source has power P. At a distance r from the source, the power is spread evenly over a sphere of surface area $4\pi r^2$. The intensity I of the radiation at a distance r is given by:

$$I = \frac{P}{4\pi r^2}$$

The intensity decreases with *distance* from the source. The intensity will decrease by a factor of 4 when the distance is doubled, and by a factor of 9 when the distance is trebled. The intensity is inversely proportional to the area – it obeys an 'inverse square law with distance'.

The intensity also depends on the *medium* through which the radiation travels.

QUESTIONS

5 Calculate the intensity of light at a distance of 2.0 m and 4.0 m from a 5.0 W light source.

6 The intensity of X-rays is 1000 W/m². Calculate the incident power of X-rays over a surface of dimensions 5.0 cm by 5.0 cm.

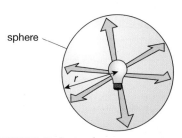

FIGURE 5: Radiation from a source spreads out uniformly over a sphere.

Q Inverse square law for light

Properties of lenses

You will find out:

> about diverging and converging lenses

> about power of a lens

> how focal length and dioptre are related

Lenses

Lenses are shaped pieces of glass or other materials that refract light. Simple converging or diverging lenses are used to correct eye defects, but many different types of lenses can be used in cameras to create unusual effects.

FIGURE 1: A fisheye lens is a wide angle lens. How has this fisheye lens distorted the image of this dog?

Converging and diverging lenses

There are two types of lens, converging and diverging.

Converging lenses

> A converging (convex) lens is thinner at the edges and thicker in the middle.

Remember!
Refraction is the change in direction caused by the change in the speed of light as it travels from one material into another.

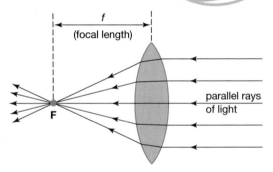

FIGURE 2: A converging lens. Our eye lens is a converging lens.

> Parallel rays of light are refracted twice at the lens. These rays converge to a point **F** on the principal axis called the **principal focus** (focal point).

> The focal length of the lens is the distance between the centre of the lens and the principal focus.

> The focal length of the lens depends on its *shape*. A fat converging lens has a short **focal length**.

Diverging lenses

> A diverging (concave) lens is thicker at the edges and thinner in the middle.

> Parallel rays of light are diverged (spread out) by the lens and appear to come from the principal focus **F**.

> The focal length f of the lens is still defined as the distance between the centre of the lens and **F**.

> A diverging lens that is much thinner in the middle then its edges has a short focal length.

> Objects always look smaller through a diverging lens.

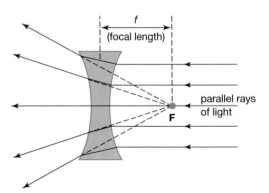

FIGURE 3: A diverging lens has a virtual principal focus **F**. What is the difference between the principal focus **F** of this type of lens and a converging lens?

QUESTIONS

1 Describe how the shapes of a converging lens and a diverging lens affect the focal length.

2 State the type of each lens shown in Figure 4.

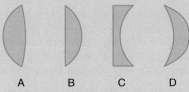

A   B   C   D

FIGURE 4: Can you identify the type of lens from its shape?

Power of lenses

The **optical power** P of a lens is defined as the reciprocal of the focal length in metres:

$$\text{power (dioptre, D)} = \frac{1}{\text{focal length (metre, m)}}$$

> As the curvature of a converging lens increases, the focal length decreases and the power increases. The power of a fat converging lens is greater than that of a thin lens.

> A converging lens has a real principal focus. By convention, its focal length and power are taken as *positive*.

> A diverging lens has a virtual principal focus. By convention, its focal length and power are taken as *negative*.

The eye lens of an average person has focal length of +5.5 cm, so its power is:

$$P = \frac{1}{0.055 \text{ m}} = +18 \text{ D}$$

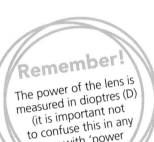

Remember!

The power of the lens is measured in dioptres (D) (it is important not to confuse this in any way with 'power in watts').

Did you know?

In laser surgery the optical power of the eye is changed by shaping the cornea.

QUESTIONS

3 An optometrist places a diverging lens of focal length 15 cm in front of a patient's eye. Calculate the power of this lens.

4 A student is holding two converging lenses in her hand. Lens A is fat and lens B is thin. Explain which lens has the greatest power.

Why do we need the power of a lens?

If you have had an eye test, then you will be familiar with the optometrist using a combination of lenses to get the correct focal length for the corrective lens in your glasses.

When lens are combined together, it is their power in dioptres that are added. This is why the power of the lens is more important than its focal length. Table 1 shows a combination of two lenses X and Y. The focal length of the combination of lenses can be found using:

$$\text{focal length (m)} = \frac{1}{\text{power (D)}}$$

TABLE 1: Using lenses X and Y.

Power of lens X (D)	Power of lens Y (D)	Combined power of lenses X and Y (D)	Focal length of combination (m)
+10	+5	+15	0.067
+8	−3	+5	0.200
+4	−6	−2	−0.500

QUESTIONS

5 Calculate the combined power of two converging lenses of focal lengths 2.2 cm and 5.5 cm.

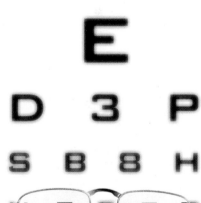

FIGURE 5: It is important that glasses have lenses of the correct powers.

Lens equation

You will find out:
> about images formed by a converging lens
> about the lens equation

Getting the best picture

The most important part of a digital camera is its converging lens. Automatic focusing is produced by bouncing off pulses of infrared waves sent by the camera to the object. Microprocessors analyse these signals and work out the distance of the object from the lens. Small motors move the lens, so that you can capture the clearest image.

FIGURE 1: This camera can take close-up images using a converging lens.

Where is the image?

Figure 2 shows an arrangement you can use in the laboratory to investigate the image formed by a converging lens.

You can draw a *ray diagram* to locate the position of the image from the len (see Figure 3):

> The object is represented by an arrow **O**.

> A ray from the top of the object and parallel to the principal axis will be refracted through the principal focus **F** of the lens.

> Another ray from the top of the object will pass through the centre of the lens in a straight line.

> The top of the image **I** is where these two rays intersect.

Did you know?

The earliest lenses were probably glass globes filled with water, and were used as 'burning glasses'.

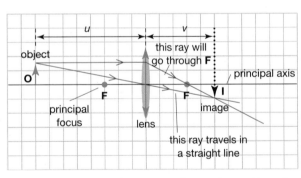

FIGURE 3: You just need two rays to locate the position of the image. What are distances *u* and *v*?

QUESTIONS

1 Describe the changes to the image in Figure 3 when:

   a the object is moved a long distance away from the lens

   b when a fatter lens is used for the same object distance.

2 Look at the experiment shown in Figure 2. Suggest what your control variable should be.

FIGURE 2: Equipment used to investigate the properties of the image formed by a converging lens.

Characteristics of the image

The nature of the image formed by a particular converging lens depends on the distance of the object from the centre of the lens. On the diagrams below, **F** is the principal focus and point **2F** is at a distance of twice the focal length from the lens.

FIGURE 4: Object beyond **2F**.

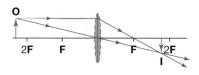

Image is:
> real
> inverted
> diminished
> between **F** and **2F**

FIGURE 5: Object between **F** and **2F**.

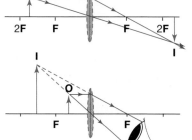

Image is:
> real
> inverted
> magnified
> beyond **2F**

FIGURE 6: Object between lens and **F**.

Image is:
> virtual
> upright
> magnified
> beyond **F**

Figure 5 shows a lens used as a projector lens in a cinema and Figure 6 shows the lens being used as a magnifying glass.

Remember!

Rays do not actually pass through a virtual image – the image is formed at the location where the rays *appear* to come from.

QUESTIONS

3 In Figure 6, explain where the object should be relative to the lens in order to get a more magnified image.

4 A lens has a focal length of 5.0 cm. A 1.0 cm high object is placed 7.0 cm from the lens. Draw a ray diagram to determine the distance of the image from the lens and the height of the image.

The lens equation (Higher tier only)

The distance u of the object from the lens, the distance v of the image from the lens and the focal length f of the lens are related by the **lens equation** below:

$$\frac{1}{f} = \frac{1}{u} + \frac{1}{v}$$

This is a versatile equation that can be used to locate the positions of the object or image or to find the focal length of the lens. Before you can use this equation, you need to be familiar with the *real is positive sign convention*, see Table 1.

TABLE 1: Real is positive sign convention

Lens	f	u	v
Converging lens	Positive	Positive	Positive for real image
Diverging lens	Negative	Positive	Negative for virtual image

Worked example

A clock is 1.20 m away from a converging lens of focal length 0.15 m. Calculate the distance of the image from the lens:

$$u = 1.20 \text{ m} \qquad v = ? \qquad f = +0.15 \text{ m}$$

The image is real and at a distance of 0.17 m from the lens.

$$\frac{1}{f} = \frac{1}{u} + \frac{1}{v}$$

$$\frac{1}{0.15} = \frac{1}{1.20} + \frac{1}{v}$$

$$\frac{1}{v} = \frac{1}{0.15} - \frac{1}{1.20} = 5.833...$$

$$v = \frac{1}{5.833...} = 0.17 \text{ m}$$

The image is real at a distance of 0.17 m from the centre of the lens. If the lens were a diverging lens of the same focal length, then the only change would be $f = -0.15$ m. This gives an image distance of -0.13 m; the minus implies a virtual image.

QUESTIONS

5 Calculate the unknown quantities in the table below.

u (m)	v (m)	f (m)
0.10	?	0.15
0.30	0.12	?

The eye

You will find out:
> about the key features of the eye
> about near point and far point
> about short sight and long sight
> about simple lenses, contact lenses and laser treatment

How do we see?

Figure 1 shows a highly magnified image of the retina. The retina helps us to see. It consists of colour-sensitive cone cells (blue) and intensity-sensitive rod cells (green). There are about 130 million rod cells and 7 million cone cells in the human eye.

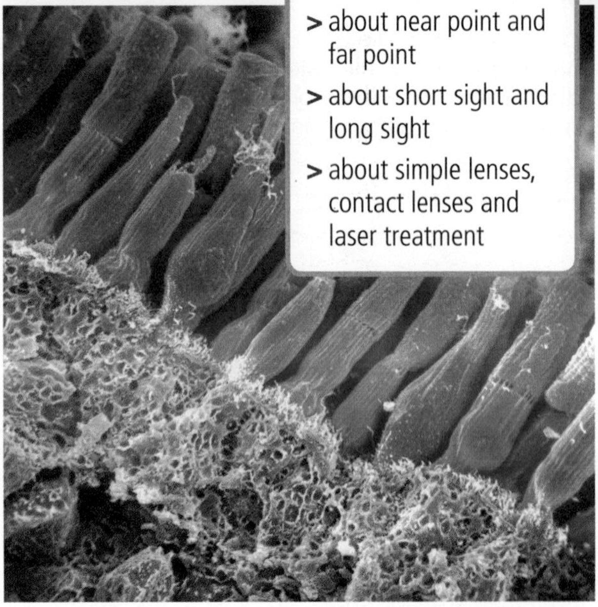

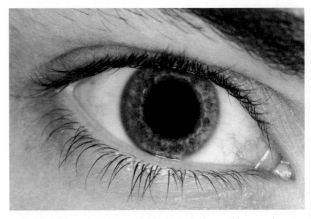

FIGURE 1: A micrograph of the retina of the eye. What does the retina do?

The human eye

Figure 2 shows a diagram of the human eye:

The **cornea** is a curved layer over the front of the eye. It is transparent and refracts light.

The **iris** is the coloured part of the eye. It automatically controls the amount of light entering the eye. Its muscles relax and contract to alter the size of the central hole called the **pupil**.

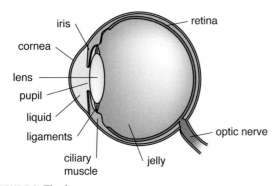

FIGURE 2: The human eye.

The eye lens is a flexible converging lens. Unlike a camera lens, it cannot move in or out.

The **ciliary muscles** change the shape of the lens, a process called *accommodation*. This change in shape allows the focal length of the lens to change.

The **retina** is where light is focused by the action of the lens and the cornea. Here, images are formed. The retina has light-sensitive cells that send tiny electrical signals along the *optic nerve* to the brain.

FIGURE 3: The pupil is small in bright light and large when it is dark.

Did you know?

The image on the retina is upside down but the brain learns to interpret it as the right way up!

QUESTIONS

1 Identify the iris and the pupil in Figure 3.

2 Explain how the eye can clearly see both close and distant objects.

Short sight and long sight

The **near point** is the closest distance you can focus an object. For an average adult eye this is about 25 cm. The ciliary muscles are tightened and the eye lens is thick with a short focal length.

The **far point** is the furthest point the eye can see clearly. For an average adult eye this point is at infinity. The ciliary muscles are totally relaxed and the eye lens is thin with a long focal length.

For some people, distant objects appear blurred, while other people cannot focus on near objects. Wearing spectacles (simple lenses) or contact lenses can correct these symptoms.

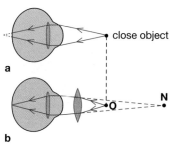

FIGURE 4: Correcting long sightedness.

Long sight

> A long-sighted person can clearly see distant objects but close objects appear fuzzy or blurred.

> A long-sighted person can suffer from headaches and have tired eyes.

> The near point of the eye is further than 25 cm and the rays from a close object are focused behind the retina (see Figure 4a).

> This may be because the eyeball is too short, the cornea is not curved enough or the eye lens is too thin.

> With the corrective converging lens, the rays from the near object **O** can be focused on the retina and the rays appear to come from the person's near point **N** (see Figure 4b).

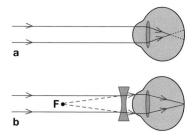

FIGURE 5: Correcting short sightedness.

Short sight

> A short-sighted person can clearly see near objects but cannot on distant objects. The far point is not infinity but much closer.

> This may be because the cornea is too curved or your eyeball is too long, meaning that light rays from distant objects focus in front of your retina (see Figure 5a). This makes distant objects seem fuzzy or blurred.

> With the corrective diverging lens, the rays from the infinity can be focused on the retina and the rays appear to come from the person's far point **F** (see Figure 5b).

QUESTIONS

3 In each case below, identify whether the eye is short sighted or long sighted:

a the eyeball is too short

b the eye lens is too thick even when the ciliary muscles are relaxed.

4 Discuss the benefits and drawbacks of wearing contact lenses compared with glasses.

Laser treatment (Higher tier only)

It is mainly the cornea that is responsible for refracting light entering the eye. The lens carries out the fine focusing, and as we have seen, the lens can change its focal length to view objects at different distances. The cornea has a focal length of about 2.2 cm and that of the lens is about 5.5 cm.

The majority of people who consider having laser correction do so because they do not want to wear glasses or contact lenses. It is a permanent treatment in which the shape of the cornea is changed using powerful lasers. The treatment can be painful for a few days, and as with any surgical procedure, laser treatment can lead to an infection.

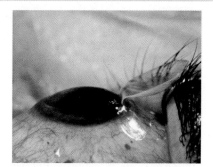

FIGURE 6: In laser surgery the outer layer of the cornea is cut open and a flap (right) pulled open. Lasers are then used to shape the middle layer of the cornea.

QUESTIONS

5 Evaluate the advantages and disadvantages of laser correction for a professional swimmer.

TIR and endoscopes

Natural glass

Scientists have found a deep-sea sponge that contains optical fibres similar to the ones used in industry and medicine. The sponge, called a Venus' Flower Basket, has tufts of glassy fibres each about the thickness of a human hair. It seems that the sponges' fibres are stronger than artificial ones.

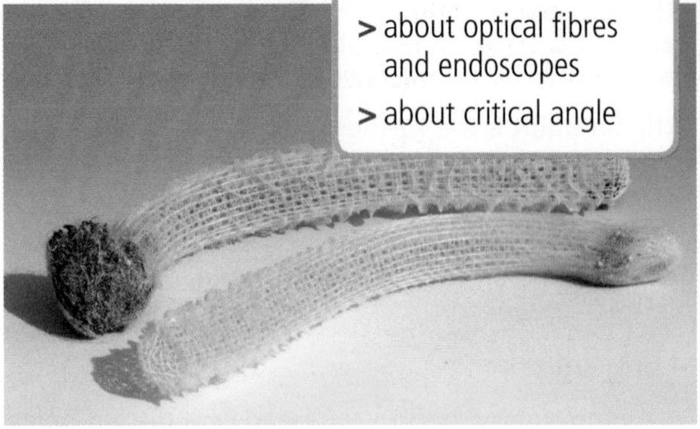

FIGURE 1: Do we have something to learn from this odd creature?

Investigating reflection, refraction and TIR

Figure 2 shows how you can investigate what happens to light as it travels from an optically dense material (e.g. glass, Perspex) into a less dense material (e.g. air).

What happens to the light when the angle of incidence is small?

> The light is reflected and refracted at the glass–air boundary.

> Light travels more slowly in glass than in air. So the angle of **refraction** is larger than the angle of incidence.

What happens to the light when the angle of incidence is increased?

> The angle of refraction becomes larger.

> At the **critical angle** c, the refracted ray runs along the glass–air boundary. The angle of refraction is 90°.

> The light is also reflected at the boundary.

> The critical angle depends on the type of transparent material.

What happens when the angle of incidence is greater than the critical angle?

> There is no refraction at the glass–air boundary.

> All the light is reflected internally inside the glass block. This is known as **total internal reflection** (TIR).

> According to the *law of reflection*, the angle of incidence is equal to the angle of reflection.

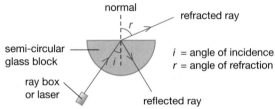

FIGURE 2: An arrangement to investigate what happens to light when it is incident at different angles inside a glass block. There is no bending of light at the curved surface of the block because the ray of light enters at right angles to the surface.

i = angle of incidence
r = angle of refraction

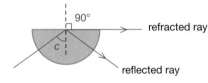

FIGURE 3: The critical angle for glass is about 42°; for water it is 49°. What is the angle of refraction at the critical angle?

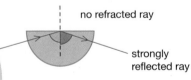

FIGURE 4: TIR only happens in the denser medium (glass). The angle of incidence is greater than the critical angle.

Remember!

Refraction is the change in direction of a wave at the boundary between two materials, caused by the change in the speed of a wave.

QUESTIONS

1 The critical angle for glass is 42°.

   a Explain what is meant by the term 'critical angle'.

   b Describe what happens to light inside a glass block when the angle of incidence is

   i 10°; ii 60°.

Q Critical angle and TIR   Uses of optical fibres

Optical fibres and endoscopes

Optical fibres are thin (0.01 mm is typical) flexible rods of transparent material. Light entering at one end of the fibre is total internally reflected until it comes out from the other end. The rays of light follow zig-zag paths inside the fibre. The light cannot escape the fibre as it always strikes the boundary between the two transparent materials at an angle greater than the critical angle.

Optical fibres are used to carry high-speed signals for broadband networks and computers.

An **endoscope** is a medical instrument used by doctors to see inside our bodies. It uses optical fibres and can be equipped with tiny scalpels and other instruments to carry out keyhole surgery.

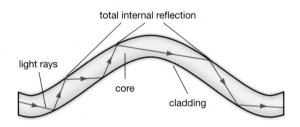

FIGURE 5: Modern optical fibres have a glass core surrounded by a special coating (known as cladding) and have critical angles as high as 80°.

An endoscope uses two separate bundles of optical fibres; one to illuminate the inside of the patient and the other to collect the reflected light so that the image can be viewed through the eyepiece. A camera is often connected to the eyepiece.

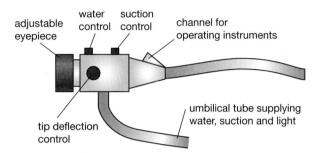

FIGURE 6: The flexible end of an endoscope has a diameter of about 1 cm and can be up to 2 m long.

QUESTIONS

2 Explain why endoscopes:

a usually have many thin fibres rather than just one thick fibre

b require a powerful light source.

Calculating the critical angle (Higher tier only)

Diamond will refract light more than glass. Diamond has a higher *refractive index* than glass. Light travels much more slowly in diamond than in glass. We can use **Snell's law** to determine the refractive index n of a material or medium.

According to Snell's law:

$$n = \frac{\sin i}{\sin r}$$

where i is angle of incidence in a vacuum (or air) and r is the angle of refraction in the medium.

At the critical angle, light travels from the denser material into air. By 'reversing' the direction of light in Figure 7 and with $r = c$ and $i = 90°$, the critical angle c at a particular boundary is given by the following equation:

$$\sin c = \frac{1}{n}$$

What is the critical angle for a medium with refractive index of 1.40?

$$\sin c = \frac{1}{n} = \frac{1}{1.40} = 0.7143$$

$$c = \sin^{-1}(0.7143) = 46°$$

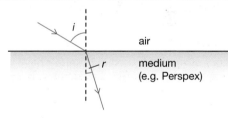

FIGURE 7: Snell's law relates the sine of the angle of incidence to the sine of the angle of refraction. This ratio is the refractive index.

Table 1 shows the refractive indices of some materials.

TABLE 1: The refractive indices of selected materials.

Medium	Air	Water	Perspex	Glass	Diamond
Refractive index	1.00	1.33	1.49	1.52	2.42

QUESTIONS

3 Calculate the critical angles for water–air, glass–air and diamond–air boundaries.

Medical uses of ultrasound

You will find out:
> about uses of ultrasound in diagnosis and treatment

Silence of the dogs

Dogs have been known to eat socks, slippers, dishcloths, their own collars, tennis balls and many other objects that would certainly not be looked on as food by humans. As animals cannot communicate with humans about their symptoms, ultrasound scanning is a very useful procedure, helping vets to see an image of the animal's insides. They can then decide whether surgery is needed to remove the object.

FIGURE 1: How can high-frequency sound help our pets?

Ultrasound in diagnosis

Humans can hear sounds that have frequencies in the range 20 Hz to 20 kHz.

Ultrasound is high-frequency sound that we cannot hear. In hospitals, ultrasound of frequency 1.5 MHz is used to form images of the insides of our bodies.

Ultrasound waves are generated and received by special devices called ultrasound **transducers**.

Thanks to powerful modern computers, it is possible to create three-dimensional images such as that of the human foetus shown in Figure 3.

Ultrasound scans are safer than X-rays because ultrasound is a non-ionising radiation. The high-frequency ultrasounds used in hospitals have very short wavelengths, typically 1 millimetre. It is possible to see minute details with such short wavelengths.

An expert radiographer can analyse images and diagnose potential problems. Among many others, ultrasounds are used to diagnose:

> cysts

> tumours

> blocked arteries

> kidney stones

> foetal abnormalities (such as spina bifida).

FIGURE 2: The ultrasound transducer sends and detects ultrasound sent into the patient.

Remember!
The higher the frequency, the shorter the wavelength.

QUESTIONS

1 Explain what is meant by ultrasound.

2 Explain why it is sensible to take an image of a foetus using ultrasound rather than X-rays.

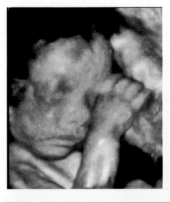

FIGURE 3: This amazing image is produced using high-frequency sound waves.

Q Diagnosis with ultrasound   Foetal scans

Ultrasound echoes

Ultrasound, like all other waves, can be reflected, refracted and diffracted. Ultrasound inside our bodies will be reflected at the boundaries between any two materials of different densities. Ultrasound images are formed using echoes. Figure 4 shows ultrasound pulses sent into the eyeball of a patient.

> Pulse A is the pulse sent into the eye from the transducer.

> Pulse B is the pulse detected by the transducer after being reflected off the back of the eye.

> T is the time taken for the pulse to travel twice the length of the eyeball.

> The length L of the eyeball can be determined from the speed of the ultrasound and the 'delay time' T using the equation:

$$2 \times L = \text{speed of ultrasound in the eye} \times T$$

The same technique can be used by a radiographer to determine the size of the head of a foetus, in order to diagnose any problems with its development.

QUESTIONS

3 The speed of ultrasound in the eye is 1060 m/s. Calculate the length of the eyeball given that the 'delay time' of the reflected pulse is 4.0×10^{-5} s.

Remember!
Ultrasound is safe because it is a non-ionising radiation.

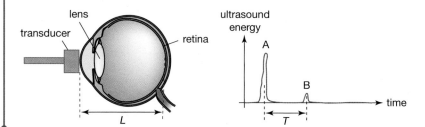

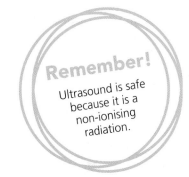

FIGURE 4: The echoes from an ultrasound can be used to determine the length of the eyeball.

Ultrasound used in treatment

Kidney or bladder stones are formed from minerals contained in urine. They can lead to serious blockages and severe pain. Fortunately these stones, which can be as large as 1 cm in diameter, can be destroyed without surgery using ultrasound. Figure 5 shows a patient receiving a dose of high-frequency ultrasound. The ultrasound waves are focused onto the stones. The machine sends a series of intense pulses (shockwaves) of ultrasound. After several treatments, the stones are broken down into smaller fragments and they pass out of the body naturally with the urine.

The rapid fluctuations in pressure caused by ultrasound can also produce heating in the body. In physiotherapy, ultrasound is used to heat injured muscles, causing increased blood flow to improve the rate of healing.

Very intense ultrasounds do have one side-effect. They can cause dissolved gases (O_2 and CO_2) in the blood to form tiny bubbles. When these bubbles collapse they can damage tissues in the body. But do not worry; in both diagnosis and treatment, the ultrasound intensities are low and very safe.

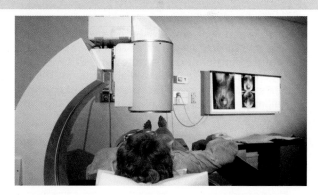

FIGURE 5: Lithotripsy is a technique where high-frequency ultrasound is used to destroy bladder or kidney stones.

QUESTIONS

4 Describe the treatment for a frail elderly patient who is suffering from bladder stones.

5 How would you reassure the mother of a young patient who thinks that ultrasound is dangerous for her child?

Preparing for assessment: Analysis and conclusions

To achieve a good grade in science, you not only have to know and understand scientific ideas, but you also need to be able to apply them to other situations and investigations. This task will support you in developing these skills.

✳ Task

Test the hypothesis that the greater the *power* of a converging lens the smaller the *height* of the image formed by a converging lens.

✳ Looking into power of a lens

Converging lenses are used in instruments such as telescopes and projectors. The power P of a converging lens is determined from its focal length f using the equation $P = 1/f$. The power of a lens is measured in dioptres (D). The focal length of a converging lens depends on the thickness of the lens in the middle. The greater the thickness the shorter the focal length. A fat lens has a shorter focal length and a larger value of power compared to a thin lens.

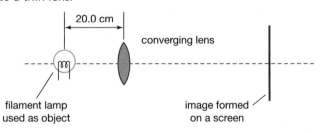

20.0 cm

converging lens

filament lamp used as object

image formed on a screen

✳ Method and results

In an experiment, a student used a variety of converging lenses to form clear images on a screen. For each lens, the student formed a clear image of a distant object. The distance between the screen and the centre of the lens was measured and this was taken to be the focal length f of the lens. The lens was then used to form an image of a filament lamp. The distance of the lamp from the lens was kept constant at 20.0 cm. The height of the image formed on the screen was measured using a plastic ruler marked in millimetres. The student carried out each experiment twice. The student repeated the procedure for converging lenses of different thicknesses.

Lens	Focal length (cm)		Average focal length f (cm)	Power P (D)	Image height (cm)		Average height h of image (cm)
A	14.8	15.2	15.0	6.67	6.2	5.8	6.0
B	12.0	13.0	12.5		3.0	3.4	
C	9.5	10.5	10.0		5.0	4.6	
D	7.0	8.0	7.5		1.0	1.4	
E	4.5	5.1	4.8		0.6	0.8	

Processing the evidence

1. Copy the table and complete the power P and average height h of image columns.

2. Display the results on a suitable graph.

3. One of the recorded results is anomalous. Identify the lens for which the result is anomalous.

4. Comment on the quality of the results.

> Make sure that your average values are given to an appropriate number of significant figures.

> Choose your scale with great care because your graph must be of appropriate size. Carefully draw the best-fit line (or curve). Joining the data points 'dot-to-dot' will lose you marks.

> You can only identify the anomalous result when you have plotted the points. How will you deal with this anomalous result when forming your conclusions? Does the anomalous result affect the hypothesis in any way?

Stating your conclusions

1. What conclusion can you draw from the graph?

2. Explain whether or not the results support the hypothesis. You must use scientific ideas and appropriate mathematical relationships to explain your observations in the light of the hypothesis.

> Describe the relationship between the two variables qualitatively (without using mathematical terms) and quantitatively. Remember to take into account the anomalous result.

> For an 'inverse proportionality' relationship doubling one quantity will halve the other quantity.

Evaluating the conclusion

1. How could you improve the evidence to better support your conclusion?

2. How might you reword your hypothesis in the light of your conclusions?

> Scientists generally expect to have six or more points close to the best-fit line or curve before drawing conclusions from a graph.

> Carefully consider the hypothesis and scientific language used to gain Quality of Written Communication marks.

Evaluating the method

1. Describe the strengths and weaknesses of the investigation.

2. Suggest two possible reasons why one of the results was anomalous.

3. Suggest how the method used to gather the results might be improved to produce better quality evidence.

> Were the filament lamp, the lens and the screen in a straight line? Did the light in the laboratory affect the quality of the image seen on the screen?

> Consider ways of minimising the risk of anomalies.

Connections

How Science Works

> Collecting and analysing scientific data.

> Presenting information, drawing a conclusion and stating this in a scientific way.

> Evaluating the best methods of data collection and considering their reliability.

> Interpreting data qualitatively and quantitatively.

> Analysing, interpreting, applying and questioning scientific information.

Maths in Science

> Carrying out calculations.

> Substituting numerical values into simple formulae using appropriate units.

> Providing answers to correct number of significant figures.

> Using proportion and ratios.

> Calculating means.

> Drawing graphs with appropriate scales.

> Interpreting data from tables and graphs.

Producing X-rays

You will find out:
> about electric currents in evacuated tubes
> about the production of X-rays
> about the equations $I = N \times q$ and $\frac{1}{2} mv^2 = e \times V$

X-rays

Wilhelm Röntgen discovered X-rays in 1895. He took the world's first X-ray image of his wife's hand. Unknown to him at the time, the intense X-rays were very harmful. Modern X-rays use low-intensity X-rays, have very short exposure times, are relatively safe and produce stunning detail.

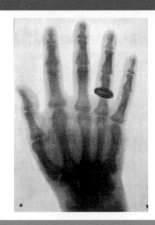

FIGURE 1: 'Hand with ring': the first X-ray.

Evacuated tubes

Figure 2 shows a glass tube with no air inside (vacuum). This evacuated tube has two electrodes, a filament and a metal plate (called the metal target). A potential difference is applied between the filament (the **cathode**) and the metal plate (the **anode**).

When an electric current flows through the filament it gets very hot. The electrons inside the filament have sufficient kinetic energy to escape. This process is called **thermionic emission**.

The electrons form a negative 'space charge' around the filament.

> The electrons are attracted to the positive anode and accelerate towards the anode.

> Current is the rate of flow of charge. Hence, the electrons moving between the cathode and anode constitute an electric current.

> A vacuum is needed because if the tube contained air, electrons would collide with particles in the air and be slowed down or stopped.

The arrangement shown in Figure 2 is sometimes referred to as a *thermionic diode*. A diode is a device that allows current to travel in one direction only.

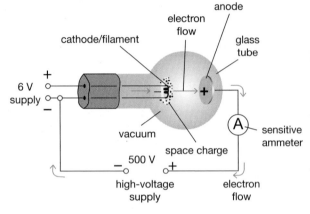

FIGURE 2: An evacuated tube. What would happen to the current if the supply connections were reversed?

○ QUESTIONS

1 Explain what is meant by thermionic emission.

2 Suggest how the current through the tube could be increased.

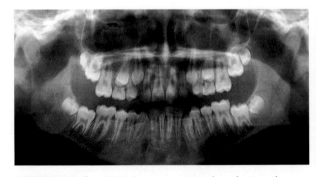

FIGURE 3: Modern X-ray images are produced using shorter exposures and are very safe.

Producing X-rays

An X-ray tube is similar to a thermionic diode. The only difference is that a higher accelerating potential difference is used. The anode is referred to as the **target**. This is usually made of a metal of high melting point such as tungsten.

The electrons strike the target at high speeds. About 1% of the kinetic energy of the electrons is converted to X-rays; the rest is converted to heat. Modern X-ray tubes have circulating water to cool down the anode. Without this coolant, the target metal can reach

2500 °C. In some tubes, the target is also rotated to spread the heat over a large surface area.

> Increasing the temperature of the filament increases the rate of electron emission from the filament and this in turn increases the *intensity* of X-rays from the tube.

> Increasing the accelerating potential difference increases the speed of the electrons hitting the target and this in turn produces X-rays of shorter wavelength or higher frequency.

Higher frequency X-rays carry greater energy and cause a greater amount of ionisation. This is why higher frequency X-rays cause more damage to the cells in our body than lower frequency X-rays.

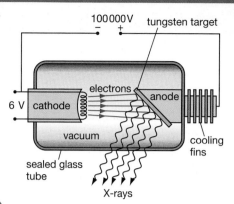

FIGURE 4: An X-ray tube is really a thermionic diode. What similarities do you notice with Figure 2?

 QUESTIONS

3 Describe the energy changes taking place when electrons strike the target at high speeds.

4 Describe how the intensity and frequency of the X-rays from an X-ray tube can be changed.

Current and kinetic energy of electrons (Higher tier only)

Current

The current in an X-ray tube can be found using 'current = rate of flow of charge'. If there are N electrons arriving at the anode per second, with each electron carrying a charge q then the current I in amperes is given by the equation:

current (ampere, A) = number of particles per second (1/second, 1/s) × charge on each particle (coulomb, C)

$I = N \times q$

The charge on a single electron is 1.6×10^{-19} C. This charge is also denoted by the letter e for elementary charge.

What is the current when 6.25×10^{15} electrons arrive at the anode every second?

$I = N \times q$

$\quad = 6.25 \times 10^{15} \times 1.6 \times 10^{-19}$

$\quad = 10 \times 10^{-4}$ A = 1 mA

Kinetic energy

For an X-ray tube, the kinetic energy in joules of each electron arriving at the anode can be determined as follows:

kinetic energy = electrical energy gained

kinetic energy (joule, J) = charge on the electron (coulomb, C) × accelerating potential difference (volt, V)

$\frac{1}{2}mv^2 = e \times V$

where m is the mass of the electron (9.1×10^{-31} kg), v is the speed in m/s of the electron, e is the elementary charge of 1.6×10^{-19} C and V is the potential difference in volts between the cathode and the anode.

You can think of an X-ray tube as a miniature particle accelerator!

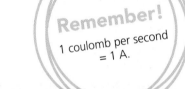

Remember!

1 coulomb per second = 1 A.

 QUESTIONS

5 What is the current when 2×10^{16} electrons reach the anode in 1 second?

6 A classmate tells you that the beam of particles in an X-ray tube is not equivalent to an electric current. Write a short paragraph to explain why he is wrong.

7 For a 5000 V X-ray tube carrying a current of 2.0 mA, calculate:

a the kinetic energy gained by an electron

b the maximum speed of an electron

c the number of electrons arriving at the anode per second.

Medical uses of X-rays

3D X-ray images

Figure 1 shows a remarkable three-dimensional (3D) image using X-rays of a patient with a brain haemorrhage. The red region shows blood leaking into the brain. These images are valuable to doctors who can accurately locate the clot and remove it using surgery.

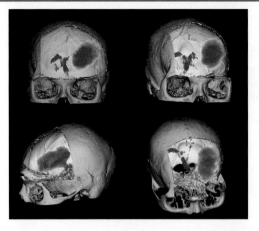

FIGURE 1: A 3D image of a patient's skull showing the location and size of the blood clot.

Using X-rays for diagnosis

CAT scanners

Figure 2 shows a sophisticated X-ray machine that is capable of producing 3D images of the insides of a patient. The machine is called the computerised axial tomography (CAT) scanner. The images are referred to as **CAT scans**.

> The patient lies on a movable table that moves in and out of a ring.

> The ring has a rotating X-ray tube and fixed detectors.

> The X-rays pass through the patient and reach detectors on the opposite side of the X-ray tube.

> The computer connected to the detectors records thousands of images or 'slices' through the patient. This helps to create a 3D image of the patient.

Unlike ultrasound, X-rays are ionising radiation. During a CAT scan, healthy cells are also damaged; the risks can be minimised by using shorter exposure times. CAT scans are used to diagnose tumours, blood clots and Alzheimer's disease. Unlike ordinary two-dimensional (2D) X-ray images, CAT scans can reveal the structure of soft tissues.

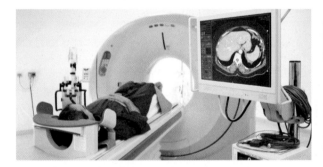

FIGURE 2: A hospital CAT scanner is an expensive machine. What is this scanner used for?

Fluoroscopes

Fluoroscopy is a technique used for obtaining real-time moving images of the internal structures of a patient.

> It is used to diagnose problems associated with the stomach and the intestines.

> It uses a **fluoroscope** which consists of an X-ray source, detector and monitor.

> The patient is given a chalky drink made from barium sulfate.

> Barium is a good absorber of X-rays.

The passage of the 'barium meal' through the patient can be viewed on a monitor and helps the doctor to identify problems.

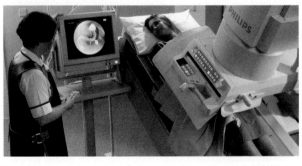

FIGURE 3: A radiographer conducts a barium meal stomach X-ray on a female patient in a fluoroscopy department. Why is the radiographer wearing a lead-lined apron?

QUESTIONS

1 A patient is complaining about stomach pains. Which X-ray technique would be advisable for this patient?

2 Explain why a patient cannot be given too many CAT scans.

Q Diagnosis with CAT scanners   Fluoroscopes in hospitals

Spreading and absorption

Figure 4 shows a point source of electromagnetic radiation, e.g. light. The power of the source spreads out uniformly, hence the intensity of the radiation decreases with distance from the source. The intensity of the radiation obeys an **inverse square law** with distance (see Table 1). The intensity I is inversely proportional to the square of the distance r, from the source and is given by the relationship

$$I \times \frac{1}{r^2}$$

TABLE 1: Intensity of radiation decreases with distance from the source.

Distance from source	r	$2r$	$3r$	$4r$	$5r$
Intensity	I_0	$\dfrac{I_0}{4}$	$\dfrac{I_0}{9}$	$\dfrac{I_0}{16}$	$\dfrac{I_0}{25}$

X-rays are absorbed by the material they travel through. For a given material, the transmitted intensity *decreases* as the thickness of the material *increases*. Figure 5 shows intensity against thickness graphs for bone and muscle.

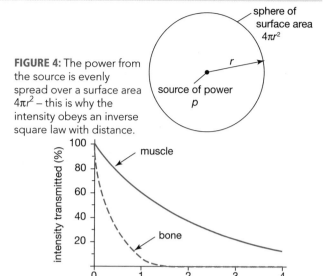

FIGURE 4: The power from the source is evenly spread over a surface area $4\pi r^2$ – this is why the intensity obeys an inverse square law with distance.

FIGURE 5: Intensity against thickness graphs for bone and muscle. Which of these two materials is a good absorber of X-rays?

QUESTIONS

3 The intensity of light at a distance of 0.50 m from a light source is 2.0 W/m². Determine the intensities at distances of 0.25 m and 5.0 m.

4 Use Figure 5 to determine the muscle thickness that reduces the intensity **a** to a half and **b** to a quarter. **C** Describe how the intensity is related to the thickness.

Using X-rays for treatment

Radiotherapy is a technique used for the treatment of cancer. Intense radiation, either gamma radiation or X-rays, is directed at the tumour to destroy the cancerous cells so that they cannot reproduce. Figure 6 shows a patient being treated for skin cancer using an intense beam of X-rays.

X-rays are produced by bombarding a target metal with high-speed electrons. In some radiography departments, the X-rays are produced using a linear particle accelerator (linac). The energy of the X-rays from a linac is comparable to high-energy gamma rays. The major advantage of linac over gamma radiation radiotherapy is that the energy and the intensity of the X-rays can easily be controlled by the radiographer. So, the patient can be given the correct dose of radiation. The X-rays from a linac can be switched off; the same cannot be said for gamma radiation from radioactive sources (cobalt).

QUESTIONS

5 Use Figure 5 to comment on the relationship between absorption of X-rays and the density of material they pass through.

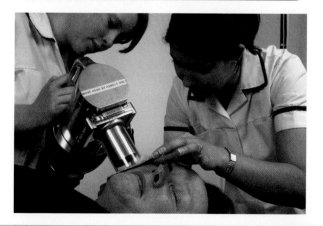

FIGURE 6: A small X-ray generator being used to treat skin cancer.

Heart action and ECG

You will find out:
> about frequency and the equation $f = \frac{1}{T}$
> about electrocardiograms and heart action
> about pacemakers

Pacemakers

A pacemaker is a small device implanted into a patient's chest or abdomen to help control abnormal heartbeat. A pacemaker helps the heart to pump blood around the body. It can help a person suffering from tiredness, shortness of breath or fainting.

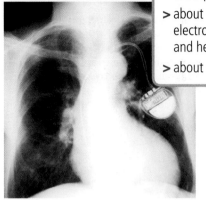

FIGURE 1: An X-ray image of a patient with a heart pacemaker.

ECG and frequency

An ECG, or **electrocardiogram**, is a recording of the electrical activity of your heart. The test takes a few minutes and is painless. Small sticky metal patches called electrodes are placed onto your arms, legs and chest (see Figure 2). In order to make good electrical contact with the body, a conducting gel is applied and body hair removed. These electrodes are connected to a monitor which displays the electrical signals that make your heart beat.

Figure 3 shows an ECG of a single heartbeat of a healthy heart. A normal heart beats regularly as it pumps blood around the body.

> The **frequency** of the heartbeat for a person resting is about 1.17 hertz or 70 beats per minute. Physical activity increases the frequency of the heartbeats.

> Frequency is the number of 'oscillations' or 'cycles' per unit time (seconds). Frequency is measured in hertz (Hz). For the frequency of heartbeats, it is convenient to talk in terms of heartbeats per minute.

> Time period is the time taken for one oscillation. You can calculate the frequency in hertz from the time period using the equation:

$$\text{frequency (hertz, Hz)} = \frac{1}{\text{time period (second, s)}}$$

or

$$f = \frac{1}{T}$$

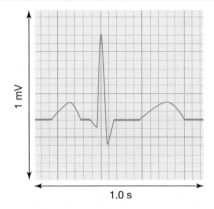

FIGURE 3: An ECG of a single heartbeat of a healthy patient. Identify the time period.

1.0 s

Did you know?

The heart rate of a hummingbird in flight is 1200 beats per minute.

QUESTIONS

1 Explain what is meant by an ECG.

2 Use the ECG below to determine the time period in seconds, frequency in hertz and heartbeats per minute.

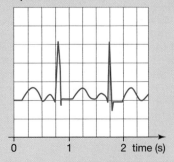

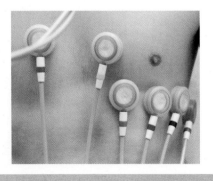

FIGURE 2: Electrodes being fitted in readiness for an ECG test. Why are the electrodes placed on the chest?

Heart action

The heart is a double pump. It has four chambers – the right and left atria and the right and left ventricles. The right chambers take blood from the body, which is low in oxygen, and pass it to the lungs. The left chambers take oxygen-rich blood from the lungs and pass it to the body.

The regular pumping action of the heart is controlled by special muscle cells. These are activated by changes in electrical potentials known as **action potentials** of the heart. Action potentials contract the heart muscles. Figure 4 shows how the various muscles of the heart are activated by the action potential.

On the ECG:

> 'P wave' is when the atria contract

> 'QRS complex' is when the ventricles contract

> 'T wave' is when the ventricles relax.

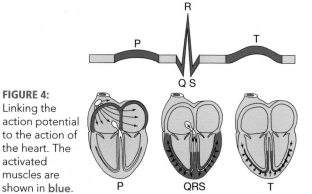

FIGURE 4: Linking the action potential to the action of the heart. The activated muscles are shown in **blue**.

FIGURE 5: Structure of the heart.

QUESTIONS

3 Explain what is meant by the term 'action potentials'.

4 Sequence the action of the heart during a single heartbeat.

Normal and abnormal ECGs

The time period for an ECG cycle depends on the demand on the body. The time period is shorter and the heartbeat frequency greater during strenuous physical activities. The shape of the ECG trace is also affected by the intake of stimulants such as caffeine or other drugs. The shape of the ECG can also be used to diagnose heart problems (see Figure 6).

Doctors can usually prescribe drugs to regulate heartbeats. In severe cases, however, the only option is to implant a **pacemaker**. Pacemakers can be quite small and run on batteries for as long as 15 years.

QUESTIONS

5 Use the ECG below to diagnose the likely heart problem and suggest a possible solution for the patient.

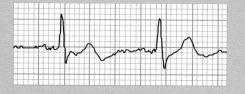

normal heartbeat

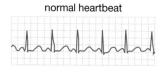

fast heartbeat (tachycardia)

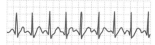

slow heartbeat (bradycardia)

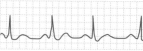

irregular heartbeat (arrhythmia)

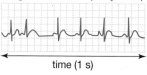

time (1 s)

FIGURE 6: You can identify heart (cardiac) problems by examining ECGs.

Pulse oximetry

You will find out:
> about the use of pulse oximetry
> about the principles of pulse oximetry

Surviving in cold water

Have you ever tried submerging your face in a bucket of icy water? If so, you will have experienced the 'dive reflex'. This is a reflex action common to most mammals, including humans, which causes your heart rate to slow down dramatically. With a slower heart rate, you would use up less oxygen. A pulse oximeter can be used to verify this.

FIGURE 1: Why does the diver's heart rate slow down on entering the water?

Pulse oximetry

Normal pulse rate

> The average resting heartbeat rate for an adult is between 60 and 100 beats per minute. World-class athletes can have heartbeat rates between 40 and 60 beats per minute.

> The maximum pulse rate is 220 minus your age in years. The target for a healthy pulse rate during or just after exercise is 60–80% of this value.

Pulse oximeters

A **pulse oximeter** is worn on the finger or earlobe. A pulse oximeter measures:

> the pulse rate in beats per minute

> the amount of oxygen in the patient's blood.

Pulse oximeters are now routinely used in the following situations:

> in intensive care

> during anaesthesia

> to investigate sleep disorders.

Pulse oximeters can be quite small and portable. These are ideal for overnight sleep screening and making measurements when walking. Figure 2 shows a tiny pulse oximeter being used on a newborn baby.

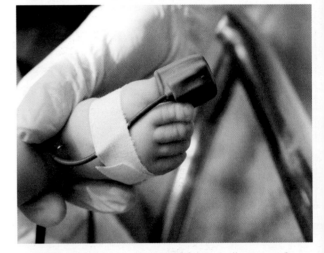

FIGURE 2: What is the advantage of this small oximeter?

QUESTIONS

1 State two things monitored by a pulse oximeter.

2 Calculate the maximum pulse rate for a 15 year old.

How does pulse oximetry work?

Haemoglobin is a protein molecule in the red blood cells that carries oxygen from the lungs to the body's tissues.

The absorption of visible light by haemoglobin varies with the amount of oxygen it is carrying.

A bright light-emitting diode (LED) sends light though the patient's finger. The light transmitted through the finger is picked up by a light detector (see Figure 3).

The difference between the incident and transmitted intensity of light can be used to determine the percentage of haemoglobin that is saturated with oxygen.

Oximeters are calibrated accurately and reliably in the range of oxygen saturations of 70–100%. Under normal conditions, blood is 97% saturated.

How does a pulse oximeter work?   Uses of pulse oximeters

Some oximeters produce an audible signal for each pulse beat. The pitch of the signal falls with reducing values of saturation.

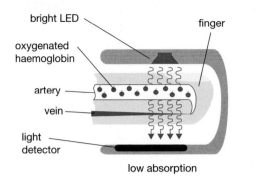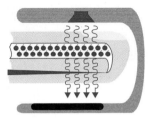

FIGURE 3: A finger in a pulse oximeter. The artery carries blood from the heart to the finger and the vein carries the blood back towards the heart.

QUESTIONS

3 In Figure 3, explain why the absorption of light is greater for the finger on the right-hand side.

4 Explain why a pulse oximeter is more helpful than frequent monitoring of a patient's pulse rate by a nurse.

5 Suggest why a pulse oximeter is usually attached to a fingertip or earlobe.

More about pulse oximeters

The haemoglobin molecules in our blood carry oxygen around the body. There are two different forms of the haemoglobin molecule – oxidised haemoglobin (HbO_2) and reduced haemoglobin (Hb). The absorption of electromagnetic radiation depends on the degree of oxygenation. Figure 4 shows the variation of the absorption of the electromagnetic radiation with wavelength for HbO_2 and Hb molecules.

An oximeter has two LEDs, one emitting visible red light of wavelength 650 nm and the other emitting **infrared radiation** of wavelength 950 nm.

> For 100% oxygen saturated blood, visible light is not absorbed as much as infrared radiation.

> For 0% oxygen saturated blood, visible light is absorbed much more than infrared radiation.

The detector of an oximeter is connected to a computer. The computer can determine the oxygen saturation of blood from the amount of electromagnetic radiation absorbed at 650 nm and 950 nm.

QUESTIONS

6 Use Figure 4 to describe how the ratio of absorption of electromagnetic radiation at 650–950 nm depends on the percentage of oxygenated haemoglobin.

7 Explain why pulse oximeters cannot use radiation of wavelength 800 nm.

Remember!
650 nm means 650 nanometres;
1 nm = 10^{-9} m.

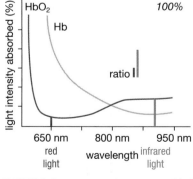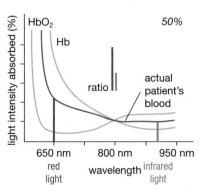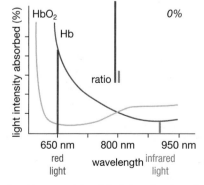

FIGURE 4: Percentage absorption of light intensity against wavelength graphs for oxidised haemoglobin (HbO_2) and reduced haemoglobin (Hb).

Preparing for assessment: Applying your knowledge

To achieve a good grade in science, you not only have to know and understand scientific ideas, but you also need to be able to apply them to other situations. This task will support you in developing these skills.

✳ The mystery of the silver spoon

It had been a terrible day for Poppy's Gran. First, Spike the dog started to act very strangely. Spike just lay in his basket groaning and wouldn't get up for anything, not even his favourite treat. Then Gran couldn't find her precious silver-christening spoon that she kept displayed on the sideboard next to Spike's treats.

Poppy and her dad came over to Gran's house and helped her to wrap Spike in a blanket. Then they carried him to the car and drove to the vet. The vet noticed that Spike's tummy was very swollen and tender to the touch, so she quickly arranged for an X-ray. The X-ray clearly showed a spoon-shaped object in Spike's stomach.

Spike had an emergency operation to remove the spoon and it wasn't long before he was home again with his appetite fully restored. Now though, Gran makes sure that she keeps the spoon and Spike's treats safely locked away.

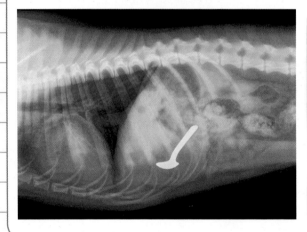

✳ Task 1

Examine the X-ray photograph closely.

> Suggest why the spoon stands out so clearly.

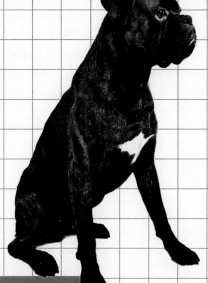

 ## Task 2

The electrons in an X-ray machine are produced by thermionic emission.

> Explain thermionic emission.

 ## Task 3

The vet could have used other diagnostic tools to investigate Spike's condition.

> Name another diagnostic tool.

> State whether or not you think it would have been a better choice and explain your reasons.

 ## Task 4

Higher tier only: The magnitude of the charge e on a single electron is 1.6×10^{-19} C. Estimate the number of electrons hitting the anode per second in the X-ray machine, if the machine has a beam current of 50 mA. (1 mA = 10^{-3} A.)

 ## Task 5

Higher tier only: The operating voltage of the X-ray machine is changed from 100 kV to 25 kV. Explain what would happen to the kinetic energy of an accelerated electron and the final speed of each electron before it hits the positive anode.

 ## Maximise your grade

These sentences show what you need to be including in your work. Use these to improve your work and to be successful.

For grade G–E, your answers should show that you can:
> relate the ionisation by X-rays to their frequency and energy
> describe thermionic emission as the emission release of electrons from the surface of a hot metal
> identify tools used to diagnose medical conditions.

For grade D–C, in addition show that you can:
> relate the absorption of X-rays to the thickness of the material
> describe current as the rate of flow of charge.

For grades B–A, in addition show that you can:
> calculate the number of electrons per second
> calculate the kinetic energy of accelerated electrons.

P3 checklist (Topics 1–2)

To achieve your forecast grade in the exam you'll need to revise

Use this checklist to see what you can do now. Refer back to pages 160–79 if you're not sure.

Look across the rows to see how you could progress – *bold italic* means Higher tier only.

Remember you'll need to be able to use these ideas in various ways, such as:
> interpreting pictures, diagrams and graphs
> applying ideas to new situations
> explaining ethical implications
> suggesting some benefits and risks to society
> drawing conclusions from evidence you've been given.

Look at pages 230–52 for more information about exams and how you'll be assessed.

This checklist accompanies the exam-style questions and the worked examples. The content suggestions for specific grades are suggestions only and may not be replicated in your real examination. Remember, the checklists do not represent the complete content for any topic. Refer to the Specification for complete content details on any topic and any further information.

To aim for a grade E	To aim for a grade C	To aim for a grade A
define 'radiation' as any form of energy originating from a source, including waves and particles	describe how intensity of radiation will decrease with distance from source and according to the nature of the medium through which it travels	*use the equation:* *intensity =* $$\frac{\textit{power of incident radiation}}{\textit{area}}$$ $$\left(I = \frac{P}{A}\right)$$
describe the refraction of light by converging and diverging lenses	explain how the power of a lens is related to its shape use the equation: power (dioptre) = $\dfrac{1}{\text{focal length (m)}}$	*use the lens equation:* $$\frac{1}{f} = \frac{1}{v} + \frac{1}{u}$$ *use the positive sign convention*
identify the cornea, iris, pupil, lens, retina and ciliary muscles in a diagram of the eye	describe how light is focused on the retina by the action of the lens and the cornea	
state that for an average adult eye the near point is about 25 cm and the far point is at infinity explain the symptoms of short sight and long sight compare and contrast the treatment of short sight and long sight using simple lenses and contact lenses		evaluate the treatment of short sight and long sight using *laser surgery*

To aim for a grade E   To aim for a grade C   To aim for a grade A

use ray diagrams to explain reflection, refraction and total internal reflection

explain refraction in terms of change of speed of radiation

explain how TIR is used in optical fibres

explain the uses of optical fibres in endoscopes

calculate the critical angle using Snell's law

---

describe the uses of ultrasound in medical diagnosis

explain uses of ultrasound in medical treatments

---

understand the link between ionisation by X-rays and the frequency of X-rays

explain the operation of an X-ray tube, including thermionic emission and collision of electrons with a metal target

use the equation:
current = number of particles per second ×
charge on each particle or
(I = Nq)
in relation to X-rays

use the equation:
KE = ½ mv² = e × V
to find the kinetic energy of electrons arriving at the anode in an X-ray

---

understand the link between the absorption of X-rays and the thickness of the material that they pass through

describe how X-rays are used in CAT scans and fluoroscopy

describe the inverse square law for electromagnetic radiation

compare the risks and advantages of using X-rays for treatment and diagnosis

---

describe how an ECG is used

identify the shape of an ECG of a healthy person

explain how action potentials can be measured using an ECG to monitor heart action

use the equation: frequency
$= \dfrac{1}{\text{time period}}$ or $\left(f = \dfrac{1}{T}\right)$
to calculate the frequency of a heartbeat

interpret the shape of an ECG of normal and abnormal heart action

explain why pacemakers are used

---

recall the uses of pulse oximetry

describe how pulse oximetry works in principle

1 a The diagram shows two types of lens, X and Y.

AO1 **i** Which one of the following statements is correct?

A ☐ X and Y are both converging lenses

B ☐ X and Y are both diverging lenses

C ☐ X is a converging lens and Y is a diverging lens

D ☐ X is a diverging lens and Y is a converging lens [1]

AO1 **ii** If lens X is made thicker in the middle, its focal length will

A ☐ increase

B ☐ decrease

C ☐ not change

D ☐ become negative [1]

b This is a scaled diagram showing the path of rays through the lens X.

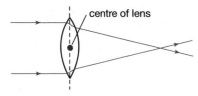

AO2 **i** Use the diagram to measure the focal length of the lens from the centre of the lens.

Give your answer in metres. [1]

AO2 **ii** Use your answer to **bi** to calculate the power of the lens. State the unit. [3]

AO2 **iii** Explain why each ray of light bends at the two surfaces of the lens. [2]

[Total: 8]

2 This diagram shows the eye.

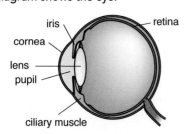

AO1 **a** Name the part of the eye that can change its focal length. [1]

AO1 **b** The image formed on the retina is always

A ☐ upright

B ☐ inverted

C ☐ magnified

D ☐ virtual [1]

AO2 **c** State the near point for the average human eye. [1]

AO2 **d** Peter is short sighted.

i Explain what is meant by 'short sighted'. [1]

ii An eye specialist suggests that Peter should have laser correction. Explain how this surgical procedure will improve Peter's vision. [2]

[Total: 6]

3 a The diagram shows a simple X-ray tube.

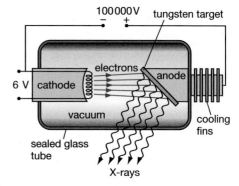

AO1 **i** Suggest why the glass tube has a vacuum. [1]

AO2 **ii** Suggest why the X-ray tube is always surrounded by lead casing. [1]

AO2 **iii** Use the diagram to explain how X-rays are produced. [6]

AO2 **b** In a hospital X-ray department, radiographers always stand far away from the X-ray tube when it is being used. Explain why they do this. [3]

[Total: 11]

AO1 **4 a** Ultrasound and X-rays are both used for diagnosis in hospitals. Describe one difference between X-rays and ultrasound. [1]

AO3 **b** Evaluate the effectiveness of using X-rays in diagnosis and treatment of cancer. [6]

[Total: 7]

Summary of Assessment Objectives

AO1 recall the science   AO2 apply your knowledge   AO3 evaluate and analyse the evidence

Worked example

AO1 **a** State two properties of X-rays. [2]

X-rays are electromagnetic waves. ✔

They can travel through a vacuum. ✔

AO2 **b** The photo shows an X-ray image of Billy's teeth.

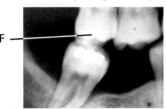

F

The darker regions show where most of the X-rays reach the film.

i Suggest why the region labelled F appears white on the film. [2]

The white bit is most likely a filling. ✔

Fillings are made of metal, which absorbs X-rays quite well. ✔

ii The grey regions on the image show the gums. Explain why the gums appear grey. [1]

The gums also absorb X-rays, so they appear a different shade. ✘

AO2 **c** In the treatment of cancer, doctors can use high-intensity X-rays from special particle accelerators called linacs. The beam of X-rays can be rotated around the patient.

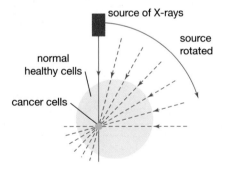

source of X-rays

source rotated

normal healthy cells

cancer cells

Discuss the advantages of using intense X-ray beams to destroy cancer. [3]

The X-rays are powerful and treat the cancer. ✘

X-rays are easy to produce. ✘

[Total: 8]

This candidate scored 4 marks out of a possible 8. The candidate was rushing and should have spent a little more time analysing the information given in the question, especially in **c**.

How to raise your grade

Take note of the comments from examiners – these will help you to improve your grade.

> This is a great start from the candidate who has demonstrated an excellent understanding of X-rays.

> This answer is well structured and the examiner has awarded full marks.

> The gums absorbs *some* of X-rays but not as much as the metallic filing and this is why the image is grey. The candidate's answer lacks detail.

> The first sentence does not provide anything new; it repeats the information given in the question. The candidate could have scored the marks by stating the following:
>
> > The beam is rotated so that fewer healthy cells are destroyed and the cancer is targeted.
>
> > The X-ray beam can be switched on and off.
>
> > The intensity of the X-ray beam can also be controlled.

1 a The diagram shows what happens to light entering a patient's eye.

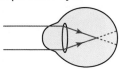

AO2 i The patient

A ☐ has normal vision

B ☐ is short-sighted

C ☐ is long-sighted

D ☐ has a missing eye lens [1]

AO2 ii What type of lens would correct the patient's vision? [1]

b An optician prescribes Ken a lens for his left eye of power −1.50 D.

AO2 i What type of lens is the optician prescribing? [1]

AO2 ii Calculate the focal length of the lens. State the unit. [3]

AO3 iii Evaluate the advantages and disadvantages of Ken correcting his sight with spectacles, contact lenses or laser correction. [6]

[Total: 12]

2 a The diagram shows a ray of light passing through a transparent block.

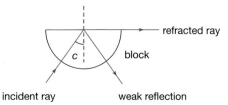

AO1 i What is the name given to the angle *c*? [1]

AO1 ii Describe what happens to the speed of light as the ray leaves the block. [1]

AO2 iii Calculate the critical angle for a glass block that has a reflective index of 1.38. [3]

b A lamp is placed 0.25 m away from a converging lens. The lens has a focal length of 0.15 m.

AO2 i Calculate the distance (in metres) of the image from the lens. [3]

AO2 ii Describe one property of the image. [1]

[Total: 8]

3 The diagram shows a typical X-ray tube.

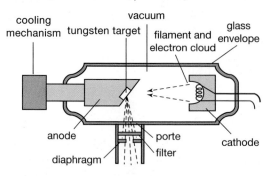

The electrons are accelerated between the filament and the anode. The potential difference between the anode and the filament is 100 000 V. The charge on an electron is −1.6 × 10⁻¹⁹ C.

AO2 a Calculate the kinetic energy of a single electron reaching the anode. State the unit. [3]

AO2 b Without doing any calculations, explain what happens to the speed of the electrons when the potential difference is doubled. [2]

AO2 c The current in the X-ray tube is 0.0015 A. Calculate the number of electrons reaching the anode per second. [3]

[Total: 8]

4 The photo shows a CAT scanner.

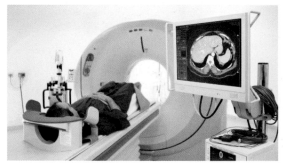

AO1 a What type of radiation is used to produce a CAT scan? [1]

AO1 b Describe how a CAT scan is produced. [3]

AO3 c X-ray machines in hospitals should not be entirely replaced by CAT scanners.

Evaluate this statement. [6]

[Total: 10]

Summary of Assessment Objectives

| AO1 recall the science | AO2 apply your knowledge | AO3 evaluate and analyse the evidence |

Worked example

AO2 **a** Lasers are very dangerous because of their intensity. A particular laser of power 6.0 mW produces a beam of cross-sectional area 2.5×10^{-6} m². Calculate the intensity of the laser beam. State the unit. [3]

intensity = power/cross-sectional area

intensity = 6.0/2.5 × 10⁻⁶ ✗

intensity = 2.4 × 10⁶ W/m² ✔ ✔

b A scientist places a gamma source on a table in her laboratory. She uses a meter to measure the intensity of the radiation at different distances from the source. The table below shows the variation of the intensity with distance x from the source.

x (m)	0.5	1.0	2.0	3.0
intensity (arbitrary units)	900	225	56	?

AO3 **i** Describe how the intensity of the gamma radiation depends on the distance x. [1]

The power of the source is spread over a larger sphere, therefore

the intensity decreases. The table shows this too. ✔

AO3 **ii** The scientist suggests that the intensity is inversely proportional to the square of the distance.

Analyse the information given in the table to show that the statement is true.

Predict the intensity at a distance of 3.0 m from the source. [4]

Doubling the distance should decrease the intensity by a factor

of 4. ✔

When the distance is doubled from 1 m to 2 m, the intensity

changes from 225 to 56 (which is a decrease by a factor of 4

because 225/56 is 4.02). ✔

[Total: 8]

How to raise your grade

Take note of the comments from examiners – these will help you to improve your grade.

> This candidate forgot to convert the power into watts. The examiner deducted 1 mark for this error and then applied the error-carried-forward rule for their subsequent work.

> This candidate's answer is comprehensive and worthy of the mark.

> The candidate has shown excellent powers of analysis by correctly doing detailed calculations to justify the relationship between intensity and distance. Sadly, the candidate has not attempted the final part of the question. The intensity at 3.0 m is 25; this would have given the candidate 2 further marks.

> This candidate scored 5 marks out of a possible 8. Not answering the final part of **bii** has cost the candidates 2 marks; this would have guaranteed a high grade.

P3 Applications of physics (Topics 3–5)

What you should know

Radiation and radioactive sources

An atom consists of protons, neutrons and electrons (P2 – Topic 1).

All isotopes of an element have the same number of protons but different numbers of neutrons (P2 – Topic 5).

Unstable nuclei are radioactive and emit ionising radiations (P2 – Topic 5).

Higher frequency electromagnetic waves carry more energy and are more dangerous (P1 – Topic 2).

Gamma rays mutate and damage cells in the body. Scientists have learnt how to take precautions when handling radioactive sources to minimise the risk of harm (P1 – Topic 2).

Ionising radiations (including alpha and beta particles and gamma rays) transfer energy (P1 – Topic 2).

 How many protons and how many neutrons are there in the nucleus of a $^{14}_{6}$C atom?

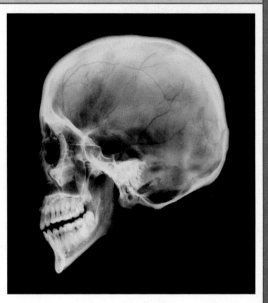

Particles in motion

The motion of an object depends on the resultant force acting on it (P2 – Topic 3)

Momentum is a vector quantity and is given by the equation: momentum = mass × velocity (P2 – Topic 4).

In all collisions, momentum is conserved (P2 – Topic 4).

Half-life is the average time taken for half of the active nuclei to decay (P2 – Topic 6).

 State the principle of conservation of momentum.

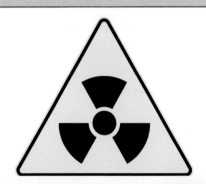

Gases and temperature

The particles in a gas are held together by weak forces and are spread out.

Heat is a form of energy.

Temperature can be measured using a thermometer.

 Give two examples of heat energy.

You will find out about

> the ethics of using radioactive techniques in medicine

> the precautions that must be taken when working with radiation

> the properties of alpha, beta, gamma, positron and neutron radiations

> beta-plus and beta-minus decay of radioactive isotopes

> nuclear decay equations

> the N–Z curve for stable isotopes

> the reasons for beta-minus, beta-plus and alpha decays

> the quark model of nucleons

> the dangers of ionising radiations on the human body

> the treatment of tumours using external and internal radiations

> PET scanners

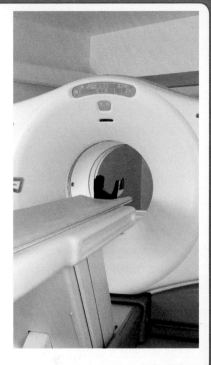

> why the scientific community collaborates to build and operate particle accelerators

> the motion of charged particles in magnetic fields

> the production of medical tracers

> particle accelerators called cyclotrons

> momentum and its conservation

> elastic and inelastic collisions

> electron–positron annihilation and PET scanners

> Einstein's famous equation: $E = mc^2$

> the three states of matter

> the kinetic theory of matter

> the celsius and kelvin temperature scales

> the importance of absolute zero

> the gas equations: $V_1 = \dfrac{V_2 T_1}{T_2}$, $V_1 P_1 = V_2 P_2$ and $\dfrac{P_1 V_1}{T_1} = \dfrac{P_2 V_2}{T_2}$

> bottled gases used in medicine

Ionising radiations

You will find out:

> about the structure of the atom

> about the properties of alpha, beta, gamma, positron and neutron radiations

> about safety of patients and medical personnel in hospitals

Helping society

The patient shown in Figure 1 is being treated for cancer. The equipment shown contains radioactive cobalt-60 which emits intense gamma radiation. This radiation destroys cancerous cells.

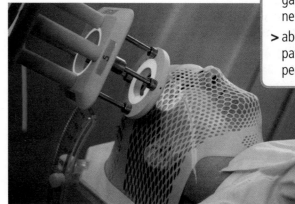

FIGURE 1: A radiotherapy patient being treated for brain cancer.

The nuclear atom

All matter is made up of atoms. Figure 2 shows a diagram of an atom.

> The atom contains a tiny positively charged nucleus.

> The nucleus is surrounded by negatively charged **electrons**.

> The nucleus contains **protons** and **neutrons**; these particles are collectively known as **nucleons**.

> A proton has a positive charge and a neutron has no charge.

> The nucleus of an atom is represented as: $^{A}_{Z}X$, where X is the chemical symbol for the element; Z is the total number of protons inside the nucleus, the **atomic (proton) number**; and A is the total number of neutrons and protons within the nucleus – the **mass (nucleon) number**.

> The **isotopes** of an element are nuclei that have the same number of protons but different numbers of neutrons.

> An **ion** is any atom that has lost or gained electrons.

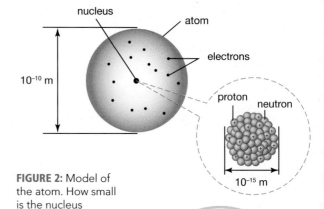

10^{-10} m

nucleus

atom

electrons

proton

neutron

10^{-15} m

FIGURE 2: Model of the atom. How small is the nucleus compared with the size of the atom?

Remember!

A neutral atom has an equal number of protons and electrons.

TABLE 1: A summary of the masses and charges of the particles of the atom.

	Neutron	Proton	Electron
Charge relative to the proton	0	1	−1
Mass relative to the proton	1	1	0.00055

QUESTIONS

1 State two particles found inside the nucleus of an atom.

2 One of the isotopes of oxygen is $^{14}_{8}O$. Work out the number of protons, neutrons and electrons for a neutral oxygen-14 atom.

Nuclear radiations

Many nuclei of atoms are stable but some are unstable. Unstable nuclei emit particles or electromagnetic radiation – referred to as nuclear radiations. Nuclear radiations can ionise the atoms of the material through which they travel. The three main types of ionising radiation are:

> alpha (α) particles
> beta (β) particles (also known as beta-minus or β⁻)
> gamma (γ) radiation.

Some heavier isotopes (e.g. plutonium-240) spontaneously emit neutrons.

Neutrons can also cause ionisation; they are particularly harmful to biological tissues.

Some lighter isotopes (e.g. carbon-10) emit **positrons**. Emission of positrons is also known as beta-plus (β⁺) radiation. A positron has the same mass as an electron but with a positive charge of 1.6×10^{-19} C. A positron is the *anti-particle* of an electron.

QUESTIONS

3 Arrange the radiations in order, from most harmful to least harmful.

4 Explain why alpha particles have a short range in air.

5 Which type of radiations will affect the charge of the nucleus?

Table 2 summarises the main properties of all the nuclear radiations.

TABLE 2: A summary of the main properties of the nuclear radiations.

Radiation	Properties
Alpha	Helium nucleus; ^4_2He Charge = $+2e$ ($e = 1.6 \times 10^{-19}$ C) Strongly ionising Stopped by paper, or skin, or about 6 cm of air
Beta (Beta-minus)	Electron; $^0_{-1}\text{e}$ Charge = $-e$ Weakly ionising Stopped by a few millimetres of aluminium
Gamma	Short wavelength electromagnetic waves Charge = 0 Very weakly ionising Significantly absorbed by thick lead or concrete
Neutron	^1_0n Charge = 0 Does not interact much with matter
Beta-plus	Positron; $^0_{+1}\text{e}$ Charge = $+e$ A positron interacts strongly with an electron to produce gamma rays

Social and ethical issues

Radioactive sources are used in the treatment and diagnosis of cancer. Because ionising radiation can potentially damage all living cells, patients are given the smallest dose possible. Radiographers and other medical personnel need to be protected from exposure to radiation. They often wear lead aprons and use radiation badges (dosimeters) to monitor the level of radiation exposure.

Modern medical techniques allow doctors to prolong life. This raises some social and ethical questions:

> Some cancer treatments are very *painful*. Should they be carried out even though there is currently no cure for cancer?

> Some treatments are very *expensive*. Should they be offered to patients to ease suffering even though there is no possibility of a cure?

QUESTIONS

6 Why do some radiologists wear aprons lined with lead, rather than cloth or plastic aprons?

7 Discuss whether it is ethical to treat a 70-year-old cancer patient with radiation.

FIGURE 3: This radiation worker has a radiation detector (dosimeter) under his gloves.

Radioactive decays

You will find out:
> about changes to the nucleus following radioactive decay
> about balancing nuclear decay equations

Using positrons

Some unstable nuclei emit positrons. A positron is an antimatter particle that is emitted from within the nucleus of the atom. Positrons do not survive long around ordinary matter. They quickly grab hold of electrons and completely annihilate themselves. The annihilation process produces gamma rays. These gamma rays are used in PET (positron emission tomography) scanners to produce extraordinary scans of the brain.

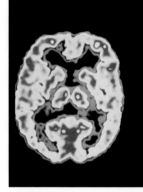
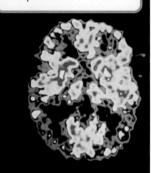

FIGURE 1: PET scans of a normal brain (left) and a patient with Alzheimer's disease (right). How can scans like this be useful in medical diagnosis?

Alpha decay

The unstable nuclei of heavier atoms often emit alpha particles. The isotopes below are all alpha-emitters:

$^{210}_{84}Po \quad ^{215}_{85}At \quad ^{220}_{86}Rn \quad ^{221}_{87}Fr \quad ^{226}_{88}Ra \quad ^{227}_{89}Ac \quad ^{230}_{90}Th$
$^{231}_{91}Pa \quad ^{238}_{92}U \quad ^{237}_{93}Np$

> An alpha particle has two protons and two neutrons.

> This means that the nucleus left behind, also known as the daughter nucleus, has its atomic (proton) number reduced by 2 and its mass (nucleon) number reduced by 4: $Z \rightarrow Z - 2$ and $A \rightarrow A - 4$.

> The original nucleus has changed or transmuted to another element.

QUESTIONS

1 Explain why a nucleus emitting an alpha particle changes into a different element.

2 A smoke alarm has an alpha source of americium-241 ($^{241}_{95}Am$). Use a periodic table to determine the daughter nucleus of americium-241.

3 Determine the daughter nucleus of the isotope $^{226}_{88}Ra$.

Worked example

An isotope of uranium-238 ($^{238}_{92}U$) is an alpha emitter. It has 92 protons and 238 nucleons.

The atomic number Z of the daughter will be 90 with a mass number A of 234.

According to the periodic table, the element with an atomic number of 90 is thorium.

Therefore the daughter nucleus is $^{234}_{90}Th$.

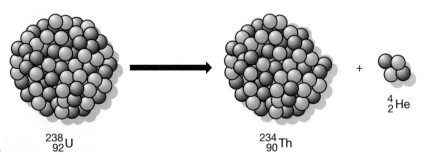

$^{238}_{92}U$ → $^{234}_{90}Th$ + $^{4}_{2}He$

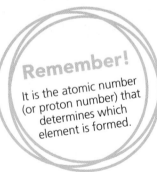

Remember!
It is the atomic number (or proton number) that determines which element is formed.

FIGURE 2: The decay of a uranium-238 nucleus. Why does the daughter nucleus change to a different element?

Q Alpha decay   Beta-minus decay   Beta-plus decay

Beta-minus (β⁻) and gamma (γ) decays

Some nuclei with an atomic number less than about 82 are unstable and are beta-minus emitters:

> A source emitting beta-minus radiation emits electrons.

> An electron removes a charge of –1 from the nucleus.

> In **β⁻ decay**, a neutron inside the 'parent' nucleus changes into a proton and an electron. The electron is emitted as a beta-minus particle and the proton stays within the nucleus.

> The atomic number of the daughter nucleus increases by +1. The mass number remains the same: $Z \rightarrow Z + 1$ and $A \rightarrow A$.

> The original nucleus transmutes into another element.

Gamma rays are often emitted from nuclei after beta or alpha emission. Gamma rays remove surplus energy from the nuclei. Gamma rays have no charge; hence they do not change the nature of the nucleus. Gamma rays are emitted because the nucleus undergoes rearrangement to get to a lower energy state.

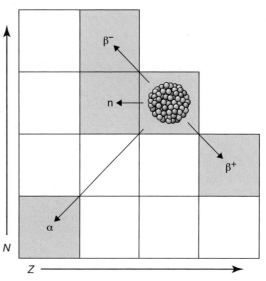

FIGURE 3: Changes that take place in the atomic number Z and neutron number N when a nucleus decays.

QUESTIONS

4 Cobalt-60 is an intense gamma emitter. Explain whether or not there are changes within this isotope when it emits gamma radiation.

5 Iodine-131 ($^{131}_{53}\text{I}$) is a useful medical tracer. It emits beta-minus radiation. Use a periodic table to determine the daughter nucleus of an iodine-131 nucleus.

Beta-plus (β⁺) and nuclear decay equations (Higher tier only)

Some 'proton-rich' nuclei decay by emitting positrons:

> A positron removes a charge of +1 from the nucleus.

> In **β⁺ decay**, a proton within the parent nucleus changes into a neutron and a positron.

> The atomic number of the daughter nucleus decreases by 1. The mass number remains the same: $Z \rightarrow Z - 1$ and $A \rightarrow A$.

> The original nucleus transmutes into another element.

In all nuclear decays, the mass (nucleon) numbers and atomic (proton) numbers are conserved. You can test these rules on the three nuclear decay equations below for alpha, beta-minus and beta-plus decays:

> Alpha-decay: $^{238}_{92}\text{U} \rightarrow {}^{234}_{90}\text{Th} + {}^{4}_{2}\text{He}$

> Beta-minus decay: $^{14}_{6}\text{C} \rightarrow {}^{14}_{7}\text{N} + {}^{0}_{-1}\text{e}$

> Beta-plus decay: $^{15}_{8}\text{O} \rightarrow {}^{15}_{7}\text{N} + {}^{0}_{+1}\text{e}$

Did you know?

Carl Anderson, who discovered the positron, was only 31 when he received the Nobel Prize.

QUESTIONS

6 Complete all the nuclear decays below:

a $^{6}_{2}\text{He} \rightarrow {}^{?}_{?}\text{Li} + {}^{0}_{-1}\text{e}$

b $^{?}_{?}\text{Ne} \rightarrow {}^{19}_{9}\text{F} + {}^{0}_{+1}\text{e}$

c $^{240}_{94}\text{Pu} \rightarrow {}^{?}_{?}? + {}^{236}_{92}\text{U}$

d $^{235}_{92}? \rightarrow {}^{?}_{?}? + {}^{4}_{2}\text{He}$

Stability of nuclei

You will find out:

> about the N–Z curve for stable and unstable isotopes

> why alpha, beta-minus and beta-plus decays occur

What is the heaviest element?

The heaviest naturally occurring element is uranium. The heaviest artificially created element is ununoctium. It was created by scientists at the Joint Institute for Nuclear Research (JINR) in Dubna, Russia. Ununoctium is considered to a noble gas. The isotope ununoctium-294 is radioactive and decays by alpha emission with a half-life of about 0.84 ms.

FIGURE 1: Particle accelerator used to create new elements.

N–Z curve of stable and unstable nuclei (Higher tier only)

Figure 2 shows a graph of the number of neutrons against the number of protons of all known stable and unstable nuclei.

> The stable nuclei lie on a gentle curve starting from the origin and increasing in gradient. This curve, shown in black, is known as the **stability curve**.

> Only stable nuclei with atomic numbers less than about 20 have an equal number of protons and neutrons.

> The vast majority of stable nuclei have more neutrons than protons.

> The protons within the nuclei of all atoms repel each other. The reason the protons do not fly apart is because the protons and neutrons exert a very strong attractive force known as the **strong nuclear force**.

> Unstable nuclei *above* the stability curve are known as 'neutron-rich' and *below* the stability curve are known as 'neutron-poor'.

QUESTIONS

1 The only stable isotope of aluminium is $^{27}_{13}$Al. Explain whether $^{29}_{13}$Al is a neutron-rich or a neutron-poor isotope.

2 According to a student, all stable isotopes have an equal number of protons and neutrons. Explain whether or not this is true.

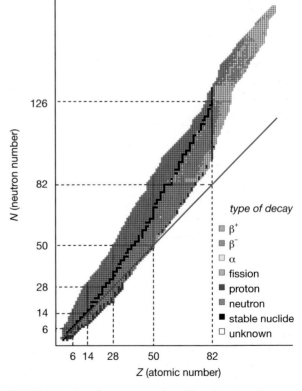

FIGURE 2: A plot of neutron number N against atomic number Z for all stable and unstable isotopes.

Is it alpha, beta-minus or beta-plus decay? (Higher tier only)

Beta-minus decay

> An isotope above the stability curve has too many neutrons to be stable (neutron-rich) and it decays by emitting an electron; this is β^- decay.

> The atomic number of the daughter nucleus increases by 1 and the neutron number decreases by 1. This brings the nucleus closer to the stability line.

> In beta-minus decay, a single neutron inside the unstable nucleus changes into a proton and an electron: neutron → proton + electron.

> Example: $^{23}_{10}\text{Ne} \rightarrow {}^{23}_{11}\text{Na} + {}^{0}_{-1}\text{e}$.

Beta-plus decay

> An isotope below the stability curve has too many protons to be stable (neutron-poor) and it decays by emitting a positron; this is β^+ decay.

> The atomic number of the daughter nucleus decreases by 1 and the neutron number increases by 1. This decay also brings the nucleus closer to the stability line.

> In beta-plus decay, a single proton within the unstable nucleus changes into a neutron and a positron: proton → neutron + positron.

> Example: $^{19}_{10}\text{Ne} \rightarrow {}^{19}_{9}\text{F} + {}^{0}_{+1}\text{e}$.

FIGURE 3: Positrons are antimatter particles. When a positron and an electron meet, they destroy each other and create two bursts of gamma rays.

Alpha decay

> Only nuclei with high atomic numbers (Z above 82) decay by emitting alpha particles.

> There is very little effect on the position of a nucleus relative to the stability curve. This is because the loss of an alpha particle (2 neutrons and 2 protons) does not change the N:Z ratio much.

TABLE 1: How some carbon isotopes decay.

Isotope	$^{10}_{6}\text{C}$	$^{11}_{6}\text{C}$	$^{12}_{6}\text{C}$	$^{13}_{6}\text{C}$	$^{14}_{6}\text{C}$	$^{15}_{6}\text{C}$
How it decays	β^+	β^+	Stable	Stable	β^-	β^-
	Neutron-poor				Neutron-rich	

QUESTIONS

3 Use the periodic table and Table 1 to write the nuclear decay equations for the $^{10}_{6}\text{C}$ and $^{15}_{6}\text{C}$ isotopes.

4 What is formed when radium-226 undergoes alpha decay?

5 Uranium-235 is formed by alpha decay of an unstable isotope. What is this parent isotope?

Neutrinos and beta decays (Higher tier only)

During beta-plus decay, a nucleus also emits a particle known as a **neutrino**. A neutrino has no charge and is one billionth of the mass of a proton. Neutrinos interact weakly with matter and hence are difficult to detect. The existence of the neutrino was predicted by Wolfgang Pauli in 1930 but it was only discovered 26 years later. The Universe is believed to be saturated with these elusive particles. Each second, about 100 million million neutrinos go through your body!

FIGURE 4: These neutrino detectors are located 1400 metres underground in Abruzzo, Italy, to detect neutrinos coming from our Sun.

QUESTIONS

6 Explain why neutrinos are very difficult to detect.

7 The decay of oxygen is as follows:

$$^{15}_{8}\text{O} \rightarrow {}^{15}_{7}\text{N} + {}^{0}_{+1}\text{e} + \nu$$

(ν is a neutrino)

Describe the changes taking place within the nucleus of oxygen-15.

Quarks

You will find out:
> about quarks
> how quarks change during beta decays

Fundamental particles

In the 1930s, physicists could explain the existence of all matter in terms of just three particles: electrons, protons and neutrons. However, in the 1950s, particle accelerators produced hundreds of new particles. Amazingly, the existence of all massive particles, including the proton and the neutron, can now be explained in terms of fundamental particles called quarks. Quarks are the basic building blocks of all matter.

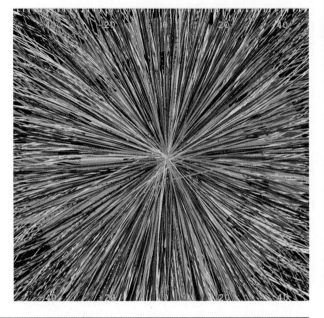

FIGURE 1: Tracks of particles produced at CERN when lead ions were smashed into each other. The particles seen here are all made up of quarks.

Quarks (Higher tier only)

The **quark** model was proposed independently by Murray Gell-Mann and George Zweig in 1964. Gell-Mann used the word 'quark' from James Joyce's novel *Finnegans Wake* to name the fundamental particle. Zweig called the particles 'aces' but this did not catch on with particle physicists.

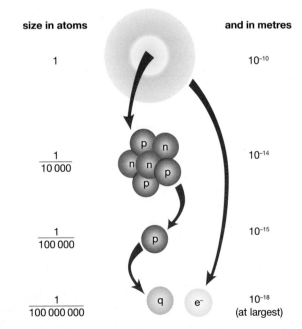

FIGURE 2: When compared to the scale of the atom a quark is a tiny particle.

> All the 'normal' matter around us is made up of two types of quarks – the **up quark** and the **down quark**.

> Experiments and theory suggest that quarks are very difficult to isolate.

> Neutrons and protons are each made up of three up and down quarks.

The total mass of a proton, or a neutron, is equal to the sum of masses of the quarks inside.

> In terms of the elementary charge e (1.6×10^{-19} C), the up quark has a positive charge of $2/3e$ and the down quark has a negative charge of $-1/3e$.

> The mass of a proton or neutron is about 80 times as great as the sum of the masses of the three quarks they each contain. To explain this scientists make use of Einstein's theory of relativity.

QUESTIONS

1 Copy and complete the table below.

Quark	Charge
up (u)	?
?	−1/3

2 Work out the charges on the up and down quarks in coulombs (C).

Fundamental particles (Higher tier only)

A particle is described as being fundamental if it cannot be subdivided into smaller particles. The electron is a fundamental particle, as are quarks:

> A neutron has one up (u) quark and two down (d) quarks.
Neutron = u d d.

> A proton has two up quarks and one down quark.
Proton = u u d.

> Physicists believe that there are six types or 'flavours' of quarks and their corresponding six anti-quarks. The six quarks are: up, down, strange, charm, bottom and top (see Figure 3). For your exams, you just need to know the details of the up and down quarks.

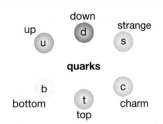

FIGURE 4: The quark model showing all the flavours. You just need to know about the up and down quarks.

FIGURE 3: The arrangement of quarks inside a proton and a neutron.

QUESTIONS

3 Explain why the neutron is not a fundamental particle.

4 Use the data and information given so far on these pages to show that a proton has a charge of +1 and a neutron has no charge.

Quarks and beta decay (Higher tier only)

In beta-minus decay, a neutron inside the nucleus of an atom changes into a proton and an electron. The electron is emitted as the beta-minus particle and the proton stays within the nucleus. This transformation can also be explained in terms of quarks. In beta-minus decay, a down quark changes into an up quark and an electron.

In beta-plus decay, a proton changes into a neutron and a positron. In beta-plus decay, an up quark changes into a down quark and a positron.

A proton inside the nucleus of an atom can decay by releasing a positron. A proton on its own is almost totally stable. However, a neutron on its own can decay to release an electron. The half-life of a free neutron is about 9 minutes.

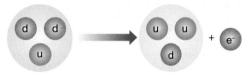

beta-minus decay
(neutron → proton + electron)

beta-plus decay
(proton → neutron + positron)

FIGURE 5: Can you describe the changes taking place within a neutron and a proton in terms of quarks?

QUESTIONS

5 The decay equation for a down (d) quark may be written as: d → u + electron. Write a corresponding decay equation for an up (u) quark.

6 Show that charge in the decay of a down quark shown in question 5 is conserved.

Did you know?

Some physicists believe that free protons decay, with a half-life of 10^{32} years.

Dangers of ionising radiations

Nano to the rescue

Melanin is the natural pigment that gives skin and hair their colour and helps to shield the skin from sunburn. Scientists in the USA carried out tests to find out if melanin could protect cancer patients from the harmful effects of radiation therapy. They found that tiny sand particles (a few nanometres in diameter) coated with melanin pigment seemed to protect the bone marrow from the damaging effects of radiation. The particles had to be so small that they would not get trapped by the lungs, liver or spleen.

FIGURE 1: Can particles 1000 times smaller than the thickness of human hair help the fight against cancer?

Dangers of radiation

Ionising radiations, such as alpha particles, beta particles and gamma rays, can be dangerous:

> Ionising radiations can damage body tissues. The cells in the tissue may mutate, die or fail to reproduce themselves.

> The effects of radiation damage include: skin burns, nausea, destruction of bone marrow, hair loss, changes in genetic material, sterility and cancers.

Precautions

To protect people who work with ionising radiations:

> Keep the distance between workers and the radiation source as large as possible.

> Keep the exposure time to a minimum.

> Use shielding, such lead-lined aprons and concrete walls.

In addition, workers are provided with **dosimeters**. These are usually made up of radiation-sensitive film within a holder worn outside the worker's clothing. The film goes dark on exposure to radiation.

FIGURE 2: How can a badge protect you?

Did you know?

A mutation is a permanent change to the DNA of an organism. Mutations can be harmful, have no effect or sometimes even be helpful.

QUESTIONS

1 State three effects of ionising radiation.

2 Design a leaflet to advise medical staff on how they can protect themselves when treating patients with radiation.

More about the damage to cells

Here are three possible biological *effects* of ionising radiation on cells:

> Cells are damaged; they repair the damage and then operate normally.

> Cells are damaged; they repair the damage but then function abnormally. These altered cells may be unable to reproduce themselves or may reproduce at an uncontrolled rate. Such cells can be the main cause of cancers.

> Cells die as a result of the damage.

The *amount* of damage caused to the cells depends on:

> the dose received

> the parts of the body exposed – rapidly dividing cells (such as blood cells and hair follicles) are most susceptible

> the nature of the radiation – alpha particles are easily stopped by the skin so they do not present a serious hazard unless the source gets inside the body.

FIGURE 3: It is estimated that thousands of people were affected by the Chernobyl disaster in 1986, some developing blood disorders or cancers.

QUESTIONS

3 Explain which type of ionising radiation is most likely to cause skin cancer and skin burns.

4 According to a student, 'radiation is not always harmful'. Discuss whether or not this is true.

Equivalent dose

The effective biological damage to human tissues by ionising radiation is known as the 'equivalent dose' and is measured in **sievert** (Sv). The higher the equivalent dose, the greater the chance of biological damage to the cells.

Here are some interesting facts:

> Radiation dose for a dental X-ray is 0.005 mSv.

> Radiation dose for a brain CAT scan is 5 mSv.

> Average background radiation dose per year is 2 mSv.

> Radiation dose up to 0.25 Sv a day causes no acute symptoms.

> Radiation dose between 0.25 Sv and 1 Sv a day can cause nausea, loss of appetite and damage to bone marrow.

Ionising radiation can be harmful and this is why in diagnosis or treatment, patients are always given the smallest dose of radiation. The maximum permissible equivalent dose for medical personnel is 20 mSv per year averaged over 5 years, with a maximum of 50 mSv in any year.

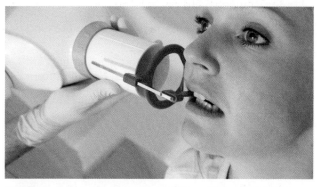

FIGURE 4: A patient having a dental X-ray. How safe is this procedure?

QUESTIONS

5 How many CAT scans can a patient be given safely in a year?

6 Discuss whether a single X-ray scan is dangerous to a patient.

7 Many dosimeters contain a range of films with different sensitivities. Suggest why this is a useful design.

Treatment of tumours

You will find out:

> about palliative radiotherapy

> about treating tumours with external and internal radiations

Brachytherapy

It is not always possible to use external gamma radiation to destroy cancerous cells. Internal radiation, or brachytherapy, works by implanting radioactive 'seeds' directly into a tumour. Brachytherapy is also known as curietherapy.

FIGURE 1: Radioactive iridium wires implanted into a man's neck to treat lymphatic cancer.

Palliative radiotherapy

Palliative radiotherapy treatment means treatment to shrink a cancer or slow down its growth. The treatment depends on the type of cancer and where it has spread in the body. Palliative radiotherapy:

> does not aim to cure the cancer completely

> can be either external radiotherapy or internal radiotherapy.

Side-effects

Palliative radiotherapy is painless. However, there are still a few side-effects after the treatment, such as:

> tiredness

> sickness after radiotherapy to the stomach, abdomen (tummy) or brain

> feeling very sore after radiotherapy to the lung or head and neck area.

To help control sickness, doctors give patients anti-sickness drugs called anti-emetics. Not all cancers respond well to radiotherapy. So other treatments such as surgery or using drugs (chemotherapy) may be more help.

> ### QUESTIONS
>
> **1** Explain what is meant by palliative radiotherapy.
>
> **2** Describe two alternative treatments to radiotherapy.

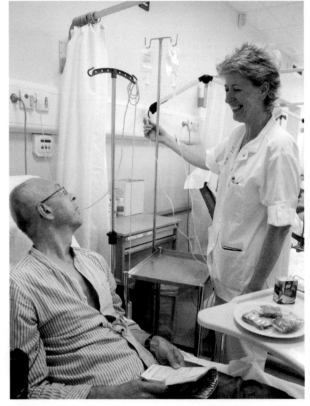

FIGURE 2: A cancer patient at a hospital receiving chemotherapy drugs intravenously.

Treating tumours using external and internal radiation

External radiotherapy

External radiotherapy works well for treating cancer cells in one localised area of the body. This type of radiotherapy uses intense X-rays from a special X-ray machine called a linear accelerator (linac) rather than gamma radiation from a radioactive source (e.g. cobalt-60). The intensity and energy of the X-rays can be controlled easily and the X-ray beam can be aimed at the specific area of the body.

> Patients can have external radiotherapy to more than one area at the same time.

> Patients can have one or two treatments or up to 10 short treatments given over 2 weeks.

Internal radiotherapy

There are several different types of **internal radiotherapy** treatment:

> Patients may have a small injection of a radioactive substance to treat *widespread* cancer in the bones.

> Patients may have a radioactive metal implant put inside the body, very close to the cancer. This can shrink a cancer.

> The patient in Figure 1 has several radioactive iridium-192 wires. Iridium-192 emits beta particles and low-level gamma rays. The radiation is close to the cancer and so does little damage to the healthy tissues around it.

Some types of internal palliative radiotherapy are given as a radioactive capsule or drink in the radiotherapy department. Patients are then usually allowed to go home. For safety reasons, such patients are told not to be close to children or pregnant women.

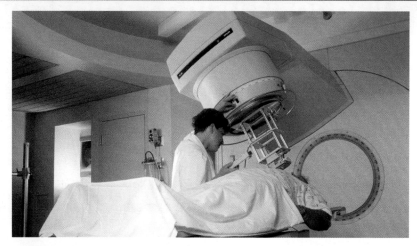

FIGURE 3: A linear accelerator (linac) used in the treatment of cancer. What radiation does this machine produce?

QUESTIONS

3 Discuss the advantages of using X-rays from a linear accelerator over gamma rays in the treatment of cancer.

4 Explain why external radiotherapy for cancer of the bones is not a viable treatment.

5 Explain why a beta source such as iridium-192 is suitable for internal radiotherapy.

Using neutrons

An intense beam of fast-moving neutrons can also be used in the treatment of cancer. Neutrons have no charge but because of their speed and large mass they have enormous kinetic energy and hence can ionise atoms. Neutrons can produce five times more ionisation than X-rays and beta particles.

Figure 4 shows a patient being treated for a tumour. Laser cross-hairs are aimed onto the site of the patient's tumour. An intense neutron beam is formed by bombarding beryllium with protons from a particle accelerator. The neutron beam will stop the growth of the tumour and could even destroy it. The patient is wearing a mask to hold her head still while the treatment takes place.

FIGURE 4: Neutron therapy.

QUESTIONS

6 Explain why fast-moving neutrons can produce more ionisation than beta particles.

7 Write a possible nuclear equation for producing neutrons by bombarding beryllium-9 (^9_4Be) with protons.

8 Compare and contrast the treatment of tumours using external and internal radiotherapy.

Did you know?

In the early 1900s, radioactivity was new and exciting – radium pendants were worn for curing rheumatism and water with radon was drunk for vigour.

Taking pictures of the brain

Figure 1 shows a gamma camera placed over a patient's head. The patient is injected with a radioactive substance known as a tracer. The active parts of the brain absorb more of the radioactive substance. The gamma radiation from the tracer passes through the patient to the gamma camera. The image of the brain produced by the camera shows the activity of different sections of the brain.

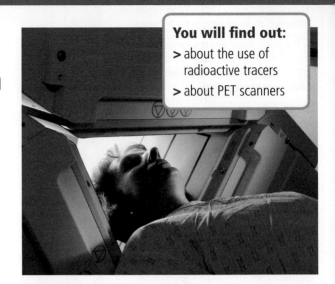

You will find out:
> about the use of radioactive tracers
> about PET scanners

FIGURE 1: A gamma camera.

Radioactive tracers

A medical **radioactive tracer** is a radioactive substance that is either injected into or swallowed by the patient.

Tracers are absorbed differently by different tissues.

Table 1 shows the properties of two medical tracers used with **gamma cameras** for the diagnosis of medical conditions.

How Iodine-131 works

Iodine-131 is a beta emitter with a half-life of 8.1 days.

Iodine is injected into a patient with kidney problems. A healthy kidney will pass the iodine through to the bladder; but if there is a blockage, the iodine builds up in the kidney.

A special counter detects the concentration of iodine and helps to pinpoint the blockage.

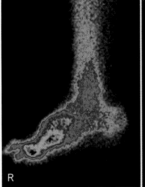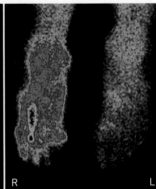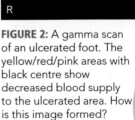

FIGURE 2: A gamma scan of an ulcerated foot. The yellow/red/pink areas with black centre show decreased blood supply to the ulcerated area. How is this image formed?

Remember!

Alpha particles are not used inside the body because they are the most ionising and will destroy healthy cells.

TABLE 1: Properties of two medical tracers used with gamma cameras.

Tracer	Half-life	Used to monitor
Technetium-99m ($^{99}_{43}$Tc)	6 hours	Blood flow in the brain
		Blood flow in the lungs
		Growth of bones
		Blood circulation and blood flow in the heart
Xenon-133 ($^{133}_{54}$Xe)	2.3 days	Function of the lungs

QUESTIONS

1 Copy and complete the sentence: Radioactive tracers must have a _____ half-life so that the damage to healthy cells can be minimised.

2 State the benefits of using technetium in diagnosing the function of the body.

Q Medical uses of a gamma camera   Medical uses of radioactive tracers

Positron emission tomography (PET) scanners

Figure 3 shows a **PET scanner** used in hospitals. The details of how it works are outlined later on pages 212–13. PET scanners are used to monitor the following conditions:

> activity of the brain

> spread of cancer through the body

> flow of blood through organs (e.g. heart).

Before a PET scan, specific radioactive isotopes are produced in a particle accelerator called a **cyclotron**. The radioactive isotopes are attached or 'tagged' to natural chemicals found in the human body. The natural tagging agents are glucose, water and ammonia. The tagged substance is known as a radiopharmaceutical. The **radiopharmaceutical** is injected into the patient.

The radioactive isotopes produced by a cyclotron include carbon-11, nitrogen-13, oxygen-15 and fluorine-18. These isotopes have short half-lives and therefore have to be manufactured just before the PET scans. For example, fluorine-18 has a half-life of about 2 hours. The cyclotrons are often located within the hospital grounds.

When the tracer is inside the body it will go to areas that use the natural chemical. Fluorine-18 is tagged to glucose to produce the radioactive drug fluorodeoxyglucose (FDG). Cancers use glucose differently from normal tissues; hence the FDG will reveal cancerous tissues.

A PET scanner detects the gamma rays produced by the *annihilation* of positrons emitted by the radioactive isotopes and electrons. For more details, see pages 212–13.

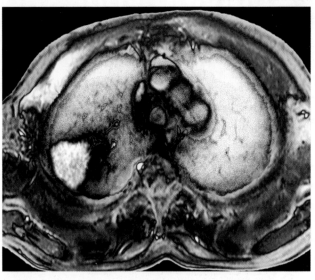

FIGURE 3: Lung cancer (white region lower left) revealed in a PET scan. How is this image formed?

QUESTIONS

3 What type of radiation is used to produce an image by a PET scanner?

4 What type of radiation is emitted by carbon-11, nitrogen-13, oxygen-15 and fluorine-18?

5 Explain why most radioactive isotopes required for PET scans are produced on-site.

World distribution of PET scanners

A PET scanner is expensive because it also requires a cyclotron to produce the radiopharmaceuticals. There are about 150 PET scanners around the world. Most are concentrated in the USA, Europe and Japan. In the southern hemisphere, only Argentina and Australia have a small number of PET facilities.

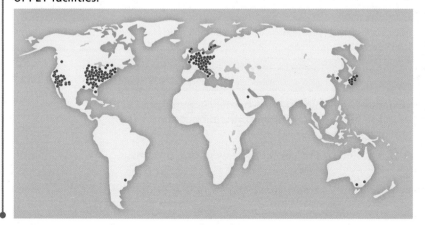

QUESTIONS

6 What are the daughter nuclei of each of the isotopes in question 4?

7 Use Figure 4 to discuss the link between PET scanners and national prosperity. Suggest how the distribution might change in the future.

FIGURE 4: Distribution of PET scanners around the world.

Preparing for assessment: Applying your knowledge

To achieve a good grade in science, you not only have to know and understand scientific ideas, but you also need to be able to apply them to other situations. This task will support you in developing these skills.

✳ End of the world?

When the Large Hadron Collider (LHC) was switched on in the autumn of 2009, it caused considerable alarm. The collider accelerates sub-atomic particles until they approach the speed of light and then smash them into one another. Some people thought that this would create black holes that would swallow the Earth.

The LHC project was set up to recreate, on a very small scale, the conditions that existing in the universe just after the Big Bang. By recreating these collisions, scientists can collect information on the nature of matter and improve our understanding of the laws of physics.

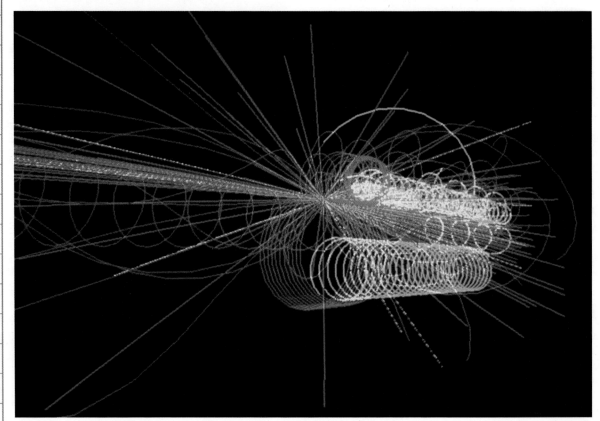

Subatomic particle tracks spraying out from a simulated high-energy collision in the Large Hadron Collider at CERN.

✳ Task 1

Over the last 100 or so years our knowledge of atomic structure has developed from J.J. Thompson's plum-pudding model in the nineteenth century to the pioneering work of the LHC project.

> Describe the structure of the atom as revealed by LHC, in terms of electrons, protons and neutrons.

> According to a student, the proton is the same as a positron. Discuss whether or not the student is correct.

Task 2

The underground areas of the LHC will become radioactive as the beams of protons circulate in the collider.

> Describe the properties of the alpha, beta, gamma and positron radiations found in LHC.

Higher tier only: A particular nucleus is radioactive and emits an alpha particle. An alpha particle has two protons and two neutrons. Explain the effect on the atomic number and mass number of the nucleus left behind.

 Task 3

The levels and duration of radioactivity surrounding the LHC vary, and this is monitored closely, particularly from a safety perspective as there are strict radiation dose limits in place for workers in nuclear installations.

> What is the name of the unit used to measure radiation doses received by the workers at the LHC?

> What sort of precautions might be used to protect people working near the LHC?

 Task 4

In large particle accelerators, like the LHC, nuclei are smashed together at very high speeds. The collisions produce a variety of new particles that can be explained in terms of specific combinations of quarks.

> Describe the quarks found in the LHC.

Higher tier only: Describe the process of the beta-plus and beta-minus decay that occurs inside LHC in terms of quarks.

 Maximise your grade

These sentences show what you need to be including in your work. Use these to improve your work and to be successful.

 E
For grade G–E, your answers should show that:
> recall that in an atom the number of protons is equal to the number of electrons
> recall that the nucleus of an atom contains protons and neutrons
> recall the properties of protons and positrons
> describe the dangers of radiation and suggest precautions taken to protect people who are exposed to radiation.

C
For grade D–C, in addition show that you can:
> describe the properties of nuclear radiations
> explain the changes to atomic and mass numbers following radioactive decay
> explain the precautions taken to protect people who are exposed to radiation.

 A
For grades B–A, in addition show that you can:
> describe the composition of the protons and neutrons in terms of up and down quarks
> describe beta-minus decay and beta-plus decay.

'God particle'

The Large Hadron Collider (LHC) is a particle accelerator that allows high-speed protons to smash into each other or into other particles. Such collisions will produce new particles, probably including the Higgs particle (dubbed the 'God particle' by newspapers). The discovery of the Higgs particle will help to explain why all particles have mass.

> **You will find out:**
> > about particle accelerators
> > why scientists collaborate in research

FIGURE 1: The CERN facilities at the French–Swiss border. The large circle marks the path taken by accelerated particles.

Particle accelerators

Particle physicists think of matter as being made up of two fundamental groups of particles called *quarks* and *leptons*. Neutrons and protons have quarks. Electrons and neutrinos are examples of leptons.

Physicists use collisions of high-speed electrons, protons and ions with matter to investigate the structure and behaviour of particles. Such experiments help scientists to develop a better understanding of the physical world.

> **Particle accelerators** are machines that accelerate charged particles to a speed approaching the speed of light.

> A particle accelerator uses magnetic fields or electric fields, or both, to accelerate charged particles.

> Linear accelerators are long and straight. The longest, at over 3 km, is the Stanford Linear Accelerator (SLAC) in California, USA.

> Some accelerators are circular. The charged particles can go around many times continuously gaining speed at every revolution.

> Small circular particle accelerators called *cyclotrons* are used in hospitals to make radioactive isotopes for PET scanners.

FIGURE 2: SLAC in California. What type of particle accelerator is this?

Remember!
The speed of light is 3×10^8 m/s.

> **QUESTIONS**

1 Explain what is meant by a particle accelerator.

2 Explain why scientists need particle accelerators.

3 A classmate says that protons, neutrons and electrons are all fundamental particles. Explain whether she is right or wrong.

Large Hadron Collider (LHC)

The European Organisation for Nuclear Research, also known as CERN (from the French words Conseil Européen pour la Recherche Nucléaire), is an international organisation whose main purpose is to provide particle accelerators for high-energy and particle physics research. CERN was established in 1954 and is funded by the European member states.

The CERN facilities are located on the French–Swiss border. It has scientists from about 580 universities and research organisations. CERN runs the world's largest accelerator, the Large Hadron Collider (LHC).

> The LHC collides protons and ions at higher speeds and energies than has ever been possible before.

> The budget for the LHC is about €8 billion, making it the most expensive particle accelerator in the world.

> The particles in the LHC travel in a circular path of circumference 27 km and make 11 000 revolutions per second.

> The LHC uses superconducting electromagnets kept close to absolute zero. These produce the very strong magnetic fields needed to keep the particles in their circular paths and to accelerate them to high speeds.

> It is hoped that the LHC will help to answer some of the fundamental questions about the structure of matter, events just after the Big Bang and why particles, and therefore all of us, have mass.

FIGURE 3: A section of the LHC. How are the charged particles made to go round in circles?

Did you know?

The World Wide Web was created in 1991 at CERN.

QUESTIONS

4 Calculate the distance travelled by a particle in 1 second in the LHC.

5 Matter produced soon after the Big Bang had enormous energy. Suggest why LHC experiments will help us to understand 'events after the Big Bang'.

Collaboration

The advantages of collaborative international research are:

> Sharing the cost between many countries and organisations; the LHC could not be run by a single organisation or country – the installation and running costs would be too high.

> Communicating our understanding of the physical world without any political barriers.

> Speeding up progress by sharing ideas among many scientists.

CERN is intended to do pure science; research for its own sake that may never have a commercial value. CERN's founding constitution states: 'The organisation shall provide for collaboration among European states in nuclear research of pure scientific and fundamental character … The organisation shall have no concern with work for military requirements and the results of its experimental and theoretical work shall be published or otherwise made generally available.'

QUESTIONS

6 Discuss the advantages of international collaborative research. Can you think of any disadvantages to this collaboration?

7 Compare and contrast the work of CERN with a research laboratory working with a car manufacturer.

Cyclotrons

You will find out:
> about the particle accelerator called the cyclotron
> how medical radioactive isotopes are made using cyclotrons

The northern lights

These bans of swirling colours of light in Alaska are caused by charged subatomic particles from the Sun interacting with atoms and molecules in the Earth's upper atmosphere. The intense magnetic field of the Earth channels the charged particles towards the poles.

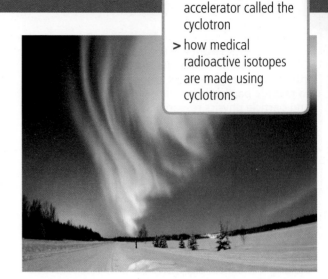

FIGURE 1: The northern lights or aurora borealis. In Roman mythology, Aurora was the goddess of the dawn, renewing herself every morning to fly across the sky, announcing the arrival of the Sun.

 ## Circular motion

Centripetal force

Figure 3 shows a person whirling a mass in a circle at a constant speed. An object moving in a circle is constantly changing its direction of motion.

> This means that its velocity is constantly changing and it must therefore be accelerating.

> The direction of the resultant force and the acceleration is towards the centre of the circle. The resultant force is known as the **centripetal force**.

> The centripetal force is always at right angles to the velocity and towards the centre of the circle.

Charged particles in a magnetic field

A magnet creates a magnetic field around it. A charged particle travelling at right angles to a magnetic field experiences a centripetal force.

> The centripetal force on the charged particle makes it go round in a circle or spiral.

> For a given magnetic field, the radius increases as the speed of the particle increases.

> Negative and positive particles travel in opposite directions in a magnetic field.

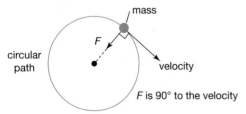

FIGURE 3: For an object to move in a circle there must be a centripetal force F acting on the object towards the centre of the circle.

FIGURE 2: What keeps the object moving in a circle?

QUESTIONS

1 Match the appropriate centripetal force with each example of circular motion.

Gravitational force	A car moving round a roundabout
Friction	A conker at the end of a string whirled in a circle
Tension	A planet orbiting the Sun

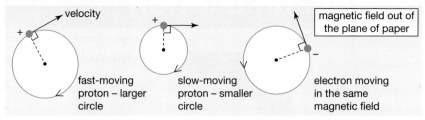

FIGURE 4: Motion of charged particles in a uniform magnetic field. How does the motion of the negative electron differ from that of the positive protons?

> **Remember!**
> Velocity is speed in a certain direction, so *velocity* can change even when speed remains constant.

Cyclotrons

Figure 5 shows a diagram of a cyclotron (a type of particle accelerator).

> It has two hollow D-shaped metal cavities called *dees*.

> The dees are enclosed in an evacuated chamber.

> A uniform magnetic field is applied at right angles to the plane of the dees by powerful electromagnets.

> The source of particles (electrons, protons, etc.) is at the centre of the cyclotron.

> The dees are connected to a very high frequency alternating voltage supply; this repeatedly changes the polarities of the dees.

Imagine that the source at the centre produces protons, with dee A *negative* and dee B *positive*. The protons are accelerated through the gap and then travel in a semicircle in dee A. By the time the protons arrive at the gap again, the charges on the dees are reversed, making dee B negative. The protons are once again accelerated, their speed increases and they travel in a semicircle of larger radius in dee B. The process is repeated many times until the protons exit at high speed.

> **QUESTIONS**
>
> **2** Explain the purpose of the magnetic field in the cyclotron.
>
> **3** Suggest why the dees are enclosed in an evacuated chamber.
>
> **4** The supply changes the polarity of the dees 30 million times every second. Calculate the time taken by an electron to complete one semicircle.

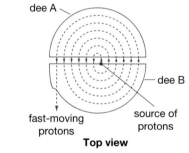

Top view

FIGURE 5: A diagram of a cyclotron showing its main components.

Making radioactive particles with cyclotrons

Cyclotrons are used to make radioactive isotopes for medical purposes (including PET scanners). This is done by bombarding certain stable elements, such as oxygen and nitrogen, with accelerated protons from cyclotrons. Fluorine-18 ($^{18}_{9}F$) is one of the isotopes produced using a cyclotron. Fluorine-18 has a short half-life of 2 hours which means that the cyclotron has to be close to the hospital where it will be used.

$^{18}_{9}F$ isotopes are made by bombarding oxygen-18 enriched water with high-speed protons. The nuclear equation for this reaction is:

$$^{1}_{1}p + {}^{18}_{8}O \rightarrow {}^{18}_{9}F + {}^{1}_{0}n + \gamma$$

The neutron ($^{1}_{0}n$) produced is not harmful. The collision of the protons with the target element also produces dangerous high-energy gamma (γ) radiation.

> **QUESTIONS**
>
> **5** Explain how cyclotrons can help hospital patients.
>
> **6** Suggest what is meant by 'oxygen-18 enriched water'.
>
> **7** Complete the nuclear reactions for the other isotopes produced using a cyclotron:
>
> **a** Carbon-11: $^{1}_{1}p + {}^{14}_{7}N \rightarrow {}^{?}_{?}C + {}^{4}_{2}He$
>
> **b** Nitrogen-13: $^{1}_{1}p + {}^{16}_{8}O \rightarrow {}^{13}_{7}N + ?$
>
> **c** Oxygen-15: $^{2}_{1}H + {}^{14}_{7}N \rightarrow {}^{15}_{8}O + ?$

Electron–positron annihilation

$E = mc^2$

The mass–energy equation $E = mc^2$ was proposed by Albert Einstein in 1905. It shows that the mass m of a system and its energy E are equivalent. The letter c stands for the speed of light in a vacuum (3.0×10^8 m/s). The Sun is a vibrant example of this equation; it converts mass into energy at a rate of about a billion tonnes every second.

FIGURE 1: Brighter than a thousand suns? A hydrogen bomb is another example of mass to energy transformation.

> **You will find out:**
> > about antimatter and annihilation
> > how gamma rays are produced in PET scanners

Matter, antimatter and annihilation

Ordinary matter consists of particles such as electrons, protons and neutrons. Particles of **antimatter** are different in terms of their charges. A positron is identical to an electron, except that it has an opposite (positive) charge of $+1.6 \times 10^{-19}$ C. An anti-proton has the same mass as a proton but it has a negative charge.

> When an electron and a positron interact or collide, they destroy each other completely. This process is known as **annihilation**.

> The total mass of the electron and positron is converted into energy, as two bursts of gamma rays. Mass energy is conserved.

> The two bursts of gamma rays fly off in *opposite* directions; this shows that momentum is conserved during the annihilation.

> Gamma radiation is an electromagnetic wave. It has no charge. In the annihilation of an electron–positron pair, charge is conserved.

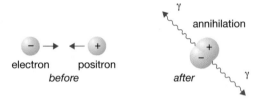

FIGURE 2: The two gamma rays move off in opposite directions. How is this related to momentum?

> **QUESTIONS**
>
> **1** Name the quantities that are conserved when an electron and positron annihilate each other.
>
> **2** Explain why a positron and an electron move in opposite directions in a magnetic field.

PET scanners

Figure 3 shows a modern positron emission tomography scanner (or simply a PET scanner). Before carrying out a PET scan, radioactive tracers such as fluorine-18 are produced in a cyclotron. The patient is injected with a compound tagged with a positron-emitting tracer. Tracers used in PET scanners include carbon-11, nitrogen-13, oxygen-15 and fluorine-18.

> The patient is placed in a ring consisting of gamma-ray detectors.

> The detectors are connected to powerful computers.

> The annihilation of the positron with an electron produces two bursts of gamma rays emitted in *opposite* directions.

> The arrival times of the gamma rays are analysed by the computer and the location of the annihilation and hence the radioactive tracer is pinpointed.

> The computer builds up a three-dimensional image of the distribution of the tracer inside the patient.

> PET scans of the brain can be used to diagnose conditions such as cancer, Alzheimer's disease, dyslexia and epilepsy.

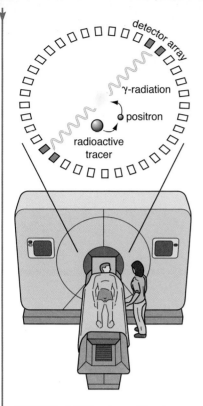

FIGURE 3: A PET scanner. The ring around the patient has gamma-ray detectors.

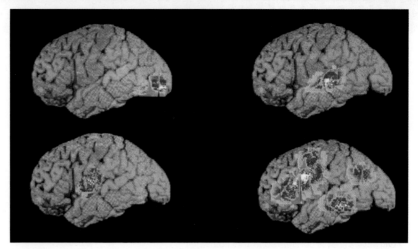

FIGURE 4: A PET scan can be used to identify areas of brain responsible for (clockwise from top left) seeing, hearing, thinking and speaking.

QUESTIONS

3 Explain how the detectors can locate the tracer within the patient.

4 Explain why radioactive tracers used in PET scans have a short half-life.

5 Calculate the difference between arrival times of gamma ray bursts travelling distances of 0.76 m and 0.75 m to the detectors. The speed of gamma rays is 3.0×10^8 m/s.

Energy released in electron–positron annihilation

When a positron and an electron meet, they annihilate each other completely. The mass of the particles is converted into energy in the form of two gamma ray bursts. The energy E of the gamma rays can be calculated using Einstein's **mass–energy equation**:

$E = mc^2$, where m is the total mass of the electron and positron

E = (total mass of electron and positron) × speed of light^2

$E = (9.11 \times 10^{-31} \text{ kg} + 9.11 \times 10^{-31} \text{ kg}) \times (3.0 \times 10^8 \text{ m/s})^2$

$E = 1.64 \times 10^{-13}$ J

FIGURE 5: The famous mass–energy equation. What does it mean?

QUESTIONS

6 Use $E = mc^2$ to calculate the energy released when 1 gram (0.001 kg) of matter is annihilated.

7 Determine the energy of a single gamma-ray burst following electron–positron annihilation.

8 In large particle accelerators, protons and anti-protons annihilate in the same way as electron–positron pairs. Calculate the energy of a single burst of gamma rays when a proton annihilates an anti-proton. The mass of a proton is 1.67×10^{-27} kg.

Did you know?

Einstein said: 'Two things are infinite: the Universe and human stupidity; and I'm not sure about the Universe.'

Q Annihilation and gamma rays   Diagnosis with PET scanners

Momentum

You will find out:
> about momentum
> about conservation of momentum
> about elastic and inelastic collisions

Collisions and momentum

What is common between the collisions of particles in a particle accelerator and the toy shown in Figure 1? In all collisions, the total energy and the total momentum of the objects are always conserved.

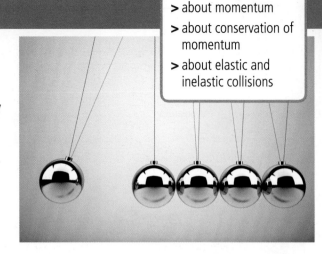

FIGURE 1: What is conserved in this collision?

Conservation of momentum

Momentum is a **vector** quantity because it has both magnitude and direction. The momentum of an object of mass m travelling at a velocity v is defined as follows:

momentum = mass × velocity

Momentum is measured in kg m/s.

We can apply the **principle of conservation of momentum** to all collisions. According to this principle:

the total momentum of the objects before the collision = the total momentum of the objects after the collision

as long as there are no external forces acting on the objects.

Figure 3 shows the speeds of two objects before and after the collision:

> total momentum before collision =
(10 kg × 4.0 m/s) + (5.0 kg × −2.0 m/s) = +30 kg m/s

> total momentum after collision =
(10 kg × 1.5 m/s) + (5.0 kg × 3.0 m/s) = +30 kg m/s.

The calculations above show that the total momentum of the objects remains the same.

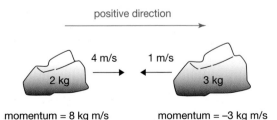

FIGURE 2: Why does the 3.0 kg object have a negative momentum?

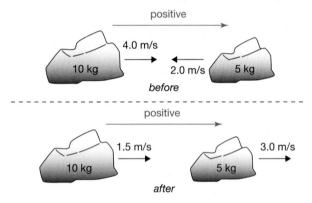

FIGURE 3: Left to right is taken as 'positive'. The 5 kg object has negative velocity and hence negative momentum.

QUESTIONS

1 Calculate the momentum of a 900 kg car travelling at 30 m/s.

2 Use the principle of conservation of momentum to determine the momentum and speed of toy car B after the collision. Each toy car has a mass of 0.08 kg.

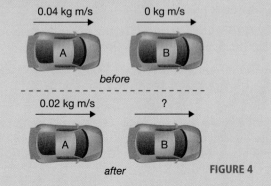

FIGURE 4

Q Conservation of momentum   Conservation of kinetic energy

Elastic and inelastic collisions

There are two types of collision: **elastic collisions** and **inelastic collisions**. Table 1 summarises the quantities conserved in these two types of collision.

TABLE 1: Elastic collisions and inelastic collisions compared.

	Elastic collision	Inelastic collision
Total momentum is conserved	✔	✔
Total energy is conserved	✔	✔
Kinetic energy is conserved	✔	✘

The collision shown in Figure 3 is an *inelastic* collision:

> total kinetic energy before collision = $(\frac{1}{2} \times 10$ kg $\times$ 4.0 m/s^2) + $(\frac{1}{2} \times 5.0$ kg $\times$ 2.0 m/s^2) = 90 J

> total kinetic energy after collision = $(\frac{1}{2} \times 10 \times 1.5^2)$ + $(\frac{1}{2} \times 5.0$ kg $\times$ 3.0 m/s^2) = 33.8 J $\approx$ 34 J.

The total kinetic energy of the objects is not the same. However, the total energy is always conserved. This implies that about 56 J of the initial kinetic energy is transformed into other forms, such as heat and sound.

Figure 5 shows a bouncing ball. The rebound height decreases with each bounce. The collisions with the ground are inelastic collisions, as some kinetic energy is being transferred into heat and sound.

Remember!
Kinetic energy is given by the equation
$\frac{1}{2} \times$ mass $\times$ speed^2.

Factors that could affect the rebound height might include the materials of the ball and the surface, and the initial height.

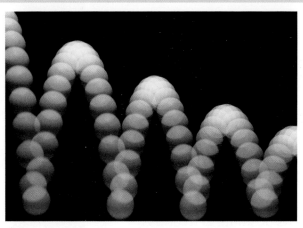

FIGURE 5: How can you tell that the ball is making inelastic collisions with the Earth?

QUESTIONS

3 Describe the main difference between elastic and inelastic collisions.

4 Explain whether the collision shown in Figure 6 is elastic or inelastic.

KE = 12 J   at rest | KE = 1 J   KE = 7 J

A →   B | ← A   B →
                                   2.0 m/s

before   *after*

FIGURE 6: Collisions.

More on momentum (Higher tier only)

Figure 7 shows the state of motion of two objects A and B before and after collision. After the collision, the objects stick together and move off with a common velocity v. The velocity v can be calculated using the conservation of momentum:

total momentum before collision = total momentum after collision

(5.0 kg $\times$ 3.0 m/s) + (2.0 kg $\times$ 0.5 m/s) = 7.0 $\times v$

16.0 = 7.0v

$v = \dfrac{16.0}{7.0}$ = 2.29 m/s

The collision between objects that stick together is always inelastic.

QUESTIONS

5 Show that the collision shown in Figure 7 is an inelastic collision.

6 A 0.16 kg snooker ball A travelling at 3.0 m/s hits a stationary snooker ball B of similar mass. After the collision, ball A stops and B moves off with a speed of 3.0 m/s. Discuss what type of collision has taken place.

5.0 kg → 3.0 m/s   2.0 kg → 0.5 m/s   5.0 kg 2.0 kg → v

FIGURE 7: Inelastic collision.   *before*   *after*

Q Elastic collisions   Inelastic collisions

Matter and temperature

You will find out:
> about the three states of matter
> about celsius and kelvin temperature scales
> about kinetic energy of gas particles and temperature

Absolute zero

The lowest temperature recorded on Earth is −89 °C (degrees celsius) in Antarctica. Outer space is much colder at −270 °C. Physicists believe that the lowest temperature possible is −273.15 °C. This temperature is known as absolute zero and is the basis for the kelvin temperature scale.

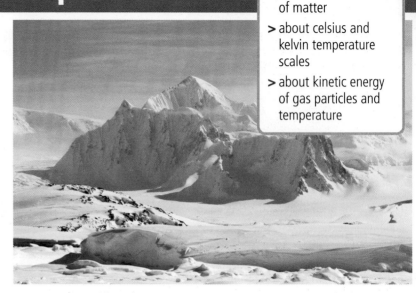

FIGURE 1: How cold is it here?

Kinetic theory of matter

The kinetic theory of matter:

> describes the behaviour of the three *states of matter* (solid, liquid and gas) in terms of the movement of particles

> explains how the average kinetic energy of the particles is related to the temperature

> explains why gases exert pressure.

A substance changes state from solid to liquid and then gas, as its temperature is increased. Table 1 summarises the three states of matter.

> **QUESTIONS**
>
> **1** Name the two states of matter where the particles (atoms or molecules) are randomly arranged.
>
> **2** Explain why you can pour a liquid but not a solid.
>
> **3** Explain the term 'random motion' of gas particles.

TABLE 1: The three states of matter.

	increasing temperature →		
	Solid	**Liquid**	**Gas**
Arrangement of particles	Regular pattern Particles are very close together	Random arrangement Particles are close together	Random arrangement On average the particles are far apart
Movement of particles	Particles vibrate about fixed positions. As temperature increases, they vibrate more quickly	Particles move around each other. As temperature increases, their average speed increases	Particles move quickly in all directions and have a variety of speeds (**random motion**)

Lord Kelvin   Kinetic theory of gases   States of matter

Temperature scales

The existence of **absolute zero** was proposed in 1848 by the physicist Lord Kelvin. At absolute zero, which is written as 0 K, all particles of the substance stop moving and have zero kinetic energy. The **kelvin scale** or thermodynamic temperature scale and the celsius scale are different.

> A temperature change of 1 °C is the same as a temperature change of 1 K. (Notice there is no degree symbol in front of the K.)

> A temperature of 0 K is the same as –273 °C.

> To change temperature from °C to K, you add 273. Example: 20 °C is the same as 293 K.

> To change temperature from K to °C, you subtract 273. Example: 100 K is the same as –173 °C.

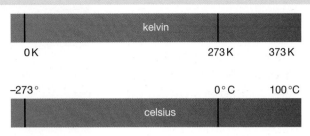

FIGURE 3: A comparison of the kelvin and celsius scales.

Did you know?

Lord Kelvin was a brilliant physicist and engineer. As well as working on heat and temperature, he was involved in estimating the age of the Earth and in the laying of the first transatlantic communications cable.

FIGURE 2: Colour temperature is important in lighting, cinema and photography and is generally measured in kelvin. Sunlight is about 5500 K and lightbulbs about 3000 K.

◯ QUESTIONS

4 Explain why a temperature recorded as –20 K must be incorrect.

5 Change the following temperatures from °C to K:

a Body temperature of 37 °C.

b Ice from a freezer at –10 °C.

6 Explain which of these two temperatures is greater: –50 °C or 200 K.

Heat and temperature

Heat is a form of energy. When heat energy is supplied to a gas, the gas particles move *more quickly*. The particles collide with each other and the sides of the container more frequently. The average kinetic energy of each particle increases and this also increases the total kinetic energy of the gas.

Heating a gas also increases the *temperature* of the gas. The temperature of the gas on the kelvin scale is related to the average kinetic energy of the gas particles. The average kinetic energy E of the gas particles is directly proportional to the kelvin temperature T of the gas, that is:

$E \propto T$

The temperature of a gas measured using a thermometer calibrated on the kelvin scale is a direct measure of the mean kinetic energy of the gas particles.

◯ QUESTIONS

7 What is the kinetic energy of a gas at 0 K? Explain your answer.

8 The average kinetic energy of gas molecules at 27 °C is 6.2×10^{-21} J. Calculate the average kinetic energy of the gas molecules at:

a 600 K

b 54 °C.

9 Use the internet to research how ideas about heat changed during the 19th century. How did the scientific community respond to these changes?

🔍 Different temperature scales   Absolute zero

Investigating gases

You will find out:
> about the origin of gas pressure
> how pressure and volume of a gas are related
> how volume and temperature of a gas are related

Spacesuit

Figure 1 shows an astronaut with a pressurised spacesuit. This spacesuit protects the astronaut by regulating his temperature and providing oxygen. Without the pressurised suit, the astronaut's blood and body fluids would 'boil' because there is no air pressure in outer space.

FIGURE 1: How does their suit protect astronauts?

 Pressure

You are constantly being bombarded by air molecules travelling faster than a jet. You do not notice these impacts because of the tiny mass of air molecules.

There are about 10^{25} molecules hitting your hand every second. Each impact exerts a tiny force and this causes a continuous pressure. We call this **atmospheric pressure**.

Figure 2 shows some molecules trapped in a container:

> Every molecule makes repeated collisions with the wall X.

> Each molecule exerts a tiny force on this wall.

> The pressure P on this wall can be determined using the equation

$$\text{pressure} = \frac{\text{total force exerted by all the molecules}}{\text{area of wall X}}$$

$$P = \frac{F}{A}$$

> Pressure is measured in newton per square metre (N/m^2) or pascal (Pa).

> Atmospheric pressure is about 100 000 Pa (10^5 Pa).

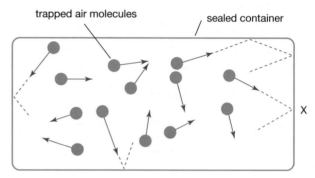

trapped air molecules   sealed container

X

FIGURE 2: Pressure is caused by repeated collisions of molecules with the container walls.

QUESTIONS

1 A container has some trapped gas. The gas exerts a force of 12 N on a surface area of 0.0001 m^2. Calculate the pressure exerted by the gas.

2 Estimate the surface area of your hand. Use $F = PA$ to determine the force exerted by the Earth's atmosphere on your hand.

 Pressure and volume of a gas (Boyle's law)

The pressure P exerted by a fixed mass of gas, kept at constant temperature, is inversely proportional to its volume V. This is known as **Boyle's law** after the chemist Robert Boyle (1627–91).

We can write Boyle's law mathematically as:

$$P \propto \frac{1}{V} \quad \text{or} \quad PV = \text{constant} \quad \text{or} \quad V_1 P_1 = V_2 P_2$$

where V_1 and P_1 are the *initial* volume and pressure and V_2 and P_2 are the *final* volume and pressure.

The apparatus shown in Figure 3 has been used to produce the results in Table 1.

TABLE 1: Results from a Boyle's law experiment. Notice how doubling the volume halves the pressure.

Pressure (Pa)	100 000	150 000	200 000	250 000	300 000
Volume (cm³)	80	53	40	32	27

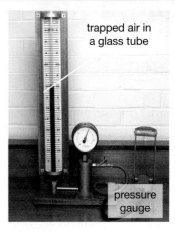

trapped air in a glass tube

pressure gauge

FIGURE 3: Boyle's law apparatus. Identify the dependent and independent variables.

QUESTIONS

3 A sealed syringe is kept at constant temperature. It contains 8.0×10^{-6} m³ of air at 1.2×10^{5} Pa. Calculate the pressure exerted when the volume is 2.0×10^{-6} m³.

4 Use Table 1 to plot a graph of P against $\frac{1}{V}$. Explain the shape of the graph.

Volume and temperature (Charles' law)

The volume V occupied by a fixed mass of gas, kept at constant pressure, is directly proportional to its temperature T on the kelvin scale. This is known as **Charles' law** after the French physicist Jacques Charles (1746–1823).

We can write Charles' law mathematically as:

$$V \propto T \quad \text{or} \quad \frac{V}{T} = \text{constant} \quad \text{or} \quad \frac{V_1}{T_1} = \frac{V_2}{T_2}$$

where V_1 and T_1 are the *initial* volume and temperature (in kelvin) and V_2 and T_2 are the *final* volume and temperature. You can calculate the volume of the gas using

$$V_1 = \frac{V_2 T_1}{T_2}$$

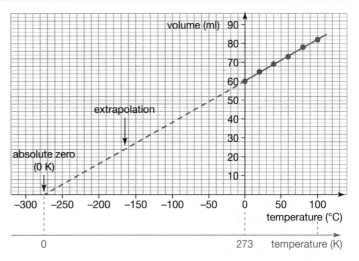

FIGURE 4: A graph of volume of a fixed mass of gas against temperature in °C. You can determine absolute zero from this graph.

You can use a plastic syringe, with its nozzle sealed, to investigate Charles' law. The syringe is immersed in a beaker of boiling water. The water is allowed to cool. The temperature and volume occupied by the gas are recorded and used to plot a graph. Figure 4 shows a typical graph of volume of air against its temperature in °C.

> The *extrapolated* graph crosses the temperature axis at −273 °C or absolute zero. This intercept is independent of the amount or type of gas used.

QUESTIONS

5 A sealed syringe, kept at constant pressure, has 5.0×10^{-6} m³ of air at 20 °C. Calculate its volume at:
   a 40 °C   **b** −20 °C.

6 According to a student, Figure 4 shows that 'volume is directly proportional to temperature in °C'. Explain whether or not this statement is correct.

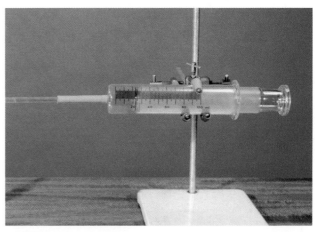

FIGURE 5: You can use a syringe to investigate Charles' law.

The gas equation

You will find out:
> about using bottled gases in medicine
> how pressure and temperature of a gas are related
> about the gas equation

Medical bottled gas

Metal cylinders are used to store gases at high pressure. The high pressure means that a large mass of gas can be stored in a small volume. In hospitals, oxygen is often given to patients with breathing difficulties, and other gases are used for pain relief and anaesthesia. Modern cylinders are made from lightweight aluminium, which makes them portable and easy to handle in emergency situations. They have a regulator that controls the flow of gas from the pressurised cylinder to the patient.

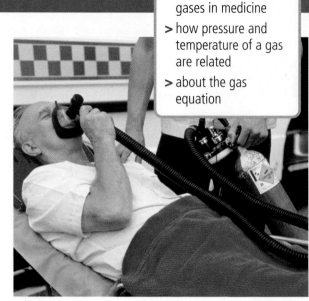

FIGURE 1: How does the gas equation help in the design of emergency equipment?

The pressure law

Imagine a gas of fixed mass in a rigid container (e.g. a gas cylinder):

> When the temperature of the gas is increased, the gas molecules move faster.

> This means that the particles collide with the walls more frequently.

> This causes the force and hence the pressure on the walls to increase.

Figure 2 shows an arrangement that can be used to investigate how the pressure exerted by a fixed mass of gas is affected by temperature.

The pressure P exerted by a fixed mass of gas, kept at constant volume, is directly proportional to its temperature T on the kelvin scale. This is known as the **pressure law**.

We can write the pressure law mathematically as:

$$P \propto T \quad \text{or} \quad \frac{P_1}{T_1} = \frac{P_2}{T_2}$$

where P_1 and T_1 are the *initial* pressure and temperature and P_2 and T_2 are the *final* pressure and temperature. Note: Both T_1 and T_2 are measured in kelvin (K) and not °C.

QUESTIONS

1 The pressure inside an oven is 1.0×10^5 Pa at 20 °C. Calculate the pressure inside the oven at 220 °C, assuming the mass does not change.

2 Sketch a graph of pressure against temperature in kelvin for oxygen in a gas cylinder. Explain the shape of the graph.

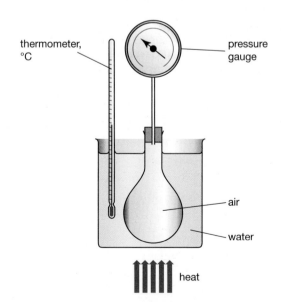

thermometer, °C

pressure gauge

air

water

heat

FIGURE 2: Apparatus for testing the pressure law. The thermometer measures temperature in °C. Is this a problem?

The gas equation

Here is a summary of the three gas laws:

> Boyle's law: $P \propto \dfrac{1}{V}$ (temperature of gas is kept constant).

> Charles' law: $V \propto T$ (pressure exerted by gas is kept constant).

> Pressure law: $P \propto T$ (volume of gas is kept constant).

The three equations above can be combined into a single equation known as the **gas equation**:

gas equation: $\dfrac{PV}{T} = \text{constant}$

QUESTIONS

3 Show how the gas equation is consistent with Boyle's law, Charles' law and the pressure law.

4 Sketch a graph of PV against T. Explain the shape of your graph.

FIGURE 3: You can use PV/T = constant to determine of volume of this diver's lungs.

Using the gas equation (Higher tier only)

We can write the gas equation as:

$$\frac{\text{initial pressure (pascal, Pa)} \times \text{initial volume (metre}^3\text{, m}^3)}{\text{initial temperature (kelvin, K)}} = \frac{\text{final pressure (pascal, Pa)} \times \text{final volume (metre}^3\text{, m}^3)}{\text{final temperature (kelvin, K)}}$$

or $\dfrac{P_1 V_1}{T_1} = \dfrac{P_2 V_2}{T_2}$

where P_1, V_1 and T_1 are the *initial* conditions and P_2, V_2 and T_2 are the *final* conditions. Pressure is measured in pascal (Pa), volume in metre³ (m³) and temperature in kelvin (K).

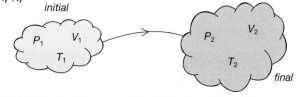

FIGURE 4: A helpful way of visualising the gas equation.

Example

A medical cylinder contains 0.0090 m³ of air at a pressure of 1.0×10^5 Pa and temperature 10 °C. Calculate the final pressure when the air in the cylinder is compressed to a volume of 0.0025 m³ at a temperature of 100 °C.

> *Step 1.* Write down what is given in the question:

$P_1 = 1.0 \times 10^5$ Pa, $V_1 = 0.0090$ m³,
$T_1 = (273 + 10) = 283$ K

$P_2 = ?$, $V_2 = 0.0025$ m³, $T_2 = (273 + 100) = 373$ K

> *Step 2.* Substitute values into the gas equation, making sure not to mix the initial and final values:

$\dfrac{1.0 \times 10^5 \times 0.0090}{283} = \dfrac{P_2 \times 0.0025}{373}$

> *Step 3.* Solve the equation to find P_2:

$P_2 = \dfrac{373 \times 1.0 \times 10^5 \times 0.0090}{283 \times 0.0025} = 4.7 \times 10^5$ Pa

QUESTIONS

5 A medical cylinder has a volume of 0.016 m³ (16 litres) and is stored outside at a temperature of 10 °C. The oxygen is pressurised to 150×10^5 Pa. It is used in the hospital ward at 25 °C to produce oxygen at an atmospheric pressure of 1.0×10^5 Pa. Calculate the volume in m³ and litres of the oxygen it can deliver to the patient.

6 Calculate the time taken to empty the cylinder in question 5 if the flow rate is 2 litres per minute.

7 Suggest why oxygen cylinders in hospitals are colour coded (black with white shoulders), made of aluminium rather than steel and have flow-rate regulators.

Preparing for assessment: Planning an investigation

To achieve a good grade in science, you not only have to know and understand scientific ideas, but you also need to be able to apply them to other situations and investigations. This task will support you in developing these skills.

✳ Task

Plan an investigation to find out how the volume of a fixed mass of air trapped in a plastic syringe is affected by the temperature of the air.

✳ Resources available in the laboratory

A plastic syringe with its nozzle sealed is available for your investigation. You can use any other equipment normally found in a science laboratory.

✳ Looking into behaviour of gases

The behaviour of gases can be analysed using the gas equation $\frac{PV}{T}$ = constant, where P is the pressure exerted by the gas, V is the volume occupied by the gas and T is the temperature of the gas in kelvin (K). To change temperature from °C to K you simply add 273.

✳ Planning

1. State your hypothesis for the investigation.

2. State the equipment you use in your investigation.
How will you set up and use your equipment to ensure that you obtain accurate evidence?

3. State the independent and dependent variables that you will measure.
Decide on a suitable range of values for the independent variable.

4. List the things that you need to keep the same in order to ensure that a fair test.

5. Write up your method as a plan for the investigation.

6. List all significant hazards in your investigation and state how each one can be controlled so that you can conduct the task safely.

> What do you expect to happen? Support your hypothesis using appropriate scientific terms to gain Quality of Written Communication marks.

> You could draw a diagram of the apparatus set-up. Remember to justify your choice of equipment.

> Secondary research – on the internet or results from similar investigations carried out by classmates – could help you to decide.

> These should be your control variables. Why is a fair test important?

> Make sure that your method is a logical sequence of steps. You can number the steps or use bullet points to communicate your method clearly.
> This is an opportunity to practice your Quality of Written Communication.

> Consider how significant each hazard is when deciding how to control it. The precaution should be appropriate to the hazard.

Processing the evidence

1. Draw a results table to display your evidence.

2. Decide how you will analyse your results by indicating what form of graph will be most suitable.
How will you label each of the axes?

3. Think about how you will interpret your graphs so that you can describe the trends shown by your results.

4. When you have completed your investigation you will need to evaluate the method and conclusions.
What will you consider in your evaluation?

When drawing your results table, think about how you are going to use the table to process your evidence.
What information will you need to see in order to evaluate your hypothesis?

Each axis will need the name and the unit; this should be the same as the headings used in the table of results.

What can you learn from the shape of the graph? What will you do if there are any anomalies?

 Connections

How Science Works

> Planning to test a scientific idea.

> Planning an experiment and answering a scientific problem.

> Collecting and analysing scientific data.

> Assessing methods of data collection.

> Collecting data accurately and safely, taking into account potential hazards.

> Presenting information and making conclusions and stating the results in a scientific fashion.

Maths in Science

> Understanding direct proportionality and simple ratios.

> Selecting the most appropriate type of graph for the experiment and appropriate scales for the axes.

To achieve your forecast grade in the exam you'll need to revise

Use this checklist to see what you can do now. Refer back to pages 192–221 if you're not sure.

Look across the rows to see how you could progress – *bold italic* means Higher tier only.

Remember you'll need to be able to use these ideas in various ways, such as:
> interpreting pictures, diagrams and graphs
> applying ideas to new situations
> explaining ethical implications
> suggesting some benefits and risks to society
> drawing conclusions from evidence you've been given.

Look at pages 230–52 for more information about exams and how you'll be assessed.

This checklist accompanies the exam-style questions and the worked examples. The content suggestions for specific grades are suggestions only and may not be replicated in your real examination. Remember, the checklists do not represent the complete content for any topic. Refer to the Specification for complete content details on any topic and any further information.

To aim for a grade E	To aim for a grade C	To aim for a grade A
recall the relative masses and relative charges of protons, neutrons, electrons and positrons	describe the process of beta-minus decay and gamma decay	*describe the process of beta-plus decay*
describe the process of alpha decay	describe the properties of alpha, beta, gamma, positron and neutron radiation	
explain the effect on atomic (proton) and mass (nucleon) numbers of radioactive decay of nuclei		*balance nuclear equations*
	describe how radioactive nuclei often undergo nuclear rearrangement by emitting gamma radiation	*describe the features of the N–Z curve for stable isotopes*
		identify when an isotope will undergo alpha decay, beta-minus decay or beta-plus decay
		describe the arrangement of up and down quarks in protons and neutrons
		explain the process of beta-plus and beta-minus decay in terms of quarks
describe the dangers of ionising radiation in terms of tissue damage and possible mutations		
explain the precautions taken to ensure the safety of patients and medical personnel		
		evaluate the ethical issues of using radiation in medicine
describe palliative care	compare and contrast the treatments of tumours using internal and external radiations	

To aim for a grade E   To aim for a grade C   To aim for a grade A

To aim for a grade E	To aim for a grade C	To aim for a grade A
describe the use of radioactive substances in medical tracers	explain why isotopes for PET scanners have to be produced nearby explain the use of radioactive substances in PET scanners	
describe how particle accelerators can help scientists develop a better understanding of the physical world	discuss the reasons for international collaboration in scientific research	
describe how particles move in a circle	explain how cyclotrons work	*explain how cyclotrons bombard stable elements with protons to produce radioactive isotopes for medical use*
state the principle of conservation of momentum	describe elastic and inelastic collisions	*analyse collisions in terms of momentum and kinetic energy, using calculations*
recall that gamma rays are produced by electron–positron annihilation	explain the conservation of mass–energy for electron–positron annihilation explain the use of annihilation in PET scanners	use $E = mc^2$ to explain the conservation of mass–energy for electron–positron annihilation
describe the movement of particles in the three states of matter describe the effect of temperature of a gas on the speed of its particles	convert between kelvin and celsius scales describe absolute zero show that the average kinetic energy of gas particles is directly proportional to the kelvin temperature of the gas	
recall what atmospheric pressure is	explain the relationship between pressure and volume using the equation: $V_1P_1 = V_2P_2$ (Boyle's law)	explain the relationship between volume and temperature using the equation: $V_1 = \dfrac{V_2 T_1}{T_2}$ (Charles' law)
understand that the gas equation is a combination of Boyle's Law, Charles' law and the pressure law	describe how the gas equation applies to bottled gases in medicine	*apply the gas equation:* $\dfrac{P_1 V_1}{T_1} = \dfrac{P_2 V_2}{T_2}$

Exam-style questions: Foundation

1 a The diagram shows how three different radiations are affected by different materials.

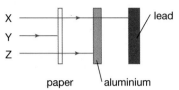

X ——→
Y ——→
Z ——→

lead

paper   aluminium

AO1 i The radiation labelled Z must be

A ☐ neutrons

B ☐ gamma radiation

C ☐ beta-plus radiation

D ☐ beta-minus radiation [1]

AO1 ii Identify the most ionising radiation. [1]

b The nuclear decay equation shows the decay of a single uranium-235 nucleus:

$$^{235}_{92}U \rightarrow {}^{4}_{2}He + {}^{231}_{90}Th$$

AO2 i How many neutrons does the uranium nucleus have? [1]

AO2 ii Identify the proton (atomic) and nucleon (mass) numbers for the alpha particle. [2]

AO3 iii Using the decay equation, describe the changes taking place within the nucleus of uranium-235. [3]

[Total: 8]

2 a The diagram shows the path of a proton in a magnetic field.

P

AO2 i On a copy of the diagram draw the direction of the net force acting on the proton (P). [1]

AO1 ii Explain why the proton moves in a circular path. [2]

AO2 iii Describe the path of an electron in the same magnetic field. [1]

AO2 b The world's largest particle accelerator is the Large Hadron Collider on the border between France and Switzerland. It is collectively run by all the European countries. Discuss the reasons for such collaboration. [4]

AO1 c Discuss how particle accelerators can help
AO2 scientists develop a better understanding of the physical world. [4]

[Total: 12]

3 a The radioactive nucleus of fluorine-18 emits a positron. It has a half-life of about 2 hours. Fluorine-18 is injected into patients during PET scans.

AO1 i Explain what is meant by a positron. [2]

AO2 ii Explain why fluorine-18 is a good choice as a medical tracer. [2]

AO1 b A positron does not survive for too long inside the body because it strongly interacts with an electron. A positron and an electron annihilate each other and produce energy.
Name the form in which the energy is released. Explain how this energy is created. [4]

[Total: 8]

AO1 4 a Describe the movement of gas particles at absolute zero. [1]

AO2 b A student does a calculation for temperature and comes up with −100 K. Explain why this temperature must be incorrect. [2]

AO2 c i The boiling point of oxygen is 90 K. Convert this temperature into °C. [2]

AO2 ii The volume of a fixed mass of oxygen is 25 ml at 20 °C. Its temperature is increased to 127 °C at constant pressure. Calculate its new volume in ml. [3]

[Total: 8]

AO1 5 a The isotope fluorine-18 emits positrons. Describe the properties of positrons. [2]

AO1 b A positron emission tomography (PET) scanner relies on the process of annihilation. Explain what is meant by annihilation. [2]

AO2 c Explain how radioactive tracers, such as fluorine-18, are used in diagnosis of medical conditions using a PET scanner. [6]

[Total: 10]

Summary of Assessment Objectives

| AO1 recall the science | AO2 apply your knowledge | AO3 evaluate and analyse the evidence |

Worked example

AO1 **a**   Complete the table below.   [3]

Particle	Proton	Neutron	Electron	Positron
Relative charge	1	0	–1 ✔	–1 ✗
Relative mass	1	1 ✔	0.00055	1

AO1 **b**   Radioactive carbon-14 is a beta-minus emitter. Describe the process of beta-minus decay in terms of changes taking place within the nucleus of carbon-14.   [2]

There is no change taking place because a particle is emitted. ✗

AO2 **c**   Old watches contained radioactive alpha-emitters such as radium. The radioactivity made the numbers and watch hands glow in the dark. Discuss whether the watches were safe to wear.   [3]

I think they were not safe to wear because alpha radiation is very dangerous. ✗

[Total: 8]

How to raise your grade

Take note of the comments from examiners – these will help you to improve your grade.

The candidate has done well to recognise the properties of the neutron, electron and positron. Sadly, the candidate has poor recollection of the positron. This particle has a relative charge of +1 and a relative mass of 0.00055 because it is the anti-particle of an electron.

This is a tough question and the candidate's answer lacks detail and precision. A neutron inside the carbon-14 nucleus changes into a positron and a proton.

There are 3 marks for this question and the candidate has simply written a single sentence! The statement from the candidate does not answer the question. The alpha particles will be easily absorbed by the watch material (glass and metal). Hence none will reach the person wearing the watch. The watches were therefore safe.

This candidate scored 2 marks out of a possible 8. A better-prepared candidate would not have struggled with **a** and **b**. This candidate should have kept an eye on the marks available and offered much more robust answers. Another 3 marks would have made a significant improvement to the candidate's grade.

1 a An electron has a charge of -1.6×10^{-19} C. Determine the charge of

AO2 i a positron [1]

AO2 ii an alpha particle. [1]

AO2 b The diagram shows the paths of a positron (red) and an electron (green) in a magnetic field.

Explain why the paths of the particles are curved and opposite. [2]

c The isotope carbon-11 is a beta-plus emitter. The decay equation for this isotope is shown here:

$$^{11}_{6}C \rightarrow {}^{11}_{5}B + {}^{0}_{+1}e + \text{neutrino}$$

AO2 i State two quantities conserved in the decay of the carbon isotope. [2]

AO2 ii Describe the changes taking place within the carbon-11 isotope when it emits a positron. [2]

AO3 d Carbon-14 is a beta-minus emitter. Using the periodic table, write the equation for the decay of carbon-14. [4]

[Total: 12]

AO2 2 a Protons and neutrons consist of quarks.

AO1 i Name the two quarks found inside a proton and a neutron. [1]

AO1 ii State the quark composition of a neutron and a proton. [2]

AO2 b The isotope fluorine-18 is a beta-plus emitter. Explain beta-plus decay in terms of quarks. [3]

AO3 c The diagram below summarises the decay of an isotope of neon-18 ($^{18}_{10}$Ne).

$$^{18}_{10}\text{Ne} \xrightarrow[\substack{\text{half-life} \\ 1.3\text{ s}}]{\beta^+ \text{ decay}} {}^{18}_{9}\text{F} \xrightarrow[\substack{\text{half-life} \\ 110\text{ min}}]{\beta^+ \text{ decay}} \text{O} \nearrow \substack{\text{stable oxygen} \\ \text{nucleus}}$$

Determine the proton (atomic) and nucleon (mass) numbers of the stable isotope of oxygen. Explain your reasoning. [4]

[Total: 10]

AO1 3 a A neutron makes an elastic collision with a boron nucleus. Explain what is meant by an elastic collision. [2]

b A 1.5 kg trolley travelling at 1.8 m/s makes a head-on collision with a stationary 3.0 kg trolley. The trolleys join together after the collision and have a common velocity v.

AO2 i Calculate the velocity v in m/s. Show your working. [3]

AO2 ii With the help of calculations, explain whether the collision was elastic or inelastic. [3]

[Total: 8]

AO1 4 a What happens to the particles in a gas at 0 K? [1]

AO2 b The diagram shows the initial and final conditions of a fixed mass of gas in a container.

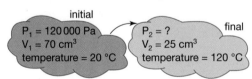

initial

$P_1 = 120\,000$ Pa
$V_1 = 70$ cm^3
temperature = 20 °C

final

$P_2 = ?$
$V_2 = 25$ cm^3
temperature = 120 °C

Calculate the final pressure P_2 exerted by the gas. Show your working. [3]

AO3 c Tina is investigating the relationship between temperature and the volume of a fixed amount of gas in a container. The gas is kept at constant pressure. Her results are shown below.

Temperature (°C)	10	20	40	80
Volume of trapped gas (cm³)	200	207	221	249

Use the data to show the relationship between volume and temperature in these conditions. [6]

[Total: 10]

Summary of Assessment Objectives

AO1 recall the science   AO2 apply your knowledge   AO3 evaluate and analyse the evidence

Worked example

In hospitals, oxygen is available in pressurised cylinders, like the one shown below.

AO2 **a** Explain how the oxygen molecules exert pressure inside the cylinder. [3]

The gas molecules move and collide (bump) with the walls ✔

of the cylinder. ✔

Pressure is force/area. ✔

b An oxygen cylinder of volume 16 litres is stored at a temperature of 15 °C. The oxygen is pressurised at 120×10^5 Pa. The cylinder is taken into a hospital ward where the temperature is 25 °C.

AO2 **i** Calculate the total volume of oxygen when the cylinder releases the oxygen at atmospheric pressure of 1.0×10^5 Pa. [3]

$$\frac{P_1 V_1}{T_1} = \frac{P_2 V_2}{T_2}$$ ✔

$$\frac{120 \times 10^5 \times 16}{15} = \frac{1.0 \times 10^5 \times V_2}{25}$$ ✗

$V_2 = 3200$ *litres* ✗

AO2 **ii** The flow rate of the cylinder is adjusted to 0.8 litres per minute. Calculate the time taken to empty the cylinder. [2]

time = 3200/0.8 ✔

time = 4000 *minutes* ✔

[Total: 8]

This candidate scored 5 marks out of a possible 8. The candidate would have picked up 2 marks and a high grade by converting the temperatures into kelvin in **bi**.

How to raise your grade

Take note of the comments from examiners – these will help you to improve your grade.

The candidate should have written a little more for this 3-mark question. The candidate could have scored full marks by mentioning that each collision exerts a tiny force on the cylinder.

The candidate has made a fundamental mistake. Both temperatures should have been converted into kelvin (K). The correct answer is 1987 litres.

The examiner has awarded full marks and has applied the error-carried-forward rule.

Carrying out practical investigations in GCSE science

Introduction

As part of your GCSE science course, you will develop practical skills and carry out investigative work as part of the scientific process.

Your investigative work will be divided into several parts:

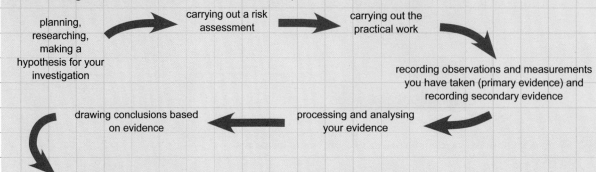

planning, researching, making a hypothesis for your investigation → carrying out a risk assessment → carrying out the practical work → recording observations and measurements you have taken (primary evidence) and recording secondary evidence → processing and analysing your evidence → drawing conclusions based on evidence → evaluating your investigation → comparing your findings with those of other scientists → discussing whether your findings support your hypothesis

✳ Planning and researching your investigation

A scientific investigation usually begins with you considering an idea, answering a question or trying to solve a problem.

Researching what other people know about the idea or problem should suggest some variables that have an effect on the problem.

From this you should develop a hypothesis. For example, you might observe during a fermentation with yeast investigation that beer or wine is produced faster at a higher temperature.

So your hypothesis might be that 'as the temperature increases, the rate of fermentation increases'.

A good starting point for your research is to use your lesson notes and textbook. The topic you've been given to investigate will relate to the science you've learned in class.

Also make use of the internet, but make sure that your internet search is closely focused on the topic you're investigating.

✔ The search terms you use on the internet are very important. 'Investigating fermentation' is a better search term than just 'fermentation', as it's more likely to provide links to websites that are more relevant to your investigation.

✔ The information on websites also varies in its reliability. Free encyclopaedias often contain information that hasn't been written by experts. Some question and answer websites might appear to give you the exact answer to your question, but be aware that they may sometimes be incorrect.

✔ Most GCSE science websites are more reliable, but, if in doubt, use other information sources to verify the information.

As a result of your research, you may be able to extend your hypothesis and justify it using scientific ideas.

> **Definition**
>
> A **hypothesis** is a possible explanation that someone suggests to explain some scientific observations.

> **Assessment tip**
>
> When making your hypothesis, it's important that it's testable. In other words, you must be able to test the hypothesis in the school lab.

> **Assessment tip**
>
> Your need to use your research to explain why you made your hypothesis.

You would then plan how you will carry out an investigation to test this hypothesis.

Example 1

Investigation: Plan and research an investigation into the effect of pH on yeast.

Your hypothesis might be 'I think that the yeast will produce the most carbon dioxide per minute at pH 7'.

You should be able to justify your hypothesis by some facts that you find. For example, 'yeast contains enzymes and I know that most enzymes work best in neutral pH solutions'.

✳ Choosing a method and suitable equipment

As part of your planning, you must choose a suitable way of carrying out the investigation.

You will have to choose suitable techniques, equipment and technology, if this is appropriate. How do you make this choice?

You will have already carried out the techniques you need to use during the course of practical work in class (although you may need to modify these to fit in with the context of your investigation). For most of the experimental work you do, there will be a choice of techniques available. You must select the technique:

✔ that is most appropriate to the context of your investigation, and

✔ that will enable you to collect valid data; for example, if you are measuring the effects of light intensity on photosynthesis, you may decide to use an LED (light-emitting diode) at different distances from the plant, rather than a light bulb. The light bulb produces more heat, and temperature is another independent variable in photosynthesis.

Your choice of equipment, too, will be influenced by measurements you need to make. For example:

✔ you might use a one-mark or graduated pipette to measure out the volume of liquid for a titration, but

✔ you may use a measuring cylinder or beaker when adding a volume of acid to a reaction mixture, so that the volume of acid is in excess to that required to dissolve, for example, the calcium carbonate.

Assessment tip

Carrying out a preliminary investigation, along with the necessary research, may help you to select the appropriate technique to use.

Assessment tip

You should always be ready to explain your choice of equipment.

Assessment tip

Technology, such as data-logging and other measuring and monitoring techniques – for example, heart sensors – may help you to carry out your experiment.

✳ Variables

In your investigation, you will work with independent and dependent variables.

The factors you choose, or are given, to investigate the effect of are called **independent variables**.

What you choose to measure, as affected by the independent variable, is called the **dependent variable**.

Independent variables

In your practical work, you will be provided with an independent variable to test, or will have to choose one – or more – of these to test. Some examples are given in the table.

Investigation	Possible independent variables to test
activity of yeast	> temperature > sugar concentration
rate of a chemical reaction	> temperature > concentration of reactants
stopping distance of a moving object	> speed of the object > the surface on which it's moving

Independent variables can be **discrete** or **continuous**.

> When you are testing the effect of different disinfectants on bacteria you are looking at discrete variables.

> When you are testing the effect of a range of concentrations of the same disinfectant on the growth of bacteria you are looking at continuous variables.

Range

When working with an independent variable, you need to choose an appropriate **range** over which to investigate the variable.

You need to decide:

✔ what you will test, and/or

✔ the upper and lower limits of the independent variable to investigate, if the variable is continuous.

Once you have defined the range to be tested, you also need to decide the appropriate intervals at which you will make measurements.

The range you would test depends on:

✔ the nature of the test

✔ the context in which it is given

✔ practical considerations, and

✔ common sense.

Example 2

Investigation: Comparing the effect of the type of lens used on the focal length.

The range of lenses you can choose will depend on the availability of the resources at your school. As a minimum though, you would choose two different lenses to compare, such as convex and plane or concave and convex.

Definition

Variables that fall into a range of separate types are called **discrete** (also known as **categorical**) **variables**.

Definition

Variables that have a continuous range are called **continuous variables**.

Definition

The **range** defines the extent of the independent variables being tested, e.g. from 15 cm to 35 cm.

Assessment tip

Again, it's often best to carry out a trial run or preliminary investigation, or carry out research, to determine the range to be investigated.

Concentration

You might be trying to find out the best, or optimum, concentration of a disinfectant to prevent the growth of bacteria.

The 'best' concentration would be the lowest in a range that prevented the growth of the bacteria. Concentrations higher than this would be just wasting disinfectant.

If, in a preliminary test, no bacteria were killed by the concentration you used, you would have to increase it (or test another disinfectant). However, if there was no growth of bacteria in your preliminary test, you would have to lower the concentration range. A starting point might be to look at concentrations around those recommended by the manufacturer.

Dependent variables

The dependent variable may be clear from the problem you're investigating; for example, the stopping distance of moving objects. But you may have to make a choice.

Example 3

1 Investigating the amount of sodium hydroxide needed to neutralise 25 cm^3 of hydrochloric acid.

There are several ways that you could establish the neutralisation point in this investigation. These include:

> using a burette to carry out a titration reaction

> using a dropper pipette to count the number of drops of sodium hydroxide added

> using a pH probe to measure the pH of the resulting solution

> using an indicator such as methyl orange.

2 Investigation: Measuring the rate of a chemical reaction.

You could measure the rate of a chemical reaction in the following ways:

> the rate of formation of a product

> the rate at which the reactant disappears

> a colour change

> a pH change.

> **Assessment tip**
>
> The value of the *depend*ent variable is likely to *depend* on the value of the independent variable. This is a good way of remembering the definition of a dependent variable.

> **Definition**
>
> Other variables that you're not investigating may also have an influence on your measurements. In most investigations, it's important that you investigate just one variable at a time. So other variables, apart from the one you're testing at the time, must be controlled, and kept constant, and not allowed to vary. These are called **control variables**.

Control variables

The validity of your measurements depends on you measuring what you're supposed to be measuring.

Some of these variables may be difficult to control. For example, in an ecology investigation in the field, factors such as varying weather conditions are impossible to control.

> **Assessment tip**
>
> Always identify all the variables to be controlled and how you will control them.

Experimental controls

Experimental controls are often very important, particularly in biological investigations where you're testing the effect of a treatment.

Example 4

Investigation: Comparing the rate of reaction between ethanoic acid and hydrochloric acid with marble chips.

There are many factors that can affect the rate of a chemical reaction, so it is important that you control all of the variables you are not investigating. You need to control the volume of acid used, e.g. 25 cm^3, and the strength of the acids, e.g. 1 mol/dm^3. You also need to control the amount of marble chips, e.g. 5 g, and the amount of time you are measuring the rate of reaction, e.g. the amount of gas produced in 1 minute.

> **Definition**
>
> An **experimental control** is used to find out whether the effect you obtain is from the treatment, or whether you get the same result in the absence of the treatment.

✳ Assessing and managing risk

Before you begin any practical work, you must assess and minimise the possible risks involved.

Before you carry out an investigation, you must identify the possible hazards. These can be grouped into biological hazards, chemical hazards and physical hazards.

Biological hazards include:

> microorganisms
> body fluids
> animals and plants.

Chemical hazards can be grouped into:

> irritant and harmful substances
> toxic
> oxidising agents
> corrosive
> harmful to the environment.

Physical hazards include:

> equipment
> objects
> radiation.

Scientists use an international series of symbols so that investigators can identify hazards.

Hazards pose risks to the person carrying out the investigation.

Many acids, for instance, while being corrosive in higher concentrations, are harmful or an irritant at low concentrations.

A risk posed by concentrated sulfuric acid, for example, will be lower if you're adding one drop of it to a reaction mixture to make an ester, than if you're mixing a large volume of it with water.

When you use hazardous materials, chemicals or equipment in the laboratory, you must use them in such a way as to keep the risks to an absolute minimum. For example, one way is to wear eye protection when using hydrochloric acid.

> **Definition**
>
> A **hazard** is something that has the potential to cause harm. Even substances, organisms and equipment that we think of being harmless, used in the wrong way, may be hazardous.

Hazard symbols are used on chemical bottles so that hazards can be identified

> **Definition**
>
> The **risk** is the likelihood of a hazard causing harm in the circumstances it's being used in.

> **Assessment tip**
>
> Your method should show how you will manage risks and make your experiment safe.

✹ Risk assessment

Before you begin an investigation, you must carry out a risk assessment. Your risk assessment must include:

✔ all relevant hazards (use the correct terms to describe each hazard, and make sure you include them all, even if you think they will pose minimal risk)

✔ risks associated with these hazards

✔ ways in which the risks can be minimised

✔ results of research into emergency procedures that you may have to follow if something goes wrong.

You should also consider what to do at the end of the practical. For example, used agar plates should be left for a technician to sterilise; solutions of heavy metals should be collected in a bottle and disposed of safely.

Assessment tip

When assessing risk and suggesting control measures, these should be specific to the hazard and risk, and not general. Hydrochloric acid is dangerous as it is 'corrosive, and skin and eye contact should be avoided' will be given credit but 'wear eye protection' is too vague.

✹ Overall plan

You should write up your overall plan – including method, equipment, variables to test and control, and risk assessment – before beginning your experiment. Arrange your plan logically. Remember, another student should be able to use it to carry out the same experiment.

✹ Collecting primary evidence

✔ You should be sure to collect evidence that is appropriate for the topic.

✔ You should make sure that observations, if appropriate, are recorded in detail. For example, it is worth recording the colour of your precipitate when making an insoluble salt, in addition to any other measurements you make.

✔ Measurements should be recorded in tables. Have one ready so that you can record your readings as you carry out the practical work.

✔ Think about the dependent variable and define this carefully in your column headings.

✔ You should make sure that the table headings describe properly the type of measurements you've made, for example 'time taken for magnesium ribbon to dissolve'.

✔ It's also essential that you include units – your results are meaningless without these.

✔ The units should appear in the column head, and not be repeated in each row of the table.

Definition

When you carry out an investigation, the data you collect are called **primary evidence.** The term 'data' is normally used to include your observations as well as any measurements you might make.

Repeatability and reproducibility of results

When making measurements, in most instances, it's essential that you carry out repeats.

These repeats are one way of checking your results.

Results will not be repeatable, of course, if you allow the conditions the investigation is carried out in to change.

You need to make sure that you carry out sufficient repeats, but not too many. In a titration, for example, if you obtain two values that are within $0.1\,cm^3$ of each other, carrying out any more will not improve the reliability of your results.

This is particularly important when scientists are carrying out scientific research and make new discoveries.

Collecting secondary evidence

As part of Controlled Assessment, you will be expected to collect **secondary evidence**. The secondary data you collect must be appropriate for the topic.

One of the simplest ways of doing this is to collect evidence from other groups in your class who have carried out an identical practical investigation.

You should also, if possible, search through the scientific literature – in textbooks, the internet and databases – to find evidence from similar or identical practical investigations.

Ideally, you should use secondary evidence from a number of sources and record it appropriately.

You should review secondary data and evaluate it. Scientific studies are sometimes influenced by the **bias** of the experimenter.

✔ One kind of bias is having a strong opinion related to the investigation, and perhaps selecting only the results that fit with a hypothesis or prediction.

✔ Or the bias could be unintentional. In fields of science that are not yet fully understood, experimenters may try to fit their findings to current knowledge and thinking.

There have been other instances where the 'findings' of experimenters have been influenced by organisations that supplied the funding for the research.

You must fully reference any secondary data you have used, using one of the accepted referencing methods.

Referencing methods

The two main conventions for writing a reference are the:

✔ Harvard system

✔ Vancouver system.

In your text, the Harvard system refers to the authors of the reference, for example 'Smith and Jones (1978)'.

The Vancouver system refers to the number of the numbered reference in your text, for example '... the reason for this hypothesis is unknown.[5]'

Assessment tip

One set of results from your investigation may not reflect what truly happens. Carrying out repeats enables you to identify any results that don't fit.

Definition

If you carry out the same experiment several times and get the same, or very similar, results, we say the results are **repeatable**.

Definition

Taking more than one set of results will improve the **reliability** of your data.

Definition

Secondary evidence is measurements/observations made by anyone other than you.

Assessment tip

Always comment on the quality of your secondary evidence – including bias.

Though the Harvard system is usually preferred by scientists, it is more straightforward for you to use the Vancouver system.

Harvard system

In your references list a book reference should be written:

> Author(s) (year of publication). *Title of Book*, publisher, publisher location.

The references are listed in alphabetical order according to the authors.

Vancouver system

In your references list a book reference should be written:

> 1 Author(s). *Title of Book*. Publisher, publisher location: year of publication.

The references are numbered in the order in which they are cited in the text.

Assessment tip

Remember to write out the URL of a website in full. You should also quote the date when you looked at the website.

✸ Processing evidence

You may be required to use formulae when processing data. Sometimes, these will need rearranging to be able to make the calculation you need. Practise using and rearranging formulae as part of your preparation for assessment.

Calculating the mean

Using your repeat measurements you can calculate the arithmetical mean (or just 'mean') of these data. Often, the mean is called the 'average'.

Here are the results of an investigation into the energy requirements of three different mp3 players. The students measured the energy using a joulemeter for 10 seconds.

mp3 player	Energy used in joules (J)			
	Trial 1	Trial 2	Trial 3	Mean
Viking	5.5	5.3	5.7	5.5
Anglo	4.5	4.6	4.9	4.7
Saxon	3.2	4.5	4.7	4.6

Significant figures

When calculating the mean, you should be aware of significant figures.

For example, for the set of data below:

18	13	17	15	14	16	15	14	13	18

The total for the data set is 153, and 10 measurements have been made. The mean is 15, and not 15.3.

This is because each of the recorded values has two significant figures. The answer must therefore have two significant figures. An answer cannot have more significant figures than the number being multiplied or divided.

Assessment tip

Remember to process all your collected evidence – primary and secondary.

Definition

The **reproducibility** of data is the ability of the results of an investigation to be reproduced by someone else, who may be in a different lab, carrying out the same work.

Definition

The **mean** is calculated by adding together all the measurements, and dividing by the number of measurements.

Definition

Significant figures are the number of digits in a number based on the precision of your measurements.

Using your data

When calculating means (and displaying data), you should be careful to look out for any data that do not fit in with the general pattern. In the table above one result has been excluded from the mean calculation because it was more than 10% lower than the other values. This suggests it may be anomalous.

It might be the consequence of an error made in measurement. But sometimes anomalous results are genuine results. If you think an anomalous result has been introduced by careless practical work, you should ignore it when calculating the mean. But you should examine possible reasons carefully before just leaving it out.

Presenting your evidence

Presenting your evidence – usually the means – makes it easy to pick out and show any patterns. It also helps you to pick out any anomalous results.

It is likely that you will have recorded your results in tables, and you could also use additional tables to summarise your results. The most usual way of displaying data is to use graphs. The table will help you to decide which type to use.

Type of graph	When you would use the graph	Example
Bar charts or bar graph	Where one of the variables is discrete	'The energy requirements of different mp3 players'
Line graph	Where independent and dependent variables are both continuous	'The volume of carbon dioxide produced by a range of different concentrations of hydrochloric acid'
Scatter graph	To show an association between two (or more) variables	'The association between length and breadth of a number of privet leaves' In scatter graphs, the points are plotted, but not usually joined

If it's possible from the data, join the points of a line graph using a straight line, or in some instances, a curve. In this way graphs can also help us to process data.

Spread of data

Plotting a graph of just the means doesn't tell you anything about the spread of data that has been used to calculate the mean.

You can show the spread of the data on your graphs using error bars or range bars.

Range bars are very useful, but they don't show how the data are spread between the extreme values. It is important to have information about this range. It may affect your analysis of the data, and the conclusions you draw.

Definition

An **anomaly** (or **outlier**) is a reading that is very different from the rest.

Assessment tip

Remember when drawing graphs, plot the independent variable on the x-axis, and the dependent variable on the y-axis.

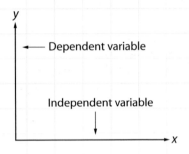

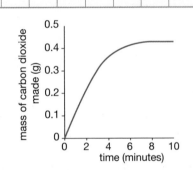

We can calculate the rate of production of carbon dioxide from the gradient of the graph

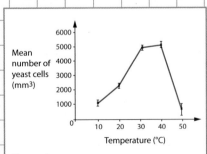

Range bars

Differences in data sets and probability

When comparing two (or more) sets of data, we often compare the values of two sets of means.

Example 5

Investigation: Comparing sweaty students

Two groups of students measured the amount of sweat they produced after exercising for 1 hour. Their results are shown in the table below.

Student	Amount of sweat produced (ml)					Mean (ml)
	1	2	3	4	5	
Group 1	15	12	17	20	12	15
Group 2	11	9	12	13	10	11

When the means are compared, it appears that Group 1 produced more sweat than Group 2. The difference may be due to the amount and type of exercise each group did, or it may be purely by chance.

Scientists use statistics to find the probability of any differences having occurred by chance. The lower this probability is, which is found out by statistical calculations, the more likely it is that tyre A is better at stopping a vehicle than tyre B.

Statistical analysis can help to increase the confidence you have in your conclusions.

 Drawing conclusions

Observing trends in data or graphs will help you to draw conclusions. You may obtain a linear relationship between two sets of variables, or the relationship might be more complex.

The graphs on the right are examples of two types of relationship between variables.

Example 6

Conclusion: As the temperature of the gas increased its pressure also increased.

Conclusion: Increasing the temperature increased the energy of the gas particles, causing them to move around faster. This means that there were more collisions between the gas particles and the sides of the container. Therefore, the pressure increased.

When drawing conclusions, you should try to relate your findings to the science involved.

> In the first point in Example 6, your discussion should focus on describing what your results show, including any patterns or trends between them.

> In the second point in Example 6, there is a clear scientific mechanism to link the increase in temperature to an increase in gas pressure.

Sometimes, you can see correlations between data which are coincidental, where the independent variable is not the cause of the trend in the data.

Definition

If there is a relationship between dependent and independent variables that can be defined, we say there is a **correlation** between the variables.

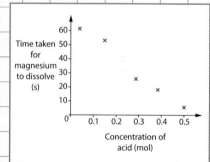

This graph shows **negative correlation**

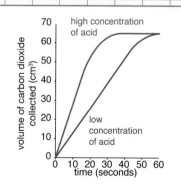

This graph shows **positive correlation**

Example 7

Studies have shown that levels of vitamin D are very low in people with long-term inflammatory diseases. But there's no scientific evidence to suggest that these low levels are the cause of the diseases.

Assessment tip

Remember to critically analyse any secondary evidence that conflicts with yours, and suggest and discuss what further evidence might help to make your conclusions more secure.

✳ Accounting for errors

Your conclusion will be based on your evidence, but must take into consideration any uncertainty in your results introduced by any possible sources of error. You should discuss where these have come from in your evaluation.

The two types of errors are:

✔ random error

✔ systematic error.

This can occur when the instrument you're using to measure lacks sufficient sensitivity to indicate differences in readings. It can also occur when it's difficult to make a measurement. If two investigators measure the height of a plant, for example, they might choose different points on the compost and the tip of the growing point to make their measurements.

Your results may be either consistently too high or too low. One reason could be down to the way you are making a reading; for example, taking a burette reading at

The volume of liquid in a burette must be read to the bottom of the meniscus

the wrong point on the meniscus. Another could be the result of an instrument being incorrectly calibrated, or not being calibrated.

Definition

Error is a difference between a measurement you make, and its true value.

With **random error**, measurements vary in an unpredictable way.

With **systematic error**, readings vary in a controlled way.

Assessment tip

A pH meter must be calibrated before use using buffers of known pH.

Assessment tip

Make sure you relate your conclusions to the hypothesis you are investigating. Do the results confirm or reject the hypothesis? Quote some results to back up your statement, e.g. 'My results at 35 °C and 65 °C show that over a 30 °C change in temperature the time taken to produce 50 cm^3 of carbon dioxide halved'.

✳ Accuracy and precision

When evaluating your investigation, you should mention accuracy and precision. But if you use these terms, it's important that you understand what they mean, and that you use them correctly.

Precise but not accurate

Precise and accurate

Neither precise nor accurate

Definition

When making measurements:

> the **accuracy** of the measurement is how close it is to the true value

> **precision** is how closely a series of measurements agree with each other.

The terms accuracy and precision can be illustrated using shots at a dartboard.

In science, the measurements you make as part of your investigation should be as precise as you can, or need to, make them. To achieve this, you should use:

✔ the most appropriate measuring instrument
✔ the measuring instrument with the most appropriate size of divisions.

The smaller the divisions you work with, the more precise your measurements. For example:

✔ In an investigation on how your heart rate is affected by exercise, you might decide to investigate this after a 100 m run. You might measure out the 100 m distance using a trundle wheel, which is sufficiently precise for your investigation.

✔ In an investigation on how light intensity is affected by distance, you would make your measurements of distance using a metre rule with millimetre divisions; clearly a trundle wheel would be too imprecise.

✔ In an investigation on plant growth, in which you measure the thickness of a plant stem, you would use a micrometer or Vernier callipers. In this instance, a metre rule would be too imprecise.

✸ Evaluating your method and conclusion

When evaluating your method, you should identify the strengths of your method and discuss how your investigation could be improved. You should consider improving:

✔ the reliability of your data. For example, you could make more repeats, or more frequent readings, or 'fine-tune' the range you choose to investigate, or refine your technique in some other way

✔ the accuracy and precision of your data, by using more precise measuring equipment.

Taking this into account, you can evaluate your conclusion – how could you improve or extend your evidence to give further support to your conclusion? An important way to extend your evidence is by carrying out repeats.

Assessment tip

Your evaluation of your method should be related to your hypothesis and reasons should be given for anomalies.

✸ Does the evidence support your hypothesis?

You need to discuss, in detail, whether all, or which of your primary evidence and the secondary evidence you have collected supports your original hypothesis. It may, or may not.

You should communicate your points clearly, using the appropriate scientific terms, and checking carefully your use of spelling, punctuation and grammar. You will be assessed on this written communication as well as your science.

If your evidence does not completely match your hypothesis, it may be possible to modify the hypothesis or suggest an alternative one. You should suggest any further investigations that can be carried out to support your original hypothesis or the modified version.

It is important to remember, however, that if your investigation does support your hypothesis, it can improve the confidence you have in your conclusions and scientific explanations, but it can't prove your explanations are correct.

Your controlled assessment

The assessment of your investigation will form part of what's called Controlled Assessment. Edexcel will provide the task for you to investigate.

You may be able to work in small groups to carry out the practical work, but you will have to work on your own to write up your investigation.

Controlled assessment is worth 25% of the marks for your GCSE. It's worth doing it well!

Your Additional Science Controlled Assessment Task (CAT) will consist of three parts:

✔ Part A – Planning
✔ Part B – Observations
✔ Part C – Conclusions

To achieve a final grade in your Controlled Assessment Unit, you must complete all three parts of at least one CAT.

Part A – Planning

In Part A you must write a plan to test a specific hypothesis.

You will be briefed with an outline of a scientific concept and task.

In your **Science** CAT you were given a hypothesis to test. In your **Additional** and **Separate Sciences** CATs you must write a hypothesis in line with the brief you have been given.

To produce a complete plan you must:

✔ Select and justify the equipment for your investigation
✔ Choose and explain the variables you will change, measure and control
✔ Identify risks and explain how you will manage them
✔ Write a plan that includes your method, equipment and variables, and reflects how risks will be managed.

Your plan must be clear and produce results that will test your hypothesis.

You will complete Part A under 'limited' controlled conditions. This means that you will be allowed to collaborate with other students and use research to complete the task.

Assessment tip

> In **Science** you ideally would have carried out Parts A, B and C in a CAT from each Science Unit – B1, C1 and P1.

> In **Additional Science** you will ideally carry out Parts A, B and C in a task from each Additional Science Unit – B2, C2 and P2.

> In **Biology**, **Chemistry** and **Physics** you may carry out Parts A, B and C in a task from Unit 2 or Unit 3 of the appropriate Science.

For each qualification (Science, Additional Science, Biology, Chemistry or Physics), if you attempt more than one task, *only your best mark* in Parts A, B and C will be submitted to Edexcel to make up your final Controlled Assessment grade.

Assessment tip

You will achieve top marks in Part A by:

> Justifying your hypothesis
> Explaining each part of your plan
> Choosing a range of data and observations to test the hypothesis
> Always showing how your plan links to your hypothesis and will produce meaningful results
> Always relating your plan back to appropriate scientific ideas
> Being clear and logical in communicating your plan.

Part B – Observations

In Part B you will carry out an experiment to test your hypothesis from Part A, using the plan you produced also in Part A.

You will use your plan to collect and record primary evidence.

You must also collect and record secondary evidence that is relevant to your hypothesis.

You may collect secondary evidence in class or at home from:

✔ the internet

✔ other students, or

✔ textbooks.

You will be expected to reference all secondary sources fully and comment on the quality of the source of evidence.

You will also complete Part B under 'limited' controlled conditions.

Part C – Conclusions

In Part C you will process and draw conclusions from the evidence you collected in Part B.

✔ Process all your evidence (primary and secondary) suitably using digital technology and maths as appropriate.

✔ Decide whether to include or exclude anomalies when processing evidence, explaining your reasons why.

✔ Produce a conclusion based on all processed evidence and appropriate scientific ideas. Does your evidence prove or disprove your hypothesis?

✔ Evaluate your method, describing strengths, weaknesses and improvements, and explaining reasons for anomalies.

✔ Suggest how you could improve or extend your evidence to support your conclusion further.

✔ Review your hypothesis in light of the evidence.

You will complete Part C under 'high' controlled conditions. This means that you must complete your write-up individually and completely under teacher supervision.

Quality of Written Communication

Be aware of the quality of your written communication in all parts of the CAT. You must ensure that the marker understands your ideas and evidence.

At all times you must communicate clearly using:

✔ an appropriate form and style

✔ clear and logical presentation, and

✔ scientific language where appropriate.

Assessment tip

If your plan from Part A was unusable – for example, because it was potentially dangerous – your teacher will give you a plan to work from for Part B. Remember, you will receive no marks for a Part A plan that is given to you.

Assessment tip

You will achieve top marks in Part B by:

> Collecting a suitable range of data.

> Carrying out repeat experiments as appropriate

> Recording all evidence – primary and secondary – appropriately.

Assessment tip

You will achieve top marks in Part C by:

> Presenting evidence so that you can draw conclusions from it

> Explaining your conclusions using maths, scientific ideas and data

> Relating your conclusion and evaluation back to your hypothesis.

Assessment tip

Your teacher will give you a copy of the Assessment Criteria so that you can see what you need to do to access all marks.

How to be successful in your GCSE science written assessment

Introduction

Edexcel uses assessments to test how good your understanding of scientific ideas is, how well you can apply your understanding to new situations, and how well you can analyse and interpret information you've been given. The assessments are opportunities to show how well you can do these.

To be successful in exams you need to:

✔ have a good knowledge and understanding of science

✔ be able to apply this knowledge and understanding to familiar and new situations, and

✔ be able to interpret and evaluate evidence that you've just been given.

You need to be able to do these things under exam conditions.

✳ The language of the external assessment

When working through an assessment paper, make sure that you:

✔ re-read a question enough times until you understand exactly what the examiner is looking for

✔ highlight key words in a question

✔ look at how many marks are allocated to each part of a question. In general, you need to write at least as many separate points in your answer as there are marks.

✳ What verbs are used in the question?

A good technique is to see which verbs are used in the wording of the question and to use these to gauge the type of response you need to give. The table lists some of the common verbs found in questions, the types of responses expected and examples.

Verb used in question	Response expected in answer	Example question
write down; state; give; identify	These are usually more straightforward types of question in which you're asked to give a definition, make a list of examples, or choose the best answer from a series of options	'Write down three types of microorganism that cause disease' 'State one difference and one similarity between radio waves and gamma rays'
calculate	Use maths to solve a numerical problem	'Calculate the percentage of carbon in copper carbonate ($CuCO_3$)'

estimate	Use maths to solve a numerical problem, but you do not have to work out the exact answer	'Estimate from the graph the speed of the vehicle after 3 minutes'
describe	Use words (or diagrams) to show the characteristics, properties or features of, or build an image of, something	'Describe how meiosis halves the number of chromosomes in a cell to make egg or sperm cells'
suggest	Come up with an idea to explain information you're given, usually in a new or unfamiliar context	'Suggest why tyres with different tread patterns will have different braking distances'
demonstrate; show how	Use words to make something evident using reasoning	'Show how temperature can affect the rate of a chemical reaction'
compare	Look for similarities and differences	'Compare aerobic and anaerobic respiration'
explain	To offer a reason for, or make understandable, information you're given	'Explain why alpha and beta radiations can be deflected by a magnetic field, but gamma rays are not'
evaluate	To examine and make a judgement about an investigation or information you're given	'Evaluate the benefits of using a circuit breaker instead of a fuse in an electrical circuit'

What is the style of the question?

Try to get used to answering questions that have been written in lots of different styles before you sit the exam. Work through past papers, or specimen papers, to get a feel for these. The types of questions in your assessment fit the three assessment objectives shown in the table.

Assessment objective	Your answer should show that you can...
AO1 Recall the science	Recall, select and communicate your knowledge and understanding of science
AO2 Apply your knowledge	Apply skills, knowledge and understanding of science in practical and other contexts
AO3 Evaluate and analyse the evidence	Analyse and evaluate evidence, make reasoned judgements and draw conclusions based on evidence

Assessment tip

Of course, you must revise the subject material adequately. But it's as important that you are familiar with the different question styles used in the exam paper, as well as the question content.

How to answer questions on: AO1 Recall the science

These questions, or parts of questions, test your ability to recall your knowledge of a topic. There are several types of this style of question:

✔ Fill in the spaces (you may be given words to choose from)
✔ Multiple choice
✔ Use lines to link a term with its definition or correct statement
✔ Add labels to a diagram
✔ Complete a table
✔ Describe a process

Example 8

a Which is the correct equation to calculate the pressure an object exerts?

Tick (✓) **one** box.

☐ $P = \dfrac{F}{A}$

☐ $P = \dfrac{A}{F}$

☐ $P = F \times A$

AO1 questions on practical techniques

You may be asked to recall how to carry out certain practical techniques; either ones that you have carried out before, or techniques that scientists use.

To revise for these types of questions, make sure that you have learned definitions and scientific terms. Produce a glossary of these, or key facts cards, to make them easier to remember. Make sure your key facts cards also cover important practical techniques, including equipment, where appropriate.

Example 9

1 Describe two factors scientists can change to affect the amount of product produced in equilibrium reactions, e.g. the Haber process or contact process.

2 Describe how DNA fragments can be separated by electrophoresis.

Assessment tip

Don't forget that mind maps – either drawn by you or made using a computer program – are very helpful when revising key points.

 # How to answer questions on: AO2 Apply skills, knowledge and understanding

Some questions require you to apply basic knowledge and understanding in your answers.

You may be presented with a topic that's familiar to you, but you should also expect questions in your science exam to be set in an unfamiliar context.

Questions may be presented as:

✔ short questions referring to an unfamiliar object, process or organism

✔ experimental investigations

✔ data or diagrams for you to interpret

✔ a short paragraph or article.

The information required for you to answer the question might be in the question itself, but, for later stages of the question, you may be asked to draw on your knowledge and understanding of the subject material in the question.

Practice will help you to become familiar with contexts that examiners use and question styles. But you will not be able to predict many of the contexts used. This is deliberate; being able to apply your knowledge and understanding to different and unfamiliar situations is a skill the examiner tests.

Practise doing questions where you are tested on being able to apply your scientific knowledge and your ability to understand new situations that may not be familiar. In this way, when this type of question comes up in your exam, you will be able to tackle it successfully.

> ### Assessment tip
>
> Work through the Preparing for Assessment: Applying your knowledge tasks in this book as practice.

Example 10

When light enters the eye from the air it first passes through the cornea – a jelly-like substance – before entering the pupil. Use your knowledge of refraction to explain what happens to the light as it passes through the cornea.

AO2 questions on practical investigations

Some opportunities to demonstrate your application of skills, knowledge and understanding will be based on practical investigations. You may have carried out some of these investigations, but others will be new to you, and based on data obtained by scientists. You will be expected to describe patterns in data from graphs you are given or that you will have to draw from given data.

Again, you will have to apply your scientific knowledge and understanding to answer the question.

Example 11

A student measured the pH of two different brands of beer over seven days to find out which one oxidised from ethanol into ethanoic acid first. His results are shown in the graph on the right.

Beer	pH on each day					
	1	2	3	4	5	6
Old Brew	6.6	5.8	4.0	3.0	2.1	2.1
Eagle Lager	6.3	5.9	4.1	3.5	2.2	2.1

a Calculate the total pH decrease for each beer over the six days.

b Ethanoic acid has a pH of 2.4. Use the graph to work out which beer oxidised to ethanoic acid first.

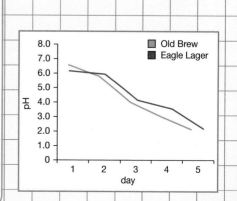

✳ How to answer questions on: AO3 Analysing and evaluating evidence

For these types of questions, you will analyse and evaluate scientific evidence or data given to you in the question. It's likely that you won't be familiar with the material.

Analysing data may involve drawing graphs and interpreting them, and carrying out calculations. Practise drawing and interpreting graphs from data.

When drawing a graph, make sure you:

✔ choose and label the axes fully and correctly

✔ include units, if this hasn't been done for you already

✔ plot points on the graph carefully – the examiner will check individual points to make sure that they are accurate

✔ join the points correctly; usually this will be by a line of best fit.

When reading values off a graph you have drawn or one given in the question, make sure you:

✔ do it carefully, reading the values as accurately as you can

✔ double-check the values.

When describing patterns and trends in the data, make sure you:

✔ write about a pattern or trend in as much detail as you can

✔ mention anomalies where appropriate

✔ recognise there may be one general trend in the graph, where the variables show positive or negative correlation

✔ recognise the data may show a more complex relationship. The graph may demonstrate different trends in several sections. You should describe what's happening in each

✔ describe fully what the data shows.

You must also be able to evaluate the information you're given. This is one of the hardest skills. Think about the validity of the scientific data: did the technique(s) used in any practical investigation allow the collection of accurate and precise data?

Your critical evaluation of scientific data in class, along with the practical work and Controlled Assessment work, will help you to develop the evaluation skills required for these types of questions.

Example 12

1 Why might there be a difference in the data collected in an investigation to measure the mass lost in the reaction between marble chips and acid, if both a conical flask and beaker were used throughout the investigation?

Your AO3 questions may also require you to demonstrate an understanding of how evidence is used and validated in the scientific community.

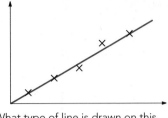
What type of line is drawn on this graph?

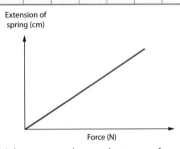
Make sure you know what type of relationship is shown in this graph

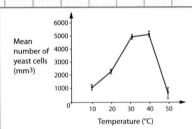
What type of relationship does this graph show?

✳ How to answer questions needing calculations

✔ The calculations you're asked to do may be straightforward; for example, the calculation of the mean from a set of practical data.

✔ Or they may be more complex; for example, calculating the yield of a chemical reaction.

✔ Other questions will require the use of formulae.

Remember, this is the same maths that you learned in your Maths lessons.

Example 13

1 10.0 cm^3 of a solution of sodium hydroxide was titrated with a 0.10 mol dm^{-3} solution of hydrochloric acid. Calculate the concentration of the sodium hydroxide solution if 15.0 cm^3 of hydrochloric acid was needed to neutralise it.

Assessment tip

Remember, you calculate the mean by adding up all the numbers in the data set, and dividing by how many numbers there are.

Assessment tip

Formulae are often given to you on the question paper, but sometimes you will be expected to recall and use these. When completing your calculation, make sure you include the correct units.

Check the specification, or check with your teacher, to make sure that you know the formulae that you have to learn and remember.

✳ The quality of your written communication

Scientists need good communication skills to present and discuss their findings. You will be expected to demonstrate these skills in the exam. Questions where quality of written communication is likely to be particularly important are marked with an *. However, this doesn't mean quality of written communication isn't important in other questions – it is!

✔ You must also try to make sure that your spelling, punctuation and grammar are accurate, so that it's clear what you mean in your answer. Examiners can't award marks for answers where the meaning isn't clear.

✔ Present your information in a form that suits the purpose. For example, think about the form, style of writing and level of complexity.

✔ Organise information clearly, coherently and logically.

✔ When describing and explaining science, use correct scientific vocabulary.

Practise answering some questions where quality of written communication is important. Look at how marks are awarded in mark schemes provided by Edexcel. You'll find these in the specimen question papers, and past papers.

You will also need to remember the writing and communication skills you've developed in English lessons. For example, make sure that you understand how to construct a good sentence using connectives.

Assessment tip

Remember, when carrying out any calculations, you should include your working at each stage. You may get credit for getting the process correct, even if your final answer is wrong.

Assessment tip

Organising information clearly, coherently and logically is the most important skill in QWC.

Assessment tip

When answering questions, you must make sure that your writing is legible. An examiner can't award marks for answers that he or she can't read.

✹ Revising for your science exam

You should revise in the way that suits you best. But it's important that you plan your revision carefully, and it's best to start well before the date of the exams. Take the time to prepare a revision timetable and try to stick to it. Use this during the lead up to the exams and between each exam.

When revising:

✔ find a quiet and comfortable space in the house where you won't be disturbed. It's best if it's well ventilated and has plenty of light

✔ take regular breaks. Some evidence suggests that revision is most effective when you revise in 30 to 40 minute slots. If you get bogged down at any point, take a break and go back to it later when you're feeling fresh. Try not to revise when you are feeling tired. If you do feel tired, take a break

✔ use your school notes, textbook and, possibly, a revision guide. But also make sure that you spend some time using past papers to familiarise yourself with the exam format

✔ produce summaries of each topic or unit

✔ draw mind maps covering the key information on a topic or unit

✔ set up revision cards containing condensed versions of your notes

✔ ask yourself questions, and try to predict questions, as you're revising topics or units

✔ test yourself as you're going along. Try to draw key labelled diagrams, and try some questions under timed conditions

✔ prioritise your revision of topics. You might want to allocate more time to revising the topics you find most difficult.

✹ How do I use my time effectively in the exam?

Timing is important when you sit an exam. Don't spend so long on some questions that you leave insufficient time to answer others. For example, in a 60-mark question paper, lasting one hour, you will have, on average, one minute per question.

If you're unsure about certain questions, complete the ones you're able to do first, then go back to the ones you're less sure of.

If you have time, go back and check your answers at the end of the exam.

✹ On exam day...

A little bit of nervousness before your exam can be a good thing, but try not to let it affect your performance in the exam. When you turn over the exam paper keep calm. Look at the paper and get it clear in your head exactly what is required from each question. Read each question carefully. Don't rush.

If you read a question and think that you have not covered the topic, keep calm – it could be that the information needed to answer the question is in the question itself or the examiner may be asking you to apply your knowledge to a new situation.

Finally, good luck!

Periodic table

Group

0
4 He 2 helium

| 1 H 1 hydrogen |

Group

1	2											3	4	5	6	7	
7 Li 3 lithium	9 Be 4 beryllium											11 B 5 boron	12 C 6 carbon	14 N 7 nitrogen	16 O 8 oxygen	19 F 9 fluorine	
23 Na 11 sodium	24 Mg 12 magnesium											27 Al 13 aluminium	28 Si 14 silicon	31 P 15 phosphorus	32 S 16 sulfur	35 Cl 17 chlorine	
39 K 19 potassium	40 Ca 20 calcium	45 Sc 21 scandium	48 Ti 22 titanium	51 V 23 vanadium	52 Cr 24 chromium	55 Mn 25 manganese	56 Fe 26 iron	59 Co 27 cobalt	59 Ni 28 nickel	64 Cu 29 copper	65 Zn 30 zinc	70 Ga 31 gallium	73 Ge 32 germanium	75 As 33 arsenic	79 Se 34 selenium	80 Br 35 bromine	84 Kr 36 krypton
85 Rb 37 rubidium	88 Sr 38 strontium	89 Y 39 yttrium	91 Zr 40 zirconium	93 Nb 41 niobium	96 Mo 42 molybdenum	99 Tc 43 technetium	101 Ru 44 ruthenium	103 Rh 45 rhodium	106 Pd 46 palladium	108 Ag 47 silver	112 Cd 48 cadmium	115 In 49 indium	119 Sn 50 tin	122 Sb 51 antimony	128 Te 52 tellurium	127 I 53 iodine	131 Xe 54 xenon
133 Cs 55 caesium	137 Ba 56 barium	139 La 57 lanthanum	178 Hf 72 hafnium	181 Ta 73 tantalum	184 W 74 tungsten	186 Re 75 rhenium	190 Os 76 osmium	192 Ir 77 iridium	195 Pt 78 platinum	197 Au 79 gold	201 Hg 80 mercury	204 Tl 81 thallium	207 Pb 82 lead	209 Bi 83 bismuth	210 Po 84 polonium	210 At 85 astatine	222 Rn 86 radon
223 Fr 87 francium	226 Ra 88 radium	227 Ac 89 actinium															

You need to remember the symbols for the highlighted elements.

 **Physics formulae**

Calculate intensity of radiation:

intensity = power of incident radiation/area

$I = P/A$

The relationship between the power of lens and its focal length:

power of lens (dioptre, D) = $\dfrac{1}{\text{focal length (metre, m)}}$

The relationship between focal length, object distance and image distance:

$$\frac{1}{f} = \frac{1}{v} + \frac{1}{u}$$

(f = focal length (m), u = object distance (m), v = image distance (m))

The relationship between current, number of particles and the charge on each particles:

current (ampere, A) = number of particles per second (1/second, 1/s) × charge on each particle (coulomb, C)

$I = N \times q$

Calculate kinetic energy:

kinetic energy (joule, J) = charge on the electron (coulomb, C) × accelerating potential difference (volt, V)

$KE = \frac{1}{2} \times mv^2 = e \times V$

Calculate frequency:

frequency (hertz, Hz) = $\dfrac{1}{\text{time period (second, s)}}$

$f = \dfrac{1}{T}$

The relationship between temperature and volume for a gas:

$$V_1 = \frac{V_2 T_1}{T_2}$$

The relationship between volume and pressure for a gas

$V_1 P_1 = V_2 P_2$

The relationship between the volume, pressure and temperature for a gas:

initial pressure (pascal, Pa) × initial volume (metre³, m³)/initial temperature (kelvin, K) = final pressure (pascal, Pa) × final volume (metre³, m³)/final temperature (kelvin, K)

$$\frac{P_1 V_1}{T_1} = \frac{P_2 V_2}{T_2}$$

Glossary

absolute zero   a temperature equivalent to −273.15 °C; all atoms or molecules stop moving at this temperature

Acheulean   a more developed stone-tool technology than that of the Oldowan but which initially overlapped with it

acid   a substance that reacts with a base

acrosome   pointed end of the sperm head containing enzymes which help the sperm to penetrate the egg membrane

action potentials   electrical signals responsible for contracting specific muscles of the heart

African Eve   the most recent common human ancestor (*Homo sapiens*)

air-lift bioreactor   a large fermenter that uses sterile air to produce upwelling, which mixes the fermenter's contents rather than using paddles

alcohol by volume   the percentage of alcohol in a standard volume

alcohol dehydrogenase   an enzyme in the liver that breaks down alcohol (ethanol)

alginate beads   inert, insoluble matrix to which an enzyme is bonded, immobilising it

alkaloids   naturally occurring, mostly bitter-tasting compounds derived from amino acids

alkanes   a family of hydrocarbons containing only hydrogen and carbon atoms, with single covalent bonds, and with the general formula $C_nH_{(2n+2)}$, e.g. methane

alkenes   a family of hydrocarbons with a carbon to carbon double covalent bond between two of the carbon atoms and the general formula C_nH_{2n}

allele   one of a pair of forms of a gene

ammonia   a gas with molecules that contain atoms of nitrogen and hydrogen

anaerobic respiration   respiration without using oxygen

anion   a negatively charged ion

annihilation   destruction caused by interaction of a particle with its anti-particle

anode   positively charged electrode

antibacterials   substances that kill or prevent the growth of bacteria

antibody   protein normally present in the body or produced in response to an antigen which it neutralises, thus producing an immune response

antidiuretic hormone (ADH)   hormone released from the pituitary gland and which affects the permeability of the walls of the collecting ducts of nephrons to water

antigen   any substance that stimulates the production of antibodies

antimatter   matter made up of anti-particles, such as positrons

aseptic   conditions that prevent bacteria contaminating surfaces and infecting wounds

aspirin   a pain-killing drug derived from salicin, extracted from the willow tree

atmospheric pressure   the pressure exerted by the atmosphere of the Earth; at sea level the atmospheric pressure is 100 kPa

atomic number   the number of protons inside a nucleus

Avogadro's law   equal volumes of all gases contain an equal number of moles of gas

bacteriophage   a virus that parasitises bacterial cells

bagasse   plant material that remains after crushing sugar cane

base   (1) either adenine (A), thymine (T), guanine (G) or cytosine (C) as part of a DNA molecule (2) metal oxide or hydroxide

behaviour   patterns of response as the result of stimuli

beta-minus (β⁻) decay   emission of an electron from an unstable nucleus

beta-plus (β⁺) decay   emission of a positron from an unstable nucleus

bifacial   having two sides or faces

biofuel   fuel produced from renewable plant or animal material

biological clock   probable mechanism of circadian rhythms related to periodic switching on and off of gene activity

biological washing powder   washing powder containing enzymes that digest biological stains in clothes

biomass   all of the organic material making up an organism's body

biomolecule   any molecule produced by a living organism

biotechnology   processes used to produce useful biomolecules

bipedalism   upright walking on two legs

bladder   part of the urinary system where urine is stored before its release from the body

blight   a disease of potato plants caused by a fungus

Bowman's capsule   part of the nephron into which urea and other substances pass from the blood by ultrafiltration

Boyle's law   the pressure exerted by a fixed mass of gas, kept at constant temperature, is inversely proportional to its volume

Bt insecticidal crystal protein   a toxin that kills insects produced by the bacterium *Bacillus thuringiensis*

canopy   unbroken layers of leaves of woodland trees, which reduce the amount of light reaching the woodland floor

carbon neutral   a product that releases as much carbon dioxide when burned as is absorbed making it

carboxyl group   the molecular group COOH, which is found in organic acids

carrier   an individual who has a mutation causing a genetic disorder but is not affected by it because the mutation is recessive

CAT scan   an image produced using X-rays from a computerised axial tomography (CAT) scanner

cathode   negatively charged electrode

cation   a positively charged ion

centripetal force   the resultant force acting at right angles to the velocity of an object that gives rise to circular motion

Charles' law   the volume occupied by a fixed mass of gas, kept at constant pressure, is directly proportional to its temperature on the kelvin scale

choice chamber   apparatus that allows an animal to choose simultaneously between alternative courses of action

ciliary muscles   muscles that help to change the shape of the eye lens

circadian   biological rhythms of activity that approximate to the daily cycle

classical conditioning   a type of learning where a response elicited by an appropriate stimulus is also elicited by a neutral stimulus

co-evolution   where a change in characteristics of one species is the stimulus that causes a change in the characteristics of another closely associated species

collecting duct   tube through which water is reabsorbed from the liquid passing through it into the blood

colour blindness   a sex-linked genetic disorder caused by a mutation on the X chromosome

common ancestor   species which is the origin of other species that have diverged ('split') and become different from it through evolution

complementary pairs   refers to the bonding between bases forming pairs of bases; adenine bonds with thymine, guanine bonds with cytosine

condensation reaction   a reaction that joins two molecules by removing a molecule of water

continuous culture   a culture that produces single-cell proteins (biomolecules) in fermenters as an ongoing process without interruption to extract product

convoluted tubules   lead into and from the loop of Henle and where substances are selectively reabsorbed into the blood from the liquid passing through the nephron

cornea   the curved layer over the front of the eye

courtship behaviour   behaviour that occurs before sexual activity that leads to reproduction

cowpox   a non-serious viral disease caught by people from cows

critical angle   the angle of incidence in a denser medium that gives an angle of refraction equal to 90°

critical period   ratio of the period of light to dark over 24 hours

crown gall   tumour-like growth of tissue produced when a plant is infected with *Agrobacterium tumefasciens*

curds   solid protein (casein) precipitated from milk in acid conditions

cyanogens   poisonous compounds containing cyanide

cyclotron   a particle accelerator used to produce radioactive isotopes used in PET scans

dialysis   treatment where blood from a person with kidney failure passes through equipment which separates the blood from a solution of suitable salts by a partially permeable membrane

dialysis fluid   a solution of salts equivalent in concentration and composition to the salts found in solution in blood

dimer   two similar molecules held together by some attractive force

dioptre   a unit for the optical power of a lens

dipole   'two poles'; the separation of charge between two covalently bonded atoms

dissociation   process by which ionic compounds split into ions

donor eggs   eggs donated by a female which are fertilised *in vitro* and transferred into another female

dosimeter   a device for measuring exposure to ionising radiation

down quark   a fundamental particle with a charge of $-1/3$

dynamic equilibrium   when the rates of the forward and reverse reactions are equal

ecosystem services   the benefits supplied by natural ecosystems

elastic collision   a collision in which momentum and kinetic energy are both conserved

electrocardiogram (ECG)   a trace of potential against time showing the cardiac cycle of the heart

electrolysis   decomposition of electrolytes using direct current electricity

electrolytes   substances that conduct electrical current when dissolved or molten

electron   a negatively charged particle found in all atoms

electroplating   coating with another metal using electrolysis

end point   the exact point of neutralisation in a titration

endoscope   an instrument used by doctors to look inside the body

enzyme   biological catalysts (usually proteins) produced by cells which control the rate of chemical reactions in cells

esterification   the reaction between an alcohol and a carboxylic acid

esters   compounds synthesised by the reaction between an alcohol and a carboxylic acid

eutrophication   the processes that occur when water is enriched with nutrients (from fertilisers) which allow algae to grow and use up all the oxygen

excess   when one substance in present in greater quantity than any other

excretion   removal of wastes produced by cell metabolism

exponential   rate of increase that is double the previous number

external radiotherapy   external source of X-rays or gamma rays used in the treatment of cancer

far point   the furthest point the eye can see clearly

fermentation   the conversion of carbohydrates to ethanol by microorganisms

fermentation reactions   chemical reactions that produce biomolecules

fermenter   large container containing a solution of nutrients and all the other substances cells need to multiply and grow

fertiliser   chemical put on soil to increase soil fertility and allow better growth of crop plants

fluoroscope   an X-ray device used for producing real-time X-ray images of the intestines and stomach

focal length   the distance between the centre of the lens and principal focus

follicle stimulating hormone (FSH)   hormone released by the pituitary gland, stimulating the development of egg follicles at the start of the menstrual cycle

food security   when everybody can obtain enough food which is nutritious and safe to eat

fractional distillation   separation of liquids in a mixture by making use of their different boiling points

free running   persistence of circadian rhythm in constant environmental conditions

frequency   the number of oscillations or cycles per unit time

functional group   the atom or group of atoms in a molecule of an organic compound that is responsible for the compound's characteristic chemical reactions

gamma camera   a special camera used to produce a three-dimensional image of the body using gamma rays emitted from inside a patient

gas equation PV/T = constant

genes   length of DNA encoding the synthesis of a protein or part of a protein

genetic marker   a mutation used to identify a biological event

genetically engineered   result of the process that produces recombinant DNA

genetically modified (GM)   an organism whose DNA has been engineered with a gene from another species

glomerulus   knot of capillary blood vessels associated with the Bowman's capsule

glucose isomerase   an enzyme that converts glucose to fructose

greenhouse gases   gases that contribute to the greenhouse effect by preventing heat radiating from the atmosphere into space

growing media   solids (agar) or liquid (broth) which contain all the nutrients and other substances microorganisms need to grow and multiply

Haber process   the process for producing ammonia from nitrogen and hydrogen

habituation   learned behaviour that decreases in response to the repeated application of the stimulus eliciting the behaviour in the first place

haemoglobin   a protein molecule in the red blood cells that carries oxygen from the lungs to the body's tissues

half equation   an equation that shows either the cathode reaction or the anode reaction in an electrolytic cell

half-life   the time taken for half of a radioactive element to decay to its non-radioactive product

hard water   water that does not lather easily with soap – a scum is formed; the water contains dissolved ions such as magnesium and calcium

herbicides   chemicals that kill plants – used to remove weeds (unwanted plants) from crops, gardens and public places

herbivorous   refers to animals that feed only on plants

herd effect   the minimum percentage of a population that needs to be immunised so that the whole population is protected from infectious disease

homeostasis   maintenance of a constant internal environment

homologous pair   pair of chromosomes that form during meiosis

homologous series   a series of compounds that have the same general formula and in which, when placed in order of increasing relative molecular mass, each compound differs by $-CH_2$ from its neighbours

hormones   substances produced by endocrine glands situated in different part of the body

human chorionic gonadotropin (hCG)   a hormone produced by a female in the early stages of pregnancy

hybridoma   type of cell produced by the fusion of non-antibody-producing myeloma and healthy antibody-producing B-lymphocytes

hydrophilic   the part of a molecule that tends to dissolve in water

hydrophobic   the part of a molecule that tends to be repelled from water

hydroxyl group   a functional group composed of hydrogen and oxygen

ideal gas equation $PV = nRT$ describes the relationship between pressure, volume, temperature and number of moles of gases

immobilised enzyme   an enzyme bonded to an insoluble inert material such as cellulose

immune response   the action of lymphocytes and phagocytes when antigens infect the body

immunisation   receiving defence against pathogens

immunological memory   the result of memory cells produced in response to first-time infection by a particular pathogen

immunology   study of the processes that establish immunity to specific diseases

imprinting   learning to identify a parent (or substitute)

in vitro **fertilisation**   eggs fertilised outside the body in the laboratory

inelastic collision   a collision in which momentum is conserved but kinetic energy is not; some of the kinetic energy is transformed to other forms such as heat and sound

infrared radiation   electromagnetic waves with wavelengths longer than visible red light

innate   behaviour that is inherited

insecticides   chemicals used to kill insects

insemination   introduction of sperm into the female reproductive system

intensity   the power of radiation per unit area

internal radiotherapy   internal source implanted into the patient used in the treatment of cancer

inverse square law   a relationship between quantities where doubling one quantity reduces the related quantity by a factor of four

ion   an atom or group of atoms with an electrical charge (can be positive or negative)

ion exchange column   a column containing an excess of sodium ions that are exchanged for calcium ions in hard water, thus softening the water

ionic equation   equation showing the ions that are involved in a chemical reaction

iris   the coloured part of the eye that controls the amount of light entering the eye

isotopes   atoms with the same number of protons but different numbers of neutrons

karyotype   image of an individual's chromosomes arranged as numbered homologous pairs

kelvin scale   a temperature scale where temperature is measured in kelvin (K)

lactose intolerant   unable to digest lactose

leach   to remove substances from rocks by dissolving in water

learning   a change in behaviour as the result of experience

leguminous   plants whose roots develop nodules when infected by the soil bacterium *Rhizobium*

lens equation   an equation that relates image distance v, object distance u and the focal length f of a lens: $\dfrac{1}{u} + \dfrac{1}{v} = \dfrac{1}{f}$

life cycle analysis   a method of calculating the impact on the environment of what we do or produce

ligase   an enzyme that makes it possible to insert a gene into another piece of DNA

limescale   an insoluble precipitate that lines heating elements and pipes, formed when hard water is heated

loop of Henlé   U-shaped part of the nephron that helps to control the amount of water reabsorbed into the blood from the liquid passing through the nephron

luteinising hormone (LH)   hormone released by the pituitary gland which completes the development of an egg follicle and stimulates its release

lymphocyte   type of white blood cell that destroys viruses and bacteria that cause disease

mass–energy equation   Einstein's equation $E = mc^2$, which links mass with the energy of a system

mass number   the number of protons and neutrons inside a nucleus

mating strategy   a part of social organisation, often based on whether the species is monogamous or polygamous

menstruation   breakdown of the lining of the uterus at the end of the menstrual cycle

metabolism   all the chemical reactions taking place in cells

methane   a flammable gas with molecules that contain one carbon atom and four hydrogen atoms

mitochondrial DNA (mtDNA)   the DNA content of a mitochondrion

molar volume   the volume of 1 mole of a gas at 20 °C and 1 atmosphere is 24 dm^3

molasses   a sugar-rich syrup produced as a by-product of refining sugar

mole   a specific number of particles (6.02×10^{23}): the relative formula mass of a substance expressed in grams will give this number of particles

molecular clock   the regular occurrence of a molecular event

momentum   a quantity calculated by multiplying the mass of an object by its velocity

monoclonal antibodies   samples of a particular type of antibody

monogamous   relationship where a male and female pair for the breeding season or even a lifetime

Mousterian   a stone-tool technology that replaced Acheulean

mycoprotein   fungus-based version of a single-cell protein (protein-rich food produced by microorganisms)

myeloma   a cancerous type of B-lymphocyte which produces a single type of antibody and which continues to divide in culture

near point   the closest distance the eye can focus an object

negative feedback   a mechanism where changes are reversed to achieve a stable level

nephrons   tubules which make up the kidney

neutralisation   the reaction between an acid and an alkali to give a neutral solution

neutrino   a particle with no charge and very small mass emitted during beta-plus decay of unstable nuclei

neutron   small particle which does not have a charge, found in the nucleus of an atom

nitrogen cycle   the cycling of nitrogen between air, living organisms and decaying dead organisms

nitrogen fixation   the incorporation of atmospheric nitrogen into organic compounds

nitrogenous   containing nitrogen

nucleons   protons and neutrons (both found in the nucleus of an atom)

nutrient solution   a solution that contains all the substances cells need to multiply and grow

oestrogen   hormone produced by developing egg follicles of the ovary

Oldowan   earliest type of stone-tool technology

operant conditioning   a type of learning where a response is reinforced by either reward or punishment

optical fibres   thin and flexible tubes of transparent material for transmitting light from one end to another

optical power   a quantity found using '1/focal length of the lens in metres'

osmoregulation   the process controlling the water content of the body

overwintering   refers to the seeds of plants which survive the harsh winter climate

oviduct   tube connecting the uterus to the ovary

ovulation   release of an egg from its follicle

oxidation   the removal of electrons from an atom

oxidising agent   substance that can remove electrons from other substances

pacemaker   a device implanted into a patient to regulate heartbeats

paclitaxel   semi-synthetic version of taxol

pair bonding   behaviour between a male and female of the same species that reinforces a relationship

palliative radiotherapy   radiotherapy treatment used to shrink a cancer or slow down its growth

parental investment   the time and energy parents spend on rearing offspring

particle accelerator   machine used to accelerate charged particles to very high speeds

permanent hard water   hard water that cannot be removed by boiling

PET scanner   a special scanner used to produce images of the metabolic functions of the body

phagocyte   type of white blood cell that engulfs viruses and bacteria, destroying them

pharmaceuticals   drugs that treat diseases and relieve symptoms

pharmacological   relating to the action of drugs on the body

phenolics   naturally occurring compounds in plants that contain benzene

pheromone   a chemical released into the environment that affects the behaviour of other individuals

photoperiod   the period of light/dark over 24 hours

pickling   a method of preserving food using vinegar

pituitary gland   an endocrine gland attached to the base of the brain near the hypothalamus

plasmids   loops of DNA found in some cells

pollination   the transfer of pollen from the anthers of a flower to the stigma of another flower of a different plant (cross-pollination)

polyclonal antibodies   mixtures of different types of antibody

polyester   polymer created by the polymerisation of alcohols and carboxylic acids using ester bonds

polygamous   relationship where an individual (usually male) mates with a number of opposite-sex partners (usually female) during the breeding season

positron the anti-particle of an electron; a particle with a mass similar to an electron but with a negative charge of -1.6×10^{-19} C

precipitation the settling of a solid substance through a liquid

pressure law the pressure exerted by a fixed mass of gas, kept at constant volume, is directly proportional to its temperature on the kelvin scale

primary immune response response of the immune system to infection by a particular pathogen, virus or bacterium, for the first time

primary stimulus stimulus directly associated with the response elicited by the stimulus

principal focus the point at which rays of light parallel to the principal axis of a converging lens converge, or the point from which rays parallel to the principal axis of a diverging lens appear to come

principle of conservation of momentum for a system of colliding objects, where there are no external forces, the total momentum before and after the collision remains the same

progesterone hormone released by the empty egg follicle following ovulation

protein compound consisting of carbon, hydrogen, oxygen, nitrogen and sometimes sulfur, and made up of many amino acid molecules

proton small positive particle found in the nucleus of an atom

puberty the period of change from sexual immaturity to sexual maturity

pulse oximeter a device used in hospitals to determine pulse rate and oxygenation of the blood

pupil the central hole produced by the iris

qualitative analysis based on appearance or description

qualitative analysis analysis of a chemical (or chemicals) to find out what's in it

quantitative analysis based on quantity

quantitative analysis analysis of a chemical (or chemicals) to find out how much is present

quark a fundamental particle within particles such as neutrons and protons

radiation any form of energy that originates from a source, including waves and particles

radioactive isotopes atoms with the same number of protons but different numbers of neutrons, with an unstable nucleus that achieves stability by emitting ionising radiations

radioactive tracer a radioactive substance injected or swallowed by a patient, used to diagnose the function of the body

radiometric dating a method of dating fossils and artefacts by measuring the proportions of radioactive isotopes and their decay products and knowing the half-life of each isotope

radiopharmaceutical a substance produced by tagging radioactive isotopes to natural chemicals such as glucose and water

random motion Motion of gas particles (atoms or molecules) characterised by motion in different directions and distribution of speeds

recognition site a short sequence of bases that is specifically cut by a particular restriction enzyme

recombinant DNA the combination of the DNA of one species with the DNA of another species

reducing agent substance that gives up electrons to other substances

reduction the addition of electrons to an atoms

refraction the bending of a wave caused by the change in the speed of a wave

reinforcer a stimulus that either rewards or punishes a response, which is then learned

relative atomic mass the mass of an atom relative to the mass of hydrogen; the mass of hydrogen is taken to be 1

relative formula mass the mass of a formula relative to the mass of hydrogen

renewables resources that are always available as a result of physical and organic processes

resazurin dye a dye that changes colour because of the substances produced by bacteria in a solution containing the dye

resin plastic beads or membranes that trap ions

restriction enzymes enzymes that cut up lengths of DNA into smaller pieces

retina light-sensitive part of the eye on which images are formed

reversible reaction a reaction that proceeds in both directions at the same time

salts ionic compounds made up of cations and anions

saponification the process of producing soap

saturated carboxylic acid carboxylic acid that has no carbon–carbon double bonds

secondary immune response response of the immune system to subsequent infection by a pathogen that it has encountered before

secondary stimulus stimulus that elicits the same response as a particular primary stimulus, but is different from the primary stimulus

semen liquid rich in sugars, produced by glands of the male reproductive system and in which sperm swim

sensitive period the time when imprinting develops in a young animal

sievert the unit of equivalent dose of radiation

smallpox a serious (often fatal) viral disease

Snell's law an equation that relates the angle of incidence i in a vacuum (or air), the angle of refraction r in a medium and the refractive index n of the medium; $\sin i / \sin r = n$

soft water water that lathers easily with soap; the water does not contain dissolved ions such as magnesium and calcium

solute the substance that is dissolved in a solvent to give a solution

solvent the liquid in which a solute dissolves

spectator ions ions that take no part in a reaction

stability curve a curve on an N–Z graph showing the positions of all stable nuclei

standard electrode potential a measure of the ease with which a substance undergoes reduction

sticky ends short, single-stranded lengths of DNA at either end of a piece of double-stranded DNA

strong electrolytes electrolytes that almost completely dissociate

strong nuclear force an attractive force between all neutrons and protons

surrogate mother a female who receives an embryo developed from a fertilised donor egg and who carries the embryo to the completion of pregnancy

tannins bitter-tasting phenolic compounds found in plants

target the anode in an X-ray tube

taxol a substance with anti-cancer properties, extracted from the yew tree

temporary hard water hard water that can be removed by boiling

terpenoids naturally occurring lipid-based compounds found in plants

thermionic emission emission of electrons from the surface of a heated metal

titration a carefully carried out neutralisation reaction to find the exact concentration of a reactant

total internal reflection reflection of light in a denser medium when the angle of incidence is greater than the critical angle

toxicity poisonous effect

transducer a device for converting electrical energy to sound and vice versa

transgenic organisms that have been engineered with a gene (or genes) of another species

ultrasound high-frequency sound waves that we cannot hear

unsaturated carboxylic acid carboxylic acid that has carbon–carbon double bonds

up quark a fundamental particle with a charge of $+2/3$

urea nitrogenous waste substance produced by the liver

ureter tube connecting the kidney to the bladder

urinary system the kidneys and their blood supply, the ureters and the bladder

urine solution of urea and other substances produced by the kidneys and removed (excreted) from the body to the environment

uterus part of the female reproductive system of placental mammals where the foetus develops

vector (1) a quantity that has both magnitude and direction
(2) length of DNA which, when combined with a gene, enables that gene to be transferred into the cells of another species

volatile organic compound (VOC) a substance that gives off a vapour at ambient temperature

voltaic cell an electrochemical cell where a spontaneous electrochemical cell generates an electrical current

weak electrolytes electrolytes that only slightly dissociate

weeds plants growing where they are not wanted

whey the liquid left after protein has precipitated from milk

whooping cough a highly infectious disease caused by the bacterium *Bordetella pertussis*

X chromosome one of the sex chromosomes, which is usually larger than the Y chromosome

Y chromosome one of the sex chromosomes, which is usually smaller than the X chromosome

yeast single-celled fungus traditionally used to make bread and alcoholic drinks

zygote fertilised egg

Index

William Collins' dream of knowledge for all began with the publication of his first book in 1819. A self-educated mill worker, he not only enriched millions of lives, but also founded a flourishing publishing house. Today, staying true to this spirit, Collins books are packed with inspiration, innovation and practical expertise. They place you at the centre of a world of possibility and give you exactly what you need to explore it.

Collins. Freedom to teach·

Published by Collins
An imprint of HarperCollins*Publishers*
77–85 Fulham Palace Road
Hammersmith
London
W6 8JB

Browse the complete Collins catalogue at
www.collinseducation.com

© HarperCollins*Publishers* Limited 2011

10 9 8 7 6 5 4 3 2 1

ISBN-13 978 0 00 741511 3

John Adkins, David Applin and Gurinder Chadha assert their moral rights to be identified as the authors of this work

British Library Cataloguing in Publication Data
A Catalogue record for this publication is available from the British Library

Commissioned by Letitia Luff
Project managed by Alexandra Riley and Gray Publishing
Production by Kerry Howie
Designed, edited, proofread and indexed by Gray Publishing
New illustrations by Gray Publishing
Picture research by Caroline Green
Concept design by Anna Plucinska
Cover design by Julie Martin
Development editors Maggie Rumble and Lesley Gray
Technical review by Dr Christopher R.J. Woolston
Contributing authors John Beeby, Sarah Jinks and Gemma Young
Printed and bound by L.E.G.O. S.p.A. Italy.

This material has been endorsed by Edexcel and offers high quality support for the delivery of Edexcel qualifications.

Edexcel endorsement does not mean that this material is essential to achieve any Edexcel qualification, nor does it mean that this is the only suitable material available to support any Edexcel qualification. No endorsed material will be used verbatim in setting any Edexcel examination and any resource lists produced by Edexcel shall include this and other appropriate texts. While this material has been through an Edexcel quality assurance process, all responsibility for the content remains with the publisher.

Copies of official specifications for all Edexcel qualifications may be found on the Edexcel website – www.edexcel.com

Acknowledgements
The publishers wish to thank the following for permission to reproduce photographs. Every effort has been made to trace copyright holders and to obtain their permission for the use of copyright materials. The publishers will gladly receive any information enabling them to rectify any error or omission at the first opportunity.

cover & p.1 Edward Kinsman/Science Photo Library, p.8t Alexander Kozachok/iStockphoto, p.8u ISM/Science Photo Library, p.8l Dmitry Naumov/Shutterstock, p.8b Scorpp/Shutterstock, p.9t Picsfive/Shutterstock, p.9u Sofia/Shutterstock, p.9l Alexander Raths/Shutterstock, p.9b Yuri Tuchkov/Shutterstock, p.10 Susumu Nishinaga/Science Photo Library, p.12t Louise Murray/Science Photo Library, p.12b Picsfive/Shutterstock, p.14 Professor P. M. Motta, G. Macchiarelli, S.A. Nottola/Science Photo Library, p.15 iDesign/Shutterstock, p.17 Eye of Science/Science Photo Library, p.18t David Nicholls/Science Photo Library, p.18b Biophoto Associate/Science Photo Library, p.20t Tim Vernon, LTH NHS Trust/Science Photo Library, p.20b Dmitry Naumov/Shutterstock, p.22 atanasija1/Shutterstock, p.24t SCIMAT/Science Photo Library, p.24b Michal Kowalski/Shutterstock, p.26t Nick Greaves/Alamy, p.26b Photoshot Holdings Ltd/Alamy, p.27 Dr. P. Marazzi/Science Photo Library, p.28t Ingrid Prats/Shutterstock, p.28b marilyn barbone/Shutterstock, p.30 DocCheck Medical Services GmbH/Alamy, p.32t Chepko Danil Vitalevich/Shutterstock, p.32b joefoxfoodanddrink/Alamy, p.32b Eye Ubiquitous/Alamy, p.40t Kiselev Andrey Valerevich/Shutterstock, p.40c alexal/Shutterstock, p.40b International Rice Research Institute (IRRI), p.41t Monika Wisniewska/Shutterstock, p.41c Vladimir Wrangel/Shutterstock, p.41b Bork/Shutterstock, p.42 Johner Images/Alamy, p.43 Brian Bevan/Alamy, p.44t nimblewit/Shutterstock, p.44b Mark Bridger/Shutterstock, p.45l Juniors Bildarchiv/Alamy, p.45r Cordelia Molloy/Science Photo Library, p.45b Gina Smith/Shutterstock, p.46t WilleeCole/Shutterstock, p.46c Bob Orsillo/Shutterstock, p.46b Mike Truchon/Shutterstock, p.47 David Parker/Alamy, p.48t James H. Robinson/Science Photo Library, p.48b dmvphotos/Shutterstock, p.49t Pete Masson/iStockphoto, p.49b fotolincs/Alamy, p.50t Peter Malsbury/iStockphoto, p.50c Roman Kobzarev/iStockphoto, p.50b James R. Hearn/Shutterstock, p.51 Jake Lyell/Alamy, p.52t Astrid & Hanns-Frieder Michler/Science Photo Library, p.52l IKO/Shutterstock, p.52r Eric Isselée/iStockphoto, p.53t Susan Schmitz/Shutterstock, p.53b David Cantrille/Alamy, p.54t Eye of Science/Science Photo Library, p.54b Jack Clark/AgstockUSA/Science Photo Library, p.55 Eponaleah/Shutterstock, p.56 John Reader/Science Photo Library, p.57t Javier Trueba/MSF/Science Photo Library, p.57b Universal Images Group Limited/Alamy, p.58t John Reader/Science Photo Library, p.58b Javier Trueba/MSF/Science Photo Library, p.60 Volker Steger/Nordstar 4 Million Years of Man/Science Photo Library, p.61 David Lyons/Alamy, p.62 Gail Johnson/Shutterstock, p.63 Jason Stitt/Shutterstock, p.64t Nattika/Shutterstock, p.64b Hellen Sergeyeva/Shutterstock, p.65t National Institutes of Health, part of the United States Department of Health and Human Services, p.65b Raguet H./Science Photo Library, p.66t Christopher Elwell/Shutterstock, p.66b Simon Owler/iStockphoto, p.68t Prof. David Hall/Science Photo Library, p.68l Bon Appetit/Alamy, p.68r Caroline Green, p.69 Prisma Bildagentur AG/Alamy, p.70t Rosenfeld Images Ltd/Science Photo Library, p.70b Lilyana Vynogradova/Shutterstock, p.72t Tischenko Irina/Shutterstock, p.72l Rosenfeld Images Ltd/Science Photo Library, p.72r Danicek/Shutterstock, p.72b Nayashkova Olga/Shutterstock, p.74t visionaryft/Shutterstock, p.74b Biozentrum, University of Basel/Science Photo Library, p.76t Drozdowski/Shutterstock, p.76b Nigel Cattlin/Alamy, p.77 M. Niebuhr/Shutterstock, p.78 africa924/Shutterstock, p.79 Patrick Duman/Eurelios/Science Photo Library, p.80t margouillat photo/Shutterstock, p.80b ahnhuynh/Shutterstock, p.81t Green Stock Media/Alamy, p.81b David Hoffman Photo Library/Alamy, p.83 IDAL/Shutterstock, p.87 blickwinkel/Alamy, p.88 Ettore Balocchi/Wikimedia Commons, p.90t Andrew Lambert Photography/Science Photo Library, p.90c Alexander Raths/Shutterstock, p.90b Charles D. Winters/Science Photo Library, p.91t Martyn F. Chillmaid/Science Photo Library, p.91c Martyn F. Chillmaid/Science Photo Library, p.91b Sashkin/Shutterstock, p.92 Bork/Shutterstock, p.93 Andrew Lambert Photography/Science Photo Library, p.94 Don Anderson/iStockphoto, p.96 Voronin76/Shutterstock, p.97 Sheila Terry/Science Photo Library, p.98t Monkey Business Images/Shutterstock, p.98b Andrew Lambert Photography/Science Photo Library, p.99t RM, p.99c Martyn F. Chillmaid/Science Photo Library, p.99b Norman Pogson/Shutterstock, p.100 Martyn F. Chillmaid/Science Photo Library, p.101 Ron Kloberdanz/Shutterstock, p.102 Robert Harding Picture Library/SuperStock, p.103 Andrew Lambert Photography/Science Photo Library, p.104 Wellford Tiller/Shutterstock, p.106 canismaior/Shutterstock, p.107r Laurence Gough/Shutterstock, p.107l donatas1205/Shutterstock, p.107r canismaior/Shutterstock, p.108 Kriss Russell/iStockphoto, p.109 tunart/iStockphoto, p.110 Bill Lawson/Shutterstock, p.112t EuToch/Shutterstock, p.112b Smit/Shutterstock, p.113 Charles D. Winters/Science Photo Library, p.114 Maurice Savage/Alamy, p.115 Robert Brook/Science Photo Library, p.116 risteski goce/Shutterstock, p.117 Andrew Lambert Photography/Science Photo Library, p.118 Oliver Hoffmann/Shutterstock, p.119 Kameel4u/Shutterstock, p.119 Alexander Raths/Shutterstock, p.120 Margo Harrison/Shutterstock, p.CUT Pslawinski, p.128t 1971yes/Shutterstock, p.128b bouzou/Shutterstock, p.129t Martyn F. Chillmaid/Science Photo Library, p.129b Ferenc Cegledi/Shutterstock, p.130 Steve Bower/Shutterstock, p.131 Charles D. Winters/Science Photo Library, p.132t Ching-Yeh Ching-Yeh Lu/iStockphoto, p.132b sciencephotos/Alamy, p.133 John Sartin/Shutterstock, p.134t Jiang Dao Hua/Shutterstock, p.134b Maddrat/Shutterstock, p.136 NASA, p.138 Zaneta Baranowska/Shutterstock, p.140t George Steinmetz/Science Photo Library, p.140b Steven May/Alamy, p.141t Monkey Business Images/Shutterstock, p.141b Jack Sullivan/Alamy, p.142t Gerad Coles/iStockphoto, p.142b Ria Novosti/Science Photo Library, p.144 Sergey150770/Shutterstock, p.145 Martyn F. Chillmaid/Science Photo Library, p.146t Daniel Wiedemann/Shutterstock, p.146b Pakhnyushcha/Shutterstock, p.147 Picsfive/Shutterstock, p.148t Terry Smith Images Arkansas Picture Library/Alamy, p.148b matka_Wariatka/Shutterstock, p.149 Tobik/Shutterstock, p.150 Korolevskaya Nataliya/Shutterstock, p.150 Anson0618/Shutterstock, p.155 Alekcey/Shutterstock, p.158t jovannig/Shutterstock, p.158b Dr. Arthus Tucker/Science Photo Library, p.159t Coprid/Shutterstock, p.159b REDAV/Shutterstock, p.160 Arno Massee/Science Photo Library, p.161 Mario Lopes/Shutterstock, p.162 Lobke Peers/Shutterstock, p.163 Franc Podgoršek/iStockphoto, p.164t Marek Mnich/iStockphoto, p.164b Andrew Lambert Photography/Science Photo Library, p.166t Omikron/Science Photo Library, p.166b BSIP, Chassenet/Science Photo Library, p.167 Pascal Goetgheluck/Science Photo Library, p.168 Susan E. Degginger/Alamy, p.170t Tony Campbell/Shutterstock, p.170c Robyn Mackenzie/Shutterstock, p.170b nutech21/Shutterstock, p.171 BSIP, Boucharlat/Science Photo Library, p.174t Mary Evans Picture Library/Alamy, p.174b AJ Photo/Science Photo Library, p.176t Zephyr/Science Photo Library, p.176c Gonul Kokal/Shutterstock, p.176b Geoff Tompkinson/Science Photo Library, p.177 Simon Frase/NCCT, Freeman Trust, Newcastle-Upon-Tyne/Science Photo Library, p.178t Dario Sabljak/Shutterstock, p.178b Bork/Shutterstock, p.180t Schmid Christophe/Shutterstock, p.180b Bork/Shutterstock, p.182l Volker Steger/Science Photo Library, p.182r Mauro Fermariello/Science Photo Library, p.183 mathom/Shutterstock, p.187 Angela Farley/Shutterstock, p.188 Gonul Kokal/Shutterstock, p.190t D. Roberts/Science Photo Library, p.190c Miguel Angel Salinas Salinas/Shutterstock, p.190b inxti/Shutterstock, p.191t Jean-Claude Revy, ISM/Science Photo Library, p.191c David Parker & Julian Baum/Science Photo Library, p.191b Ingvald Kaldhussater/Shutterstock, p.192 Mark Kostich/iStockphoto, p.193 Health Protection Agency/Science Photo Library, p.194 Dr Robert Friedland/Science Photo Library, p.196 Ria Novosti/Science Photo Library, p.197t Lawrence Berkeley Laboratory/Science Photo Library, p.197b Volker Steger/Science Photo Library, p.198 CERN/Science Photo Library, p.200t Medi-Mation/Science Photo Library, p.200b Martyn F. Chillmaid/Science Photo Library, p.201t Ria Novosti/Science Photo Library, p.201b Monkey Business Images/Shutterstock, p.202t Dr Karol Sikora/Science Photo Library, p.202b Imane/Science Photo Library, p.203t Doug Martin/Shutterstock, p.203b Fermilab/Science Photo Library, p.204t James King-Holmes/Science Photo Library, p.204b BSIP, Cavallini James/Science Photo Library, p.205 Sovereign, ISM/Science Photo Library, p.206 L. Medard/Eurelios/Science Photo Library, p.208t CERN/Science Photo Library, p.208b David Parker/Science Photo Library, p.209 David Parker & Julian Baum/Science Photo Library, p.210t David Lyons/Alamy, p.210b muzsy/Shutterstock, p.212 Rex Features, p.213t Dr Robert Friedland/Science Photo Library, p.213b marekuliasz/Shutterstock, p.214 Orla/Shutterstock, p.215 Adam Hart-Davis/Science Photo Library, p.216 Volodymyr Goinyk/Shutterstock, p.217 Robert Gray, p.218 NASA, p.219t sciencephotos/Shutterstock, p.219b Andrew Lambert Photography/Science Photo Library, p.220 Adam Hart-Davis/Science Photo Library, p.221 JonMilnes/Shutterstock, p.222 omers/Shutterstock, p.227 Robert Gray, p.228 Lawrence Berkeley Laboratory/Science Photo Library, p.229 Ingvald Kaldhussater/Shutterstock, p.246 Martyn F. Chillmaid/Science Photo Library..